Contents

WHEN MEN MEET

HOMOSEXUALITY AND MODERNITY

Henning Bech

Translated by Teresa Mesquit and Tim Davies

Polity Press

First published in Denmark as *Når Mænd Mødes* 1987 © Gyldendal.
This translation from the revised Danish text first published 1997 by Polity Press in association with Blackwell Publishers Ltd.

Editorial office:
Polity Press
65 Bridge Street
Cambridge CB2 1UR, UK

Marketing and production:
Blackwell Publishers Ltd
108 Cowley Road
Oxford OX4 1JF, UK

ISBN 0-7456-1420-5
ISBN 0-7456-1559-7 (pbk)

A CIP catalogue record for this book is available from the British Library.

Typeset in 11½ on 12½ pt Times New Roman
by Ace Filmsetting Ltd, Frome, Somerset
Printed in Great Britain by Hartnolls Ltd, Bodmin, Cornwall

This book is printed on acid-free paper.

Preface

The English text is a translated and revised version of the original Danish edition of 1987. The main argument of the book is basically unchanged. The line and steps of progression have been more clearly elaborated, implying also some reorganizing of the material and some cuts in sub-arguments. The metatheoretical framework, methodological guidelines, theoretical specificity and epistemological status of the work have been made more explicit (in new introductory sections on 'Aims' and 'Approaches', as well as in the opening and concluding sections of the main chapters and in the notes). Examples too specifically Danish to make sense to an international readership have been left out or replaced by other material.

Although the basic argument of the book remains unchanged, the English edition contains some important additions and elaborations. In chapter III, I have dealt more extensively with the spatial implications of 'absent homosexuality' in relation to the geography of everyday life. I have also added an explicit discussion of the concept of 'homophobia', criticizing its focus on the negative and destructive sides of male resistance to physical-orgasmic homosexuality, and problematizing widespread notions that a cultivation of cultural masculinity and male–male relations is necessarily equivalent to 'misogyny'. These concerns are the object of the new sections on 'Closets' and 'Homophobia', as well as of additions to the subsequent sections (18–21). In chapter IV on 'The Homosexual Form of Existence', I have detailed my critique of 'discoursive constructionism' as well as pointed to a certain doubleness in the concept of 'identity'. I have described in more detail the specifics and the importance of urban sexualization (sections 13 and 17), and I have added a new section (19) on the pleasures and problems of male homosexual couples. I have also stressed the material 'sedimentatedness' of the homosexual world and its influence in giving 'form' to homosexual existence (sections 22 and 23). Chapter VI on 'The Disappearance of the Modern Homosexual' has been substantially enlarged, including discussions of the legislation on 'homosexual marriages'; of national differences in the trends towards the disappearance of the modern homosexual; and of the phenomena of the 'queer' (section 2). I have also added a discussion of the changes in 'non-homosexual' mens' relations to male–male sexuality – changes amounting to a tendential 'disappearance of the modern heterosexual' (section 4). Along the way (and particularly in the notes on chapters III.17, IV.2, IV.3 and IV.17) I have specified some implications of my analyses for research on non-modern forms of male–male sexuality and erotics, as well as on the historical development and specific subforms of modern homosexuality. Above all, these implications concern questions related to gender.

In general, I have had the opportunity of re-thinking my theories and analyses in the light of the impressive amount of scholarly literature which has appeared in the field since I first wrote the original Danish text during the mid-1980s. This new literature has been important in relation to the additions and elaborations mentioned above. It has also allowed me to flesh out my arguments with references to additional empirical material, as well as forced me into discussions of what would or would seem to contradict my theories and analyses. In accordance with the principles on which the book is written (see n. 8 to the Introduction), these discussions have been primarily conducted in the notes; in general, the fleshing-out and the critical reflections deriving from the impact of this new literature can easily be identified by paying attention to the publication dates of the works referred to. (On the principles for selection of the reference literature, see n. 22 to the Introduction; following these principles, I have also reduced references, given in the Danish edition, to the literature published before 1986/7.)

Quotations from texts not written in or previously translated into English have been translated by my translators and myself.

The Danish Social Science Research Council has kindly given financial support for the work of revising the book and translating it into English. My special thanks for providing me with, among other things, approval, books, chocolate, criticism, dishes (rich or – sometimes as essential – simply clean), encouragement, inspiration, invitations or money go to Zygmunt Bauman, Margareta Bertilsson, Michael Bochow, Matthias Duyves, Anthony Giddens, Gert Hekma, Preben Hertoft, Rüdiger Lautmann, Klaus-Jürgen Lüttjohann, Karin Lützen, Jan Löfström, Frank Mort, Mehmet Necef, Arne Nilsson, Poul Poder Pedersen, Ken Plummer, Wilhelm Rosen, Bente Rosenbeck, Hans Soetaert, Ulla Thorborg, Jeffrey Weeks, Øystein Ziener; and to Anders Møller. None of whom, of course, are responsible for the contents of the book.

Henning Bech
Copenhagen
April 1996

I

Introduction

1 A woman passing

Before going out one evening, a woman puts on men's clothes, cuts her nails square, practises a male gait and glues on a moustache. She wants to pass as a man, and thus resembles those of her fellow sisters, especially from the nineteenth century, about whom Jonathan Katz writes and whom he calls 'passing women': women who – for economic or other reasons – dressed and worked and lived as men.[1] This woman – her name is Rita Mae Brown – is not on her way to work, however, and neither is she, as some readers may suspect, heading for a lesbian pub. She is on an expedition to an unknown territory, a land of men and men alone: she wants to visit a gay bath house. She manages to get in; and unlike the others she doesn't take off all her clothes but puts on a short robe; after which she investigates the premises: the TV room, the maze, the orgy room, the cubicles, the steam bath, the sauna. She notices how the usual social hierarchy is replaced here by another – condition of body, size of penis, age – and the tension, competition, anxiety that go along with it; but also the possibility of total abandon in the darker rooms, of losing oneself in anonymity and carnal desire. She registers the obsession with penis, erection and orgasm, but also senses other needs, for human contact, for love, though more disguised. She is struck by the silence and the direct way these men look at each other and engage in each other, but also by the security and the ease with which they accept refusal. A few hours later she leaves and reflects on the experience. Perhaps there is a risk that, for some of these men, life narrows down to sex, as much of it as possible with as many as possible who look the best, but she wants to have this option for herself as well: to be able to choose between – or choose to combine – deep long-term relationships, bath house sex, and short-term affairs. She wishes this type of refuge existed for women: it would resemble the baths, but there would perhaps be less competition, more laughter, and people would touch each other not only to have sex but just to touch.[2]

2 Aims

This book is about the conditions and possibilities of life in contemporary modern societies. The theme is explored through a discussion of the relations between homosexuality, masculinity and modernity. And, of these, the point of departure and reference will be the exemplary, as I shall argue, phenomenon of male homosexuality.[3]

This is not a field uncultivated by science. Indeed, it might have seemed devastated and scrubby after decades of exploitation by medicine, psychiatry and psychology. However, methods of cultivation were revolutionized from the 1960s by the scholarly approach eventually labelled *social constructionism*. The homosexual, it was argued, is not a particular type of human being to be found in all societies throughout history. He is essentially a social and cultural construction first produced in north-western societies in recent centuries.[4]

The debate between social constructionism and its critics, often labelled 'essentialists', quickly grew impassioned, even rancorous; and it has recently become near-mandatory in advanced studies to kowtow in the opening lines and asseverate that one's work can neither be placed in one category nor the other.[5] As for the present book, 'constructionism' constitutes a major theoretical background and source of inspiration, both for the original Danish edition of 1987 and for this revised English one. However, I do think there have been, and still are, substantial problems at the very foundations of much constructionist scholarship.

One problem concerns the conceptualization of what is the modern male homosexual – a question so often answered in terms of a homosexual 'identity'. A further difficulty concerns the relations to homosexuality among 'non-homosexual' men. Insofar as this area was not simply left aside, it has often been theorized in terms of 'latent homosexuality', 'repression', 'sublimation', or 'homophobia'. Third, there is the question of what constitutes the 'sexual' and 'male' qualities of modern male homosexuality, and to what extent these can be addressed within the intellectual paradigms and with the analytical tools traditionally considered appropriate in science and scholarship – to say nothing of normative canons and political correctness. There may, sometimes, have been simplifications or omissions concerning the representation of passion and sensuality, as well as of the attraction to and attractiveness of *men*, and accordingly of masculinity. Fourth, there is the question of which phenomena in modern societies hold the greatest importance for the existence of modern homosexuality, as well as the problem of the relations between this homosexuality and the other phenomena of these societies. Very often, the emphasis has been put on the constitutive significance of such entities as 'discourses', 'categories', 'meanings', 'labels', 'scripts' or 'roles' and the possible reinforcement of these by the social institutions of 'medicine', 'law', 'the media', 'the nuclear family', 'patriarchy', 'masculinity', 'capitalism', 'the state' or 'power'.

On these four, fairly substantial points I do not think that the perhaps most favoured ideas, theories and concepts of constructionism are entirely satisfactory from a theoretical and metatheoretical point of view. Nor do I think that they are quite in tune with the subject matter, the 'empirical material' of homosexuality and modernity – and often not even with the material presented by the constructionist scholars themselves.[6]

These problems are among the major theoretical driving forces of this book. But it should not be forgotten that its broader interest is to explore, by way of a particularly instructive phenomenon, the conditions and possibilities of life in contemporary modern societies – a concern of some relevance, I hope, for women as well as men, 'heterosexuals' as well as 'homosexuals'.

3 Approaches

In the rest of this introduction, I shall enter into a fairly technical discussion of the framework, methods, style, and practical interests of the book.[7] Readers who want to get down to business may wish to skip to chapter II. Similar advice should be given concerning the notes. They contain various kinds of discussions and references – vital to the academic reader, but perhaps less interesting to others.[8]

Frame The general frame of investigation – scholarly stance, world view, overarching approach – of the book is highly influenced by Anglo-Saxon traditions of cultural studies, social history and symbolic interactionism. However, an equally important impact stems from the continental European traditions of dialectics, materialism, phenomenology, existentialism and critical theory – that is, the works of Hegel, Marx, Simmel, Husserl, Heidegger, Sartre, Kracauer, Horkheimer, Adorno, Benjamin and Foucault. These authors are present throughout the book, as expert guides, objects of criticism or interlocutors – be it by name, or implicitly in wording, touch or tone.

Branch The book belongs within the realm of social science and cultural studies. Although specifying its objects to be historically constituted, it is not a work of history in any traditional sense. The task is to investigate the modern phenomenon of homosexuality as one that *exists*, examining its basic features and the conditions without which it couldn't exist and couldn't continue to exist. In this process, certain points will emerge from which one may take one's bearings in studying the origins of the phenomenon; but it is not the principal aim of the book to answer this question. We are investigating, as Marx might have said, the already existing homosexuality, not its coming into existence.[9] Neither is it the objective to write the story of what happened, year by year, from the point at which the phenomenon was established up till now. Instead, it's a matter of producing, insofar as this is possible, a still picture, a kind of snapshot of the basic features which have remained constant over the years. (I write 'insofar as this is possible', as one cannot presuppose that such a pattern of basic features does in fact exist or is particularly substantial.) In another wording, the task is to identify a specific *configuration*, *conglomeration* or *formation*. In that particular sense, the analysis is structural. This, however, includes the identification of basic trends of development which, *as trends*, have also remained constant over the years.[10]

Methods The study combines a number of traditional methods of social science and cultural studies: participant observation of various spaces and ways of life; analysis of primary texts and images; critical discussion of existing theoretical and empirical work.[11] On a more general level, however, the approach can reasonably be characterized as a phenomenological analysis. It's a matter of *sticking to the phenomena*.[12]

Obviously, one cannot simply read or record the phenomena without bringing along methodological and other equipment. Moreover, it is well known by now that the method cannot avoid being co-constitutive of the object.[13] But I do not agree with those who claim there is nothing left of the object outside the method. It would be difficult to deny that there are more or less adequate methods to study an object; and what characterizes adequate methods is precisely that they discover more than their own shadow. Accordingly, the methodological guideline of sticking to the phenomena implies respecting the 'primacy of the object'.[14] Exactly which methods can reasonably be put to use, and how they are to be arranged in relation to one another, should ultimately depend upon the unique characteristics of the phenomenon studied. Moreover, upon these will also depend the extent to which a phenomenon can at all reasonably be subjected to the paradigms of conceptualizing, interpreting and explaining that are constitutive of science and scholarship. It is essential to pay attention to the limits of these, point to the dimensions of the object which transcend them, and, occasionally, switch to other, 'non-scientific' forms of intercourse and writing.

One aspect deserves particular comment. Phenomenological analysis is often considered synonymous with 'understanding' the 'hidden meaning' of the phenomena. This is not the position taken in this book. For instance, style, life, sexuality and pleasure are not reducible to 'meaning', and phenomenological analysis should not simply try to 'understand' them or explain them as the expression of something other.[15] The same applies to 'tunings', which make up a basic and inescapable dimension of existence.[16] Moreover, tunings are not merely a substantial part of the phenomena studied; they are co-constitutive of the acts of phenomenological cognition themselves. This does not leave the analyses to pure subjective mood and whim. But it does imply that in their execution and their claim of validity they depend, in part, on whether they manage to *re-present* the tunings. Obviously, this puts quite some stress on matters of style (to which I shall return).

There is a further and significant sense in which the overarching approach can adequately be characterized as a phenomenological analysis, in accordance with major traditions of continental European phenomenology. It moves within the realm of lived life and experience, or, in another term, the life-world.[17] Its point of departure is some surface phenomenon of the social world as given to human subjectivities. It may, for instance, be a 'tuning' or mood – such as *Angst*; a figure – such as the whore; a gaze; or the design of a space.[18] The analysis tries to apprehend these 'surface' phenomena in their full specificity, however multifaceted and indeterminate they may be. Further, it moves towards unfolding the broader context in which they are situated, as well as discovering constitutive features of the life-world. A guiding question is the following: since this particular phenomenon can appear as a part of the life-world, which other characteristics may we infer apply to the latter? Thus, for instance, at the 'bottom' of the gaze we find the city.[19]

The phenomenological analysis used in this book, then, enters into lived experience to unfold it. In the process, it snuggles up to what is quotidian and recognizable, even trivial, for the inhabitants of the life-world; however, it does not stay within the already existing boundaries of their conscious or acknowledged experience. Furthermore, specifying the particular characteristics of a phenomenon implies considering it from the outside as well, in order to determine its difference from other phenomena and the extent to which it is a historical and social creation.[20] Accordingly, phenomenological analysis can often shift advantageously between insider and outsider perspectives, going into and out of the life-world; as well as tack between levels of concrete experience and abstract theory.

Status The analyses of *When Men Meet* are in the nature of interpretations and presentations, readings and displays, illuminations and suggestions. As a whole they constitute what might be termed a *qualified story*. I intend it to be in accordance with the existing relevant, empirical research material (others' as well as my own); and I intend it to have been subjected to a reasonable degree of critical theoretical reflection.[21] But the story – like all scholarship and science, whether they realize their 'storied' nature or not – has dimensions transcending this, and to that extent, not least, it might well be assessed in the light of its ability to lend some measure of perspective, its capacity to make one see things in a different light, opening up new possibilities.

Many of the book's topics, and much of the material for its analyses, have of course been discussed in other studies. And indeed, I have made extensive use of others' work.[22] However, the reader will find that I usually ask somewhat different questions, apply a somewhat different perspective and arrive at somewhat different results. Thus the book is a contribution to ongoing dialogue and mutual inspiration, on the basis of what a tradition of scholars has achieved.

Presentation and style A number of different organizational principles are at work, crossing paths in the succession of chapters. There is the more traditional one of first introducing other researchers' understanding of a topic, then presenting one's own investigation and finally concluding how far this had led to other results. But there is also a principle of 'development' (or, in the Hegelian term, *Entwicklung*). The presentation follows the movement of thought dependent upon the object's 'own logic' as well as upon the methodological and discoursive necessities of an adequate representation of this. A third organizational principle is that of montage. In part, this device of textual construction likewise reflects the characteristics and movements of the object and of cognition – but here, notably, the ruptures and lack of coherent completeness in both. It further offers the possibility of exploiting certain cognitive effects. The 'space' between the individual pieces of the montage becomes one of reciprocal commentary, elaboration and friction that may, perhaps, spark off additional dimensions of cognition, and help make the text *move*.

The exposition moreover makes use of a number of aesthetic and rhetorical devices such as ambiguity, irony and other features of style traditionally associated with literary fiction. Although these are sometimes rejected as not belonging to the domain of sociology and cultural studies, they have proved essential and ineradicable,[23] and I shall take the stance that the trick is to utilize them instead. In addition, there are special reasons for using such literary devices in a study like the present one. It is phenomenological, trying to represent as adequately as possible the phenomena of lived life in their very concreteness and their tunings; in Kracauer's words, it aims at performing 'interpretations in the concrete material'.[24] Moreover, some particular groups of phenomena are those of pleasure ('sexual', 'erotic' or other); the representation of this places special demands on the style of the exposition if it is not simply, in Adorno's words, to commit conceptual violence against its subject matter and perhaps thereby double the violence that has already been committed in reality.[25]

All in all, then, the style of the book does not really conform to conventional approaches, particularly not to conventional social sciences. Instead, it has some affinity to what has come to be known as postmodernist forms of writing, although they might perhaps more adequately be termed modernist. It attempts to make use of the variety of styles represented in the history of sociological and cultural studies, and of the experience accumulated by using them.

Interest and politics The structural-phenomenological focus of the book may provoke the objection that it forgets the active human agent and is not political enough. As most would agree, however, seeking a political relevance by making appeals to the working class seems to be a hopeless gesture by now (which is not equivalent to claiming that the working class is 'dead'). In the wake has come the attempt to identify movements of protest and resistance at various levels, down to individuals' actions and indeed their inner motions. However, I believe that this paradigm of critique, in Europe at least, had largely exhausted its politicizing as well as cognitive potentialities already by the mid-1980s, given the political and intellectual conditions and developments in that part of the world. (Which is not equivalent to claiming there no longer exist any social movements or individual acts of protest.) This situation incited me to search for new forms of not-politically-irrelevant writing when I was working on the Danish edition of the book during the early and mid-1980s, and I have not altered my stance on this. Consequently, the 'active human agent' may not be as prominent as some might wish; but I do think that the book has substantial political implications – although its political *style* is not one of lecturing, but rather of showing, dialogue, irony and persuasion.[26]

4 Short outline

Each of the remaining five chapters is divided into a number of sections. It is very well possible to start with any section that may attract immediate interest. Many of them (particularly in chapters III–V) are moreover conceived in a way so that they 'mirror' the whole, though from a particular angle. The sections, however, are also combined and counterpointed into the much larger units of the chapters, and in the last instance, of course, of the book. Given the variety of the methods and styles employed, as well as the complexity of the argument pursued over sometimes more than twenty sections per chapter, readers may lose track and come to wonder what precisely I am aiming at and where precisely my argument differs from others'. Here is a brief outline to facilitate overview; and I strongly advise any 'lost' reader to move to the concluding sections of the chapter and read them first.

Chapter II relates three different patterns of sexual relations between men in 'non-modern' societies; they will serve as a contrast medium for the investigation of modern homosexuality. Chapters III–IV concern homosexuality and modernity. Chapter III deals with the relations to homosexuality of men not separated out as 'homosexuals'. Section 1 introduces the theme, which is further developed and analysed in the following sections. Results are summarized in section 21. Chapter IV deals with men separated out as 'homosexuals'. Sections 1–3 introduce the theme; sections 4–20 analyse it from various angles; and the results are summarized in sections 21–4. In both chapters modernity appears as a constitutive background for homosexuality. Chapter V proceeds to discuss the mutual reproductive relations between homosexuality and other factors and phenomena of modernity. Section 1 introduces the theme, which is analysed in sections 2–6, and the results are summarized in section 7. Finally, chapter VI discusses the possible disappearance of the formations of modern homosexuality.

II

Homosexualities Out of Date

1 Sambia

> The first time it tasted bitter. Later you can feel that it tastes sweet.
>
> 'Kambo', in Herdt, *Guardians of the Flutes* (1981)

When the boys are between the ages of seven and ten, they are removed from their mothers, indeed from any contact with women and girls, and initiated into the men's cult. During the next ten to fifteen years they engage in fellatio daily. At first they fellate the older boys and young men; later, from puberty on, they are fellated by a new group of boys. Between the ages of sixteen and twenty-five they marry, and for a while they may engage in sex both with their wife and with boys. But once the wife has had her first menstruation, or once they have become fathers, they are expected to have sex exclusively with women.

The above summarizes observations made by the American anthropologist Gilbert H. Herdt in Papua New Guinea in the 1970s, among a people he has called Sambia.[1] It corresponds in many respects with the material gathered among other peoples on New Guinea and the neighbouring islands by numerous anthropologists over the years.[2]

This fellatio, according to the Sambia men, is necessary. Only by ingesting semen can boys grow up and become *men*: muscular, strong, aggressive, brave, daring, courageous, tough, warlike, assertive, and dominating women and children.

It is beyond doubt that these sexual relations have a coercive nature: the boys are removed from their mothers and enlisted in the fellatio activities of the male cult without regard to what they themselves may wish; no one can escape; and the entire process is regulated in detail, as well as integrated with a great many other highly regulated practices and ideas into the Sambia overall cultural system. It is always decided from without, by a system of norms for which the adult men are agents, exactly when who should or should not do what.[3]

But this sexual activity is not coercion alone. If it is good to be a man (and, in Sambia, it is *the best*), and if a boy can only become a man – and survive at all – by ingesting semen, then semen is a gift, and the relation between the one who is fellated and the one who fellates is a relation between one who gives and one who receives.[4] Fellatio is not only that which makes boys men, but that which makes them *fellow* men; creating a certain bond between men: generosity and gratitude, obliging and being obliged, solidarity.

And finally, Herdt stresses, these sexual relations have an erotic and desirous nature. Although the roles as fellator and fellated are defined in advance, there is a certain leeway as to how often one does it, with whom, and how one interacts with the other in general. Most, however, engage in fellatio on a regular basis, and the young men joke with each other about particularly attractive boys they'd like to have fellate them; most also carry on this type of sexuality as long as the norms allow (that is, also after the norms no longer require it). And at least the young men who are fellated are erotically aroused by it – for otherwise they wouldn't be able to achieve an erection and an orgasm, Herdt concludes with a certain scientific pedantry.[5] One runs the risk of sounding a bit foolish when *arguing* the issue of desire, even though, as here, it is merely to show that desire does exist. The fact that it is necessary – here and elsewhere – is owing to the usual scientific practice of arguing it *away*.

2 Athens

> Now I am no good at measuring beautiful people; almost everyone who has just grown up appears beautiful to me. This time, moreover, the young man appeared to me a marvel of stature and beauty; and I felt everyone in the room

> was in love with him, such was their astonishment and confusion when he came in; and there were also many other wooers who were following after him. On the part of men like us it was not so surprising; but when I came to observe the boys I noticed that none of them, not even the smallest, had eyes for anything else, but that they all gazed at him as if he were a statue on display. Then Chairephon called me and said – 'What do you think of the young man, Socrates? Doesn't he have a handsome face?' – 'Immensely so', I replied. – 'Well', he said, 'if he'd strip, you'd forget he has a face at all, he is so overwhelmingly beautiful and shapely.'
>
> Plato, *Charmides*[6]

At least in the sixth to fourth centuries BC it was customary, at least in certain parts of Greece and among certain social classes, that men had sexual relations with 'boys' or 'young men'.

Just how old would a 'man' be and how old was a 'boy' or 'young man'? It isn't easy to answer such questions (nor so many other questions regarding Greek 'pederasty'). In the first place, the indications given by the sources are not comprehensive enough to allow us to come to any general conclusions about this great stretch of time and this considerable area; it is likely that the relations varied accord-ing to time and place. Secondly, the existing indications are not necessarily direct expressions of rules or norms. At least in Athenian society of the fifth and fourth centuries, the norms themselves are the object of public debate. Moreover, the aim of this debate is not so much to lay down strict rules to be followed to the letter by all; rather, Greek ethics seeks to give guidelines, which in turn must be specified differently under different circumstances. In a text, an indication of how old the boy or man should be in a sexual relation (and of a great many other circumstances concerning such relations) should therefore be read more as a commentary than as a direct expression of a rule.[7]

But there is in any case an age difference between the partners in these relations. The biological or chronological age is not decisive here; the essential is a perceived difference in development or maturity, and connected to this also one of social position: in other words a difference in one's status as a *man*. One of the partners should be so young that, although no longer a child, he does not yet fully count as a man; correspondingly, once the young man has become a real man it is no longer fitting for the partners to continue the relation.[8]

This Greek pederasty resides in a tension between desire and morality. It may have been associated at one time with notions that only by ingesting the adult man's semen did a boy become a man, but such notions did not exist among the educated and reflective Athenian upper class of the fourth century. (And it may in fact be that semen never made its way into the boy or young man, either orally or anally. The preferred position was perhaps *intercrural*, i.e. frontal, with the man's penis between the boy's thighs.) The man does not imagine that his sexual interplay with young boys makes them into men, or that his interest in them derives from pedagogical motives; on the contrary: it is driven by an entirely natural desire for sexual pleasure. This is precisely what makes it problematical, seen with Greek eyes: it threatens to make 'the boy', who is after all to become a man, *unmanly*. A man should be able to assert himself, be superior to others, take initiatives and make decisions, give orders and resist – which he cannot do convincingly if he has been pliant in sexual respects, submitted himself, been the simple object of another man's desires. Here, then, is a system of meanings and a logic which may seem to be just as self-evident in the modern world as in the Greek (by which they don't necessarily become 'natural'): a polarization of significance as to top and bottom, active and passive, penetrating and penetrated; a logic which joins certain sexual positions with certain values and certain social positions. In other words, men's desire for young men poses a danger for the latter's development into men; therefore it must be associated with morality, i.e. pedagogical interests, precisely in making the young man into a full-grown man by training him in sporting competition, hunting, discussion, etc. This was all the easier because it was precisely the young man's budding manhood that aroused the erotic interest of the man, not any potential likeness to women.

From this tension between desire and morality – between this particular desire, and this particular morality with its imbedded norms of masculinity – proceed a number of the phenomena characteristic of Greek pederasty: that the young man is not too willing, too forthcoming, doesn't have – i.e. shouldn't have – a *sexual* interest in the relation, and only submits to the adult man's desires in a kind of acknowledgement of his moral qualities. Hence also the intercrural position: a compromise between the adult's 'self-evident' desire to have sex with young men and the equally 'self-evident' imperative of securing the young man's honour as a prospective man. And hence the discussion itself of how one should act towards the young man: an extensive discussion which in turn produces a wide-ranging erotic awareness and sensibility towards young men.[9]

To say that sexual relations between men and boys were commonplace in ancient Greece is not synonymous with claiming that sexual relations between men – 'adult men' – were not. And in fact, references to them can be found in Greek literature and painting. The sources, however, do not permit us to say they were widespread, and it is reasonable to imagine they weren't. Based on what has been said above, it is clear what the problem would be: hardly that a man would want to penetrate another man, but that the other man would thereby lose in masculinity.[10]

3 The Indians

> During the time that I was thus among these people I saw a devilish thing, and it is that I saw one man married to another, and these are impotent, effeminate men and they go about dressed as women, and do women's tasks, and shoot with a bow, and carry great burdens . . . and they are huskier than the other men, and taller . . .
>
> Alvar de Vaca (*c.* 1530)

> But we place our trust in God and expect that these accursed people will disappear with the growth of the missions. The abominable vice will be eliminated to the extent that the Catholic faith and all the other virtues are firmly implanted there, for the glory of God and the benefit of those poor ignorants.
>
> Francisco Palóu (1777)[11]

When the white conquerors came to America they encountered in many places men who behaved more or less like the women, and who engaged in sexual intercourse with men. The missionaries, of course, were right: *it couldn't go on that way*; still, these particular figures could be found well into the twentieth century.

Among the Mohaves in south-western USA, however, these conditions were already passé when the French-American psychiatrist and ethnologist George Devereux visited them in the 1930s. He had to seek his information from those who could recall the days of old: a toothless and semi-senile man who still remembered the initiation songs, people who in their youth had known an *alyha*. This is what he learned.

The alyhas were men who behaved like the women as much as possible. They wore women's clothes; they simulated menstruation, pregnancies and births (the children, unfortunately, being stillborn and buried in private); they married or had affairs with men who would penetrate them anally or orally; and they pretended to have female genitals and demanded these were respected.

It was no coincidence that alyhas existed. 'From the very beginning of time' they were meant to be. Neither was it accidental who became an alyha. There were pregnant women and fetuses having dreams about it; there were boys who would rather wear women's clothes and play with dolls, rather cook than hunt. But not until the boy came to puberty was the ceremony arranged which would be the final test as well as the public affirmation.[12]

Aside from a little teasing – especially if they overplayed – the alyhas were not harassed. On the other hand, they weren't held in particularly high esteem, writes Devereux. Still, people could see their merits: they were exemplary cooks and housekeepers. Certain parts of Devereux's material (which he stresses less) however indicate a higher status. It was mentioned that only members of prominent families could become alyhas, that they were particularly gifted shamans (medicine men), and that they had luck in gaming. Moreover, it was told, only those other men possessing special powers – particularly shamans who were specialists in curing venereal diseases and known for being lucky in love – succeeded in procuring an alyha for wife.[13] Most likely, the alyha had once been of high standing (socially, religiously, with respect to the arts of healing and warfare), which had since been diminished.[14]

Any man could initiate a relationship with an alyha (if the latter was willing). There was nothing strange about this; contact was often established at ordinary social gatherings where flirting went on anyway between men and available females: widows, divorcees and women of easy virtue. A man who *married* an alyha however was likely to be teased, Devereux notes; but as stated, there are indications pointing in another direction: the option of marrying an alyha was not bestowed upon anyone; it demanded special status, even luck in love.[15]

Many other American cultures had figures similar to the Mohave alyhas, though perhaps not identical to them.[16] For example, the *nadles* among the Navahos in the southern Rocky Mountains. They seem to have enjoyed greater freedom than the alyhas: they could dress as men as well as women, perform male as well as female activities, and have both casual and lasting relationships with both women and men. Their standing was high: they were thought to bring wealth to their families and the nation in general; they performed important tasks in economic and social life; they were considered holy and shown great reverence. Even their promiscuity was respected; and there was complete social acceptance if a man had a relation to a nadle.[17]

It seems that, despite their efforts, the missionaries and authorities failed in eradicating the Indian man-women entirely. The anthropologist W. L. Williams encountered two of them in the flesh in 1982 while doing field work on the Lakota reservations (in South Dakota). The accounts he gathered are in line with those sketched above.[18]

III

Absent Homosexuality

1 Possibilities

> By studying sexual excitations other than those that are manifestly displayed, [psychoanalysis] has found that all human beings are capable of making a homosexual object choice and have in fact made one in their unconscious.
>
> Freud, *Three Essays on the Theory of Sexuality* (1915)

> The data . . . seem to offer little support for the theory that large proportions of the population harbour unrealized fantasies about same-gender sex. 2.2% of men report having felt attracted to, but having no experience with, someone of their own gender . . . 6.1% of men have had some kind of homosexual experience . . . Those who . . . describe their sexual experience as *mostly* or *exclusively* with others of the same gender is small, making up barely 1% of the total sample of men.
>
> K. Wellings et al., *Sexual Behaviour in Britain* (1994)[1]

What happened or happens between men in Sambia, in Athens or among the Indians does not resemble what is usually associated with homosexuality in modern societies. Here, as every child is (or was) supposed to know, there are the homosexuals, who are only after sex with other men, and the heterosexuals, who are simply incapable of that sort of thing. Or if they do it nonetheless, then only because they are not in full possession of their faculties (but dead drunk, sub-normal or not yet fully grown), or because they are deprived of their full freedom of movement (as being put in prison or in military camps).

The sexual relationships between men in these other societies, then, seem too different to tell us much about modern homosexuality – other than that it is historically specific and not universal. However, the cases do indicate that sexuality between men – and not just the behaviour or the interest, but also its acceptance – is a universal possibility in the sense that there are no biological or other not historically conditioned obstacles to it. If such obstacles did exist, it could not be universal in any society. Or at least, these societies indicate that certain *types* of sexuality between men are possible for all men. Provisionally, we can distinguish between two main types: *pederasty* (such as in Sambia and 'classical' Athens) and sexuality related to *berdache* institutions (such as among the American Indians).[2] 'Pederasty' is here used as a generic term for sexual relationships between a man and a young man/youth/boy. 'Berdache' – the term has a long history with changing meanings – has become a common generic term for a number of social roles, identities and ways of being where a man lives, perhaps *as* a woman, perhaps as an intermediate gender or a mixture of genders, a man-woman: whatever the case, in accordance with some of the norms that, in a particular society, apply for life as a woman. Of relevance in our present context are the varieties of the berdache institution where any man (perhaps any man of a certain social status) can have sexual relations with the berdaches.

The classification of many varied forms of male sexual relationships in two main categories is of course, problematical, as are all superficial classifications of this kind. It glosses over a number of differences between the phenomena that are shoved together in the same category and accentuates, more or less arbitrarily, one single feature at the expense of others. If we are clear about this, the consequences need not be serious.[3] The characteristic accentuated here as generic to pederastical institutions is age difference (in a biological or social sense) between the partners; for berdache institutions it is difference in gender identity and gendered ways of being.

Hence, what these societies demonstrate is that sexuality between men is a universal possibility *provided that* those involved experience each other as being different; more specifically, *as not being men to the same extent*. But is sexuality between men a universal possibility when they do experience one another as equally male (i.e.

not totally equal but in the sense that neither of them is experienced as a 'non-man' or a 'not yet man')?

There are many examples of societies in which boys of the same age in puberty, or very young men, have sex with each other.[4] There is also a host of indications, from the most varied cultures, of different kinds of sexual relations between adult men.[5] But often the accounts consist of but a few sentences which are in themselves ambiguous; besides, it is difficult to determine what is reliable and what is just rumour or accusation. In any case, it has not yet been determined that societies exist or have existed in which sexuality between 'equals' is universal.

So far, we have confirmed that there are no biological or other not historically conditioned obstacles to sexuality between men; at any rate, as to certain forms of sexual relations. To that extent, 'homosexuality' is a universal possibility in modern societies too. But is it also a universal *reality* in such societies, or to phrase the question differently, to what extent does it actually exist here, and how?

These questions were for a long time left comparatively uninvestigated by constructionists. During recent years, however, the field has been increasingly analysed and theorized. Primarily, it has been done in three (perhaps combining) ways: by employing psychoanalytic theories and analyses; by elaborating concepts of homophobia; and by researching the possible coexistence of, on the one hand, the particularly modern dichotomy of homosexuals and heterosexuals, and, on the other hand, previous distinctions which allow for different forms of male–male sexuality (perhaps somewhat similar to those connected with berdache institutions).[6] I shall discuss all of these approaches in the course of the argumentation pursued in this chapter; each of them, I think, contains a number of problems.

In any case: the historical and cross-cultural material does not help in answering the questions of the actual prevalence and forms of homosexuality in modern societies. If we want to explore the issues more thoroughly, we have to use sources of knowledge that specifically concern homosexuality in these societies. The most obvious of such sources are *population surveys*, *prison studies*, *psychoanalysis* and *social phenomenology*.

2 Population surveys

'In these terms (of physical contact to the point of orgasm), the data in the present study indicate that at least 37 per cent of the male population has had some homosexual experience between the beginning of adolescence and old age', writes Kinsey. To really get his point across to the stunned American readers of 1948, he adds: 'This is more than one male in three of the persons that one may meet as he passes along a city street.' Moreover '13 per cent of the males (approximately) react erotically to other males without having overt homosexual contacts' (i.e. physical contacts with orgasm).[7] Kinsey's method permits him to transcend conventional beliefs by a simple trick: the personal interview on behaviour and reactions, collected in mass quantity. His overall conclusion, then, is that about 50 per cent of the male population has homosexual experience (in one form or other).[8]

However, the other side to this conclusion is obviously that '50 per cent of all males (approximately) have neither overt nor psychic experience in the homosexual after the onset of adolescence.'[9] Moreover, there are methodological problems with Kinsey's sample, with the likely consequence that the percentage for men with homosexual experience is too high.[10] It is also possible that the figures are an expression of specific American circumstances in the 1930s and 1940s.[11] As to the question of whether the partners experience each other as equally male, this is not dealt with in the study.

There have been many other attempts to measure the prevalence of homosexuality in the population. However, none of them exceed Kinsey in percentage. If one is to believe the majority of these studies, homosexuality is very uncommon, affecting only a small percentage of all men.[12]

3 Prison studies

Sex between men in prison is widespread, and many researchers have studied it. Why?

According to their own answers, they've been concerned, and as such they represent a broader concern: society's. An *evil* is abroad.

The task of the researcher is to find an explanation, i.e. the cause, so that society can intervene and eradicate the evil.[13]

The explanations vary, but they all are cut of the same cloth. However, two basic types of explanation can be identified (even if they often occur side by side). One runs like this:

1 Men possess a sexuality (or it possesses them) which is pressing and demands release.
2 The object of men's sexual interest is women.
3 If men are cut off from access to sexual satisfaction with women they will therefore seize on surrogates: hence, in male prisons, on men.
4 A number of circumstances in the functioning of prisons (too few or too negligent personnel, uncertainty due to conflicting crime policy directives, etc.) entails that this form of sexual release is not prevented.

The cure is directed at point 3 or 4. Men must have access to women; or changes must be made in prison conditions so that these acts can be prevented.[14]

The second basic kind of explanation starts in roughly the same manner:

1 Men who land in prison typically bring with them a particular form of sexuality.
2 The object of this sexuality is women.
But then comes this conclusion:
3 If men are cut off from access to sexual satisfaction with women (as happens in prison) they will then *have no sexuality at all.* Hence, if they nonetheless have sex with men in prison this cannot be in order to satisfy sexual need. But then, why?

We must start all over again.

1 Men who land in prison typically need emotional ties to other people and need to confirm their masculinity.
2 In social life outside prison, these needs are met via a mix of non-sexual relations with men and sexual relations with women.
3 If men are cut off from the usual pattern of satisfying these needs – as happens in prison with the atomizing of inmates, the absence of women, the impossibility of self-determination, the insecurity

– they will seize on surrogate satisfactions: hence, in male prisons, sex with other men. In this way the needs for emotional ties are satisfied as well as the needs for the demonstration of masculine dominance and potency, or for security.
4 Thus, homosexuality in prison is a product of the very forms of oppressive control: atomizing, alienation, loss of self-determination, insecurity; accordingly, an increase in oppressive control merely risks increasing homosexuality.

Consequently, the cure is directed towards point 3: it is a matter of 'providing those activities for which the homosexual contacts are serving as substitutes'. If not, there is 'little opportunity for adequate control of homosexual activity in the prison environment'.[15]

As we can see, the two explanations are variations of the same basic pattern:

1 + 2 Men's sexuality is (in fact) heterosexual.
3 Homosexuality in prisons is therefore a surrogate, a substitute for *other and different* needs and activities which prison precludes.

Is this explanation valid? Can homosexuality in prison be explained on the basis of this pattern of drive and deprivation, compensation and substitute? Query: if in the relations of these men it is *simply* a matter of finding a substitute for sex with women or of satisfying non-sexual needs, then any man could surely be used, or at any rate it should not be important for such relationships whether a man is *sexually attractive as a man* (is good-looking, tough, looks like James Dean, is big and silent, hairy, has a special gleam in his eye, etc.)? Further, the most effeminate would be the most popular. But is that the way it is?

Before we pursue this question further, we should have a closer look at a specific 'class distinction' that seems widespread in prisons. Some men are categorized, and categorize themselves, as 'Men' (or 'jockers', or 'studs'): they dominate, they are the ones who penetrate, fight, procure the material goods and are waited on. Others are 'punks' (or 'kids'): they are dominated, penetrated, serving. These labels have a high degree of stability: once attached – and this occurs rapidly after arrival at prison – they stick. Not all perform these roles, and they are not equally widespread in all prisons. But they are rather extensive and we have to take them into consideration when examining whether a man's 'sex appeal' as a man plays any part in homosexual relationships in prison.

One might argue in advance that such a study was superfluous or even improper, since a great deal of prison homosexuality starts with rape and other forms of violence, as appears to excess from the literature. I am, however, interested in studying whether, *apart* from the violence, or for that matter *in relation to* it, there are also forms of erotic attraction, both in relationships that do not contain violence and in those that do. I shall disregard what is repellent in violence, not because I'd claim it's rare or inessential or indeed acceptable, but because I want to investigate something else.

Does, then, the sexual attraction of a man *qua* man play a role in prison homosexuality? It is not surprising that prison studies have rarely posed this kind of question. Their point of departure virtually precludes it. But there are in fact a few newer studies that do raise the issue. They ask the prisoners, who immediately respond that it's the *feminine* in other men that attracts them; and the researchers instantly take note of this without further questioning. Moreover, some studies investigate the issue *objectively* and conclude that the men subjected to sexual assault, on average *weigh less*, *are younger* and *are less violent* than the assaulters. The matter, then, is perfectly plain: 'The aggressor sees himself as a male; therefore, he selects targets who look, to him, like females.'[16] Elementary. As all agree it's no problem that the evidence is less than thin and the reasoning totally mindless. Did they expect that an aggressor would choose, as objects for his sexual attack, men who were bigger, more strongly built and more violent than himself? Can a man really overlook that it is another man he is penetrating? Are there really that many feminine men who land in prison? Aren't prisoners, now and then, *too* eager to assure us that they are only interested in the effeminate, and too inconsistent?[17] Would anyone expect that an ordinary male prisoner, faced with a seriously concerned researcher who, on behalf of state and prison authorities is engaged in studying the problem of homosexuality and consequently incarnates power in a multitude of forms: The State, The Prison, Science, Morality and The Heterosexual Norm – would anybody expect such a prisoner to say that he got a hard-on at the thought of other men?

Let us therefore turn to those studies which never even raise the question of what it is in a man that attracts another. The absence of the question does not preclude illuminating material shining through in the reports, so to speak without the researcher noticing it, all the while he is aiming to show something else.

Let us first look at the punk. Some 'Men' boast that all punks run after them with flattering offers.[18] Whatever the truth in this (and the punk can have good reasons which have very little to do with sexual attraction), it seems that many punks, even though they may have originally resisted sexuality with a man, come to 'like it' – and to like the man; and sometimes continue to have sex with men after they leave prison.[19]

Next, the Man. Is the other man's sexual attractiveness *as a man* of importance to him? Certain factors seem to preclude this in advance. The Man is labelled and experienced by others and by himself precisely as Man, whereas the other is labelled punk, that is, in one or other sense, 'not-Man': at any rate, not as much a man as the Man. In some cases, but clearly not all, these punks perform a pronounced female role: dress in women's clothes (to the extent that they can get away with it), adopt women's names, imitate women's speech, walk and gestures. (In such cases the class of non-Men can be subdivided in two: queens and punks.)[20] These distributions of roles and public perceptions of oneself and others are probably important in order to make the relationships work; at any rate, they prevent the Man from falling into the socially condemned role of homosexual even though he practises homosexuality.[21] But do *we* have to accept them at their face value?

In any case, these men know very well that it is other men they are penetrating. It's possible, and very likely, that in many cases when they penetrate strongly feminine or feminized queens, they do so precisely because these remind them of women; they can fantasize they are with women.[22] But it is also possible that the gender mix, i.e. not-only-woman but also man, has a sexually exciting effect on some; or that the feminine in a man may serve to justify the enjoyment of his masculinity. Besides, most punks are not feminine.[23] But is this an unfortunate detail to be disregarded as quickly as possible? Let us see what slips through in the texts. In fact they often speak of it, though it's never the subject.

'Men' tell (or it is told of men) that they have sex, or want to have sex, with men who they think 'look good' or 'attractive', who are 'special' and whom they 'spot', have their 'eye on', 'choose', etc.[24] But it's not just a matter of a few individuals' special inclinations, but also of more general assessments. Prisoners, researchers and prison authorities state that the punks who are 'sexually' or 'physically' 'attractive', 'desirable', etc. are often the object of conflicts between Men, are often subject to sexual assault, are those who obtain relationships with the Men of the highest status and –

for one or more of these reasons – should be kept separate from the other inmates.[25] And in such contexts, there is no indication that it is the femininity of the punks which attracts. Besides, there are often relationships with less pronounced divisions of role, more mutuality of interest – in sex, in love.[26]

Thus it seems that men in prison do not merely have sex with other men *despite* the fact that these are men but also *because* of it. But, it will be objected, to the extent that this is actually the case, it's precisely because, as the second type of explanation emphasizes, there are other needs than the sexual at stake: to affirm masculinity, to feel secure, etc. In other words, when a prisoner has sex with another prisoner it is because, by doing so, he is boosted, so to speak. For example, the more manly the other is, the more man you become by penetrating him. Or, the stronger his arms, the more security he gives.

But in this sense, these relationships are in principle no different from other homosexual relationships. To counter that there is the difference of desire and pleasure is, according to the above analysis, obviously unfounded: in both cases there is sexual excitement, erection, orgasm, positive attraction, interest in precisely this man as a man or in the manliness he symbolizes.

These studies of sex in prison are interesting. They show that men are capable of arousing the sexual interest of other men, and indeed positively so, *as men*; not merely negatively, as substitutes for women. They show that men have sex with men in prison not merely because they lack women but because other men are there. They show that the problem is not so much to explain why there is sex between men in prison as why there isn't outside. The studies show the opposite of what they claim; what they don't want to say they blurt out all the same.[27]

4 Psychoanalysis

'By studying sexual excitations other than those that are manifestly displayed, [psychoanalysis] has found that all human beings are capable of making a homosexual object choice and have in fact made one in their unconscious', writes Freud.[28] This claim rests at first on 'empirical' material drawn from the client analyses conducted by Freud and his colleagues. However, the cases are simply too few and too specific to corroborate such general conclusions, let alone the reservations one might harbour as to the analytic procedures applied to this material. We should therefore take a closer look at whether the claim has any further foundations.[29]

Freud proposed yet another type of argument from empirical material. Whereas the above draws general conclusions from the homosexuality of a few individuals, this line of argument takes its starting point in phenomena which are clearly universal (e.g. social feelings), seeking to prove they are of a homosexual nature. This type of reasoning is the topic of the next section.

In addition to these arguments, proceeding more or less directly from empirical material, yet another kind of reasoning could be applied. If one can hypothesize the existence of homosexual interests in all men on the basis of analyses of empirical material, then this proposition will be theoretically reinforced if universal homosexuality is a necessary or likely consequence of *other* – and plausible – assumptions in psychoanalytic theory. There are, for Freud, typically two possibilities: if homosexuality is present in all adults it is because it was constituted in everyone's *childhood*, or because it is carried along in everyone's *biology*.

Let us look at the latter first. Homosexuality, we are told, exists in all human beings because it is there by nature, humans are constitutionally bisexual. Freud refers here to *anatomy*: the sexual organs of one sex bear traces of the other. Based on this observation Freud now makes the particular manoeuvre of rendering improbable the likelihood of inferring bisexuality in partner choice from this 'anatomical hermaphroditism', *and* inferring it just the same.[30]

This, then, is one line of thought from biology. There is another, though it was never worked out in detail by Freud. It leads us back to *the evolution of the human species*.

Freud's idea is that what appears as constitutionally given was once historically acquired. Biological heredity is historical experience, stored throughout evolution, a sort of memory bank of humanity. Therefore, if it can be proved that during the evolutionary history of the human species there were experiences which would effect homosexual proclivities, it would follow that all humans are constitutionally endowed with such dispositions.

Thus we are led back to the *primal horde*, at the transition from ape to man. The despotic father ensured his monopoly on women by banishing his young sons from the flock; within these groups of exiled brothers emerged homosexual feelings and activities. But even prior to this banishment there was homosexuality: the sons feared and hated the father, yet they loved him as well.[31]

One can, of course, raise fundamental objections to this theory, both as a historical construct of mankind's distant past and as a biological theory of the heredity of acquired properties. But even if we disregard these objections, the theory does not explain how homosexuality would be a necessary or plausible consequence of relations within the primal horde: how can it be that male children become sexually interested in their fathers or brothers?

The excursion into biology thus brings us, via the evolutionary history of the species, back to the *childhood of the individual.* Is it possible to find circumstances here that must bring about the formation of homosexual proclivities in all?

The material for an answer is found in Freud's reflections on the principles for the child's – in this case, the male child's – choice of sexual 'object'. The fundamental options are seen to be determined by the phases and relationships through which every boy must pass in his development. Accordingly, these various forms of object choice play a (greater or lesser) role for all boys; and at least six of them are of a homosexual nature.

1 The boy chooses as a sexual object those persons who nurse him, and he does so because they happen to stimulate his pleasure zones in the process, that is, they seduce him. According to Freud this does not merely concern the mother – who suckles (etc.) the boy – but also the father who protects him.[32]
2 The boy chooses as a sexual object those persons who resemble him, and he does so because he loves himself (and not least his penis). In this context, the father takes first place. Freud terms this type of object choice 'narcissistic'.[33]
3 The boy chooses as a sexual object persons of the same sex and gender as himself because they resemble what he once was (and was happy to be) or what he would like to be. Freud sees this form of object choice as a variation of the narcissistic form, a kind of compensation for 'damaged' narcissism.[34]
4 The boy chooses as a sexual object those persons whom he regards as rivals in the struggle to attain the mother's favour. He hereby avoids fruitless conflicts and achieves at the same time an outlet for his energies in a slightly different fashion. Here, too, the father would surely be in prime position, although Freud speaks primarily of the brothers.[35]
5 The boy chooses males as a sexual object because his mother has done so. Having been forced to forfeit the mother as sexual object he now seeks to recoup himself by identifying with her, including

her object choice and not least her love for him; he seeks objects he is able to love just as his mother loved him.[36]

6 The boy chooses males as a sexual object because he wants to feel the pleasure of having his anus and rectum stimulated, and males are active and have something to stimulate with.[37]

All of these lines of argument pose problems. Concerning (1), how can the father become a sexual object when he typically plays no part in the boy's personal hygiene? (2) Does the boy really love himself in any sexual sense, and can it be made credible that he *therefore* will transfer this sexual interest to persons who resemble him? (3) Can fractures in narcissism be healed through the choice of a specific sexual object, and if so, how should one further grasp the process? (4) Is it plausible that the boy's feelings of hostility can be substituted by sexual interest? (5) Can the boy really identify with the mother to the extent that he chooses the same (types of) sexual objects she has chosen? (6) Is it reasonable to assume that desires for anal pleasure lead to a homosexual object choice (and not the other way round, for example)? Finally, there is the problem of whether the boy's homosexuality (and homosexuality *per se*) can be adequately described – as is virtually always the case with Freud – on the basis of the conceptual dichotomy of passive–active, feminine–masculine (homosexuality, what would one expect, being the passive and feminine: the boy wants his penis to be touched, he wants to be penetrated by his father just as his mother is).[38]

I will refrain from pursuing this discussion here, not only because it implies such theoretical and empirical problems (which Freud tries to take into account, although only to a certain degree), but primarily for three fundamental reasons.

First, the framework that Freud establishes for the discussion makes it more difficult than necessary. The setting, the gallery of characters, the time frame of the plot, the repertoire of potential interpersonal relations inherent in the roles, in short, *the scenery of the Oedipal theatre*, limit the scope of material for discussion and place it beyond the test potentials of our own life-world.

Secondly, Freud's arguments, even if they could be made tenable, are not sufficient for our present aims. *Maybe* all boys are sexually interested in their father or brother; without further qualification, however, we cannot infer that these childhood wishes continue on as homosexual interests in every adult man.[39]

And finally, explaining by way of childhood implies a certain reductionism with respect to homosexuality (as with so much else).

Homosexuality is not allowed *to be*: it is not simply there, in sheer presence; it exists only insofar as it existed in childhood, only because it existed in childhood, only as an expression of what existed in childhood. It has to be explained, that is, explained away.

No one within the psychoanalytic tradition has produced more convincing arguments for the universality of homosexual interests.[40] On the contrary, many exponents (not least in the American versions of psychoanalysis) have been concerned with revising Freud in this respect, such that homosexuality could be strictly limited to a minority.[41]

Although Freud's arguments in favour of a universal homosexuality are problematic, it can hardly be doubted that he has made a decisive contribution to our knowledge of the prevalence of homosexuality: where Kinsey and prison studies have shown that homosexuality is more widespread and capable of spreading even wider than generally known and conceded, Freud has shown that it may be found even when those involved are not consciously aware of it.

5 Social phenomenology

As mentioned in the previous section there is yet another way of confronting the issue of the universality of homosexuality in modern societies. This approach addresses phenomena which are in one sense or other general but seemingly have nothing to do with homosexuality – ordinary patterns of feeling and action, social institutions and roles – and seeks to reveal a hidden homosexual content. Again, the main source of inspiration has been psychoanalysis.

Thus, in Freud we find homosexuality underlying such phenomena as religion, morality, social feelings and jealousy. To a large extent, we are told, the connection was originally established through events in the primal horde, but it is re-established in reality or in fantasy in the developmental path of each individual.[42]

Behind *religion* with its father figure hides the son's love (and hate) for his father. The son had to give up this love object, not least because the father was also his rival in relation to the mother and threatened to castrate him. He therefore killed the father more or less literally: and the beloved father is now resurrected truly deified.[43]

Underlying *morality* and its anchor in the individual psyche (self-examination, ideal demands and conscience) is also the son's desire for the father. He loved his father but had to give him up as a sexual object and tried to compensate himself by resurrecting him (and his commands) in his own psyche.[44]

Behind the *social feelings* too – friendship, fellowship, solidarity, charity – hides a homosexuality that, in the end, originates in childhood, especially from the sexual interests which the boy – to avoid useless conflicts yet nevertheless get something out of the situation – developed in his rivals during the struggle for the sexual favours of the mother.[45]

Behind *jealousy* – which on the surface is only about grief at the loss of the beloved woman and hatred of the rival man – we also find grief at the loss of the beloved man and hatred of the rival woman; once again in a repeat of the patterns of emotion in childhood relations to parents and siblings.[46]

Homosexuality is not the only factor underlying these phenomena but it is, in Freud's view, the decisive one. One can almost say that were there no universal homosexuality, there would be no culture. Yet Freud's reasoning is weak. The point of departure is a phenomenon which is analysed – turned and twisted – so that its distinctive features may appear. Next, an attempt is made to demonstrate that these special features can only be understood if we assume that they are, in one way or another, expressions of an underlying homosexuality. These 'phenomenological reductions', however, follow a special zigzag course. Sure enough, a phenomenon is turned and twisted; a fairly simple example is the relationship between the 'primitives' and their totem animal. Here, naturally, Freud can be phenomenal: the incredible acuteness known from the analysis of dreams and symptoms, the capacity to see what has been overlooked. (For instance, in the above example: why both celebrate the killing of the totem animal *and* grieve over it?) But, having ascertained the various special features of the phenomenon, it is abandoned. We move on to *similar* special features in neurotics, psychotics, the perverse, or children (little Arpád had a similar relation to *chickens* during his summer holiday in the countryside in 1910). The next step is to remind the reader that psychoanalysis has traced these particular features in children etc. back to homosexuality in childhood (yes, it was the *father* that Arpád loved and hated). The final conclusion is that the phenomenon under analysis can be traced back to the homosexual relationship to the father.[47] (The components may appear in a different order, the logic remains the same.) This reasoning, too, is not cogent. Once again, childhood is the centre of gravity. But even if we do accept this, it is not the phenomenon that is traced back to homosexuality, but at best something which *resembles* it. Psychoanalysis here (as everywhere else) tends to become an automatic application of preconceived frameworks to the part of the real world under study: to possess the answer before the analysis. The phenomenon has hardly been made to speak before theory shuts it up.

The same zigzag course is found in Hocquenghem's attempt – via Freud and Ferenczi's analyses of paranoia – to trace the social persecution (and prosecution) of homosexuals back to a universal persecution mania that, again, is an expression of a universal and universally repressed homosexuality.[48] The analysis is fantastically astute and suggestive but it remains an argument by analogy: Hocquenghem is able to see interrelationships that no one else can discover, one may affirm – or object.[49]

6 Proofs

Is homosexuality a universal reality in modern societies, i.e. is it found in or among all men? Neither population surveys, nor prison studies nor psychoanalyses have provided the material to *prove* it. But one might venture to say that, taken together, they have made it conceivable by demonstrating that homosexuality, in various forms, is more widespread and spreadable than is generally known and acknowledged.

Possibilities, but no proofs. If scientific investigations and arguments can take us no further regarding the universality of homosexuality in modern societies, it is not necessarily because much remains to be studied, nor necessarily because what was to be demonstrated does not exist; it is perhaps because something about this object precludes such scientific argumentation beyond a certain point. Indeed, it may be a constitutive trait of homosexuality in modern societies that it exists primarily insofar as its existence can be denied.

In the following pages we shall further investigate the possible existence of such a homosexuality: its prevalence, its nature, and its specific forms. In the process we shall reflect upon the methods by which it can be investigated, as well as upon the rationale – or perhaps *ir*rationale – of pursuing this type of investigation. First, we shall delineate the theme by way of an example.

7 The torturer

Thy Neighbour's Son, a film about torture under the junta dictatorship in Greece, is an attempt to grasp what makes a man into a torturer.[50] It reveals a remarkable ambiguity in these efforts to explain. On the one hand, a number of statements are delivered directly to the camera in interviews with 'experts' (psychologists) as well as with 'ordinary' victims and henchmen. The main thrust of these statements is that torture training functions primarily via a mechanism of compensation: when first recruited, the future torturer is subjected to severe subordination and humiliation by his superiors; then suddenly one day he is informed that he has completed training, is treated as an equal by his former tormentors, granted their privileges and initiated into their fellowship. The sudden change, one gathers, unleashes a number of needs and reactions. There is a reaction of emancipation: it is once again possible to move about 'freely' and according to will; related to this, in turn, is a reaction of gratitude to the former superiors, involving a desire to live up to their standards; finally, and most importantly, there is an accumulated need to compensate for the humiliations endured during the harsh period of training. *Summa summarum*: torture. This mechanism is all the more effective because the trainee is kept in a state of chronic mobilization: everyday rhythms are disrupted, drills are constantly pushing beyond the usual bounds of physical performance, commands are issued in impenetrable and unpredictable ways. The result: inner reflection is thwarted, the scene is left to the artificially isolated autodynamics of physical-emotional reactions. And once the result has been achieved, it is fortified by a series of more prosaic reinforcements: access to material goods, fearful deference on the part of civilians.

This, then, is one of the explanations for the transformation of man into a torturer. Besides it, and separate from it, are a number of instances in the film which *could* be pieces of an explanation; they are hardly ever articulated directly to the interviewer and the camera, but they form an integral part of the – reconstructed – scenes from the everyday life of torturer socialization and profession. At work are a number of games concerning the signifiers *man/*

homosexual. A recruit is commanded to stamp on the picture of his girlfriend, to fornicate with a sack in front of the others; 'a man should fuck and fight' is the officer's maxim (that, it seems, is the *definition* of a man); the word homosexual (more precisely: Greek slang for a man who lets himself be sodomized)[51] is an indispensable prop in all relationships of violence and humiliation between officers and recruits as well as between torturers and victims: it is what one is *not* and may not be; what one disavows, makes use of in training, uses as humiliation, uses to legitimate the humiliation. These parts of an explanation do not actually contradict the explanation that is presented explicitly, but they are not integrated into it, not articulated by it.

8 'Latency', 'sublimation' and 'repression'

If homosexuality is found among all men, yet not explicitly so, what then is its mode of being and how can it be identified?

These questions lead us into a field largely occupied by psychoanalytic theory. Homosexual drives, this conception has it, are held in contempt in modern Western societies and by and large not allowed to take on explicit or 'manifest' expression, but must remain 'latent'. They are 'repressed', i.e. kept as much as possible from conscious life and from being acted out. Or they are 'sublimated', i.e. gain expression in interests and activities which in certain ways resemble homosexuality, but which still have a significantly different character and are socially acceptable. This is how the Freudian leftist tradition apprehends the issue (Altman, Hocquenghem, Mieli, and Freud himself as well).[52] But to some degree this way of thinking has also spread. Thus, many gays are of the opinion that men play soccer because they're afraid of having sex with each other.

One problem with the concepts of repression and sublimation is that their meanings are unclear and harder to keep separate than may appear at first glance.[53] These difficulties, however, can be remedied through interpretation and qualification; and to the extent that the concepts may, by then, seem too specific to accommodate all relevant phenomena in the area, one can try to supplement them with still others taken from the Freudian repertoire of defence mechanisms. In the following explorations, however, I will avoid any use of such concepts as repression, sublimation and latency, primarily because they are so intertwined with the basic notions of libido, drives and childhood that make up the general fabric of psychoanalysis. Since I have already dealt with this complex of problems in other contexts, I will only briefly summarize it here in relation to the themes of the following investigations.

Thus, the concepts of latent, repressed or sublimated homosexuality are heavily entwined in a particular base-superstructure model: the various acts and experiences of eroticism, love, pleasure, etc. are considered to be merely distorted – repressed or sublimated – expressions of what it ultimately is all about, i.e. a physical orgasmic release, repeating or reworking patterns of behaviour and experience rooted in childhood relations to the parents. Moreover, this basic essence is conceived as a drive: an ever-present force that endeavours to push its way out, always prepared to assume these distorted expressions.[54] Finally, the base–superstructure and drive of sexuality are thought to exist in all people; and consequently sublimation and repression are common to all.

As noted before, I am not convinced that such conceptions can be considered adequate and well founded. Rather, we must keep open the possibility that e.g. soccer and other social relations between men – even insofar as they may have sexual dimensions – are not necessarily distorted expressions of underlying drives to achieve sexual release and reiterate childhood, nor of any underlying sexual essence whatsoever. Conversely, when something is indeed the object of 'repression' or another form of 'defence', it is not necessarily a sexual matter, but whatever interest that happens to be charged with danger. Furthermore, there are not necessarily any 'homosexual' wishes present prior to a given situation – they could conceivably emerge in the situation itself; neither is it certain they would occur among all participants.[55]

Since we are unable to accept the theoretical framework of psychoanalysis, we can scarcely accept the general analytic guidelines implied in the concepts of latency, repression and sublimation: that it is a matter of identifying an underlying homosexual drive, or vice versa, of revealing where and how it is hidden, i.e. in fact filling in a previously defined grid.

The following explorations, then, differ from the conceptual and analytic apparatus of psychoanalysis. But Freud's actual analyses, as well as the moves used in them, remain a source of inspiration.

9 Mikaël

'Poignant in its pain, this book is Danish literature's principal work on jealousy and by far the most pronounced portrayal of "another kind" of love', wrote Hakon Stangerup, the literary critic, in commenting upon Herman Bang's *Mikaël* (1904).[56] The novel has twice been adapted for the screen, in 1916 by Mauritz Stiller and in 1924 by Carl Th. Dreyer; the former version is sometimes referred to as the first 'gay' film ever.[57] But how, indeed, do Stangerup and others know it is a story of 'another kind' of love, that is, of *homosexual* love?

Seemingly, the book is lacking in any reference at all to homosexuality. The *word* is not mentioned, nor are comparable terms; there is no discussion of the *problems* of being homosexual, no description of homosexual subculture, its locations or its doings, no physical – *sexual* – intimacy, no touching of forbidden parts. (Is it *really* necessary to impose a sexual symbolism on Mikaël's rubbing of the old man's feet one cold evening?)

Granted, the novel displays a number of characteristics which can't help but raise suspicions in the minds of sensitive readers that the narrator, and indeed the *author*, is a homosexual: his indulgent relation to nobility, this strange predilection for the world of princesses, grand dukes and dowager duchesses (as a rule, the more noble in standing, the more noble of spirit); his preoccupation with the ladies' garb; the extravagant opulence of the settings; the posing pathos ('How – and her voice had the sound of someone whose thoughts seek longingly towards something long since passed – beautiful it is'; 'with a smile like someone who, far too young, has seen far too much')[58]; the accentuated ambiguities combined with the penetrating insight ('perhaps he had not noticed the change in Lady Adelsskjold's tone, or possibly he had timidly ventured to divine what it might conceal')[59]. In a word: *camp*, albeit unintentional. But even if the author is homosexual, this is no guarantee that the *novel* is about homosexuality.

In any case: an ageing celebrated Parisian painter ('Maître') has taken the seventeen-year-old Mikaël into his home, in part because the boy may have a bit of talent, but primarily because he himself is bored, feels confined, lacks contact with life. At the age of twenty-two, the young man falls madly in love with a Russian princess, becomes secretive, takes to contradicting Maître (which, to any outsider, seems to be high time). He no longer respects regular hours for meals, usual conventions, all those snug habits that become entrenched when people live together over a long period and which lend hominess, familiarity, Maître-and-Mikaëlness, intimacy, at least presence to life. Mikaël sells a personal gift Maître has given him; he also 'borrows' a few valuables (they seem in abundance) to finance his freedom and his infatuation. The painter responds with anger and sorrow, and a certain amount of jealousy, of course: he is left with loneliness, absence, old age, death.

In short: a story of a generation conflict, of conflict between two sets of social values (capital vs nobility and peasantry, money vs land, buying vs gifts – the avaricious Princess de Zamikoff originates, of course, from a family of merchants, Mikaël is of undefined proletarian background and Maître of peasant ancestry), of conflict between art and life, of everyday human dependencies. What, then, is *homosexual* about it?

The innocent reader is fictitious. In spite of, or rather *because of* the absence of homosexuality in the novel, and the silences, denials and double entendres in the secondary literature, it is known what the text is about.[60] Even if the heterosexual reader *knows nothing* (and because he or she doesn't know), he or she knows it just the same.

How is it that we know what we don't know? First, there is the issue of *passion*. Maître overreacts to Mikaël's breaking away, all the way through to the very end: a man does not *die* because his foster-son leaves him for a woman, even when the man doesn't like her. In any case, it's *abnormal* to do so.

Further, Maître paints Mikaël, uses his naked body as a model for his paintings, and this is apparently not what it seems, even when we carve away all vulgar-Freudian interpretation of symbols (the paintbrush): not only does he paint him as Alcibiades and Eros, but the relation elicits a number of situations charged with overwrought ambiguity. Mikaël to Maître: '. . . I say to myself – and suddenly Mikaël spoke very quickly, almost as someone who is ashamed – it is *your* body he is painting . . . But then you must also, well, understand that my body (he searched for a word and came upon the most peculiar) should not be befallen as with the others', etc. On another occasion, to Mikaël's aggressive outburst that, for Maître, he has never been more than 'an object to be painted', Maître responds: 'Do you really believe so?' after which Mikaël averts his eyes and 'a moment later' Maître adds: 'But Mikaël, I shall never give you an answer.' And when the servant enters straight away, they continue eating as if nothing had transpired – although the servant 'knew everything'.[61]

Moreover: a number of impertinent remarks, primarily from the somewhat cynical but clear-sighted participant observer Mr Schwitt. For example, to Mikaël, to whom Maître has given an Egyptian ring: 'No doubt he'll soon present you with a pair of anklets' (as slaves would wear, perhaps, but prostitutes as well).[62] To Maître, who mentions that Mikaël 'entered' his life: 'That is to say, you took him into your life' – an innocent correction, one would think, if it weren't for the agitation it arouses in both men. Again, to Maître: 'It's been quite some time since you painted a woman' – the inappropriateness appearing in Maître's lack of response.[63]

Fourth, the pronounced parallelism between the development of the relationship of Maître–Mikaël–Princess de Zamikoff and of the clearly erotic domestic triangle of Adelsskjold–Lady Adelsskjold–the Duke of Monthieu: the yearnings, sufferings and jealousy of Maître and Adelsskjold flow together and merge.

Fifth, allusions or overtures to open homosexuality, relatively plain talk, followed by neutralizing: excuses, rationalizations, denials, erasures. Mr Schwitt, on women who want it all: ' "There are fewer and fewer men left who are able to give all." The duke slowly turned his head: "Do you think so?" he said. "I know. And the reason is very simple. Men nowadays", said Mr Schwitt, "must first take care of the finances. The women get whatever remains." '[64] (Naturally, these sentences have several connotations in the text, as others do in general; I only wish to stress one aspect of meaning here.)

Sixth, certain words, themes which – for larger or smaller groups of people, and for them more or less consciously – have particular homosexual connotations. During a tense exchange between Maître and Mikaël, Maître begins to conjure up memories of happier moments and places, speaking of visits to 'foreign countries and regions where they have been together'. Happiness is not now, at most it exists in memory or in yearning; and it is not found here but in another country, a foreign country – a stock theme in the homosexual experience. And *where* might that place be? In this novel, it is Prague, London, Rome, Norway, Algeria, Egypt – above all, the last two, the *Arab* countries ('But there is nothing as wonderful as the desert', the Egyptian ring, the Oriental anklets, a life of abandon, the shrouded women, men together, Arabian nights, Gide, Lawrence).[65] Moreover, Maître often laments his confinement: his cage, bars, cell, prison, etc.; he is closed off from life, can only hope to watch *the others* live, observe *the others*' love, he is a stranger and alone, others do not know him as he really is – again, stock themes in the homosexual experience.[66]

There are, of course, combinations of these ways, e.g. of the special themes and the neutralized overtures. About the Duke of Monthieu, a whole series of these: his face 'had the pale tint brought out by creams and essences'; he is, in yet another inappropriate remark by Mr Schwitt, 'truly a work of six centuries' – in other words, degenerate; he 'seems confused' when Mikaël meets him at night on the promenades near the Tuileries Gardens along the Seine – allusions that are all quickly negated by his glances towards Lady Adelsskjold's bosom, etc.[67]

And finally, there is absence. Mikaël is the absence that is present all the same: although possessing the title role, he is absent as the leading character, absent over long passages of the text, absent when Maître is dying and needs him most, perhaps even absent as erotic love in Maître's consciousness. Nevertheless, he is present at all times, implied, if you will, as that which lends meaning to the text – and to life. This absent presence is homosexuality. The fact that Mikaël, that homosexuality, is not there indicates that indeed it is; it is present in that it is not present; that is its way of being.

No doubt it holds true – even today, and not just in 1966, when Stangerup wrote his review – that *Mikaël* is 'by far the most pronounced portrayal of "another kind" of love', i.e. of homosexuality. It is the most pronounced portrayal of homosexuality precisely because it does not speak of homosexuality. It is the exposition of homosexuality's most common mode of being in modern societies: the dialectics between presence and absence, knowing and ignoring, desire and denial. Bang is part of and departs from this dialectic, exploring and exposing the poles, transitions, mechanisms and methods by which he is produced, and reproducing them in turn.

This game of presence and absence, knowing and not knowing, desiring and rejecting that Bang plays, and which plays Bang, plays the playing reader as well. It is a game that is part and parcel of the basic mechanics of modern society, and accordingly one that he or she, living in this society, cannot help but be inserted into – as pawn and player, simultaneously. That is why he or she – even the heterosexual reader – knows very well: precisely because he or she doesn't know.[68]

10 Ways

In the preceding section I have delineated a particular type of homosexuality and suggested it may be the most common in modern societies. It is characterized by being something which is both everywhere and no place at all, something everyone wants and doesn't want, something everyone knows about and knows nothing of. I suggest we call this phenomenon *absent homosexuality*. In choosing this term over 'latent' homosexuality, I want to avoid any secondary meanings from psychoanalysis that might cling to the latter. 'Absent homosexuality' is more in keeping with the phenomenon, rather than reducing it to mysterious underlying drives; 'phenomenologically', then, it is a more suitable expression.

In our reading of *Mikaël*, we arrived at some insights into the particular mechanisms or 'forms of movement' belonging to this homosexual dialectic of being and nothingness. Some of these we studied more closely: homosexuality does not exist, nevertheless it exists

1 in the form of the unmotivated, the inappropriate, the rupture in relation to conventions, norms, contexts, etiquette governing what is allegedly the issue: nothing where something should be; something where nothing should be; something where there should be something else; too much; too little – e.g. interest, shame, arousal, confusion; furthermore, it exists
2 by being neutral – non-erotic, non-sexual, non-passionate – yet leaning against, placing itself near something non-neutral, thereby appropriating meaning;
3 by coming out yet letting itself be negated;
4 via a word, a theme, a prop loaded with some special significance referring to the universe of homosexual existence;
5 by virtue of the indication itself of absence.

We have found, then, a number of ways in which homosexuality is present even though it isn't; at the same time, these ways point to a number of guidelines for what one should pay attention to if looking for absent homosexuality: the ruptures, the parallels, the disavowed outbursts, the metaphors and metonyms, the conspicuous absences.[69] But these are merely some preliminary guidelines;

there is no reason to believe that this list exhausts all of the possibilities for absent homosexuality to be present. One must assess carefully what goes on in every case.

In the following analyses we shall look more closely at some of the forms, movements, spaces and consequences of absent homosexuality. In this chapter, however, we will not concern ourselves with the reasons behind its existence.[70]

11 Persecutions

'One day I was asked by a lawyer to examine and declare sane one of his clients, the recorder of the town X, who was being unjustly persecuted by his compatriots', writes the psychiatrist Ferenczi in 1911. 'Soon after, the man in question announced himself. It made me suspicious to begin with that he handed me a mass of newspaper cuttings, documents and pamphlets, numbered and sorted in the most exemplary order, all of which he had written himself. A glance at the papers convinced me that he was a paranoiac with delusions of persecution.'[71]

It appeared from these documents that the man – owner of a newspaper as well as a municipal recorder – had complained about his neighbour opposite, a lieutenant colonel, in a vast number of letters to military and civilian authorities as well as to the general public. Said neighbour had been shaving at his window in shirtsleeves or bare-chested; furthermore, he had hung his gloves to dry on a cord strung across the window; finally, he had been seen in undergarments, dressing without pulling down the shade. Not that this bothered the plaintiff; but he was obliged to protect his sister and other females in general.

In that the authorities refused to take action, the matter had escalated (surely they regarded him as 'an old woman who has nothing else to do but discover objects of her curiosity', the municipal recorder thought); in his newspaper he called for the punishment of officers who offended young girls in the street, demanded protection for defenceless women against propositioning, tried to incite the civil authorities to take action against the military ones, organized petitions, filed lawsuits, etc.

Ferenczi has no doubts. It is a case of homosexual desires which the man refuses to recognize and which are repressed from consciousness, but they return, doubly denied: it is *not me* that loves him, it is he who loves me; no, he does *not love* me, he hates me, persecutes me. The paranoiac 'seeks until he has convinced himself that he is hated. He can now indulge in his homosexuality in the form of hate, and at the same time hide from himself.'[72]

Underlying all paranoia, Ferenczi maintained, and Freud agreed, are found homosexual wishes.[73] Not least, their conclusion was based on the characteristic pattern of symptoms displayed by the patient: he feels persecuted by men with homosexual aims, he feels obliged to fight them, monitor them, compile evidence, etc. In this way, he in fact brings about and legitimates a form of homosexual contact and satisfaction.

However, this pattern of symptoms, claims Guy Hocquenghem, is not limited to a few individuals who are 'ill'. It is a general pattern in modern societies. No 'heterosexual' man meets a proclaimed or supposed homosexual without feeling threatened; there is a 'tension immediately produced by the questions posed by the "normal" man: Is he after me?'[74] In public imagination, homosexuality is inextricably linked with criminal behaviour, disease, moral decadence, political subversion; there are fantasies of homosexual conspiracies, homosexual contagion. More: homosexuality, personified in the homosexuals, is fought; evidence is sought, police monitor urinals behind false mirrors, penetrate homosexual meeting places, conduct raids, frisk those present and take them to jail; plainclothesmen frequent public toilets and incite homosexuals to make a proposition so the police, in turn, can arrest them; lawyers and judges interrogate them on the precise nature of their sexual acts; medical and psychiatric scientists test them, conduct experiments on them, study their bodies, measure their penis and the reaction of their pupils when shown homosexual pornography; psychoanalysts question them regarding their fantasies and dreams; surgeons castrate them; journalists and sociologists enter their milieux in order to report on the dangers to beware of.[75] All in all, then, modern society as such appears to be a gigantic, homosexually desiring and repudiating machine.[76]

Hocquenghem's demonstration of a paranoia-like pattern of symptoms even at the institutional level of society is strikingly persuasive. It is difficult to deny that, in modernity, the conceptions held by the media, the law, the police, health authorities and science have taken on delusory dimensions in their insistence on the danger of the homosexual; and that the zealous fight against homosexuality brings with it extremely intimate contacts. The question, however, is how one should grasp such a far-reaching social paranoia. Underlying Hocquenghem's reasoning is a vision of the human world as made of streaming desires. The pleasure of these is linked to their freedom of flow; they can, however, become arrested, incarcerated and thereby deformed, in personalities and institutions. Obviously, this view is critical of Freud and Lacan in wishing to 'liberate' 'desire' from its imprisonment in the 'oedipal triangle' which they consider a necessary constituent of childhood as well as of personality and social structures. But it nonetheless sticks to the psychoanalytic notions of libido and energy. To the extent that these notions are too metaphysical or inadequate, they do not corroborate the idea of a paranoid homosexual desire inherent in social institutions.

Such desire, however, seems possible as an expression of the homosexual 'paranoia' which individuals may bring along into the institutions. It may further be related to the fact that certain institutions have been assigned the special task of fighting homosexuality; and it may be connected with particular formal traits in some institutions: they are social worlds of men and masculinity. In both the latter instances, homosexual paranoia, insofar as it is present, is produced in and by the institutions, in that homosexuality is both conjured up and repudiated in ways we have yet to consider more closely.[77]

The analysis of paranoia, then, points to the existence of absent homosexuality at various levels of society. Further, it has delineated another form of absent homosexuality than the one presented in *Mikaël*. The emphasis is on the negative pole: not on the passionate desire for homosexuality, but on the impassioned averting of it.

12 Justification

'Homosexuality concerns everyone, yet everywhere it is banned. This repression itself demands analyses in which desire partakes. There are no neutral or objective standpoints in connection with homosexuality; there are only situations of desire in which homosexuality plays along', writes Hocquenghem.[78] This description is particularly fitting in our present context. If indeed homosexuality is everywhere, it is there, as we have seen, mostly as that which isn't there, that which is known and not known, that which one wishes and will not tolerate. Thus, it is present only insofar as its presence can be denied. Consequently, neither reasoning nor 'evidence' can prove its existence.

The same conditions that render argumentative proof impossible would seem to make such a procedure necessary. Insofar as homosexuality is something people wish yet will not tolerate, they must not merely deny its existence in themselves but also persecute it in others. In this way, homosexuality, personified in the homosexuals, is placed in a defensive position in relation to the modern argumentative institutions of the police, the courts, public opinion and science. The homosexuals are forced into trying to defend themselves with arguments that are both substantial and may qualify as scientific, for instance attempting to prove that homosexuality is not a special malformation of a peculiar minority but a wish and a reality found in all men. In this manner, the reasoning runs the risk of being caught in a game which it seems doomed to lose from the outset, since the universal presence of homosexuality in modern societies *cannot* be proved. Furthermore, one easily ends up reinforcing the social conception that homosexuality is suspect and should be controlled through science, in addition to reinforcing the homosexual in his notion that he is the sort of person who must legitimate himself. It seems, then, we are clamped into a negative dialectic of passion and paranoia, persecution and justification.

However, *any* investigation of this field – no matter how scientific it may present itself – will be trapped in this jam. Insofar as the present analysis is correct, homosexuality is not some *thing* lying there between us and independent of us. What may appear as a thing is the denied reification of a social relation, including reader and writer. Further, what may seem an impossible point of departure turns out to offer distinct advantages. It compels us to acknowledge that there are limits to science, and that scholarship cannot suffice with scientistic methods and criteria of proof, but must instead adapt its ways according to the particular nature of the object of inquiry. To this extent, the epistemological status of the analyses in progress does not differ from that of much other scholarship, since large and interesting areas of social life would be left aside if empiricist methods of verification were to reign supreme. Moreover, the particular passionate-rejective character of absent homosexuality provides the incentive to invent methods of analysis and ways of arguing not practised by others, and for trying unorthodox styles of representation in attempting to deal with paranoia and rejection as well as sharpen the sensitivity for quite paradoxical phenomena.

13 Male spaces

Let us consider an account from the early 1980s, still bearing the afterglow of the Gay Golden Years, at a point when everything might still seem beautiful, powerful, full of the future; and let us ignore the moralistic remarks that appear all too easy.

> The bath house has a whole row of cubicles fitted with cots and discreet lighting. You can enter from the hallway, lock the door, and pursue common interests in private. A darkened room surrounds three walls of one of the cubicles, to which there is an entrance from the hallway but not from the dark room. Through small holes in the three walls you can peer into the cubicle and watch what goes on via mirrors on the cubicle walls. From the cubicle you would hardly notice the small holes in the walls if you don't know they are there, in other words: either you know they're there or you don't; in the dark room the holes are registered via the little spots of light; you can peer through them routinely or encouraged by sounds emanating through the thin walls, or because others are standing and watching. A man, dark, hairy, moustached, muscular, is there with another guy, a little younger, blond, slender. The dark man is standing, fucking the other, who is lying on his back on the cot while the dark man forces his legs in the air. Various sounds: the dark man spits in the blond one's face, slaps him hard on the buns while he fucks him, the blond man is panting. Through the holes a group of men, each on his own, each through his separate hole, watch the scene, steaming, masturbating; each of the others is simultaneously a new scene for any one of them: each one of us registers – senses/observes – the others registering what is going on in the cubicle and around them. A special form of separate participation, of 'audience-oriented privacy', a system of Chinese boxes of see-through mirrors, this witnessing/staging, which by virtue of your reading of my writing is now quadrupled. For the original image is also staged; not just because it isn't *natural* to spit on the person with whom you're fucking: hardly ever have people, not even our grandparents in the country or 'primitive' people for that matter, fucked without certain fantasies being projected on inner screens and certain positions and accoutrements being arranged; but here, deliberately calculated staging predominates, the pleasure perhaps lies primarily in the staging.[79]

Let us briefly consider yet another account from the early eighties.

> When you see a group of *men* standing in front of a shop window you know very well what they are watching: boxing on video. *Hear* they can't, so you'd think what they're watching must be fascinating enough to hold them captive: two men jumping around in shorts, slugging each other, preferably to a pulp. Evidently, there must be some kind of pleasure they derive from watching.[80]

Here we have another of those little everyday situations, so different from the first: men stopping on their way home from work, fathers passing by, a street in front of a shop window. Let us take a closer look at this situation. For the clinical eye, it turns out to share a number of traits with the first.

Thus, all the participants are men. The space constituted on the street by the shop window is, like that of the bath house, a pure male space.

Secondly, the space is divided into a stage – or an *arena* – with two actors, plus a space for the audience. In this case the stage is unlike the theatre but more like a cinema: a *screen* – though this is not important; here, the screen is primarily a technical wonder universalizing time and place so that the boxing match can take place somewhere else and some time other than just that particular evening at Madison Square Garden.

Thirdly, a series of movements or waves pass between these men. If we look first at the two actors on the stage, most of the movement takes place between them, frontally and in the form of body contact or attempts at body contact. But there is a certain measure of movement in relation to the audience, an awareness of being watched, and an exploitation of, a playing on this relation: an amount of *showing off*; of course, these boxers have no direct relation to these men standing on this street, but they do to the audience and the cameras present at the event, and thereby to all potential audiences. As for the spectators' space, the main movement proceeds towards the stage, in the form of glances, or perhaps rather an engrossed staring, gaping, gazing; moreover, there is a certain movement, certain currents, between the spectators themselves: a particular being-with, sharing, being next to, communion; each man is the next man's *fellow spectator*, is aware that the other is partaking in the same thing, is the sort of man who takes part in the same thing as oneself.

It is hereby implied that the activity proper takes place on the stage: that's where the action is. This, of course, is linked to an activity within the spectator, but he does not perform it with the others in his part of the space, at least not in the same manner as performed on the stage. They merely *stand* there on the pavement. For the spectator, then, there occurs a special combination of witnessing and participation: he witnesses a form of male relationship (in which he also participates on his own) while participating in another with those standing around him.

There are still other traits that the space around the boxing video shares with the baths: *the desire for action*, something has to happen, just tooling around is no good, that gets boring, then they leave; there's *fascination*: the fact that they're standing there, riveted gaze; and with that, a certain *arousal*: the bated breath, the gasps.

Soccer – again another situation altogether: the turf, the expectations, the beer, and so forth. Nevertheless, the traits we found at the baths and around the boxing video recur: a pure male space (or at least almost pure: entirely on the field and predominantly in the stadium); the separation of stage and spectator space; the directions and forms of movement: the frontal activity between the two parties on the stage; their showing off and awareness of being seen; the spectators' attention directed towards the stage, as well as their feeling of togetherness; the combination of witnessing one male context while participating in another; the desire for action; the fascination; the arousal.

There are, of course, special variations of these features here. For instance, twenty-two men on the stage instead of two, though certainly it remains the case that two parties are acting with and against each other. It also happens, as we know, that the movement on the stage transplants itself to the audience, though it is not really in good taste, and preferably limited to manageable levels. Furthermore, there is no physical contact between these actors – in any case, this is not the object of the game; when in fact contact does take place – and this happens regularly, of course – it is either against the rules (tripping, shoving) or it takes place in the intervals of the game (kissing, hugging, piggy-backing after scoring a goal). But even though the bodies are not meant to touch, they are in constant movement towards each other.

The variations may therefore seem unimportant, and, if anything, the conspicuous features common to these three male situations are especially pronounced in this case: the primadonna in a cocksure parade of showing off along the sidelines following a goal; the much-lauded togetherness ('the atmosphere') in the stadium; the audible discontent with lulls and sluggishness; the hissing of gasps multiplying and returning.

Even if the observant reader may not have noticed, I have not voiced the view that soccer (or boxing on video) is merely another form of homosexuality – repressed, sublimated or the like. *I* have said nothing about getting it in, haven't asked what kind of hole it is the goalie protects, or what is lost if the others succeed in scoring.[81] Soccer is soccer. What we see repeated in these little scenes is a special type of male space, with specific elements, structures, forms, etc. We can sketch a diagram, as is customary in scientific analyses, expressing certain features graphically though bypassing others.

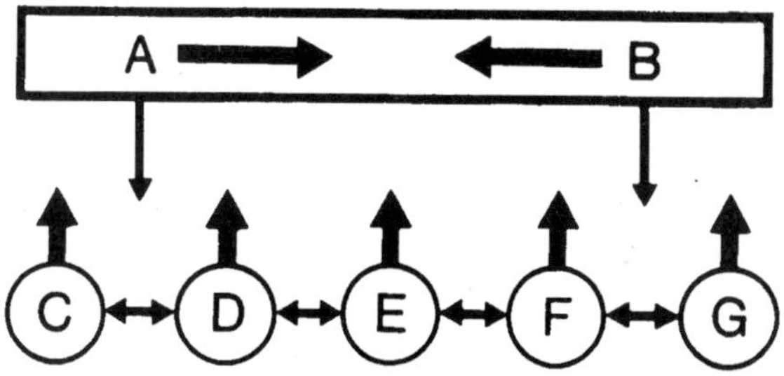

With this diagram we are able to apprehend the divisions of space, the directions of movement, the force of the movements. What we don't capture are the types of movement (glances, etc.) and its modes (excitement, fascination, the desire for action).

This space reappears in many situations: in the context of various other kinds of competitive sports – basketball, baseball, ice hockey, tennis, badminton, etc. (and this spatial structure seems to be by far the most popular: more than any others, sports having this type of space are candidates for becoming national sports); also around the videos in gay bars and leather clubs; and around the countless men's movies, such as those of Howard Hawks or Paul Newman.[82]

We are accustomed to viewing the specific contents of a situation as the most important (be it sex, boxing or soccer), while its forms, structures and spatial dimensions are secondary. If we, as here, redirect our attention towards the latter features – and certainly the reiteration and popularity of this space make it reasonable and interesting to do so – the 'contents' fade into the background; the crucial part, then, becomes this space with its forms and structures, plus that which sustains and structures it: *an interest between men in what men can do with one another*. This interest is overdetermining, if you will; in relation to it the issue of homosexuality, or not, in a sense recedes into the background.

We can compare it above all to taste, but of a particular kind, an epicurean one. This kind of taste, as we know, prides itself on transcending those barriers – e.g. refusing to eat carrots – which can be so annoying in children and so childish in adults; it 'likes anything if only it is well prepared'. Every content is equally valuable, though by no means exchangeable. On the contrary, there is an interest in each and every thing precisely for what it is, its particular features, and therefore, too, its difference from other things: carrots, for their fine taste, *baby* carrots, that is, with a squeeze of lemon, or because they can be used in a *crème Crécy*; broccoli, for its lovely colour, and as a complement to dishes that are mildly seasoned (and because they don't 'taste like asparagus, thank God. For the sake of variety, it's nice that all of those vegetables termed "poor man's asparagus" have a taste of their own and not like asparagus.')[83] Specificity and difference are important. On the other hand, there is an interest in all kinds of things ('provided they are well prepared'); one cannot stick to plaice every evening, but must move from one thing to the next. Variety and transition are important. Likewise with the interest between men in what men can do with one another: soccer is appreciated for what it is, but there are other things to be tried and enjoyed as well.

This interest, which our clinical gaze has identified, is situated within the realm of aesthetics. It wishes to try all, without inhibitions or concerns, to enjoy the differences and cross the barriers. In actuality it cannot fully unfold, even within the aesthetic field. Here, too – and precisely here – barriers and differences abound, already in the kind of taste which prides itself on its liking for everything 'provided it is well prepared': a pinch of sugar in the oil and vinegar dressing, a squirt of ketchup in the sauce, and everything is ruined.

So, too, with the interest between men in what men can do with each other. A barrier runs from spaces with unambiguous homosexuality to those lacking it, a barrier which appears as boredom: many 'homosexuals' can't be bothered watching soccer matches, they find men's movies dull, unless such diversions can be experienced as camp (or a turn-on). Conversely, there is a barrier running the other way which appears as fear, dizziness, disgust. And some like to watch soccer matches but don't care for movies. Such is the case with aesthetics: it is intrinsically idiosyncratic and subject to many social and moral restrictions as well.

These barriers are not equally impenetrable. Everyone knows that those running from spaces without homosexuality to spaces with it are the most difficult to pass through. Nonetheless, homosexuality can be observed in the former sort of spaces, e.g. those of soccer. The hugs, the kisses, the piggy-backing – it isn't homosexuality, they do it only because they are beside themselves with glee, people say, thereby reiterating the common reassurance that homosexuality only takes place in special enclaves and never because one is glad. Ironically, the very denial that this is homosexuality somehow seems to end up as its confirmation: what else do the rules introduced against kissing and hugging bring to mind?[84] And then there are the insults: why, of all things, are the visiting players called homosexuals?[85] Once again we see the same pattern: exists – does not exist; knows – does not know; wishes – rejects. Apparently these sports situations lend immediacy to the possibility of homosexuality and with it the prohibition: it is expressed so that it may be repudiated, or repudiated so that it may be expressed. Under these circumstances it becomes impossible to determine whether it is in fact a goal the goalie strives to guard. It would be foolish to think that soccer *is* 'repressed' or 'sublimated', i.e. displaced and distorted homosexuality; but not that it is so *as well*.[86]

Boxing videos, soccer, bath house sex and men's movies are not the same; however, they turn into each other, as we've seen in the case of soccer; and they do seem to be sustained by the same broader phenomenon: the interest between men in what men can do with one another.[87] This interest, then, 'precedes' the boundary between homosexual and non-homosexual relations. So far we have tried to delineate its distinct character by drawing an analogy to taste and aesthetics; in the next chapter we shall take a closer look at its construction or constitution in relation to homosexuality and masculinity. We shall consider this relation in three tempi: masculinity as *decision*, masculinity as *nature*, and masculinity as *appropriation*.

14 Male constitution

Men can practise bodybuilding. It needn't be to the extreme of flexing one's rippling muscles but in the more moderate version, like the men who frequent 'Taurus'. Here, the weights are not lifted directly but via the push and pull of handles and bars, mounted on 'machines' *à la* dentist's chairs. What makes these men toil away at the machines? Surely not just any desire to keep their bodies operative and avoid muscle aches and other such ailments; nor the mere wish to keep age and death at bay. If so, they would surely jog, do callisthenics or take classes in modern dance. What is at stake is a *decision to be a man* (more of a man than one thinks one is); more precisely, it is about *modelling* oneself as a man.

Does this decision to be a man imply a relationship to other men? In no distinctive way is Taurus a social space. It happens once in a while that two men work together to talk to each other, but that is rare. *If* a special relationship to other men lies in the decision to be a man it is apparently not to be found in collaboration or conversation.

How, then, could a potential social relation between these men be conveyed? Perhaps via the senses, via sensing *per se*. It's possible to, or impossible not to, have indirect contact with another man's sweat or body heat, it's possible to *smell* one another, and to hear one another, these orgasm-like groans of exertion, and in that sense one could say there are social relations; it is even possible that attractions come about through this particular smell, this groaning; but these seem to be accidental results of the decision to be a man – and not implied in it. It is not a matter of wanting, above all, to smell like a particular man or to become like another man whose smell one likes, nor to be like the one who groans in a special way – if he is a shrimp. If there is any relationship to other men inherent in the decision to model oneself as a man, apparently it has to be conveyed via *sight*.

At first glance, however, it doesn't seem that sight is used for social purposes at all. People look for the machines, but not at each other; each is apparently minding his own business. And yet, a few glances can be observed. Rarely direct and almost always brief; other kinds of looking are met by the other's gaze and averted. What do these glances signify, and what is signified by their absence?[88]

Pure observation will hardly help us any further: there is nothing more to see. We must return to this very decision to be a man and examine it more closely. Is it a matter of becoming like a particular other male whom they know or have known, or is it a matter of becoming a Man, as a cultural fantasy, as the sum or abstraction or epitome of the masculinity of actual men? Never mind; in any case the decision places a man in a relation to a male figure of one kind or another, whether this is a certain other man or the category

Man. That is, a relation of man to man, a *social* relation. Moreover, it is a certain kind of social relation. At one pole is an ideal, something valued as positive: that is what one would like to be (like). At the other is a lack: one who isn't man enough, who wants to be more of a man. At the same time, however, he *is* a man, to some degree; accordingly, not only a lack and something valued as negative, but also a *something* and something valued as *positive* – otherwise he wouldn't be capable of wanting to be more of it. Between the poles a *comparison*: I am not as he; and a *wish*, a *longing*, a *desire*: I *want to* be like him.

Thus, in the very decision to be a man there is a relation to another man (concretely or as a category); the decision implies a certain and interested social relation. This relation to another man exists already before they walk into Taurus, and they bring it along with them. How does it affect Tom's relation to the other men at Taurus that he wants to be (more of) a man?

It is likely that at least one of these other men resembles – in one or more ways – the man Tom would like to be (like). The social relation, the longing towards another man inherent in his decision to be more of a man, must therefore simultaneously establish and reappear in a relation to this other man: if Tom wishes to be (like) Mick/Male, and Harry is like Mick/Male, then Tom would like to be (like) Harry.

But here seems to be a problem. We have just seen that the only medium by which the relation could be conveyed in all certainty was sight, *and* that no looking took place, at any rate no glances were sent, at least not very many. We therefore have to specify: Tom wants to establish a relation to Harry – if he *sees* him. But is there any reason to believe that he does?

Tom comes there in order to be like Mick/Man. His labour with these machines makes sense to him by reason of this will to be (like). Mick/Man is therefore present *for him* constantly, in his mind, in his being, lodged in his sight as well. Someone who is like the man he wants to be is therefore someone he can't help but notice. But Tom must also be more actively on the lookout for someone who is like Mick/Man. He needs to be able to rate himself: to measure the degree to which he is like him. For this reason, he must watch for others who are perhaps more like Mick/Man than he is himself. He also needs to be able to actualize the picture he has of him – that, indeed, is what he wants to be like.

We have found that the decision to be male implies a relation from man to man, that this relation must reappear in relations to other actual men, and that it must be conveyed via sight. On the other hand, we have also found that, apparently, there is very little looking.[89] Everyone knows the reason: the imperative of repudiating homosexuality. The first commandment: thou shalt not look at another man. And it is reasonable to assume that denial becomes particularly crucial in a situation like this, where desire is particularly near.

Thus: looking *must* take place, and looking *must not* take place. From this follow a number of distinct features in men's view of men.

1 *Colluding glances*. There *are*, as stated, gazes. Rarely frontal, and almost always brief, only when one's gaze has a fair chance of evading the other's. But if he doesn't see it (and others don't), he can be viewed. If he refrains from seeing it, more precisely, if he disregards his seeing it, he can let himself be viewed, permit the gaze; perhaps he will be permitted to do the same in turn. But he can only disregard it if the other's gaze is sufficiently discreet. If not, it must be evaded – the Gaze Police steps into action. (This is also a problem for the participant who wants to observe observing.) The counter-gaze: What are you looking at? What is the matter with *you*? How dare you think I'm up to something with you – that I'm *like that*? Keep your gaze to yourself!

2 *De-centred vision: seeing without looking*. It is unlikely that seeing takes place only in the few glances being sent. Rather, it is plausible that men develop a capacity to see others without looking at them. Every man knows it. You head for your locker in the locker room (or whatever and wherever it is), keeping your eyes off the others. But you don't look *at* the locker either. The act requires a special kind of attention. I'm not referring to what's called looking out of the corner of your eye; that demands another kind of effort: the pupils are 'deliberately' turned to one side while the head is kept in another direction, as if looking at something else. That is in fact a gaze, a focusing via the pupils, a centring, a looking at. Here, though, is another kind of effort altogether, a de-centring, a kind of dis-traction. Perhaps an easing of the pupils such that they don't focus but rather take more in. On the other hand, neither is it relaxation: looking straight ahead without seeing, staring into space. It is still a matter of seeing something particular. A strained non-straining of the eye.[90]

For the most part these decisions to be a man pass unnoticed.

Nonetheless they must be made. A man's life is made up of a lengthy series of them. At one point or another he must decide to move his hands just so, stand, walk, *spit* just so.[91] Such decisions are doubtless made for the most part already in childhood, even in early childhood – as a kind of 'primal decisions' which one may continue to build upon and develop (though usually doesn't alter).[92] And each of these decisions to be a man implies a relation to other men, a wish, a longing.

But of course it isn't all just decisions. Some of it is nature no doubt: the way muscles develop, the way bones are connected, etc. In any case, nature is but a game board: in setting limits it also defines a free space. The rest, and that which isn't decision-making, is learning, encoding, appropriation – automatically and imperceptibly.

A man has never truly decided to put on men's clothes. He has always had them on. The mother was there from the beginning and first he was dressed; later, he dresses himself, but she'll usually continue to buy his clothes. And later still, the girlfriend or the wife or the institution, if not the mother, will see to it that he continues to dress the way he should. He may at some point confirm this 'choice' of clothes (not this specific one – which must often be revolted against – but the species: men's clothes) by going out and buying trousers himself; but basically this is not a matter of making a decision. What does this mindless 'putting on' signify for him as a man, and what does it imply for his relations to other men?

What happens when I – without further ado, mechanically – put on the daily men's attire? I become or reaffirm that I am a man (as opposed to woman); in other words, via the clothes I enter into a relation with the category *man*. I thus become a specimen of a species. In so doing, I have already entered into a relation to every other man who is also wearing men's clothes (and who is thereby a specimen of the same species). The relationship consists not only of an outward likeness ('others can see that I look like him'), nor only an externally experienced likeness ('I know I look like him'). It is also intimate: through the clothes I get close to him. This intimacy is embarrassing in extreme situations: confronted with the man in full riding gear buying a loaf of bread at the supermarket, far from the track, holding a whip. Via the clothes you gain insight into the way the other person relates to himself; in general – in the case of another man's ordinary male garb – an insight which isn't distancing (or fascinated), but affirmative, not one brought to attention, but rather an immediate one: I experience him as someone who experiences himself in the same way that I experience myself (that is, as a man). I *am* as he is with regard to being a man: I am a man just as he.[93]

These identifications can sometimes be cultivated deliberately: one guy chooses to wear something similar to what the other has on, in the same cut and the same colour, with only a matching difference of shade. Two guys can by way of their clothes achieve or reaffirm a conscious pleasurable identification with each other. But what we are considering at present are no such 'conscious' wishes for identification, no intentional experiences of identification, but mechanically produced identity effects.

Men's clothing is something appointed by others at first, after which one simply puts it on 'self-actingly' and continues to wear it, more or less reinforced by the effects it produces. Clothing is but one example of these semi-automatic appropriations of male identity. Another is that of referring to and addressing someone as he/boy/guy/sir/Mr/man. These identifications become self-identifications and, in each case, a relation to other men is brought about in the process. And there is no reason to try to draw a line here between what is learning and what is nature, for the same effect comes about: by registering one's own biological gender (e.g. the genitals) one stands in relation to the category man, and consequently, as we have seen, to other men.

Thus, to wear men's clothes, to have become a man, is something *social* in and of itself: he is thereby always already in a relationship to, a being-with other men. Being a man is nonetheless uncertain: he can never fully know what it implies. But it is *joyful*, or good, so they say. From this follows an *interest* in other men: he is engaged in the uncertain yet perhaps rewarding project of being a man, and they are men and therefore persons he can *feel secure with, learn from, share with, mirror himself in*. In actuality, all sorts of barriers may stand in the way of this interest. Some men he finds repulsive; he would despise the idea of being like them, would definitely have nothing to do with them – for one reason or another. But in principle, the interest in other men is there, it is included in having become a man.

It may seem high time to point out that one thing is to want to be like another man, but quite another to want to have sex with him.[94] However, in the above analysis I have in fact taken pains not to imply that the social relations inherent in the wish to be a man and in the experience of being a man were at bottom 'homosexual' relations. Indeed, I have been interested in the *specificity* of these relations, their unique and distinctive character. But the connections between wish, longing, body, male images, togetherness, sharing, security, excitement, equality and difference in relation to other men which are intrinsic to identification make it impossible to keep it apart from eroticism. It is with this concept just as Hegel wished for all of his: once it is thought through, it segues into something else. Identity wish and identity experience are not the same as erotic wish and erotic experience, but they turn into one another, unless one prevents them from doing so – because one cannot make love or have sex with others any time, any place, or because one has chosen to be faithful to someone special, or because of any number of reasons.

In modern societies there is, of course, one particular barrier which overshadows all the others, not even allowing them to be brought up, namely the imperative of repudiating homosexuality. This is what prevents identity wish and experience from becoming truly erotic. Paradoxically, this necessary denial of the possibility of physical-orgasmic sex in turn affects the wish for identity and sexualizes it, precisely by emphasizing the possibility. It is this duality of sexualization and denial that reappears in the stolen glances and de-centred vision of the gym.

In the course of sections 13 and 14, a certain connection has appeared which can be summed up as follows: being or wanting to be a man implies an interested relation from man to man. This *male interest* includes the pleasures of mirroring and comparing, as well as of companionship and apprenticeship. (There is more to it than pleasures, as we shall see in section 20 on violence.) The interest between men in what men can do with one another is a specification of this. In any case, male interest can turn into erotic interest, by which is meant a relation of attraction, desire and pleasure not necessarily focused on physical-orgasmic sex, although it may include this. Thus I draw a distinction between male interest, eroticism, and sexuality, although at an abstract basic level one may freely turn into the other. In modern societies, however, male interest is *sexualized* – precisely, *homosexualized* – inescapably and in specific ways. With the analysis of these we shall proceed.[95]

15 Homosexual pictures

The question is not so much whether homosexuality exists throughout, but how it is there. You can see it at the cinema.

In *St Elmo's Fire*, you see it already in the advertisement. Seven smiling faces meet the photographer's lens: three girls and four boys. Anyone can add and subtract. Granted, he will neither admit it nor deny it through the first two-thirds of this endless pubescent film, but the rest of the group as well as the audience is increasingly aware that it can't be any other way. He actually looks very nice and ordinary and is always kind and helpful and understanding; and they aren't at all prejudiced and think it's perfectly all right; one of the girls has even had her apartment done entirely in pink by her neighbour best friend the interior decorator – to whom she providingly introduces him, but what's the use: in the end it turns out that all along he's been secretly in love with one of the girls who was dating one of the other boys. Whew. Is – isn't; wants to – doesn't want to; gone – there! just as the most famous ear of our time heard his grandson say as the child threw the bobbin behind the drapes and pulled it back again; or rather, the other way round: *there – gone!* The trick isn't to pull a rabbit out of the hat, but that there isn't any. Why won't the film let him be gay when its characters are so tolerant; why must homosexuality be dragged out when it must be conjured away all the same? Who takes pleasure in this little game? Not the homosexuals in the audience, at least. That is, only the heterosexuals; and for them it is enjoyable only if and because they might wish and fear that they weren't.

In *Dead Poets Society* we are at a boys' prep school, USA, 1959. A new teacher upsets the school's rigid discipline and mandatory cramming, transforming poetry classes into gestalt sessions and thereby instilling the American Dream ideals: individualism, self-confidence, ambition, initiative. The boys are enthused, resurrect a secret 'Dead Poets Society', and idolize their new teacher and 'Captain'.

However, one of them takes the teacher at his word: he decides to follow his stage dreams against his despotic father's will and without his knowledge. But the father finds out and takes his son out of school, intending to pack him off to a military academy; the boy commits suicide. Major school scandal. A scapegoat must be found; the boys are intimidated into informing against their favourite teacher, who is dismissed. But in the end the cowed raise themselves – up onto the desks – and salute their departing 'Captain' goodbye.

Am I to insinuate that these prep school boys are 'homosexual', or that the poetic teacher has seduced a vaguely sensitive lad, knocking him up with actors' whims? Not at all. Nothing in the film points in that direction. The word is never mentioned, the thing is never shown. On the contrary: any time a suspicion might crop up that something homosexual was involved, the film makes great efforts to exorcise it. 'We don't read or write poetry because it's cute!' the teacher assures. He's also able to demonstrate how vigorous and terse Shakespeare can be when recited by men like Marlon Brando and John Wayne – and how tacky it sounds with the trademark saccharine lisp no one could imaginably attribute to anyone but gays. Moreover, he coaches the boys in soccer; indeed, back in high school he was himself the team captain and by no means a sissy. Besides, he keeps a photo of his wife on his desk. Granted, she lives in London, but this, too, has a reason: 'I love teaching, I don't want to be anywhere else.'

True enough, the comely aspiring actor puts his arm around the shoulder of the inhibited yet budding little cutie who has become his roommate; and yes, the latter sends him a long glance in the bathroom – from behind, tracing his legs below the towel. Yet pin-ups as well as live girls are introduced into the society of dead poets, and both the aspiring actor and his inhibited roommate seem satisfied at the sight. 'Don't you guys miss having girls around here?' one of these asks. 'Yeah, because then there wouldn't be so much wanking around,' a boy remarks, to the others' applause.[96]

But doesn't this repeated dismissal of any suspicion of homosexuality itself become – suspicious? Why should we see the photo of the wife when the husband chooses to work among young men an ocean apart from her and she plays no role but that? Why should we know that he once captained a soccer team? Why should he be coaching the boys in kicking a ball when he is teaching them passages from the dead poets? Why should a scene in which the two roommates are chasing each other from bed to bed end with the other boys coming in, so that the two aren't left alone? Why should the headmaster, as the repugnant opposite of the popular teacher, be shown spanking a boy from behind in rhythmic motion on the raised bottom with a substantial bat?

Further, why is the list of brilliant poets who are mentioned by name – Shakespeare, Byron, Shelley, Thoreau, Tennyson, Whitman – as if it were copied from the famous-gay-poets list-of-kings of old homo-history?[97] Why, finally, do the hitherto so inhibited youngster's feelings for his dead roommate turn out to be so passionate that first he breaks down and sobs, then gets not only the other boys to rise up in the end but perhaps even the film? Is the detestable father perhaps on the right track when he shouts those familiar words to the poetry teacher, 'You stay away from my son!'? Isn't it all, after all – just as the dazed and confused boys describe their new teacher in the beginning of the film – rather *weird, different* and *spooky*?

It is indeed a ghost that's rummaging about. All of the questions posed above can, if you wish, be rejected or answered in ways that have nothing to do with homosexuality. Only in two cases might a broader readiness to identify the spectre be awaited: namely the scene in which the detestable headmaster bats the bum of the poor little boy in rhythmic swats, and that in which the teacher ridicules a rendition of Shakespeare by a certain type of actor. This art of suggestion has enchanted millions of viewers in the western world. There is a *basic* need, it seems, to see homosexual interests shown as something that concerns anyone (for these high school boys can, in principle, be anyone, apart from 'homosexuals') *and* to see them exorcized straight away. Homosexuality can and must be shown for everyone as that which everyone might perhaps like to experience; that is, if it can remain unarticulated and one ends up revolted or disgusted.

Quite differently in *A Chorus Line*, where the men line up, as it were, and confess they're homosexuals. That's calling a spade a spade, one would think; here, homosexuality isn't dragged out of the closet only to be stuffed away again, but rather to be cemented as the eternal essence of these individuals. Not for the purpose of making them disgusting – but the opposite. One of them is from a cultivated background so he might as well be gay; that's just the way it is and he's happy enough so we might as well be. The other has a harrowing past: as a child he was once pawed by some dirty old men in a theatre, and to satisfy an irrepressible craving for the theatre in later life, he finds himself compelled to seek an engagement with a drag show, and one evening his parents happen to see him *en grande toilette*, his father in pained silence and his mother in quiet tears; isn't it a crying pity? Nature or childhood, swing-along or suffering: both of them are nice and likeable. They're homosexuals and they should be allowed to be.

From this game of confession it appears not only how vulnerable homosexuality is, but also how absent it is in everyday life even when it is set apart and makes no demands on being universal; how much it can be that which isn't there even though it is: otherwise it couldn't be made into the main ingredient of the material supposed to nourish the film (and the producer). And it's boys from a chorus line who are confessing: to whose surprise really? The shock lies in the fact that one knew already. From this it appears how much homosexuality can be that which one knows nothing of, even though one knows. At the same time this confessing, by its very selectiveness – only a few come forward, and they are none other than chorus boys (and not mechanics) – ensures that nothing's wrong with the rest of them, of us; if homosexual interests are presented unequivocally and without emetics, then they are presented as what only a few want.

A Passage to India takes place in India in the 1920s, during the period of British colonial rule. It is one of those films that portray how people, when beyond the bounds of accustomed civilization – on excursions into nature, travels to foreign countries – also come into contact with uncivilized sides of themselves, sexual ones in particular. In this case, a frustrated Englishwoman is confronted with her sexual desires during a visit to India. Here, though, no man comes out to confess he's homosexual; there is no mention of homosexuality at all; nor any sexual advances from man to man. Homosexuality is unmistakably absent; so let's take a closer look.

One of the few likeable Englishmen in the film is a bachelor and headmaster. He is the only person who lets the natives visit his home, among them the leading male character. The first time this Indian comes to visit, the headmaster is just getting ready: he is seen taking a shower through a matte pane of glass. The spectators – and the Indian – thus see him naked, and yet they don't. While waiting, the Indian walks about looking at odds and ends, and at one point he lies down in rapture on the Englishman's bed. And when the latter comes out of the bathroom – half-naked – a semi-physical exchange takes place between them: one gives a collar stud – though not a tie – to the other.

This can of course be discussed backwards and forwards. What's *homosexual* about it, one may ask; isn't it me reading more into it than there is? Indeed, both of them get married in the end, and the

Indian is quite hectic in his interest for the Englishwoman. But I might try to use the old trump card. The film is based on a novel by E. M. Forster, and he was homosexual, a closet homosexual. He did write a novel with an openly homosexual topic as early as 1914, and later a number of short stories – none of which, however, were published till after he died.[98] In his other works, homosexuality never comes out. Yet that doesn't mean it isn't there; it is merely camouflaged.[99] But, you may object, if by some strange coincidence one had managed not to learn that Forster was a closet homosexual,[100] there wouldn't be the least bit of sense in seeing anything homosexual in the relationship between the headmaster and the Indian; besides, even though Forster wrote the novel, he did not make the film. Yes, I might say, but why should the Englishman be shown taking a shower when the Indian arrives, why should the Indian lie on his bed, etc.? And you may interject that these things have other functions in the film. And so forth.

But this ambiguity is precisely the point. Forster's novel, like Bang's *Mikaël*, is an example of what has been termed 'traditional homosexual culture', or more precisely: traditional homosexual culture produced by homosexuals.[101] It is a culture that wishes to express homosexuality – erotic interests from man to man – and hide it, all at the same time. What we see is deliberately coded; gaining access to the hidden contents requires a decoder which only other homosexuals ordinarily possess, at least if the contents are to be translated into pure words.

What is interesting here is the question of what is gained by retaining this homosexual code from an early 1920s novel all the way through to a mid-1980s film, i.e. post-Gay Lib and post-Fassbinder. Let us consider the possible alternatives for the sake of argument. (a) The headmaster and the Indian could be cast as homosexuals. This, however, would drag so much down with it that the entire plot would have to be rewritten. (b) It could be made clear and unambiguous that these ordinary men were not only erotically interested in women, but also in men. However, the more directly homosexuality is shown as something everyone wishes, the fewer will see it. (c) This camouflaged homosexuality could be dropped altogether. Actually, the story about the frustrated woman's confrontation with her sexuality and the British oppression of the Indians would not become absurd; it could very well be told without the headmaster taking a shower, etc. However, the camouflaged homosexuality has not been dropped, but carefully retained; and thereby the fourth and last possibility has been chosen.

Apparently, this homosexuality and its camouflaging code are hard to get around; in any case, it seems that something is achieved that wouldn't otherwise come about. Is it a matter of appealing to a homosexual audience without offending the heterosexual viewers? Or is this camouflaged homosexuality retained because the ageing director needs to give expression to his closeted homosexuality? Perhaps. But it is also possible to view the matter from another angle and ask: how can 'the heterosexuals' help but register that one man lies down on the other man's *bed*? The answer is of course that they can't. What is achieved in relation to the heterosexual audience is that the film becomes more realistic: they are more able to recognize and identify with a situation when the erotic interests are present. And that can be achieved precisely on the condition that they are also not present. *The code still works*, and it is still needed; not so much any more so that the homosexuals can express their specific interests in safety, but so that 'the heterosexuals' can reclaim their ordinary homosexual interests without risk.[102]

Code of Silence, as indeed it is called, is a cop film; a typical B-movie. The 'plot' is that the honourable policeman manages to get scores of criminals on his own. In other words: a real men's movie. They beat each other, shoot each other and help each other, but they don't have sex with each other, of course. Nevertheless, homosexuality is alluded to repeatedly throughout the film – always in relation to a contact of some closeness or intensity between two men, and always in the form of crude jokes or insults. An example: a couple of gang members have gone to see another gang to buy drugs and are frisked before being let in. Having been searched, one of them says to the guy who frisked him: 'Hey, you oughtta marry me.'

Why is it that this kind of remark occurs so often in men's films? One would perhaps hazard that it's *precisely* because these men are *real* men – indeed, they *repudiate* homosexuality through these remarks; it is precisely in insults and crude jokes aimed at *other* men that homosexuality is brought up, isn't it? But if they truly *are* real men, that is, 100 per cent guaranteed free of homosexuality, without the least homosexual thought or the least homosexual feelings, why then can't they just *mind their machismo*, why can't one man let another frisk him in the course of serious male business without having to bring up homosexuality? To frisk someone is to frisk someone: there's no reason these men should think of homosexuality in this connection – unless, of course, such close contact between two men makes homosexual interests present. Otherwise the remark wouldn't make sense, either in the film's social setting or for its audience.

In the James Bond movie *A View to a Kill*, James Bond is up against something truly evil: a domineering he-woman who is black to boot, a super-intelligent and bespectacled man (not black, obviously) who seems to like his woman on top in bed – a true intellectual. Moreover, he has homosexual tendencies: in one scene he fantasizes the destructive consequences of his evil inventions; and he is seen putting his hand affectionately around the neck of his fellow conspirator – a former German Nazi doctor – while the world falls apart around them. It is the only scene in which two men touch each other – aside from the fights – and this contact has the end of the world as its setting, if not its consequence.[103]

In this case, then, James Bond is up against incredibly monstrous evil forces. (The question, of course, is if he ever wasn't.)[104] Nonetheless, he – and the film – succeed in putting things in their place.

Here we see homosexuality situated in a mythological universe, in a *company* no less fantastic than those from the late Middle Ages and the Renaissance in which sodomy was situated: there, were-wolves, basilisks, witches, Jews, papists and agents of the king of Spain communed;[105] here, he-women, intellectuals, blacks and Nazi doctors. Then as well as now, men's desire for other men belongs to the forefront of the evil forces, of the chaos that threatens the existing cosmos, the established order; it must therefore be destroyed.

In this film, then, homosexuality is not only that which is so present that one is forced to repudiate it constantly; it is that which is so dangerous that it must be wiped out entirely – otherwise the end of the world is nigh. This *dread* of homosexuality makes, of course, no sense if homosexuality really *could* be limited to those few per cent that most population surveys suggest. Homosexuality can only be a global threat if it is globally present.

Cop au Vin. The worst villain in this Chabrolian idyll turns out to be the local doctor. He is the one who, out of pure greed, has cast his wife in the base of a garden statue and set fire to another woman so that her charred hand can be shown to us at the morgue. And who else could it possibly be: at the very start, we've seen him with his slimy, effeminate frills circling about an innocent young man who, for the record, is lugging around a massive maternal fixation (carrying, indeed, his lame mother). For the benefit of the dense the point is spelled out in the final scene: we see the only-naturally-violent policeman who, in the absent father's place, has unravelled murder mystery as well as maternal meddling; with one hand, he sends the arrested doctor off to be punished – with the words that he was probably bisexual – and with the other hand, he sends the young man straight into the melon-banging mailgirl's embrace. Homosexuality is so obtrusive that it cannot be excepted even if one cannot accept it; it *must* be let out and it *must* be led off.

In the jolly family movie *King Solomon's Mines*, the *Germans* are the villains – the Germans and the Turks and the Blacks, and guess who else. The learned American professor who has discovered the way to the tremendous treasures in King Solomon's mines is captured by the Germans, who rule – or rather, are attempting to rule – the area. (The problem with Germans as imperialists, one gathers, is that they're so inept.) But the noble American professor of course refuses to tell these bratwurst-bellied bandits where the treasure lies (besides, he intends to keep it himself); they therefore try to coerce him, with German thoroughness: each time they hit him, they reproachfully hold the broken whip up in front of him and say: 'Now see what you've done!' Until one of them drops the whip, announces that he likes the venerable old professor, and pulls out his cock for sucking. *Relax!* – it has been filmed so discreetly that nothing is really seen, yet the meaning cannot be mistaken. It all ends on a merry note as the hero shoots the man's cock off through a hole in the floor – a real *blow-job*, eh? By now the pattern is rather trite: once you say villain, you've got to say homosexuality, the villain has to be homosexual, or homosexuality has to be made villain, so that it can be both pulled out and shot off.

The Shooting Party is a different kind of shooting altogether. English nobility gathered at the manor for the autumn hunt, a foreboding air shortly before the first World War, distinguished character actors, autumn shades and soft-focus images, a colour and bouquet like fine old sherry – in short, *Dallas* for the cultured. But see if it isn't there just the same; infinitely discreet of course. There is a Jew among the guests, which is suspect in the first place; wealthy he is, of course, a bachelor at that, perhaps a bit of a libertine. Over dinner he is asked jokingly whether it was perhaps time he got himself an heir; he makes light of it. At a little festivity for which everyone appears in costume, he poses as – Oscar Wilde.

And one night he pays a visit to another man's wife – a voluptuous and warm-blooded yet neglected woman – in her bedroom; having fondled her breasts with his big hairy sensual Jew-hands, he voluntarily ducks down and – licks cunt. I never spoke a truer word – even though you don't ever see it. Again, the old code; though here, ultra-discreet: only the faintest suggestions, the finest touch, interactions so ambiguous that they negate themselves.[106]

If indeed homosexuality is everywhere, you should be able to go to the cinema and see it in any film. And you can.[107]

The selection of films presented here does not, of course, fulfil the prerequisites for representativity in any statistical sense. On the other hand, it is not atypical of the films one can see in the late twentieth century. It represents many different kinds, from many different kinds of surroundings, for many different kinds of audiences. Nor have I selected the films because they were known or rumoured to feature homosexuality. In fact, I've seen some of them because I was at one time intent on testing the hypothesis of a ubiquitous homosexuality and carefully chose those films in which one would least expect it to be. I found a certain satisfaction in sitting there with a clinical gaze, observing just how elegantly or clumsily the film managed to show what it didn't show and want what it didn't want; a purely scientific-aesthetic treat. At one point it wasn't fun any more; I simply wanted to go to the movies to enjoy myself or to do something different; I wasn't up to watching more ambiguities or listening to more insults. But it was impossible to escape.

Moreover, since I first formulated the main ideas of this chapter in 1985, I've had the opportunity to test them against a large number of diverse films. And there seems no reason to believe there isn't absent homosexuality in practically all films, particularly so since the Second World War.[108] In some cases, it is likely that the most absolute absence of even the smallest and most ambiguous suggestion of homosexuality should be seen as an indication of its presence. This, for example, is the case with films about adolescent boys in European new men's cinema. Another case is the Batman movie of 1989: why else is Robin the Boy Wonder – *absent*?[109] But it can, of course, be imagined that there are also films which don't feature homosexuality at all. As a rule, they'd belong to the following categories: they may come from countries which are not quite 'modernized' yet and hence do not partake in the particular mechanics of modern homosexuality; or they may cater for women in particular; and/or they may be characterized by an unusually high artistic quality. In all of the cases, however, it is impossible to know whether the absence of homosexuality is in fact a way for it to be present.

In sum: homosexuality can be present in a more or less distinct or ambiguous manner, it can be associated with individuals, speech or actions, have a relatively positive or severely negative tinge, be present in a single scene or from beginning to end, but *it is there* – or, in any case, you never know if it is not.[110] In that respect, the examples discussed above are undoubtedly representative of the vast majority of films. But of course, they are not representative of *how* homosexuality is present; in this sense, each film has its own particular traits, each story its particular logic. Yet they present certain possibilities and suggest a certain pattern: homosexuality can be shown *camouflaged*, or it can be shown blatantly, but then only as *clearly separated* (that is, as 'homosexuals') or *clearly denied*: it is pulled out only to be conjured away, thrown up, put down, kicked out, led away or blown off. Not without good reason does Vito Russo conclude his book on homosexuality in the movies with a *necrology*, a list of homosexuals who met their death on the silver screen and how it happened.[111]

This massive presence, the fact that homosexuality is present in practically all films, shows something about the actual prevalence of homosexuality despite its official limits: it is at least so widespread that it cannot be evaded. And the ways in which it is present show that it is *universal*: otherwise it is incomprehensible that it must be dragged out when it's going to be negated anyway.

16 Closets

The 'celluloid closet' is Vito Russo's term for films in which 'gay characters' are hidden away like dirty secrets and never allowed to come out with their life or dignity intact.[112] But as we have seen, there isn't always *a homosexual man* locked up in the film closet, rather an ever-present *absent homosexuality* among 'non-homosexual' men. And the closet of absent homosexuality does not shut around the characters of the film, but extends to include the spectators. In this sense, the movie closet is coextensive with the space constituted by and between the men on the screen and the ones in the audience, i.e. the space of the cinema. 'Closet', then, can be used as a name for the special spaces structured or occupied by absent homosexuality. Given the omnipresence of the latter, it is to be expected that the social world is studded with such devices.

The closet as a life space must accommodate the positioning and movement of presence and absence, knowledge and ignorance, desire and disavowal. It is therefore no surprise if closets are often square in shape as well as structured around a spectatorial and specular axis as in the cinema (and generally in structures of the type depicted in section 13). In such space, both passion and its denial can be demonstrated vicariously: i.e. between the two parties on the stage or screen, thus simultaneously involving and not involving the spectator. Further, the relation between the audience and those acting is conveyed by way of the eyes and thereby through the simultaneity of distance and intimacy intrinsic to the gaze. Moreover, the audience constitutes potential partners-in-eroticism, just as they are witnesses of the non-involvement of the individual spectator – the more witnesses the better, which is a reminder that the four-sided structure of this type of closet is not dependent on the number of 'spots' or 'points', i.e. persons present, but on the lines and angles constituted by their positioning in space.

This male quadrangle of the closet, however, readily becomes pentagonal, or perhaps hexagonal, to the extent that *a homosexual man*, or the spectre of one, is conjured up in the interaction on the stage or screen (and perhaps yet another among the audience). Moreover, the closet may become multidimensional and Chinese box-like, as in televised sports, where one particular kind of closet – that of the athletes and the stadium crowd – is contained in another closet constituted between the TV-viewer and those appearing on the screen; which in turn is mediated by a third closet (or rather, range of closets) related to a number of 'narrators'. These possess special options for staging a version of 'the male paranoid theatricization of the male closet'.[113] The cameraman may move the eye of the lens from certain parts of the body where it has come to linger; the editor may, through freezing, zooming, slow motion and instant replay, elevate the performing body beyond the earthly laws of irreversible time and spatial constraints and turn it into an object of intense contemplation – and cut away; the commentator may babble to distract from any sexualized visual excesses as well as point to their possibilities in his description of bodies and performances.[114]

A further complication – or mitigation – of the geometry and kinetics of the closet is the ever-increasing incorporation of women in these spaces. From the viewpoint of the mechanics of absent homosexuality, it is in fact an issue of incorporation (whether women are straightly brought into this territory or are included through simply being present there): they may function as witnesses as well as evidence of the absence, ignorance and rejection of homosexuality among the male spectators and participants. This, too, can be seen projected onto the cinema screen, if one is unable to perceive it elsewhere. An almost sure-fire rule of thumb is the following: as soon as men are about to become absorbed in doings with each other (and how often isn't this the case – in films), a woman will be introduced with whom at least one of the men must, implicitly or explicitly, enter into intercourse. Obviously she may, at the same time, mediate a staging of inter-male erotic and sexual interests. Another example is the insertion, into the lulls and hugs of televised male sports, of pictures from a camera entrusted with the task of finding a woman spectator.

The polygonal, multidimensional and Chinese box character of many closets should not blind us to the virtues of simpler, triangular ones. Again, these are often of a spectatorial and specular structure, whether the apex is manned by the lecturer, the entertainer, the priest, the bartender, the crucified Christ, the newscaster, the hanged man, the boss, the sergeant, or the corporate director at the head of the table. And again, the erotics of the triangular closet may be relayed and rejected by the intimacy yet distantness of the gaze; by the incorporation of homosexual spectres or real women; by reference to the urgencies of work and war. Nor should we forget the dyadic, interspecular structure of a number of relations, although such male tête-à-têtes are often avoided when not highly formalized or staged by a third party into some kind of a triangle. We merely mention these forms in passing; the main objective was not to examine the infinitely intricate variations in the layout and workings of closets, but to point to their very real presence and prevalence in the geography of everyday life.

17 'Homophobia'

In recent years, the term *homophobia* has gained currency in analyses of 'non-homosexual' men's relation to homosexuality. Loosely, we may translate it as 'dread of homosexuality'; however, it can be used to cover a larger or smaller area of relations, and its meaning can be vague or carefully specified as well as connected to one theoretical framework or the other.

Insofar as 'homophobia' is intended as an explanatory concept, useful for identifying the causes and conditions of certain phenomena, it is very often associated with a psychoanalytic framework. We have already indicated the problems of this theoretical structure (chapter III, sections 4–5, 8); however, concepts of homophobia are not necessarily related to this matrix, as Jonathan Dollimore has pointed out in his informative distinction between psychoanalytic and socio-cultural or 'materialist' notions of homophobia.[115] Since it is not the topic of our present concern to give explanations – as opposed to explications – of non-homosexual men's relations to homosexuality I shall postpone further discussion until later (chapter V, section 6).

In the present section I shall concentrate on the explicative or phenomenological level of the concept of homophobia, i.e. as a concept intended to identify particular patterns – or *the* particular pattern – of the relations of 'non-homosexual' men to homosexuality. Very often, the term is used without much specification and tends to be empty of cognitive effect, although rhetorically important in ways I shall return to in a moment. Yet the concept of 'homophobia' has also been used in such penetrating and sophisticated studies as those by Eve Sedgwick and Jonathan Dollimore.[116] In exploring the dialectics of homosexual presence/absence, knowledge/ignorance and desire/denial, these investigations largely address the same field of study and basically conceive of it in much the same way as I have done in this section. And at the level of phenomenological explication, many of our analyses are, I think, compatible and complementary.[117]

A point of discussion arises, however, concerning the choice of category to be used as *the* main concept covering the scope of this field.[118] 'Homophobia' (and the related notion of 'homosexual panic') is characterized by terminologically privileging the *passionate* dimension of the dialectics as well as the *negative* pole of the passionate: repulsion, fear, hatred, anger, disgust. The authors might want to include other aspects under this heading as well, or even prioritize these. Thus, Sedgwick specifies the concept by means of the more passionless notion of 'blackmailability', and in fact stresses the 'epistemological' dimension, i.e. the axis of knowledge/ignorance.[119] Dollimore follows Sedgwick with respect to 'blackmailability', and further stresses issues of social control related to the constitution of identities by way of exclusion.

However, the choice of words is influential in shaping the reader's relation to the text and to the world. Terms like homophobia may easily end up drawing one's attention away from apprehending that the negative pole of passion is not always decisive or dominant. Rejection is not always particularly passionate; it may be a fairly conventional manoeuvre, much like greeting someone or obeying traffic lights, making it easier to pursue interests of a completely different nature. Rejection may also be a device for making sexuality possible (from prisons to paranoia) in that it abides by conventional standards of dealing with the subject matter, much like the Latin terms and other such rhetorical gestures of medical texts. Further, rejection may sometimes be an integral *part* of the erotics of homosexuality.

This last point leads us into what may seem dangerous waters (not to mention the whirlpools of 'political in/correctness'). But it also brings us close to points made in recent critiques of the regime of sexuality, of 'King Sex', namely that the joys of eroticism may very well have to do with *reluctance*, *distance*, *resistance*, *longing*, *postponement*, *obstacles*.[120] Should we accept such insights, it would follow that this may also be the case, to some extent and in some way, with eroticism from man to man. The contrapositioning of Bang and Ferenczi, Maître and municipal recorder at the beginning of the discussion of absent homosexuality also served the purpose of indicating this: not all erotic desire between 'non-homosexual' men is marked primarily by 'paranoia' or 'homophobia'. The emphasis may as well be on the pole of protecting and developing. Not surprisingly, these more 'positive' dimensions of absent homosexuality can most easily be approached by way of homosexuals' literature. This, however, does not mean that they are not to be found among non-homosexual men as well; the difference is mainly in the weight and type of negation.[121] From this point of view there is no radical difference between the 'homosexual' and the 'non-homosexual' men of modernity. Bang's work may even be said to be too much in the negative mood: longing and want are part of erotics, but so is being-with. Indeed, erotics is, among other things, very much about presence: dwelling in the other's nearness; feelings of unity and being together; glimmering eyes; sharing a bottle of wine; walking along the Elbe; starlit skies above a roof terrace in the Mediterranean. Sentimentality is part of it, and so is heart-throbbing. And male resistance to 'homosexuality' – the physical-orgasmic act – may well, sometimes, be enhancing the erotic; this becomes more passionate precisely because the sexual possibility is not known or not wanted – or because *perhaps* it is.

A further reason for avoiding 'homophobia' as the main concept to cover the scope of the field is related to this: it has a tendency to turn into *male-phobia*, i.e. an unspecified hostility towards any kind of masculinity that differs from the qualities attributed to women, as well as towards any kind of relations between men which do not include women, or alternately, are not proclaimedly 'gay'. This tendency is often recognizable in the vague uses of the term referred to above: precisely because it is empty of cognitive effect, 'homophobia' functions as no more or no less than an invective against men and masculinity. Indeed, some academic regimes of discourse seem to require this as a necessary device for the legitimation of the text, a guarantee of its political correctness; such appears to be the case with some versions of 'men's studies', of 'feminism', and of 'gay studies', each having interiorized the rhetorical demands of the others at least to the point of lip service.[122] Clearly, this is not a position advanced by a good deal of men's, women's and gay studies (and certainly not by Sedgwick and Dollimore). Nor is it the position taken in the present study. 'Closets' of absent homosexuality may, in actual fact, be coextensive with 'male spaces' (how is one to *know*?), but it seems reasonable to emphasize that, in terms of a phenomenological constitution analysis, a passionately rejective 'absent homosexuality' is not coextensive with sexual interest among non-homosexual men, and further, that such sexual interest is not coextensive with 'male interest' and its corresponding spaces.[123]

Nor do I see how, as a gay man, I could take this route of undifferentiated condemnation of masculinity and men without too much *bad faith*. Male homosexual attraction is intimately and inextricably entwined with attraction to masculinity. Advancing this claim is not equivalent to advocating the charms of queer-bashing or celebrating a supposedly never-changing ontology of heterosexual male dominance over gays and women. Nor does it leave one unprotected against the facile accusation, lurking just around the corner, which equates male homosexuality with fascism. It is one of the main purposes of this book to attempt an analysis and to point to possible futures not entrapped in these equations, without sacrificing the power and the joy of the attractions of masculinity.[124]

The assumption, however hidden and implicit, that sexual attraction of men to men might *as well* be an attraction to women is senseless, and indeed as violently offensive as the assumptions underlying any attempt at curing homosexuality. Masculinity does make a *difference* in matters of male–male sexual attraction. And it is senseless to claim that this difference does not, or should not, have to do with quite a number of cultural dimensions of masculinity, but merely with the existence or non-existence of a penis. The latter is simply too insignificant to make a difference.[125] An analysis of male homosexuality that doesn't acknowledge this difference of masculinity is indeed – homophobic.[126]

18 The friend

The most striking thing about modern friendship is the lack of it.

Everyday language is indicative. A (non-homosexual) man can talk about other men as his 'good friends' in the sense that they are acquaintances whom he knows somewhat better than others. Yet would it be fitting to call them his 'friends'? Perhaps he'd rather refer to them as 'some friends of mine'. It is problematic enough in the plural form, but even worse in the singular. Another man can be referred to as 'my good friend, Peter Smith', or as 'a good friend of mine', or at a pinch as 'a friend of mine', but it is hardly fitting to say 'he is my friend.' Some form of modification is required, either by 'good' or 'best', which curiously enough seems to weaken what follows in this case, and/or by combining it with a plural form which detracts from the singularity of the relationship. For it is precisely this singularity that comes to mind with the word 'friendship': a relationship to another man which is cultivated for its own sake. Not that the two cannot do something together, but primarily they are together because they enjoy each other's company.[127]

Friendship, then, does not exist in modern everyday speech. But does it exist in real life? In the nature of the case, there is some difficulty in investigating this empirically, since one cannot simply ask a man whether he has a friend because language itself forbids him to say so. One could however try to calculate the probabilities. *Where* might such a friend be in a 'heterosexual' man's life? Not at home, since that is reserved for the wife and kids. Nor at work, because there he is mostly together with more than one man, and in any case work itself is the primary concern in that context. Where then? In the gaps between home and work he is usually either with his family (at the movies, for example, or on a Sunday outing); or he is alone (in the car, in the supermarket); or if he is ever with other men, it is always in the plural or always subordinated to some other purpose (soccer, politics). If there is room at all for a friend in a man's life, it must apparently be found in the interim between the family he was born into and the one he will later enter, in other words, in the relatively unguarded niches of boyhood and youth; and even there the possibility is vanishing, since nine-year-olds are now expected to have girlfriends. Friendship between men is a social impossibility in modern societies, at least for most males.[128]

In fact, men's friendships may have been rare throughout history. Even in those periods when friendship was cultivated, it was reserved for special social strata, as in medieval monasteries, and in practice perhaps even for special age groups, as with the 'Romantic' or 'intimate' friendships of the eighteenth and nineteenth centuries.[129] However, the absence of friendship in modern Western societies appears against the backdrop of a period in which such relationships were relatively widespread and accepted.

If the friend is nowhere to be found in modern speech, nor in real life, then is he there as a *wish*, dream, fantasy? A possible source here is *fiction*, of which films and TV series are probably the most suitable survey material since they reach a wide audience. And indeed, many of the films with a leading male character do feature some trace of friendship. Television does not abound with series in which the relationship between two men plays a major role, but in at least one important case it does: *Miami Vice*. It is tempting to view this show as an indication of the status of friendship in modern societies, both because there aren't *more* of such series with friendships, and because there isn't *more* friendship in it. Even though the two leading characters are together almost constantly, they do little else than drive, watch for possible criminals, and shoot at them. The friendship is amputated, but it's *there*; one way or the other, it *is* reaffirmed in every episode that these two men feel something special for each other, a special belonging and a special responsibility.[130]

The remarkable thing is that despite the actual absence of male friendships, particularly in the latter half of the twentieth century, they are still dreamed about in films and on television. It seems, then, that a general need for friendship exists in modern societies as well, though relegated to the realm of fantasy. We have seen in this section how homosexuality tends to affect all relationships between men and forces them into repudiations. Friendship stresses the close relation itself between two men; in addition, it closes in on itself, has no spectatorial structure and no witnesses; it therefore seems logical enough that not only must such relationships continually repudiate homosexuality, but they must be avoided altogether. The absence of friendship is thus an indication of the presence of homosexuality; homosexuality is present by being absolutely absent – again, a conclusion that obviously cannot be proved.[131] And to the extent that dreams of friendship are presented in the fictions of film and TV, they must of course partake in the general denial whose various forms we have analysed in the preceding chapters: they are in fact being transformed in themselves by being situated in a spectatorial space; further, at least one of the two men must end up in bed with a woman; the enemy whom they are combating must not only be a criminal but also a homosexual; insults or jokes about gays must be fired off; a ridiculous 'real' homosexual must make an appearance, and so on. These processes soon become self-aggrandizing: the more one has to assure oneself that one's relationship with another man is not homosexual, the more conscious one becomes that it might be, and the more necessary it becomes to protect oneself against it. The result is that friendship gradually becomes impossible, in real life as well as in language. When the homosexuals from the 1920s to the 1960s so frequently used words like 'friendship' and 'friend' in the names of their organizations and journals, it was no doubt also because they could thus borrow support from a phenomenon still socially respectable.[132] But as time went by, these words turned into purely homosexual terms, just as the reality they designated disappeared from everything but homosexuals' relations.[133]

The denial of suspicions of homosexuality not only affects friendship, but all social intercourse between men having no other purpose than the intercourse itself and lacking a formalized and regulated pattern and a spectatorial structure. If pubs have a bad reputation it is not merely because they violate work morale and threaten family life, but also because unregimented and suspicious male pleasures can run rampant here. Professional solicitude has openly expressed this suspicion and turned it into a science under the heading 'Alcoholism and Homosexuality'.[134] A comprehensive attempt to purge life of homosexuality is thus operating, in that these aimless, unregimented or non-spectatorial relationships between men are avoided. They simply don't *exist*: and no one would know they might were it not that the culture industry still presented the fantasy of them and that language still kept homeless words.

19 Heterosexualization

We have seen in the preceding chapter that one may try to avert homosexual suspicions by avoiding male–male situations where they might arise. As noted in passing, though, a fundamentally different mode of avoidance exists. Again, the realm of fantasy may provide a particularly intimate insight. The pivotal critique raised against the *Tintin* adventures in the late twentieth century, is quite simply:

> Not enough women!
>
> Not enough in relation to real life, not enough in relation to desires, not even enough in relation to the small handful of males who comprise the main body of characters.
>
> That is the nature of this universe, it's no use denying it. Nor pointing a finger of reproach aimed at improving the work. For it can become neither better nor any different: the creator passed on four years ago.
>
> Yet *would* it perhaps have improved by itself? Was it that Tintin, for the first time – in his creator's seventy-sixth year – was on the threshold of a bona fide romance, replete with ponytail and lipstick and a pent-up Catholic energy?

writes Søren Vinterberg, literary critic, in a deadpan commentary.[135] Perhaps the objection cannot be taken quite seriously by the one who advances it; perhaps he'll have to ironize discreetly in the process. But how on earth can he arrive at it, succeed in writing it in the newspaper, and still be regarded as right in the head? This communication, and its discreet irony, require a certain congeniality between writer and reader, a common feeling that one *perhaps really should* feel guilty here. *There is a norm* one has perhaps transgressed: *if there are men, there should also be women, and preferably just as many, otherwise something is wrong.*

This norm is not new; in any case, its origins date back as far into the nineteenth century as does the homosexual; and it is not floating in thin air, but like him, has spread and lodged itself in people's lives and their being together. One of the more striking aspects of modern societies, when compared to other or earlier ones, is the relative absence of 'monosexual' – single-gender – domains.[136] Modern societies have no great life-encompassing and widely respected institutions for men which could correspond to the medieval monasteries; and the modern world is not partitioned off in two spheres with but tangential points of contact, as is still the rule in some Arabic countries, where 'public life', from pavement cafés to government agencies, is a male enterprise. And in more and more of the domains in Western societies previously reserved for men, women are now actively engaged, from education and plumbing to political institutions, the police and the military. Modern societies are *gender-mixed*. Granted, in many places there are still more men than women, but seen in relation to the situation in the mid-1800s, a great change has come about. There is practically no place where there aren't women; and there no longer exists any norm which excludes them; on the contrary, it is more and more the norm that something is wrong if women are absent where men are present.

But what, exactly, is wrong? Is it that social intercourse between men, in and of itself, is living proof that women are, in actual fact, excluded from equal access to privileged positions? If so, there shouldn't be any reason to worry with respect to Tintin, for the road to women's equal rights is hardly the one which allows them to go gallivanting about in Africa and other such strange places with the rather ridiculous Tintin and his entourage. We can let this example serve as an indication that anxiety about men's social intercourse is a matter that involves more than women's access to equal rights.

What then? No doubt there are many factors; for example, the fear of what men might concoct when on their own, and the disastrous consequences this might effect; a fear that is historically justified, it seems, and therefore part of the reason why it is a quite natural assumption today that women, at bottom, are good, while it is suspect to be male. What is of particular interest here, however, is of course the role of 'absent homosexuality', which is by now too obvious to require further discussion: in a situation where homosexuality is conjured up in each and every instance of male social intercourse *and* must be denied at the same time, the presence of women naturally serves this denial as well. And the denial is most effective if women are not only present, but the men also penetrate them.

This is, funnily enough, also what is demanded of Tintin. As we have seen, the possible 'improvement' in relation to the lack of women in this series would not simply consist of including more women, but would precisely require that Tintin experienced 'a bona fide romance, replete with ponytail and lipstick and a pent-up Catholic energy'. Romance, it reads (and 'a pent-up Catholic energy', whatever that is); but later it becomes clear what exactly is implied: namely that 'the Boy Scout loosened up his tight knickers a bit.' Only in this way can Tintin and his male aficionados avert the suspicion that they might, even fleetingly, be more interested in men than in women. *Tintin out of Snowy*, as the graffito reads above the gay bar john. It *is* rather mind-boggling to imagine there might be even the faintest shade of homosexuality in this sterile universe, but these days one can never be certain. And it isn't enough to act out the ritual repudiations, such as letting the aria accompanist be bossed around by the old *fag hag* Castafiore, and letting him swoon with the ladies, or letting the overly identical goofs Dupond and Dupont dance a *pas de deux* on the moon or scramble onto tables and chairs, clutching each other and screaming for help because they've seen a mouse.[137] For these repudiations of a queer masculinity are perhaps expressions of a suspect interest in real men. More effective agents are needed: women.

But again: the incorporation of women into male relations cannot merely serve as a guarantee against or a public repudiation of homosexuality, but must also establish and mediate it. This may take the shape of various sorts of triangles, expressly sexual or otherwise.[138] The triangles may also be established via telemedia: e.g. the relations of visual pornography between the man and woman on the screen and the man watching. And the number of persons involved may of course be multiplied, as in the gang fuck. Obviously, such relations mediated by women are not identical to non-mediated sexual relations between two (or more) men. But there is nonetheless a sharing of sexuality, as well as a participation in and arousal by the sexuality of the other man and his masculinity gear, a form of sexuality floating in the indeterminate middle range between identification and desire. It is important to *respect* the particular qualities of these forms of (homo)sexuality, analytically as well as in real life. In scholarly works and other literature, the relations established by way of such mediations are usually approached with a copious and indiscriminate use of the vocabulary of alienation, fetishism, reification, pathology, assault, violence, gynephobia or homophobia. However, there are at least three crucial distinctions to be considered here: whether or not the relation is consensual – there is a distinction to be made between *gang fuck* and *gang rape*; whether or not it belongs to the realm of fantasy and play; and whether or not it is pleasurable.[139] Again, the experiences of gay pornography may be elucidating, detailing the pleasures of the *man-in-between* other men, in the more or less sophisticated settings of the prison, the houseboy at the all-male party, or the services to be performed beneath the poker table.

The dialectic of absent homosexuality is thus a contributing factor with regard to the normative and factual decline of monosexual domains, as well as to the actual – and fundamentally ambiguous – heterosexualization of all relations in modern societies. However, this onrushing gender mixing and heterosexualization also provokes reactions and attempts at evasions. Precious little is able to hold its ground in modern societies; in fact, there is only one institution which is effective in evading gender mixing, and that is sport. Confronted with the attack that men's companionship brings about horrible consequences in and of itself, it parries that it's just play. And faced with the possible objection that this sort of play, as well, should be gender-mixed, it holds a terrible weapon, the mere existence of which is so deterring that the objection need rarely be uttered: what is worse, not to be allowed to play on equal terms, or in fact to be? Sport appears as the last bastion of pure masculinity, its ironic revenge against an onrushing civilization, and the only place where it can safely celebrate itself in its crude naturalness.[140] Beyond sport, masculinity turns truly fantastic.

20 Violence

It is impossible to overlook the *pleasure of violence* that forms part of many relations between men: in boxing, torture, soccer, the pursuit of criminals, prison sex, etc. What is the more specific connection between pleasure and violence here? Let us briefly and schematically review the preceding cases, now with special regard to illuminating this question. No doubt there are a number of possible relations, which are hardly mutually exclusive but often enter into combinations.

1 *Violence as denial.* We have repeatedly noted a particular relation between violence and pleasure – most manifest in films and soccer, but also in torture, prison sex and police pursuit of homosexuals. Each time the possibility of homosexuality presented itself – i.e. when some form of physical contact or emotional intensity arose between men – it would be simultaneously rejected with a violent disavowal of one kind or another. Denigrating jokes or insults against gays would be made, a real or fantasized homosexual person

would be introduced who was ridiculous, suspicious or disgusting, or who could be ridiculed, made suspect or denigrated; or arrested, maimed or executed. In this manner, not only those directly involved are purged, but also anyone who may have come close enough to feel an arousal. As we have seen, it is often impossible to discern whether it is the proximity of homosexuality that leads to denial, or if it is denial which is used to evoke homosexuality. Accordingly, this form of connection between violence and pleasure turns into the next.

2 *Violence as a pretext.* In many cases, violence is a socially accepted institution, a setting used to legitimate the practice of erotic male interests that are otherwise tabooed. In the previous examples, we have observed this link perhaps most clearly in connection with the role-playing found in prisons (Man vs punk); this establishes a framework that can legitimate sex between men in relation to the surroundings as well as for those involved. The same no doubt applies to torture, where erotic tensions between the soldiers themselves or between soldiers and victims can be discharged in socially respectable forms, thereby lending torture sexual over- and undertones. (In these contexts, violence is of course often used not only as a pretext but also a *means* to attain sex.)

3 *Violence as surrogate.* Homosexuality, as we have seen, becomes imminent particularly in contexts in which there is physical or intense emotional contact between men, and where masculinity is stressed. This applies to such institutions as the police and the military, where men are literally rubbing up against each other, all the while their interaction with physical strength and virility boosters (canons, pistols, batons) turns them on. This sounds like homosexual wishful fantasy, and most likely that's just what it is. Still, a directly sexual acting out is often socially impossible in these contexts (except such special situations as torture and prison). It is probable that this sexual tension seeks release in violence, which is also socially accepted behaviour in precisely these surroundings. The same no doubt applies to team sports. The sexual tension built up from within can seek to come out as aggression against the opponent or as violence.[141]

These various combinations of violence and pleasure, which are by no means mutually exclusive but often come together, are not specific to modern societies. They can be found wherever male institutions and socially acceptable forms of violence have existed together with taboos against erotic/sexual acts between men.

Nevertheless, there are special characteristics which distinguish the modern form of male erotics, that is, of 'absent homosexuality'. Not only does it produce and deny physical pleasure at one and the same time, but it does so ever more directly and ever more comprehensively. The possibility of physical-orgasmic sex between men is explicitly conjured up and denied (verbally, visually); and this happens everywhere and constantly, as soon as men are together. This dissemination and intensification of the possibility of physical-orgasmic sex acts between men *and* of its denial must necessarily have some impact on the violence of male relations. It must – other things being equal – lead to an escalation of the violence which is used to deny sexual interests, the violence which is used to legitimate transgressing the taboo against sex, and the violence which is used as a surrogate for sex. In other words, an escalation of the various forms of violence that are irrational and aren't really aimed at the other's pleasure, aren't really play.[142]

4 *Violence as play.* Violence – domination/submission, strength/surrender – is one of many games men can play together. As we have seen in connection with soccer and boxing, it is one of the ways by which *the interest between men in what men can do with one another* is enacted. As men, they are by definition equal, and in actuality always unequal. And as 'men' they are – by nature and by culture in an inextricably entangled hotchpotch – directed at enjoying the extremes of their physical strength and the capacities of their body (or their mind). Hence, the pleasure in testing this strength, testing this equality, balancing or maintaining this inequality. Let us hasten to add that these games are not the only ones that men can play with each other, and furthermore that they can be played in a multitude of ways and in more or less civilized forms. In many cases, they are but an entertaining pastime; in some cases the pleasure of the other's pleasure is essential; but they can easily turn unpleasant, because the parties are often in different positions of power, and because someone *must* lose, and it's not certain he finds this very entertaining.

5 *Violence as counterbalancing and as limit.* In the analysis of male identity, I stressed the 'positive' aspect in the relation to other men which is inherent in the decision to be a man and the recognition of being so: wishes, longings, desires to be like another man;

security, fellowship, the desire to learn from and to mirror oneself through being with other men. I also mentioned the close link and the blurred boundaries between the experience of identification and eroticism. However, I discreetly chose to ignore the more 'negative' aspects of these relations of identification, even though these negative aspects are always present, or at least are always close by. On the one hand, the distance and inequality can seem too great in relation to the wish to be like another man; he becomes envious or jealous of the other, hating him at the same time as he is attracted to him. On the other hand, the equality can seem too great, so that he fears being engulfed by the other and not being anything himself. Between these extremes lie all kinds of transitions and links. In both respects, violence can pose a solution, in the one case by establishing a balance, in the other by drawing a limit. In either case, it is an issue of setting oneself off in relation to the other. This 'violence' does not, of course, have to be physical, but can be vented in all kinds of assaults, threats, attacks and competitions; it moves between attempts to undermine the other's position from the outside and attempts to surpass him within his own domain. Insofar as these possibilities of disquieting inequality and disquieting equality are intrinsic to male identification *per se*, there is good reason to expect that this violence must also be a dominant trait in many cases. When heterosexual relationships have been relatively stable, it is attributable not least to the fact that it was possible (to pretend) to maintain a *fundamental* difference between the partners. But if such forms of violence are perhaps unavoidable between men, they can assume varying dimensions and more or less unpleasant forms.

6 *Violence as pleasure.* The link between violence and pleasure in relations between men can be explained and understood in such a way that the violence *really*, *essentially*, *at bottom* is pretext or surrogate, tug-of-war or entertainment, counterbalance or demarcation. Thus it is full of significance and swollen with meaning. On top of, or beneath or beside this is surely a violence that itself is pleasure; just as meaningless, or just as meaningless to analyse as other types of pleasure between men, and within certain limits just as harmless.[143]

In all of the cases mentioned, violence does not exclude sexual pleasure, but is indeed easily connectable with it. This can seem disquietingly confusing; some help may be found in the three sets of criteria we listed in section 19 above: whether or not the relation is consensual, whether or not it belongs to the realms of fantasy and play, and whether it is pleasurable for both parties. From this point of view, not all violence connected with inter-male sexuality is 'homophobic'; it may be a desirable part of sexual pleasure, intensifying it, indeed constitutive of it.

21 Homosexualization

In the previous sections I have been exploring what happens with the rest of the men when some are separated out as 'homosexuals'. It is time to sum up the results of these investigations and considerations.

I have presented a particular theoretical framework and conceptual apparatus for this field, in contrast to and in a dialogue with psychoanalytic notions of 'latent', 'repressed' and 'sublimated' homosexuality, as well as with various notions of 'homophobia'. To cover the whole of the field I have suggested the term 'absent homosexuality', more in line with the phenomena than 'latent homosexuality', less potentially male-phobic and more differentiable than 'homophobia'.

More specifically, I have identified the contours of a *dialectical machinery*, bearing some resemblance to that of capital as analysed by Marx.[144] In absent homosexuality, there is a triad of oppositional poles: being/absence, knowledge/ignorance, desire/denial. Further, there is a number of 'forms of movements' and transitions between these poles, such as sequestration, displacement, camouflage, disavowal, evasion, safeguarding. Often, it is impossible to discern whether the movement proceeds from one pole or the other, since the demands of both end up being honoured. Moreover, there is a propelling dynamic of reciprocal reinforcement and amplification. The more homosexuality is present and emphasized, as a reality or a possibility, the more energetically and expressly it must be denied. Conversely, however, denial has the unfortunate – or fortunate – consequence that it conjures up precisely what was to be rejected. When one must be aware of what to avoid because it can be construed as homosexual, one becomes aware that it could actually be so. And when one wishes to repudiate homosexuality through an express denial (in words or behaviour), one ends up emphasizing it in the selfsame act, thereby also subjecting oneself to suspicion.

Consequently, these various phenomena affect and amplify each other in a continually more rampant spiral.

In this sense, absent homosexuality is a tendentially self-reproducing and self-expanding abstract 'logic', which, however, can exist and actualize itself only by materializing in the substances of socio-cultural life, which it connects to, and in part creates and shapes according to the rules of its own inner dynamics.[145] In the preceding sections we have considered the articulation of this in a number of phenomena: in ways of seeing and the structure of social spaces; in the working of institutions such as science or the police; in the male milieux of sports and torture; in the symbolic worlds of scholarship and journalism, film and comics; in the eradication of certain forms of male relations and the ambiguity of the inclusion of women; in violence against homosexuals.

In sum: absent homosexuality is potentially omnipresent and tendentially ever-expanding and ever-intensifying, materially embedded and embeddable in social spaces and bodies, relations and institutions. It is *the* typical form of sexuality among non-homosexual men in modern societies. Unequivocal homosexual acts (physical-orgasmic) also occur among men who are not separated out as homosexual, yet these acts, too, are drawn into the logic of absent homosexuality. This is a major organizing power of modern societies, on a par with other great agents such as capital and bureaucracy.

We have found no reason to conceive of all of this as the repressed and sublimated expressions of a homosexual drive, neatly established in every man's childhood and always lying in wait to vent itself. Instead, I have suggested that the phenomena of absent homosexuality may be a historically specific formation of a certain – not always sexual, but sexualizable – interest, inherent in masculinity, in what men can do with one another. Thus an analysis of the constitutional relations of masculinity and homosexuality has been delineated, alternative to that of psychoanalysis as well as to studies conducted in terms of a homophobic constitution of masculine identity. This analysis has implications also for considerations on the future of masculinity and male–male sexuality (as we shall see in chapter VI). I have taken care to avoid any wholesale condemnation of this 'male interest' (as it is sometimes found in connection with the notion of homophobia). Specifically, it seemed necessary to point out that male interest and relations among men aren't necessarily reprehensible merely because they do not involve women or declare themselves as 'homosexual'. Moreover, it should be remembered that sexual or erotic attraction to men is somehow an attraction to masculinity; and that this should be acknowledged in any study that is not anti-gay. In this context, it was also reasonable to point out that, in absent homosexuality, the emphasis may as well lie on the positive and affirmative pole as on the negative one, and that male resistance to physical-orgasmic homosexuality is not always in opposition to inter-male erotics, but may intensify it or indeed produce it.

As for the method of analysis, I have delimited my approach from any hasty reliance on (psychoanalytical) sexual symbolism. More fundamentally, I have severed the analysis from the methodological 'guarantee' implied in the psychoanalytic idea that there is always a homosexual drive underlying the phenomena and that, accordingly, the task merely consists of finding where and how it has concealed itself. It is crucial always to investigate whether, how far and how homosexuality is present – which requires a certain measure of ingenuity, flexibility and persistence since absent homosexuality is indeed an elusive matter. Consequently, there is no guarantee for the analysis: on principle, it cannot be verified, since absent homosexuality is characterized precisely by being present only insofar as its presence can be denied.[146] On the other hand, the analysis, on principle, cannot be falsified. It is inescapably, self-consciously and stubbornly uncertain. Moreover, the relations of presence/absence, knowledge/ignorance, desire/denial are not limitable to an objective 'object' of investigation. Precisely insofar as the analysis is correct in identifying the tendential omnipresence of the dialectics of absent homosexuality, these also include the relations of reader and writer of the present text. For this reason as well, the analysis of absent homosexuality is far from being a simple game of cognition, of overcoming ignorance by disseminating knowledge; it is inextricably entangled in the logic of desire and denial. There is no Archimedean point of exploration outside the dialectic of reciprocal passion and paranoia. Self-reflectively uncertain and passionate, the analysis must draw stylistic consequences from this state of affairs in attempting to sharpen attention to rather paradoxical phenomena, in trying to re-present that which is absent. But I do believe that a number of persuasive arguments have been offered here, not least this pivotal one: *why is homosexuality incessantly dragged out when it is going to be negated anyway?*

To speak of 'homosexuality', and more explicitly 'absent homosexuality', in connection with a great many male relations might seem an unreasonable abstraction from the actual diversity of different individuals' different relations. However, it is not merely a 'formal abstraction', stuffing phenomena with only a superficial resemblance into the same category, but a *real abstraction*: the uniformity and homogenizing conveyed by the notion exists in reality.[147] On the one hand, it appears in a certain weeding of the diversity of male relations: some of them simply become impossible. On the other hand, it appears in a certain pruning of the remaining relations: all of them are regimented and subordinated to other primary purposes, or they are situated in spectatorial spaces; and they are all potentially homosexualized – not only in the sense that wherever men are together, the possibility of eroticism is always close by, but in that all of these relations are charged with the *emphatic appeal* to *physical-orgasmic* sex, while at the same time a compulsory gesture of disavowal is imposed upon them. All relations between men tend to be caught in this cramp of actuation and denial.

'Absent homosexuality' is thus present in real life, all the while it retains its ghost-like character – as that which exists and does not exist, that which is desired and denied, that which is known of and unknown. This mode of being of absent homosexuality can only be comprehended in its relation to the other pole in the modern form of male–male eroticism, i.e. *the homosexuals*, in its simultaneous connection to and demarcation from them. Its phantom-like character is indeed related to the fact that it is a reflection emanating from the homosexuals.[148]

IV

The Homosexual Form of Existence

1 Grocer in the crush

'It was during the exhibition period that he had been arrested in the Tivoli Gardens because, in the crush outside the open-air theatre where he was standing alongside a young person, he had proceeded to finger him in an indecent fashion,' Dr Knud Pontoppidan, a consultant, reports in his clinical lecture in December 1890 about a 39-year-old grocer who two years previously had been committed 'for observation' to Pontoppidan's ward at a Copenhagen hospital.[1] During the police enquiry, it had emerged that 'in the course of the summer, he had been guilty of a whole series of that kind of immoral outrage, and he was chastised with five days' bread and water.' Now he has been recommitted for observation,

> having recently been encountered in a public lavatory under suspicious circumstances together with an adolescent lad. Once again it transpires that for some time he has been paying visits to public conveniences or lurking in the vicinity of such in order to find an opportunity for indecency. He states that he has always been able to see from the young passers-by who was willing to be used in this respect; no persuasion was required, and usually only trivial utterances would be exchanged, whereafter, in tacit agreement, he had achieved his intention in the form of mutual masturbation.
>
> In a short while, you will be allowed to see the patient; however, it would be inhumane of me to coerce him in the presence of a large gathering to give further particulars of this embarrassing matter. I shall therefore confine myself to reproducing for you the content of our confidential conversations.

From these conversations, and from his observations generally, Pontoppidan concludes that we are faced with a case of 'contrary sexuality', indeed that 'one would be hard put to find a more typical example.'[2] The sexual urge here is focused exclusively on individuals of the same sex as one's own; thus, when the grocer

> attended balls and social gatherings, he ascertained to his amazement that he remained completely cold in the face of the ladies; it did interest him to talk with a vivacious and witty woman, but he could feel nothing of the disquiet and anxiousness of heart of which his comrades spoke. Later he attempted coitus on repeated occasions, but to no avail; he even felt out-and-out disgust at intercourse. He has often pondered on the possibility of being rescued through marriage, but he has never been capable of working up the requisite tender feelings towards the opposite sex.

The preference for the young is perhaps a special penchant on the part of this particular grocer, whose 'lascivious dreams' revolve around 'butcher's boys with bare arms and tight-fitting trousers'. But in all other respects, there is no doubt that Pontoppidan considers him a typical example. Thus, as regards the *cause*: the grocer's 'anomalousness' is congenital; it 'manifests itself the very instant sexuality awakens' and is 'an expression of a degenerative predisposition'. Admittedly, the grocer displays 'no other distinct signs of degeneracy'; however, 'some hereditary disposition is in evidence, a maternal aunt having been mentally disordered.'

The contrary-sexual, then, is different from the start. 'Already as a boy' the grocer 'felt that he was not like other people' in sexual matters, 'though it was not till he was grown up that he fully realized his exceptional status'. By then, however, the drive is uncontrollable. 'Generally speaking, this perverse sexual urge appears early on and exerts a powerful hold over the individual; often, it is also quantitatively increased and torments the patient like true ruttishness.' The grocer has thus 'struggled for many years against his abnormal craving, until of late he has succumbed to it and fallen foul of the law'.

The perverse sexual predisposition also finds other expressions in personality. Though not in the form of bodily abnormalities, Pontoppidan states. 'I shall now give you an opportunity to see the patient while I exchange a few comments with him. The first thing you will notice is that, with his ample beard and altogether strong build, he is completely representative of the virile type. I can also inform you that the genitalia have developed altogether naturally.'

It is in fact characteristic of these contrary-sexuals that the 'anatomical hallmarks of the sex are present. Sometimes, however, it is possible to detect in the entire emotional make-up and mentality a character type reminiscent of the other sex, viz in the male patients something soft and sentimental (which can also be detected in our patient).' The intelligence, however, 'remains generally unscathed'.

Another characteristic personality trait in the contrary-sexual is his depression. This is not a direct corollary of his peculiar sexual urge, however, but rather a natural reaction to it. 'When the perverse sexuality is present in indubitable and pronounced form, the patient cannot avoid becoming fully cognizant of his exceptional status and perceiving it as the bane of his life.' Thus the grocer, too: he wishes 'not to live, yearning only for the time when he may dare hope that old age will put an end to his abnormal sexual proclivities'.

In many instances, the contrary sexual urge can hide, so that it is not clear to others that this is what really underlies actions and appearances. Such is the case with 'those old fellows who invariably gather handsome young men around themselves and regale them'. Most people would presumably think that these are variations within the framework of the norm; yet medical science refuses to be satisfied with the superficial impression: 'I am, however, inclined to believe that if I am given occasion to penetrate more closely into the nature of such a case, I shall generally be able to prove that the phenomenon occurs in tandem with other neuropathic symptoms on a common degenerative basis.'

Indeed, these 'contrary-sexuals' belong entirely within the purview of medical science. They are cases not of moral depravity, but of disease proper. Hence, the physician is the expert and authority in this field. Accordingly, it is perfectly appropriate that the judicial system consult precisely him on the question of whether the contrary-sexual offender is *compos mentis* and thus punishable. And so it is in this instance, too: with his expertise, the physician is in a position to determine that the grocer suffers from a 'decidedly morbid, congenital and by its very nature incurable abnormality', and must consequently be regarded as being of unsound mind. The contrary-sexual does not belong in jail but in hospital.

2 The species

From the second half of the nineteenth century, a new *species* is described in the scientific literature. Initially, there was some disagreement about what to call it: the 'contrary-sexuals' was one attempt. Gradually, however, the term 'the homosexuals' came to dominate.[3]

The sciences that studied this species – i.e. medical science, above all – described it with the following cohesive series of characteristics, as epitomized in the case of the crushed grocer:

1 The homosexual is *sexually attracted to other men.*
2 This attraction is an *end in itself* and not just a substitute for a dearth of women – thus, a prisoner would not be considered homosexual simply because he has sexual intercourse with other men in prison.
3 The attraction has an *emotional* aspect, not just a physical one – thus, Arab men will not be considered homosexual merely because sex between men is (or was) a widespread practice in the Arab countries.
4 The attraction segregates the person in question from other people, makes him *different* – not just in the way red-haired people differ, but in a more fundamental and comprehensive sense.
5 *Either/or*: either one is homosexual or else one is not, i.e. one is heterosexual.
6 *Constancy*: the homosexual *is and remains* homosexual.
7 *Fate*: homosexual is something the homosexual *is* and *must be*.
8 *Cause*: at some juncture, something has happened to cause the homosexual to be homosexual – a specific change in his biological equipment or a special event in relation to his environment in the course of his psychic development.
9 Whether what has happened originally comes from within or without, the result now resides inside the homosexual as an *inner nature*, *essence* and *nucleus*: his homosexuality. This nucleus:
(a) *is concealed and not readily accessible*: it may even hide from the person himself; many years may pass before he discovers that he 'is' homosexual;
(b) *presses* and seeks out – it is scarcely possible to curb it;

(c) is *uncontrollable for the person himself*: he cannot control it; it controls him;

(d) *radiates and usurps larger or smaller parts of the person*, thus creating:

10 *A special personality* with a series of external physical and psychological traits (e.g. gait, gestures, physical build, artistic interests).

11 The personality of the homosexual is altogether rather *feminine*.

12 The homosexual is *obsessed with sex*; at any rate the sexual plays an uncommonly important part in his life.

13 The development of the homosexual's homosexuality and the features related to it gives him a *special life history*.

14 It is *wrong* to be homosexual; first and foremost, it is a *disease*: his homosexuality:

(a) is something which *inhibits his life development*;

(b) is an *affliction*, something he is subservient to and tormented by;

(c) has natural, 'objective' *causes*, i.e. causes which in principle can be identified with the precision of natural science (it is not a result, for instance, of his own free choice or the devil's whims).

15 It is a *tragedy* to be homosexual.

16 The homosexual's homosexuality is *dangerous*.

17 It *requires exploration*.

18 It *requires supervision and control*.

19 It *requires scientific specialists* for its exploration, supervision and control.

Such, at any rate, was the opinion of the scientific enterprise that had specimens of the species for observation and examination in its clinics and laboratories. And its ideas gradually became common wisdom; they can be identified as the predominant trend in all the scientific, fictional and popular literature on the subject from the late nineteenth century to at least around 1970; and they also appear from newspaper writings and attitude surveys. Even in the 1990s, they are often presented by the media as *the* opinion of science; and a random group of same-sex lovers will also be able to confirm today that these are attitudes they often encounter in their family or at work. This is not to say that the various features of this species characterization have not been subject to discussion and problematization; on the contrary, it was disputed from the start.

But its continued importance is evident, not least from the fact that by and large it still constitutes the framework for the discussion and determines what problems can be raised at all.[4]

Such was – and largely still is – the opinion of *the others*. But what about the species itself? It, too, can speak and write.

3 Confirmations, refusals

From the end of the nineteenth century onwards, the medico-scientific view of 'the homosexuals' was also largely the self-perception publicly articulated by the men who nurtured intense erotic interests in other men. In fact, they co-authored it; what may be termed its *Urtext* was written in the 1860s by one of them, the German jurist K. H. Ulrichs.[5] In this manner, those affected confirmed the existence of the species and classified themselves as specimens, whether they opted to call themselves 'homosexuals' or not: from Ulrichs's 'Urnings' through the 'inverts' of the turn of the century to the 'homophiles' of the 1950s and the 'gays' of the post-1960s.[6]

Nevertheless, there are individuals who refuse to accept they are 'homosexuals' in this sense, although they have strong erotic interests in other men and to that extent would seem to belong within the category. One early example is Walt Whitman, who had written so ardently of his desire for men in the mid-nineteenth century. As time passed, it became clear how his work would be understood, and Whitman denied it was *that sort of stuff* he had been writing about.[7] This was done in a private letter; in fact, the refusal to be 'homosexual' has mostly not been expressed publicly, since standing up and declaring one has such interests yet is not 'homosexual' is to condemn oneself as a homosexual who will not admit it. So it is wiser not to say anything at all.

However, some people have attempted to formulate an alternative framework of understanding, though often displaying a certain fuzziness about its erotic or sexual nature (as well as about their own preferences in that respect). The most extensive attempt was made in Germany during the early decades of the twentieth century. The experiment backfired; the picture portrayed by medical science won through in the long run, and indeed, the intended alternative never seriously emancipated itself from the modes of thought of the medical and natural sciences.[8]

Elements of this resistance to being 'homosexual' can usually be encountered even in those who claim to be so. Often they have opposed the outrightly negative characterizations, disputed whether it was really all that dangerous and necessarily a disease and a tragedy, or questioned whether it was in fact particularly feminine. Many have asserted that such common features are due merely to the negative reactions of society: without these, 'the homosexuals' would be just as normal and ordinary as anyone else, apart from their sexual preference. Others passionately refute that their sexual preferences should be of any significance whatsoever: *they*, at least, 'have no problems on that score, since there is in fact nothing to *stop* one from showing some degree of regard for other people: after all, the heterosexuals don't go round advertising who they sleep with, and the so-called homosexuals have nothing at all in common, other than this immaterial sexual preference, unless they absolutely insist on being ostentatious and provocative.' These people *refuse to be homosexual.*

This mixture of advocacy and adverseness points to an existential problem, correlating more or less directly to a *theoretical problematic* with a number of prevalent positions.

1 Does the idea of a homosexual species capture the essence and nature of a certain subgroup of human beings? This, as has emerged, has been a dominant conception during the past hundred years, whether it was couched in the vocabulary of biology, psychology or psychoanalysis.
2 Or is this allegedly common nature a result of society's discrimination and oppression? This has been a favourite or auxiliary explanation from the 1950s onwards.[9]
3 Or is the alleged essence of the homosexual merely an 'essentialism', an ideology constructed by certain agents, supported by certain powers and interests, and assumed or transformed into an identity? This has been the view of the 'constructionist' approaches that gained momentum from the 1970s, conducted in terms of homosexual discourses, roles, labels, categories, definitions, concepts, scripts, ideas and identities.[10]
4 Or are the essentialist notions, rather, an illusory albeit successful discoursive device of power, a 'master narrative' beneath which teems almost infinite difference? Again, this can be termed a constructionist view, but one following the more 'deconstructionist' or 'postmodern' turn of the 1980s, pointing to complex and

changing constructions and deconstructions of identities and desires.[11]

These are, in an ideal-typical stylized form, the main theoretical positions and analytical approaches prevailing and competing in the study of homosexuality since the later nineteenth century.[12] The following sections aim at investigating how far they are appropriate, and whether they should be substituted or supplemented by other theories and approaches. I shall take as my starting point certain *moods* (or 'tunings') and convictions related to being homosexual.

4 Wrongness

> It is only reasonable that there are people who disdain us. We must learn to understand that, but *we*, too, have a right to be and to live (. . .). We, who are born to solitude, *must* show kindness, preferably goodness, to all. Thus we pay for our right to be, our place in society. We must seek in our dealings, in art or in practical life, to achieve the greatest and the best, thus creating esteem for ourselves and for the type to which we belong. We must not feel disgraced that we were born to solitude, but we must judge ourselves more seriously and severely than we judge others. We should preferably be gentle and quiet and turn our contempt on – ourselves.
>
> C. Houmark, *Naar jeg er død* (1926)[13]

Anyone can try being an outsider. Chancing to do so may be less simple in a contemporary Western city, where to all intents and purposes you can walk down the street (almost) naked without anyone bothering to look at you. But, providing you can afford it, you can, for example, rent a reasonably exposed beach house in a better-class second-home area, catch the train and bus there, walking the last part of the way, and spend a week alone reading and sleeping and going for walks. You will soon develop a special relationship to the occupants around. You are odd – you can see it on their faces. To start with, one (their 'one') arrives by car, not trudging along with all one's kit; and one does not walk to the grocer's. Secondly, one does not stroll around alone, but together with one's wife or a medium-sized dog. Finally, one goes around in shorts during the day, however cold it gets. Anything else is suspect. They *gape*; and if they think no one is there, they come over and stare through the window, if possible to get a shock. When you ask what they are looking for they retreat, with the comment that they just wanted to take a look around; without apologizing, for they were well within their rights. We are dealing here with forces so strong and a right so compelling that it invalidates even private ownership. After a few more days, they call the police.

Once the massive majority in one's surroundings takes a disapproving view, one begins to feel wrong oneself and sets to work trying to detect shortcomings in oneself. Clearly, it has something to do with being different from them, but in what exactly, and how much? (Is something amiss with one's jacket, too?) And once one begins to feel unwelcome, the effect quickly snowballs: one feels frowned upon, even when they are just being curious; petty incidents turn into weighty evidence.

So what do I do?

1 I *adapt*, change or pretend; I dress decently and don't leave the dishes lying around messily in front of the kitchen window; I acquire a dog or a wife or both.
2 I *avoid* them, draw the curtains and only go out at night (but cannot fail to realize that it simply heightens suspiciousness).
3 I *rationalize*; I am a bit of a character, but for *highly respectable* reasons; the fact that I have neither a dog nor a wife is because it would disrupt my work, which is very important and to which I am utterly devoted.
4 I *assure myself* – and possibly them – *that I have the right to be there*; I have paid the rent, have the receipt in my wallet and can present it, should they ask; I have done nothing illegal.
5 I *pretend to ignore*, I certainly give no thought to being strange and to their watching; I have more important things to attend to.
6 I *defy*: I do what I want, 'am' what 'I am'; *dogged*, I straighten my posture and walk down to the grocer's with head held high.
7 I *persevere*, exaggerate, put on extra-provocative clothes, flash in front of the windows.
8 I *sneer* at them, their wretched normality; I am terribly venomous.
9 I *lord it over them*, I have breeding, I do not listen to music with the windows open and when I do so, it is classical; I mow the lawn every day, and the instant you lay a finger anywhere, I am there like a flash with a dishcloth; I jaunt into town and send money to the starving in Africa.

10 I *rage*, or I *cry*, at their stiff-necked norms or my own stiff-necked deviancy, or at the circumstances that have brought this about, and fantasize about things being different.
11 I *contact like-minded people* in order to buttress myself, look out for them in the area, walk to the phone box and the letter box, relate my trials and tribulations, and ask people round.
12 I *flee*, return to the city.

Anyone can rig up that kind of experiment with themselves, thereby establishing this tense relationship with others on a miniature scale for a while. In the homosexual, it is a chronic state. In his world of experience, the others are always there as a disapproving shadow; he *inhabits* this antagonism, pinched in this unease of wrongness and distended in this network of reactions. In this way, the homosexual's form of existence is preceded by a negative sign, without which it would not be, and by which no part of it remains unaffected, but from which the remainder does not simply follow.[14]

5 Uneasiness

> Regrettably the type to which I belong from birth is frequently in possession of an unfortunate disposition – qualities such as mendacity, shiftiness, a taste for finery, jealousy and capriciousness, as indeed I know from myself. It is as if the awareness of being an exception, without daring to be so in the face of the world, impairs the character, rendering it feeble, fumbling and dishonest! Having to live a lie, seek what one *believes* is happiness, in the dark and among the shadows, and never being able to savour one's happiness in the full light of day, speak of it and stand by it, must leave its mark on the man externally as well as internally. His look often turns to a scowl, unsure and evasive; the voice snuffling, frail and vapid; and the speech either, as with me, prim and meticulous to the point of affectation, or faltering and desultory. The gait becomes swaying or undulating and the handshake limp – for fear of exposing, betraying the truth which we dare not confide in anyone, which at times we attempt to conceal from ourselves and which we deny, adamantly and harshly, to the shame and misfortune of the thousands who are born with the same morbid inner self.
>
> C. Houmark, *Naar jeg er død* (1926)

One lament recurs over and again in the hundred-year history of the homosexual: that he cannot be himself. For fear of the reaction from his surroundings, he passes himself off as something other than he is; he may even have adopted their attitude to the extent that he seeks to hide it from himself as well. He does not stand by it, dissembles, acts out a role.[15]

Thus, being homosexual involves a distance and discrepancy between what one is and what one pretends, a dishonesty *vis-à-vis* the world that rebounds on oneself as uncertainty about who one really is – in a word, an existential *uneasiness*, whether it manifests itself in feelings of distaste or not.

Houmark has a keen eye for the consequences of this uneasiness. Not only does it find expression in a series of character traits, it seeps out into the external behaviour: the affected speech, the mincing walk, the insecure handshake. Everywhere artificiality, uncertainty, covering up.

Houmark thus explains a whole series of the traits traditionally considered to be typically homosexual from this uneasiness. A later age may have been inclined to put the emphasis on another aspect of uneasiness – on the psychological strain, the experience of distaste, apprehension, fear – tending somewhat to gloss over the, at first sight, not too flattering social characteristics and traits it gives rise to; in relation to this, Houmark has a sharp sociological eye.

No matter whether the emphasis was put on one side of this uneasiness or another, *the advice, the remedy* was always the same: *be yourself, come out, out of the closet.* Houmark again:

> It is, I feel, our duty to *be ourselves* in the right place at the right time. I do not – of course not – think that we must propagandize, display ourselves in defiant candour, yet *we ought to be ourselves.* It is only reasonable that there are people who disdain us. That we must learn to understand; but *we*, too, have the right to *be* and to live . . . However unhappy I may have felt, however much I know that my yearning, my hope and my trust will be a perpetual series of disappointments, I nonetheless wish to live and to die as the one the Creator determined me to be.[16]

For Houmark, then, coming out is a matter of choosing the lesser evil; for the gay activists of the 1970s, it was both an immediate personal emancipation and a means in the fight that was to end with the final liberation of homosexuality. And just as it is a matter of course for Houmark that homosexuals should not advertise their homosexuality and be provocative, so too it was obvious for the gays of the 1970s that they should.[17] In any case, however: '*Be yourselves*, and get rid of your uneasiness.'

Funnily enough, they didn't. Houmark's text already indicates that: he knows mendacity and the other dubious characteristics from himself; his own speech is affected, even if he did attach importance to 'being oneself'. It is not possible to get rid of uneasiness by coming out. Anyone who has tried to dance with another man at a heterosexual party knows it; the room turns into a zoo, viewed through the cage bars; there is no liberation from the look the others so carefully keep to themselves.[18] Even in gay bars, in the reserves, there is no way of avoiding this uneasiness and having its expressions made clear: the homosexual who enters and says hello to the 'girls' is not *just* greeting: he is acting greeting, playing a homosexual greeting. The affectation, the artificiality, the attitudinizing is still around.

Some may try to take comfort in the thought that this is a backlog of uncertainty and anxiety, of conditioned reactions and old habits that will disappear as familiarity with the new situation grows. There is surely some truth in that. But homosexual uneasiness in itself, the problem that it is not possible to be what one is, runs deeper.

What was supposed to be the real homosexual self, underlying whatever role he may have had to play, is not there. It is itself a role; moreover, a role which is not fixed.[19] Admittedly, there are in society a number of prescripts for what 'the homosexual' has to be – different, with a special personality, a special life-history, etc.; but that is only an empty frame without contents, a part without lines. Moreover, it is a role he can never be completely at ease with, identify totally with – because it is negative. From the uneasiness of not being able to be himself as a homosexual, he progressed to the uneasiness of having to be himself as a homosexual. There was no self to be.[20]

It is, of course, not only the homosexual who has that sort of problem. There is no way of being oneself these days at all. What is a farmer who has gone bust, a teacher who may lose her job, an out-of-work person attending a course? Even fathering has become a problem, being a man has turned into a role. It is no coincidence that existentialism became a fashionable philosophy during the first half of the twentieth century and that role theory was a great hit in sociology. It will never be natural to be homosexual, but there is no longer very much that it is natural to be; roles preponderate: you can enter into the spirit of them and you can make an identity out of them, but never become one with them.

Some roles are easier to identify with than others, however, as they are written out in detail and enjoy the backing of society; it is easier to forget the uneasiness. Otherwise it can become importunate. 'Unemployed', for instance, is a strange role, not something from which to carve an identity in a work-oriented society; it is merely an absence and an insufficiency, not something to be. Still worse is 'homosexual': one can cease to be unemployed (or hope to do so); but into the part of the homosexual is written that he is doomed to be so for ever.

The homosexual, then, is close to the uneasiness that clings to modern existence in general: the impossibility of becoming one with what one is, the compulsion constantly to play a part. He is a born existentialist and a practising role-theoretician. Therefore he could not help discovering the other side of the impossibilities and the compulsion of this uneasiness: the possibilities and the freedom. If it is not possible to be oneself anyway and one has to play some role, one is free to play *various* roles, try out, experiment, change. And if one cannot become one with the role anyway, one is free to *act* it, calculate the effects, overact, enjoy the acting and the contact with the audience and fellow actors. If one is free, one must create.

6 Loneliness

'We are *born* to loneliness', Christian Houmark wrote in 1926; fifty years later, we read of the homosexuals that they 'tend to have more close friends than the heterosexuals'.[21] Despite such brilliant overtaking of the heterosexuals on the socializing scale, 'we' *are* in a way lonelier.

The homosexual – insofar as he wishes to be homosexual, however he may have hit upon that idea – must leave the safe and self-evident socialness he has otherwise become embodied in. He must go out to 'realize himself'. He is no longer with *them*; what he does now is somewhere else, in another world: a *demi-monde* of which the former knows nothing and is unwilling to know anything. To this extent he becomes a stranger; by leaving their world he becomes an outsider; he steps out of their fellowship and becomes alone.

And even when he does not separate, he does not remain one with it. Insofar as he wants to be homosexual, he cannot tell them about it or show it; even if he dares, they can't be bothered to listen; and even if they do, they still can't really understand it. Part of him is not social. To this extent he is lonely.

The moment he steps out of the given social world (family, workplace and so on) in order to 'realize himself', he steps *into* another. He comes out in the city. Though full of strangers, it is nevertheless social: one cannot help but notice them, see them, perceive signals from them – and be noticed, seen, send out signals. A unique social world; it unites within itself distance and closeness, anonymity and involvement: you can drown in the crowd and remain yourself; you can be together with others yet free of them, and free to them. Here, the homosexual can *be*; here, his peculiarity can vanish in the blanket anonymity, his strangeness in the general strangeness; and here, he can make contact: either in the common urban space or in the special areas that, so to speak, concentrate the social space of the city: railway stations, urinals, parks and bath houses.

The city is the social world proper of the homosexual, his life space; it is no use objecting that lots of homosexuals have lived in the country. Insofar as they wish to be homosexual, the vast majority must get out into 'the city' one way or another, into the open mass of strangers, whether on the streets of London, at the railway station toilets in Northampton, at the coach station in Salisbury or in the small-ads world of newspapers; via communication and transportation the entire country has become urbanized.[22]

The city, with its crowds of mutual strangers, is the place where the homosexual can come together with others; and – at the same time and for the same reasons – it is the place that confirms his loneliness. And though it is not necessarily his only social world, it is there as a background: that which he started out from, that which he can fall back on, that which is always there as an alternative. It can be cultivated for its own sake: its contradictions and possibilities captivate, it incites and entices.

In the city, the homosexual's loneliness is dissolved while at the same time preserved. He dissolves it himself, if and when he makes all the close friends and acquaintances that the recent scientific literature allots him. With them he can then share his sorrows and his joys and live his life as a homosexual; and to them he can confide even his most intimate homosexual secrets, if he wishes. Yet he can never be one with these friendships. He carries around the basic experience that togetherness can come to an end, that it is not covered by a guarantee. He can be thrown back on 'himself'; this empty 'self' remains outside. To this extent, he is doomed to be alone.

Of course, the heterosexuals, too, have to leave the initial community; they, too, have to come out in the city, and for them, too, the new communities are not so safe and self-evident that they can devote themselves entirely to them. In the modern world, it is altogether impossible not to know that the social life one lives could be different, that it is not covered by a guarantee, that it is therefore impossible to become one with it and to that extent one is an outsider; if not known from oneself, this is known from others, or from the media. In this way the heterosexuals know loneliness, too. But for the most part their break-away is less radical: they go from one social world to a similar one, or the various worlds merge into each other with no great dividing lines. And they do not come so close to the city: typically they go there only when they are young, or when *in transit*, that is, when they are on their way from one safe and self-evident community to the next; they scarcely get the first one out of their head before they enter the next one. They have to go home to the family. The homosexual, on the other hand, is typically travelling and typically out in town: he sits there at the café table, alone, gazing out of the window.

7 Observedness

The minute the homosexual gets out into town and wants to realize himself, he runs up against the police. Streets, parks, urinals, foyers, stations – all the spots where he can make contacts and, if lucky, satisfy his lusts are under surveillance, if not by the police themselves then by other guards and supervisors in their place and ultimately, of course, by other onlookers.[23] Unlike the personal surveillance in the country or at home in the family, this surveillance is neither total nor constant: it does not know everything about a person, only what it can see on the spot; and it is not always present, only sporadically. There is thus the possibility of eluding it; conversely, one has to reckon on its being present any time. One cannot be homosexual, therefore, without feeling potentially monitored.

Certain other consequences for the homosexual follow on from this. He learns *vigilance*; his brain kits itself out with radar, which simultaneously records his actions and scans the surrounding terrain for hazards – like birds feeding, though his eyes do most of the work so the head need not rock so much. He learns to refine his contact actions, make them discreet, suggestive, silent, etc. And since his desire is thus associated with secrecy, danger and the police, he learns to associate desire with secrecy, danger and police (an association he may cultivate for other reasons as well).[24] It adds a thrill that someone may come along, that one risks being taken by surprise, that they may catch you with your trousers down and have the authority to punish you.[25]

The potential surveillance on the part of sentinel authorities is thus answered by surveillance sensations, self-surveillance, evasive efforts and surveillance pleasure on the part of the homosexual. But just as the urban police need only monitor people's external conduct and ensure that 'all is well', the homosexual's reactions merely concern his external behaviour. It is radar he has installed, not X-ray.

The relation to the police, then, is purely superficial and does not lead to any self-examination or to any 'self' for that matter, unless it was there for other reasons. But it is. From the outset, the homosexual is related not only to the police but to medicine and hence to the inner forces of his body, to psychiatry and hence to his soul. In this regard he is *split* into an inner and an outer.[26] Innermost a nucleus – his homosexuality – concealed and morbid, manifesting itself in the most uncontrollable ways; outermost, then, a series of bodily and mental traits that are the external signs of the inner nucleus. Inner forces whose morbidity and perilousness command that they be identified and controlled, but with which he himself cannot get to grips without the practitioner's help; external signs and traits which house the secret significance and point to the concealed cause, but which he himself can scarcely spot and whose meaning and cause are so cryptic as to elude him without the aid of the practitioner's objective expertise and analysis, just as, conversely, the practitioner cannot unearth the key without his help: it may be possible to open people's bodies without their volition, but not their souls.

This special supervisory relationship between the homosexual, his interior and the physician (psychiatrist, psychologist, etc.) is, as we have seen, inscribed and prescribed even in the medically authorized conception of the homosexual. In fact, this is *the* point where 'discourse', 'role' and 'script' are most specific, directly instructive of action and productive of a particular mode of experience and existence. They are conveyed to the homosexual not merely through the face-to-face admonitions and exhortations of the practitioner, but also through manuals of medicine and manner books of psychology, as well as through the general spread of the ideas of medicine and psychology. But the relation is consummated not merely by reading and rumouring. In practice, it is often engraved in his body and soul through the very hands-on procedures of observation and examination, as well as through the physical equipment and spatial layouts of the hospital, laboratory and consulting room. Accordingly, these belong to the spaces that form the typical background to his existence, associated with their own tunings and rhythms of coming and going, hope and despair, reticence and intimacy. In this way, then, the otherwise magical transubstantiation of the word into flesh, the 'taking-over' of a 'discourse' and the ensuing 'assumption' of an 'identity' can take place; again, the case of the grocer, crushed in the auditorium as well, is instructive. 'Labelling' is a very heavy-handed procedure indeed, but nevertheless just a minor part of what goes on even in the medicalized making of the modern homosexual. And again, such practices and spatial structures have proliferated to the point of becoming commonplace, and to that extent transforming the social world into a generalized consulting room and auditorium.

Thus, by dint of his concealed and dangerous interior, the homosexual is related to the physician; or he is related to the physician and hence to a concealed and perilous interior. In any case, he is reliant not only on surveillance and analysis but also on self-examination and self-exposure. Whereas the police are a danger and a limit he attempts to avoid (or perhaps nuzzles his body surface against), the physician is allegedly a friend, a confidant. He can safely be told everything, for his only wish is to help; and he needs to know everything, or he cannot help. He it is one visits (or submits to be sent to) with the first tender doubts or the crushing certainty; he it is to whom one addresses one's confessional writings.[27] If not for the individual homosexual himself to be helped and immediately so, then at least in the longer term the *species* to which he belongs; if not to the individual physician, then at least to the *institution* he represents. For the physician is a doctor, and thus communes with the powers on high. He is not just a medicine man but also a man of science; and it is as much in this latter capacity that the homosexual is obliged to give away himself to him.

Through the physician, then, the homosexual is placed relative to the medical and psychiatric sciences. And not only must one address science, it also addresses one: the place to read about oneself is writings whose content ultimately originates from it. It is impossible to be homosexual without knowing that one belongs to science.

Of course, the homosexual is not the only one to have been positioned relative to the physician (psychiatrist, psychologist, etc.) and to science, and to have been equipped with significant manifestations of inner, sexual forces and made reliant on observation and analysis. This gradually came to be true of all modern people.[28] However, it has made itself particularly felt in the case of the homosexual. He was prejudged morbid or abnormal, and thus belonged to the machinery *par excellence*. And he can scarcely avoid conceiving of his sexuality as a particularly comprehensive and meaningful part of himself – this, after all, is the very thing which defines him as a homosexual and thus sets him apart from the rest of mankind.

Accordingly, it is impossible to be homosexual without asking about the reason, without relating to one's body and one's behaviour as if they are signs of some inner, without feeling obliged to give oneself away.[29]

8 Zoological problems

Before proceeding, and against the backdrop of the foregoing expositions, it may be useful to outline a provisional answer to the questions posed at the beginning of this chapter and to delineate the direction in which the following investigations will move.

Is there any basis whatsoever for speaking of and describing homosexuals as a 'species', as people who have something in common other than a particular sexual preference? I think so. For existing as a homosexual is synonymous with existing under certain *conditions* (such as disapproval, medical practice and the city) which bear on that existence in at least three ways. In part, *they leave certain imprints*, directly and ineluctably. In part, *they are there as conditions one is forced to relate to*, 'answer', in some way or other. And finally, *they invite certain specific answers*, though it would be incorrect to say they have rendered them necessary. And once these 'answers' (e.g. associations or signals) have been provided and have assumed a more or less stable form, they themselves eventually form part of the series of conditions that exert an influence. In these ways, the conditions *form* the homosexual existence, moulding it into a specific *form of existence.*

A series of qualifying statements will surely be apposite.

1 *I do not maintain that all homosexuals are identical.* Indeed: they are very different. But as men with strong erotic interests in other men, they are subject to certain conditions they cannot help being affected by and relating to. For each individual, however, the outcome depends on the multitude of other factors that also play a part in his life. What I am describing, then, is *trends* – which, while undoubtedly present, nevertheless assert themselves to very different degrees and in highly different ways in the individual person.[30]

2 *I do not maintain that there always have been and always will be 'homosexuals' with features like those I describe.* Indeed: homosexuals are a specifically *modern* phenomenon; and one of the intentions of this chapter is precisely to delineate the particularly modern conditions of life without which this form of existence would not be possible. On the other hand, nor am I saying that before the second half of the nineteenth century there may not have been ways or features of life reminiscent in certain respects of the homosexual. The homosexual form of existence is a jumble of many different factors, of effects from and answers to a long string of conditions of life; and these conditions and answers did not all arise at the same juncture. Some of them (e.g. the existence of cities) predate others (e.g. the psychiatric attention paid to erotic interests from man to man). But it is the peculiar *hotchpotch* of these conditions of existence and answers that makes the specifically modern homosexual form of existence.

3 *I do not maintain that the homosexuals,* since entering the world in the nineteenth century, *always have been and always will be the same.* Indeed: a historical development has taken place in both the conditions under which they exist and the 'answers' they provide to them. To take just a single example by way of illustration: it is general knowledge now that the shift in self-description from 'homosexual' through 'homophile' to 'gay' (and, indeed, to 'queer') is not purely superficial but altogether expresses a modified historical situation.[31] Nonetheless, a number of fundamental and significant conditions and answers are the same, and hence a number of basic features about the homosexual form of existence as well. And it is primarily to these that I direct attention in this

section. It is precisely in order to emphasize this historical homogeneity that I have chosen the term *homosexuals* (or 'the homosexual' or 'the homosexuals', to stress the species character). 'Homosexual' is best here, since it has been commonest throughout the period as a whole. It is not that I have anything particular against the words 'gay' or 'queer' or cannot hear that 'homosexual' has clinical and sex-centred overtones – on the contrary, as appears.

One may well ask whether the fundamental conditions that make up the background to the homosexual form of existence have also changed during the past twenty or thirty years, or at any rate are in the process of changing, even though they have been pretty constant for a long period. I shall revert to this question in chapter VI; for the time being, there is reason enough to freeze the picture.

4 *I do not maintain that the homosexuals are simply the results* of certain conditions that have a bearing on them and saddle them with a particular life. Indeed the relationship is much more complex. As I have already emphasized, the homosexual form of existence is also a creative *answer* to specific conditions. Moreover, the homosexuals – in many different ways – bear on the conditions that bear on them; I shall elaborate this in chapter V.

In the current chapter, then, we are off into the world of zoology. It may be reasonable here to recall what I wrote at the beginning of the book: it is not a matter of investigating how and why 'the homosexuals' arose historically; it is not a history of the evolution of the species that is about to be written. The objective is to elucidate the particular characteristics of this species: the special form of existence that typifies it and makes it a species as well as the conditions that make up the background to it. We shall continue to take as our starting points certain surface phenomena, trivial or scintillating points of concentration, exemplary instances to be developed and unfolded towards broader dimensions of this form of existence and its conditions.

9 The gaze

> Do you know what it is as you pass to be loved by strangers?
> Do you know the talk of those turning eyeballs?
>
> Walt Whitman, 'Song of the Open Road' (1856)

At gay bars many things go on, but making sexual contact is certainly one of them, whether it's intended to end in orgasm or not. However, you don't just go up to the person you're interested in, raise your hat and introduce yourself. Or, if you do, you're asking for the consequences. You *can* have a drink served to the object of your attentions, though these days at least that's regarded as being somewhat over the top, or in any case it's unusual. You *use your gaze*; but in the right way, for a right way there is.

Naturally, you have to let your eye wander around until it finds something attractive or at least acceptable, but then there are certain rules of good form which you do well to follow; this requires delicacy, self-control and practice, i.e. good manners – a qualification in itself. Without it a person is either innocent – which may be very charming; or stupid, which definitely is not.

You must *never* start letting your gaze rest on the man you're after. You look away *almost* as soon as his eyes hit yours; and after a moment, you look back to see if he's looking at you. Now it's his turn to shift his eyes; this must happen quickly, in any case, and the very speed of it – i.e. whether the pace is a little slower or a little faster – will map out the likelihood of further developments. It can easily happen that he merely glances back just to make sure he's being looked at; in that case it will lead nowhere. He just wants your gaze, but won't give anything in return. If these reciprocal glancings repeat themselves, however, you can start fixing your gaze a little longer and see what happens.

The process is not altogether without sources of error and not completely foolproof. The other may corroborate your gaze quite by chance, e.g. because he's looking for something else and his line of vision is so close to you that you think it's you he's looking at, thus encouraging you to engage in more persistent efforts of the eyes which you should really have avoided. Or if you keep – I mean if another person keeps staring, because he mistakenly feels encouraged or is simply stupid enough to do so even if you *have* been ignoring him, it can be impossible not to look and see if he's still standing there staring, which only encourages him to carry on. Or a self-perpetuating process can arise which neither party really wants: a couple of chance eye contacts *en passant*, while the eyes are scanning the place anyway, may be enough to set off the magnetic spiral – as is known from the train, where one sometimes has to resort to the window, both to escape the other person's gaze and to see if it's still there.

There are many ways of contacting people; there is something *democratic* about the gaze, insofar as it ensures a certain equality, independence and free choice between the parties. It neither compels nor commits the other one to any counter-performance; I have no right to nurture expectations of another unless he reciprocates my gaze of his own free will; and if he does, it's because he thinks that one look is equivalent to another.

But the gaze is also unreasonable, arbitrary, *despotic*: it sees the exterior only and overlooks all other qualities; and by removing his gaze, the other person can rise above you, humiliate you, crush any dream of equality. Thus it is ruthless, yet at the same time gentle, providing you know how to observe the rules of usage: not a word has been uttered, not a 'no' has been voiced, *it could be* that he simply has not seen you and is preoccupied with something else (someone who arrived earlier, his friends, his own thoughts); you don't have to face the fact that he *wants nothing* to do with you (unless you've been so idiotic, or chance has been so cruel, that the other person has felt justified in evading your gaze with demonstrative faces and relocatings).

Not that the gaze need always be used as a means to achieve *further* contact. It becomes enough in itself; from being a means of contact, it becomes the end. The reciprocal glancing turns into *the* contact. This has its advantages. One avoids the countless risks of error and repulsion that may arise if you have to listen to each other, smell each other, have sex, wake up together; it's not nearly so strenuous. Besides, it offers its own rewards: pleasure, excitement, affirmation.

Out in the city – on the street, the stations, the foyers, etc. – the objective may sometimes be the same: to establish contact with other homosexuals through gaze. Here, outside the reserves, gaze carries the additional task of identifying the other homosexuals by sifting through the welter of signs: dress, companions, the way a glance meets your own. But otherwise the situation is the same as at the gay bars, apart from the fact that the space of the city can now be exploited. The gaze is combined with a different mobility; you can track, you can stop and pretend to be looking at windows, you can sit down on a bench and get up again, you can end up out at Chiswick. What is called *cruising* is this combination of gazes and movements, which at gay bars takes place in an enclosure and finds its proper territory out in the city.

Here, you can also cruise those who do not perhaps consider themselves homosexuals but who might nevertheless be made interested, or at least uncertain – about what is happening, about themselves. Again, it is incumbent on the gaze to identify this category by outward signs (that they're on their own, that they move awkwardly or hunch up uneasily or bristle with narcissistic desire for experience, etc.); moreover, the gaze must again establish the contact. But because this is a different category, the gaze also has to be used differently; here it's a matter of seduction, so the gaze must be more audacious, it must *linger* – not too long, but longer than otherwise, then be taken away again slightly slower than otherwise, as if sticking voluptuously to the other's and only reluctantly tearing itself away from its string of toffee.

A third category (there are transitions, of course, and these are no less exciting) are those whom the glance spots as being impossible to make interested but nevertheless can't keep its eyes off and can't help trying to make eye contact with. The risk of violence is present here; the gaze becomes alert but also insistent, asserting its right to see; in this case, the art is not to remove the eyes quickly or elastically but to dare keep them there as long as possible.

Finally, there are also those gazes not interested in being seen but only in seeing – concealed glances, stolen glances, as the phrase goes. It is not the other's eyes that are looked for but his face, his body, his behind, his trousers or whatever else it might be. In a way, the gaze does want to have sexual contact, but not mutually and only with a body or part of a body or clothing, not with anything like a person and not, therefore, with the eyes in which a soul is said to be mirrored. It is purely fetishistic. The gaze wants to caress buttocks and bulges, it wants to take its pleasure *through* the other person but not with him, and to keep its pleasure to itself, a pure treat for the eyes. The surface is far too interesting to be spoilt by any 'interior'. This gaze is in a way the easiest one to feed; on the other hand, it is a macroconsumer, cannot get enough, but there are also plenty in the city.

The homosexual is equipped with a gaze. He is sometimes said to have big eyes; if that's true, it's surely because they would otherwise be incapable of coping with everything they're supposed to. The homosexuals are virtuosos at using the gaze; it can discern almost imperceptible signs; it can fine-tune and flit around in endlessly different ways; it has an enormous cruising range – look at them come biking, for instance: the eyes can rotate in directions one would have thought impossible. One may occasionally wonder whether it's the homosexual who has a gaze or his gaze which has him. The gaze has made itself independent, and not just by becoming the end instead of the means. It has turned into a self-actuating radar that automatically launches into action whether you want it or not, realize it or not; the homosexual has turned into an appendage to his gaze. It becomes impossible to walk down the street without the gaze starting to carry out its functions; it becomes impossible to go to a gay bar without the eyes immediately engaging in these games. It can become a torment to have to let oneself be dragged along by one's gaze; but of course, it's also convenient that it works by itself: you gain pleasure without needing to puzzle over it or exert any effort to get it.

The gaze belongs to the city. Only when there is mutual strangeness does it exist; and the city supplies strangers galore. In the country, there is no gaze, but instead an all-embracing visibility. At the same time, the city hampers other forms of contact: the flow, the crowd, the strangeness, everyone going about their own business, what to do with all these people if not look at them; besides, their surfaces captivate the glance, they are indeed designed to do so. The very flicker, too, captivates the eyes. There is always something to look at.

The city is not the only factor which favours the development of the gaze: a number of other determinants in the formation of modern subjects are at play. For instance, the emergence of feelings of privacy, self-surveillance, self-control and closeness threshold, all of which impede other forms of contact, whereas they don't obstruct the gaze to the same degree. You are free to look at others: no private thresholds need be overstepped, no norms offended (provided you stay within certain limits). The gaze is a crafty escape from the prison of the body and soul. And modern generalized surveillance – police, science – can (or will) not prevent it either; even good old-fashioned social control has trouble with it: even when you are with someone, your gaze still has a certain freedom. Democratization also plays a part: *everyone* walks down the street, and everyone is free to look at everyone.

The modern world is voyeuristic. As a citizen of that world, the homosexual takes part in that general voyeurism; besides, he has his own particular reasons for evolving the gaze since, as we have seen, more so than others he has the city as his life space and the inner self as his essence.

The homosexual, then, develops the gaze. Conversely, it may be that the gaze develops the homosexual: another man's surface captivating one's glance, another man's gaze meeting one's own and arousing interest. Whatever the case, it is impossible to be homosexual without having a gaze.[32]

10 Signals

'Well, those kinds of people can recognize one another from their glances across the length of a crowded room. If there are 500 men at a knees-up, the homosexual ones will have sussed out those with the same inclinations in less than an hour. We straights can't even begin to imagine how it comes about', Himmler notes in his jovial speech in February 1937 to the SS squad leaders on the problem of homosexuality and its solution.[33] And true it is. But how *do* they go about it? Herman Bang:

> Antagonized by society, threatened by laws, most homosexuals club together, making themselves mutually recognisable by means of a series of signs which – heaven alone knows how – are the same in every country . . . Very often, however, these signs are not necessary at all. Homosexuals can recognise one another, literally, before they have seen one another's faces. I myself do not comprehend it, but it is a fact. It is as if they are connected by some electrical current. A homosexual is capable of identifying another person as homosexual even if he only sees the person from behind at a great distance.[34]

Thus, the media involved extend from distinct signs to extrasensory perception, it seems. Or perhaps it is simply a matter of signs so subtle that even homosexuals have difficulty acknowledging them as such? In fact, they *might* be the subtler manifestations of what I have called uneasiness: clumsiness, anxiousness, acting – 'natural signs', so to speak, not consciously intended. Many signals lie somewhere between the intended and the unintended: this clothing, this manner of speaking, these gestures may not be chosen primarily for their sign value; yet because they have for some reason or other become 'typically homosexual' they can function as signs, and it is or becomes impossible not to be aware of this. In other instances, the sign is clearly intended, selected with a view to signalling as unambivalently as possible the carrier's homosexuality to a larger or smaller circle. These signs vary with time and place, ranging from secret codes – such as suede shoes, red socks and an earring in the right ear – to the open declarations of the 1970s, like badges proclaiming 'Glad to be Gay' and 'How dare you presume I'm heterosexual?'

Regardless of what happens to function as a sign of the carrier being homosexual, the sign is surely never completely arbitrary, but meaningfully linked to what it denotes: being homosexual. Often it is something which traditionally belongs to a feminine context – like jewellery and particular gestures; precisely because, as we shall see, being homosexual is inextricably bound up with femininity. And often, it is something belonging to a masculine context because, as we shall see, being homosexual is just as inextricably bound up with masculinity. The widespread clone look of the 1970s is one example of signalling through masculine accessories: Levis, lumberjack shirt, crew cut, moustache with or without a trim beard, and so on.

One may wonder how indeed an outfit from the universe of masculinity can be used to signal that someone is homosexual, at any rate if it's consistent. But often it is not consistent, being mixed with a little, unbecomingly 'feminine' detail (a natty little scarf, for example); and when it *is* consistent, it may still be a signal by being *too* consistent: the hair *too* cropped, the beard *too* designer-stubbly, the wear-holes in the Levis *too* precise.

It is altogether impossible to live in the modern world without emitting and capturing signals. The city, the strangeness, the role-awareness, the development of the inner self, the glance: under these circumstances – and in mutual interaction with them – people become surfaces for one another, and their surfaces signals. The homosexual, however, pre-eminently co-exists with these modern circumstances of life, in addition to being especially dependent on the possibility of emitting and receiving signals. Thus, he is an expert in the study of signs, a self-evident semiologist.

11 Meetings

In the city, the homosexual makes contact. It is usually established by means of glance and signals – or in instances where glance cannot be used, by touching or listening. It is possible of course to meet strangers anywhere – at work, at friends' and acquaintances' – but the city is *the* proper place for that kind of meeting, and there are also special places here particularly well-suited or even tailored to the purpose.[35]

Many of these meetings are of a certain nature. They are transitory; the parties come from a mutual strangeness and return to it again afterwards. Nonetheless, the actual meeting is highly intimate: the person lets his surface be pawed or exposes his innermost self or becomes another person altogether, in a way that is rarely possible with those nearest and dearest. And finally, it is repeated over and over, with new strangers.

Within the framework of these common denominators the meetings can vary, depending on what is shared: conversation or sex or romance; for how long: a few minutes, a night or a weekend; how many persons: closed two-man relationships or more open 'public' ones; where: at home, random nooks (a gateway, a bench, a café), specially suitable places such as parks and urinals, or places particularly made for this kind of contact: bars, bath houses, back rooms.

Some may wonder at the voluminous consumption of such meetings. It's perhaps reasonable that the homosexuals have to go out into the city to make contact, but why do they *keep on* doing so? Why don't they stick to the contacts they make and embark on a lasting acquaintance; and if they make only transitory contacts anyway, why don't they stop repeating them?

It is not unusual to hear that they do so out of *need.* Because of the condemnatory attitude of their surroundings, they must fear being recognized and unmasked, and must seek contacts which are as brief and anonymous as possible; or they make this condemnatory attitude their own and end up disparaging their partner and having to replace him; or they simply lack the social backing in the form of good will and rights necessary for more lasting one-to-one relationships.[36] If society changed its attitudes, the homosexuals would also leave off their brief and anonymous contacts, and establish stable and decent relationships just like anyone else. Or perhaps homosexuals are for more psychological reasons unstable, disinclined to enter into lengthier, committed relationships.[37]

There may be something in it all.[38] But as all-in explanations, they are also typical rationalizations, having decided in advance that such meetings should not exist and therefore refusing to recognize their special quality and general background.

Thus, these explanations ignore the fact that the city is there. It can surely, to some degree, be repressed and no doubt also forgotten about to a certain extent, the more you are at home with your family or enclosed in the workplace. But none of this is entirely successful; the steady stream of people attracting your glance resurfaces on the internal screens of the imagination or they loom forth from the television in the evening, just as you are getting ensconced in the bosom of the family. The city is there. Instead of trying to get away from it, you can enter it; instead of closing your eyes to it, you can open them, and see what comes of it. The brief contacts and one-off meetings are one way of tackling the reality of the city: the fact that you are among strangers; that there are lots of them and that there are constantly new ones; that you yourself are exposed surface and hidden interior, clandestine receiver and live signal; that the mixture of proximity and distance, surface and depth, crowd and loneliness is at once attractive and alarming. The city lays down needs; you only have to dial a sex hotline to convince yourself of the common 'need for contact' and the desire to meet and be intimate with complete strangers, at the same time realizing how much the whole country, through the communications media, has become a meeting place for masses of mutual strangers and in that sense has turned urban. It is particularly the marginalized groups, of course, that have cultivated these needs, those out of a job and those on the periphery of the family: single OAPs have their benches in the parks and squares, the young their discos, cafés and burger bars, suburban wives their department store restaurants. And the homosexuals have been out in the city, forced to as well as free to experiment with meetings for more than a hundred years.

Nor should what actually goes on at these meetings be overlooked. We are accustomed to viewing them in the light of long-term, binding 'personal' relationships, against which they stand out as something purely negative, an absence and an evil: they are *not* long-term, *not* binding, *not* 'personal' – and that is *not good*. They are *alienated*, not authentic: there is no giving of the self, only enactment of a role and maintenance of distance; they are *reified*: the other person is treated as a thing to be used and disposed of, and only appearance counts in selling and buying; they are *instrumentalized*: it is a matter of pursuing purely selfish interests and making the other person into a means for them, instead of both persons becoming a common end for each other; they are *fetishized*: only the surface of the other person, or only a part of him, is given attention and worshipped – that whole vocabulary of invectives and distancing phrases, formulated by the last couple of centuries' theoreticians and poets as fascinated and frightened witnesses to the development of the capitalist market, the state bureaucracies and the modern city. In short: these meetings are purely and simply the negation of what they should be; there is, so to speak, *nothing* left.[39]

Yet obviously something does go on; and something, at that, which cannot be reduced to the mere trading of commodities. You might say that a special kind of exchange is taking place, though 'exchange' (swap, circulation) is not really a good word here. Even in these anonymous park 'bangs', in these semi-anonymous one-night stands, or even in the pure eye contacts, a *being-together* is established, overstepping the border between one and the other, or at least playing with it, balancing on it and swaying from side to side, opening and closing. There is an intensity between them that envelops them and occasionally transcends beyond them to others; an excitement or vibration beyond what is normal. Time stands still.

> The observer, Mr. X, another middle-aged man, and two youths stood face-to-face within the small, dimly lit leafy enclosure. The two young men reached out and fondled one another without regard for the others present, obviously resuming a transaction that our arrival interrupted. One pinched the other's nipples, while the latter concentrated energies on the penis. Grabbing each other, they kissed vigorously, grinding pelvises together.
>
> X walked over to them and without forewarning touched the buttocks of each. They parted slightly, looked at X, and gradually absorbed him into the action. The two youths opened each other's trousers and pulled out respective cocks. They turned to X and did the same. X grabbed both penes. Meanwhile, the older man had commenced rubbing his penis through the trousers. His head turned inquisitively toward the observer who, anticipating a 'rush,' maintained a studious visual involvement with the evolving threesome to cue the middle-aged man that he was not interested. However, the man slowly inched his way around the narrow area so that he stood within touching distance of the observer. From the corner of his eye, the observer noticed the guy's hand slowly reaching for his groin. Equally paced, the observer cupped his genitals with the hands. The man 'read' the message and transferred his attention to the threesome. Rather than close in on them immediately, he moved to about 18 inches from one youth. He pulled out a large penis and stood motionless, masturbating. He waited to be seen by one of the three. By this time, however, they were too engrossed to notice, alternating between fellatio and kissing. X pulled one youth's pants down to the knees and tried to penetrate the anus with his penis while the other youth fellated him. Receiving little notice, the older man closed in on the side of X and thrust his penis into X's hand. X grabbed it, turned toward the older man, squatted on his knees and lustily fellated him. Noting that orgasm would no doubt conclude this four-cornered arrangement, the observer terminated his observation.[40]

The intensity spreads to the scientific observer and onwards; science turns into pornography. (Obviously, in situations where two people close around each other, the intensity cannot spread to an observer in the same way. Here, the corresponding literary genre is confession rather than description, fiction rather than sociology.)

Insofar as the intensity spreads, opens up to and embraces others present, these meetings are democratic, solidary, 'comradely'. The formal equivalence and equal right to participate, prevailing in the modern world on the market, in politics and in the city, becomes more real here.

Thus, the meeting is often more democratic than the gaze establishing it; this is related to the closeness and intensity that arise, as opposed to the distance and strangeness of the gaze. Meetings confined to two persons often also bear this mark of democracy, fellowship, friendliness, which is not just 'common courtesy' to ward off embarrassing incidents and ensure that everything runs smoothly, but also has to do with the feeling that this intensity is something enveloping both parties, something shared.

> Sexual invitations [in bath houses] follow an etiquette involving simple and nonabrasive rituals . . . that are characterized by their gentleness; usually they are not forceful or persistent. Nonacceptance is ordinarily communicated in a way that is nonabrasive and that masks rejection. In the hallways, one declines another's invitation by avoiding eye contact or by smiling but not sustaining eye contact. In private rooms, such simple scripts as 'I'm just resting,' 'Sorry, I've just come,' or 'Not now,' accompanied by a smile, are customary forms of not accepting an invitation. In the orgy room, one gently removes the hands of the solicitor and/or moves on. If group sex is occurring, a participant merely turns his head, shifts his body, or raises his arm to signify that a newcomer is not welcome.
>
> During the sexual activity itself, concerns over sexual performance do not disrupt an atmosphere of congeniality to the degree that they often do in other contexts. For example, since trial-and-error positioning is routinized, it does not communicate rejection or a sense of incompetence . . . Participants also note that after sexual episodes verbal and nonverbal communications of congeniality are not uncommon (e.g., an embrace or expression of thanks).
>
> Since participants expect the interaction to be restricted to sexual activity, departures after a sexual episode are also simple, routine, and nonabrasive. Participants melt away with little or no ceremony. And since participants expect as much, such departures do not ordinarily engender feelings of disappointment or emptiness.[41]

The being-together, the intensity and the companionship are established, consummated and completed by means of a language, often a 'silent' language, body language; moving hands, lips, and so on become signs, of liking.

These meetings are one answer to the realities of the modern world, and they have a particular quality of their own. This is also what pulls, just as much as the need pushes; and what makes them, including the sexual ones, continually sought after, despite the dangers and damnations associated with them.

It is not always that the meetings run equally smoothly. The longer they last, the more they involve, the greater the danger of imbalance and dysfunctions, of one party becoming more interested in the other than vice versa, of his being unable to cope with parting again without further ado. And just as the meeting concentrates the intensity, it can also concentrate the feeling of expiration, of potential dissolution and nothingness, which belongs to all relationships in the modern world.

12 Associations, neighbourhoods, networks

As a 'homosexual', one is from the outset a specimen of a species, and thus enjoys a ready-made association with the phylum of fellow members of that species: *the* homosexuals. Just as the homosexual is 'born to loneliness', he belongs by definition to a group. However separately he lives and however segregated he remains from these others, indeed if he never in all his born days meets another homosexual, he cannot identify as a 'homosexual' without first having heard or read about them.

But of course, these individuals have good reasons for seeking out members of the same species and *associating*, making the 'speciesship' to which they belong virtually into a reality for themselves. On the one hand, they can find in a community *protection* from the others and *strength to resist*, enabling them to assert a territory and generally fight to improve the ecological conditions of the species. On the other hand, they can find and create a *social life* here, a life with the other homosexuals.

With such good reasons, it is only a matter of time – a short time – until homosexual associations invariably emerge, however small, fictive and secretive. The social history of the homosexuals is rich in unions, leagues, federations, clubs, lodges, movements, groups, societies, coalitions; sometimes associated with internal information media, sometimes more or less commercial.[42] The structure varies from the strictly formalistic to the basic-democratic, and the content spans from gay choirs and hiking to the struggle against capitalism. Ultimately, however, their common background also endows them with the purposes mentioned above: outwardly to protect or enhance the living conditions for the homosexuals, and inwardly to construct a social life based on the homosexuals' 'own' terms. Hence also a certain uniforming of the members: either the emphasis is consciously placed on developing the species-specific or else this is the inadvertent outcome because only homosexuals are assembled. The associations are thus hothouses for the special features that typify the existence as a homosexual.

Yet they also add a new dimension to it – and not merely that of conviviality and fellowship. Being together with other homosexuals allows one to mirror oneself in them and find self-affirmation. It allows one to share and interpret one's experiences. It allows one to learn in more detail what it means to be homosexual: how to act, what to think, thus lending substance to one's proclaimed identity, as well as assimilating certain techniques that may help bridge the gap between this identity and one's actual experiences and conduct. At the same time, being homosexual is normal here, loses its negatively laden value; perhaps one may even receive confirmation that it is better than being heterosexual.

The association is a place where being homosexual makes sense. What is more, it is a habitat, created by oneself and one's own kind for oneself and one another; in principle, a place of one's own. Here the homosexual is allowed to be, and to make something of himself as a homosexual.

So he can, more or less, in the spots of the city that are frequented by those of his own species – in the sun, neon or darkness of cafés, bars, baths, beaches, cottages, cinemas, bookstores, clothes shops, parks, streets and squares. Of course, the greater the number of such places and people, signs and rituals, concentrated within a specific area, the more homosexual can he become. That fellow members of his species also *live* there is obviously a factor extremely conducive, though not necessary, to such a concentration; in order for a homosexual neighbourhood to actualize, the individuals will in any case have to leave their dwellings and enter the city or other people's places. But living close to others also has a significance for one's awareness of the *potentialities* of community and opportunity, and in urban living this is often just as important as actualization itself.[43]

In the associations or in the city, the homosexual gets to know people, often people he can socialize with in other places as well. And when a relationship comes to an end – as it frequently does – it is not uncommon for the parties to continue their acquaintance. Through those one knows, one gets to know others; together, therefore, a *network* of friends and acquaintances often forms for the individual.[44] This may well include a few heterosexuals, current acquaintances from this or that context or a backlog from previous periods; but it may be difficult to make *this* work in the long run.

A network of friends is no 'substitute' for family; it is altogether something quite different from a family.[45] It is not a unity, rather a 'plurality': there are more people one can be together with, either tête-à-tête or in changing combinations; and one derives different things from them as well as developing different things with them. There's one to joke with and one to confide problems in; one to live with and one to romance with; one to go to the cinema with and others to dine with.

Furthermore, those in a network of friends are not pre-positioned, without the question of desire or duty even arising. They have been chosen; further, you are with those you feel like being with and when you feel like it (hopefully they feel like it, too; otherwise things are in a bad way, unless there are plenty of them to choose from); or else you are with them because you feel bound to them. Or out of boredom and for want of better.

And finally, you live both inside and outside the network of friends. You are constantly leaving it again, not only in a physical sense but also in a more fundamental one; for, once out of it, it ceases to exist for you: it will probably still be there tomorrow, but there is no telling. Perhaps they will have made other friends, better friends, no longer feel bound. Its existence needs continual re-establishment; it is not *simply there*.

The network of friends and the association, together with the pub or bar, are the most important social institutions in the homosexual's life. Only through these is it possible to develop a more concrete and more positive identity as a homosexual; these are where a large part of one's life is spent; and these are the places that one can fall back on alongside a relationship or when it ends. Behind them, in turn, is the city; it remains the social basis for life as a homosexual; both in the sense that its concentrations of people and diffuse social control enable associating and networking, and in the sense that its common spaces and special venues provide the last resort to fall back on, alongside networks and associations or when they break up; it is *always* there.

13 Sexualization

Cab drivers, it would appear, are very horny. As they drive around town, they keep their eyes constantly peeled for girls (we are assuming they are Men, as indeed they are for the most part); they discharge torrents of horniness to the female fares they get in their cabs and look them up and down in the rear-view mirror; and when they talk to one another at the cab ranks it's smut-speak, full of stories about sex on the back seat and implied raunch. They also have a game in which they grab each other's bums and think it is very funny.[46]

But if cab drivers are horny, what about homosexuals? They move in the same urban world as the cab driver, but come even closer to it than he, remaining in his cab for the most part as he does. And the city is *stimulating*. We have already seen how its spaces are exploited in various forms of sexuality. However, the city is not merely a stage on which a pre-existing, preconstructed sexuality is displayed and acted out; it is also a space where sexuality is generated. What is it about the city that stimulates? Surely that altogether special blend of closeness and distance, crowd and flickering, surface and gaze, freedom and danger. Others are defenceless vis-à-vis your gaze and you yourself are on display to theirs; you come so close to them that you can actually touch them, yet ought not to: a distance that incites you to overstep yet still maintain it; surfaces intercept gazes and turn into signals, and the flickering vibrates; the crowd generates feelings of supply and possibilities; the anonymity and the absence of immediate social control amplifies the feeling, and the risk of nevertheless being monitored and uncovered increases the tension. You sense this omnipresent, diffuse sexualization of the city and confirm it by designing your surface accordingly and by taking up a position, perhaps also by engaging in cruising and brief encounters.

But what indeed does 'sexuality' mean here?[47] It is a matter of change and alteration, corresponding to the constant circulation of new and different stimuli. It is a sexuality of following the whims and caprices of what attracts, trying out what has not yet been tried, and thus of transcending barriers. It is a sexuality of parts and pieces: not of relating to the other as a whole human being, but only to those delimited parts of the bodies and outfit that happen to attract – a forearm, a smile, blond hair – ignoring the rest. It is a sexuality of distance and strangeness, not of the familiar and the secure.[48] It is a sexuality of surfaces – not primarily wishes for deep and intimate union, but the desire for rubbing and perhaps for penetration, not in order to find out what is behind but merely to leave impressions, like slashing seats on the tube. It is a sexuality of styling and staging: not primarily a matter of entering into a union with the other's body and soul and having an orgasm, but of playing the game, of following the rules and rituals of dressing, posing, glancing, of staging a performance and a sequence, of knowing that there are spectators and of being oneself a spectator of others' performance. Sociological literature about gay men's sexuality in public places may, on first reading, cause one to stagger, as it is common practice there to use a current sociological jargon and speak of 'actors', 'scripts' and so on. But what we have here, in fact, is an area in which life lives up to sociology. This sexuality is also, however, one of the smells from body and materials which it is 'normally' attempted to camouflage or eliminate, of transcending the barriers of the visual, the distance, the surfaces, of allowing oneself to be knocked out by the odours of armpits, feet, genitals. However, smells are usually secondary to the visual in the sexuality of the city; if looks attract, smell may provide an extra kick. The same goes for the qualities of tactility and sound – of leather, silence, skin, nipples. Furthermore, urban sexuality is a sexuality of power and danger, of exposing to and exposing oneself to; as well as of the *potentiality* of violence and supremacy. And as a male homosexuality, it is a sexuality of the attractions of maleness: of the parts, surfaces, smells, touches and fantasized power of masculinity. It is also a sexuality of sentimentality; it happens – perhaps not so rarely – that one feels a sinking wild dream of eternal unity: 'On the corner of Sixth Avenue, he watched and waited, the lights banged on and off. A truck came by; he looked up into the face of the truck driver, and felt an awful desire to join that man and ride in that truck wherever the truck was driving' (James Baldwin, *Another Country*).[49]

By having the city as his primary life space, therefore, the homosexual easily becomes more sexualized than other people, even cab drivers.[50] What is more, in his case – in contrast to, or at least to a more pronounced degree than them – sexuality does not merely come from 'without' – from the city – but also from 'within', from the very bottom of his soul. He is, precisely, homo*sexual*; the self-image offered him first by science and then by common wisdom presents him as one whose sexuality is his innermost nucleus, radiating and usurping larger or smaller parts of his person: i.e. as a sexual being *par excellence*.[51] (He is surely the only living creature to be explicitly defined and identified in this way by his *sexuality*; 'heterosexual' is much the same as *non*-homosexual, a reflection that only strikes on bumping into homosexuals).[52] And this definition as a creature determined by sexuality is, as we saw, not merely an externally affixed label, but embedded in his body and soul through his interaction with medicine and psychiatry, whether it is they that examine, analyse and monitor him or he himself and his surroundings that take on the job. The homosexual's sexuality thus appears to become both his very essence and his special field of experience; in addition, it is the basis on which he is segregated and opposed to the others.[53] Accordingly, there is no avoiding his ascribing importance to it. Thus, all in all, sexualization is a fundamental way of experience and conduct in his existence, a fundamental mode of openness to the world and of trying out its possibilities.

14 Stagings

The discotheque is the space for a series of stagings.

1 Of course, the room has its fixed limits: walls and doors, floors and ceilings – in themselves designed in one way or another. But they are primarily a skeleton to support another space that moves and has no fixed boundaries. The walls are a fastening place for mirrors and a projection surface for changing images, the floor a foundation for mass in motion, the ceiling a bearing structure for *the light*: the razor-edged laser light that can plot out a space and parcel movements into snapshots, the ultraviolet light that makes white luminous and tones the rest dark, the suddenly brash yellow and the warm red dream rays, the fleet light that can flash, gyrate, zoom down from the ceiling like a fireball and scatter stardust across the walls. In addition the music, the soundscape. No, that's not it; the sound does not form scenery, but substance, fleshing out all gaps, and more; in which you are and move; as dense and airy as whipped cream. Light and sound, images and body of waves, all in all a staging of artificial space, of *stage*. A stage for what? For additional stagings, not least.

2 Self-staging. You dress up to go to the disco. You choose a *style*.

You present yourself as a nice, regular kind of guy with jeans and a polo shirt, or you overdo it, from the more discreet *Marlboro* look to the painstakingly rigged-out, like black clothes and a red scarf, black eye-shadow and red lips. You strike up a pose when at the disco. You assume a 'masculine' position, for example, standing with your legs apart, holding the cigarette between the tip of your thumb and your forefinger, the glow hidden by your *fist*, and don't let it hang and flap around between the fore- and middle finger; or you act in a 'feminine' manner. (Everyone knows what an effeminate gay is like, don't they; so there's no need to go into that.)[54] You communicate, as rehearsed, perform a greeting scene with those you know (rush over, for instance – 'Ha*llo* there!' – and 'give them a big hug'); you follow the etiquette for eye contacts; you act, if you have succeeded in learning it, that you are a sex object dancing.

3 The discotheque is also the stage for separate shows which in themselves stage 'reality': slides, video films, live performances. Some are separated into particular times for more concentrated attention (performance proper), but most of it runs while the rest of the disco is operating, forms an integral part of the staging of fluid space. These various kinds of image – stills, moving and real live ones – each have their special features: common to them is the staging, not just in the sense that an image cannot avoid staging what it depicts, but also in the sense that the staging is accentuated: stylized aestheticized female figures and stylized sexualized male figures. The artificial, shocking, grotesque, oversized, refined, perfect, chiselled is decisive. Often, pictures of stagings from earlier periods are quoted, old models' photos or poses struck by great stars of the twenties, thirties, forties, fifties, etc., in a multiple staging over time.

4 Duplications. These pictures, shows, are not just stagings in their own right and components of the staging of the disco space as a whole; they duplicate it, like the mirrors; the disco reflects its own staged-ness in them. But the room reduplicates 'inwards' as well, into a stage proper facing a spectators' space – the dance-floor as seen from the sides, from raised platforms or from the *balcony* that is indeed the logical corollary of many discos. The participants double as actors and audience; one part mirrors its own ornate configuration in the other's eyes or appearance.

5 This series of stagings not only *are* staged and not only duplicate one another, they themselves also *stage*, *teach* staging. Partly in a more general sense by demonstrating the significance of stylistic forming, outfit, performance, superficiality, and partly in a more specific sense by providing a model for particular stagings. The porn videos, for instance, teach him to stage himself and another person as actors and spectators in front of a mirror, so that they can see themselves do the same things they have seen others do in porn films; even without a mirror, he positions himself and the various parts of the bodies so that an imaginary audience may look as directly and protractedly as necessary; his eyes look at you in the same self-absorbed/inviting way as they look at the viewer through the camera. Sexuality is duplicated: there is acting and refracting.[55]

The disco is a concentration point for the stagings of the modern gay world. Not that there haven't been stagings *before*: the grand balls at the *Magic Hall* in the Paris of the twenties or the 'Urnings balls' in Berlin around the turn of the century were also lavishly mounted productions, at which people not only styled themselves up but surely also used the engineering available to stage spaces and performances; and it will be eternally difficult to surpass Oscar Wilde.[56] And homosexual (art) porn has always simultaneously staged both the reality/fantasy it depicted and that to which it gave rise: from von Gloeden's stylized 'natural' still-lifes of Sicilian adolescents through the mid-century dream texts about the two of them alone in the forest cabin: *that* was how it was to be consummated, once they had enjoyed the throes of mutual excitement while chopping firewood or having a swimming match in the stream, one physical contact topping the next, without them actually understanding how, as the sun glistened on the water or coloured the evening sky red.[57] There were stagings before the disco, and obviously there are still stagings outside its realm: posing also goes on at gay bars and in the street and privately. Both external and prior to the disco, homosexual existence is staged; all the disco did was concentrate it, duplicate and propel it, using the most advanced high-tech engineering and the calculated exploitation of the historical stock of earlier stagings.

Homosexual existence is altogether staged existence. Not in the trivial sense that human life is inconceivable without a particular style, a particular form – e.g. it is not possible to greet or dance without some stylizing of the motions – but in the sense that, in homosexual existence, staging is *accentuated*, as we have seen it prototypically expressed at the disco. But after all, heterosexuals eventually got their discos;[58] more or less *all* modern existence can be said to be staged in an accentuated way. The homosexuals, however, as has been seen from the above sections, have been living particularly close to the circumstances that engender and promote staging: the existential uneasiness, the role that calls to be acted out yet cannot be identified with, the city, the emphasis on signals and gaze. To these must be added a shot of energy from the tense rapport with the outside world: the more the staging outdoes itself, the more outrageous is it to the common sense of common people; aggression is satisfied through the symbolic revenge of shocking, scandalizing, non-plussing.

It would be wrong to portray the disco as if it were nothing *but* staging. Gazes are also exchanged, cruising proliferates, encounters are initiated, relationships disintegrate; there is chatting, drinking and dancing with friends and acquaintances. To this extent, the disco can be said to be one of the homosexual life-world's most typical spaces: it concentrates a large number of the elements characteristic of this form of existence. And not least, it is a space of energy, *high-energy*, a space for discharging and recharging, for motoric activity; the signs of the cables with their 'Danger – High Voltage' become symptomatic. The energy of light and sound fuses with the physical energy of those present. Sexual energy? – not really, or kind of. *Sensual* energy, rather: emotions turn into energy, pure energy, stylized energy.

15 Camp

It is by no means unusual for people nowadays to sit down and enjoy something on television *because* it is awful. There *are* people who take royal weddings, Guy Fawkes, or the Fourth of July seriously (or the news for that matter), and who identify with *Dallas* and *Dynasty*, or get wrapped up in whether one Eurovision Song Contest melody is better than another; but there are probably just as many who watch these programmes without doing so. The enjoyment consists in experiencing them contrary to what they set out to be; as delightfully dreadful.[59] This is camp.

In Denmark, one of the annual camp highlights is the Queen's New Year speech on TV. There the monarch sits, resplendent in her exquisite royal setting, in what is ostensibly one of the most solemn moments of the year, addressing the whole of the Danish people gathered in their thousands of little homes – and then she says nothing. It is made extra camp by the fact that she is really so nice and every year attempts to say something, and something new at that, and say it so beautifully; indeed, it is graceful camp. Not only is the Queen's New Year speech camp; the Queen herself is camp, altogether camp, in her essence and all her appearances: because at the same time she absolutely is not and may not be anything and is/is not so with so much taste and such exquisite care, *at such a high level. All* modern Queens are camp – albeit scarcely all with the same elegance, but we will go no further into that, for reasons we shall return to in a moment.

Clearly, not everything can be perceived as camp. Some mismatch is required; some incredibility between what a thing purports to be and what it is, between surface and essence, form and content, ambitions and outcome. And it requires the final result to be grotesque, yet also a little touching, in order to be camp proper; it must be possible to identify slightly with the futile exertions made, while still being able to laugh at them indulgently.

The necessary discrepancy may come about in many different ways. Queens are camp on account of the mismatch between the magnificent staging and the absolute absence of content, combined with the dedicated commitment. In Herman Bang's *Mikaël*, the converse is true, if anything. Here one senses pain and passion in the content, but it is throttled (occasionally, at least) in theatrical gestures and swollen pathos.

> 'Ah yes, so young', said the Duke, and with his svelte body bent deferentially forward in the chair, he told once again of the castle back home. No trees were as dear to him as oaks. They were so *strong*, oaks. And with a smile so lugubrious as can only be found in people of ancient breeds that appear to have seen and to bear everything in this world that their eighteen ancestors together saw and bore, he said . . .[60]

There are endless examples from stage and screen in which both the sentiments and the expression lack credibility, but in which the mismatch nevertheless exists owing to the energetic overacting: the old Ealing comedies, with their hearty butch matrons and spindly male protagonists; soap opera series like *Emmerdale Farm*, full of dialectal overkill and endless cosy chats over pots of tea around the hand-embroidered kitchen tablecloth; early Hollywood classics like *Hush, Hush, Sweet Charlotte*, with Bette Davis's eyes smouldering among the old flames of her splendid past life. The same is true of *Dallas* and *Dynasty*: all those meaningful glances, all those close-ups of dismayed faces to wrap up scenes. And the Eurovision Song Contest is camp, not because the songs are either worse or better than any others, but because of the sumptuous staging, the orgy of staircases and platforms and smiling hostesses with or without long gowns and long gloves. Over time, the scenery and get-up have swung from the decorously elegant to the hectically jerky – and partially back again; but it remains A1 camp; the effort makes it so.

Many different things, then, can be perceived as camp, but there are limits. On the one side, various forms of unease lie in wait. The danger with *Dallas* and *Dynasty*, and even with the Eurovision Song Contest, is that they so easily become *boring*. Watching the same discrepancy for *so* long is not funny. The problem with many entertainment programmes is that the *embarrassing* becomes pushy; you get too close to these people who take what they are doing seriously: when they make such a point of replaying the most vacuous and hackneyed clichés from everyday usage in front of the entire nation – as if they were saying something; or when they get flustered at not being able to guess a particular capital; when they sit there as part of the studio audience in their Sunday best, clapping away and enjoying themselves during the designated slots. It is *too* much. Camp, in a way, is fuelled by people's fatuity – and one's own ability to identify with their inanity – but it must not reach the point of threatening their dignity; then it's not fun any more. With time, however, the embarrassment can become less insistent; if these entertainment programmes are repeated in the 2000s, they will surely become the camp of the time. Witnessing the Red Army Choir's recent tours in the West has, *per se*, many camp qualities, whether they happen to be performing with the Finnish 'Leningrad Cowboys' – sporting the world's pointiest shoes and highest quiffs – or are providing backing vocals to dancing Cossack children in French television's lovely children's Sunday afternoons. Yet the associations evoked by this army bring the experience dangerously close to another of camp's limits: that of human suffering. There are other, related forms of experience which do not observe this limit and which, if anything, live off overstepping the mark: e.g. certain forms of *kitsch*, delighting in the pure sumptuousness of extravaganza, whatever its background, or perhaps even being stimulated by shuddering at the sinister character of this.

On the opposite side, camp experience is threatened by *quality*. (Of course, it is not wrong for something to be good, but then it is just not camp.) Wagner operas, with their nimbus of valkyrie horns and gross female singers, virtually in advance epitomize the cliché of camp; yet occasionally, they *sing* so beautifully that one is uplifted. The French art of the ballad teeters on the edge of being camp, with its sonorous sensitivity and pompous passion, but it captivates as well. Or the *play-acting* can be too good, the dramatic skill despite the content, as every now and then with Bette Davis in the old Hollywood films: there may be no one emotion proper to express, but she certainly does *express*. Conversely, historical distance may exert an influence and show up weaknesses in what was once thought to be good; many of the 1960s programmes on art and culture would undoubtedly be rather campy now.[61]

Camp experience is bound up with a mismatch in what is experienced; but consequently it is also bound up with the person experiencing, for not everyone is likely to experience the same mismatch. What is camp – and perhaps the very possibility that *something* is so – is, if not individual, then at any rate group-specific (as the reader may have noticed), including nation- and generation-specific. But even in another sense it is intimately connected with nation and with time. A special affinity exists between a lot of camp and *aura*, i.e. the particular awe-inspiring nimbus and action-binding power surrounding certain phenomena. *What used to be aura is in the process of becoming camp*; to this extent, camp is aura de-auraticized. These 'decaying' aural phenomena[62] include royalty and other national symbols. Many of them are only known or best known to the natives concerned; accordingly, these enjoy a privileged status when it comes to witnessing and participating in the development of certain phenomena into camp. Moreover, the experiences of camp and aura are not mutually exclusive, but mostly form combinations; it might even be argued that camp experience – of royalty, for instance – is frequently dependent on the continued presence of a certain aura. In that sense, too, camp is often a national affair; this becomes manifest, for instance, when non-natives highlight the camp aspect of a national symbol, and the natives react by feeling that the dimension of aura is violated. For this reason, we will not comment on the cut of the Queen's dresses in other countries.[63]

In the glide of aura towards camp there is, as we have also seen in the preceding examples, a built-in temporal dimension. This is a contributory force in making camp experiences generation-specific. For instance, when various national song and folk-music traditions are in danger of turning into camp, or even further into *corny*, *kitsch*, *crap* or *junk*, this is partly related to the decay in national auras, though also to the degree of aura different generations have had the chance of associating with these traditions. If Anglo-Saxon pop music (whatever country the performers come from) is not generally considered camp, one of the reasons is that it has been successful in presenting itself as international and not just local and national. It is not immune to the erosive effect of time, however. *ABBA*, I suppose, was wonderful disco in the 1970s, or *bad taste*; revived in the 1990s, the experience scale moves rather between 'wonderful disco' (with some distance of nostalgia) and camp.

The camp mode of experience never occurs in isolation; it is a special version of an altogether broader sense of surfaces: the sense that the surface, form, style of phenomena have detached themselves from the essence, content, message, and gained their independence, and hence can be experienced *as* surfaces, i.e. as something else and more than just expressions of an inner essence.[64]

This sense is not equally widespread; but there is reason to believe that camp and similar experiences are becoming more and more universal. Modern societies are increasingly seeing the evolution of a surface to people, things and situations – a surface with an autonomous existence; thus, a common background for such experiences is established. I shall return to this in chapter V and will therefore make do by briefly mentioning three of the most important factors at work: urbanization, industrialized mass production, and the emergence of the visual media.

It is not just the homosexuals, then, who have camp experiences – not any longer at least. But they have lived with them longer and more intensely. The actual word 'camp' – as a term covering various types of such experience – seems to originate from homosexuals' subculture, although some of its roots go back further.[65] They have had a special basis for developing this sense of the surface as surface, with their special affiliation to the city, their role-awareness, their camouflage-demanding relation to the surrounding world, their sense of staging and visual shaping. They have thus been able to record more quickly than so many others the evolution in surface that accompanied the mass production of things and pictures; and conversely, this array of detached and designed surfaces, pictorial or material, has reverberated on the development of this sense in the homosexuals. Furthermore, they may have a special interest in emphasizing the importance of the surface: the more something is a question of surface, the more it is an *aesthetic* matter, a question of taste and enjoyment – and the less a moral one. The emphasis on surface is a defence against the others; it wards off.[66]

Camp – and similar phenomena, such as kitsch – is primarily a way of *experiencing*; but it goes without saying that it must immediately become a way of *presenting*, too – presenting oneself and the things one deals with. Nothing is simply what it is: always already is a distance built in, between surface and essence, between form and content, and thus it relates back to itself. Therefore, it's impossible to produce and present something without being conscious of that relationship and without relating to it. The surface has been liberated from simply having to express the inner, and the job is to decide what is then its purpose.

16 Sensitivity

The homosexuals are so sensitive. That's what it is, even though it may not be suitable in a man. But in their case, it gets to be too much: they are *hyper*sensitive, always picking up on remarks as if they were directed at them personally and uttered maliciously. They are touchy, *paranoid*, as common parlance would have it; they are for ever on the lookout for injustices, *collecting* them, the way others collect stamps.[67] So people say, forgetting that what is thus called paranoia is often the ability to see the things beneath the surface that others wish to deny.

But this sensitivity is not reserved to the homosexuals, particularly hypersensitive as they may be. The ability to register what is going on beneath the surface, which comes to the fore so clearly in hypersensitivity, is an important aspect of modern sensitivity generally. It goes hand in hand with three other aspects. Thus, with what is registered beneath the surface, which is not just anything but precisely sensations and feelings (one's own or others'): impulses, sentiments, urges, inklings, yearnings, moods, motions. Often, they do not emerge directly and unequivocally, either because they are suppressed or because there are, as it were, more of them than expression can accommodate (there is a *scarcity of signs*, as Goffman says). The third element of modern sensitivity is empathy, the ability not only to register others' feelings but to identify with them. And finally, there is the amount of the sensitive subject's own feelings: if one says of a person that he is sensitive, it implies that he has a lot of feelings; yet that in itself is not enough for us to call him sensitive. These four 'elements' or poles belong together, interacting with and reinforcing one another. The more feelings one has oneself, and the more subtly differentiated those feelings, the better equipped one is to register their likes in others, and the other way round; further, the more capable one is of registering one's feelings – sensing them, distinguishing them from one another, naming them – the more they develop and differentiate, thus being cultivated. The very act of talking about feelings and devoting attention to them plays an essential role in developing this sensitivity; and even though it certainly has roots stretching far into the past, it does not really unfold until the 1700s and during the 1800s, with all the attention that feelings then received, not least in literature.[68]

Fiction – with its ability to express the individual, the shimmering, the ever-changing, the ambivalent, the unuttered and the rigidly unutterable – was the very medium for elucidating fragile and volatile feelings and their infinitely subtle and tortuous paths and strayings; and indeed, it sought precisely to develop itself technically so as to become capable of it, with ever more virtuosity. Thus, it was far better suited to bringing out feelings than the academic psychology and psychoanalysis that were evolving contemporaneously or slightly later and which, with their stodgy schematics and reductionism, distorted and smothered rather than developed them. Fiction was able not only to go off in pursuit of feelings and confine them, but to follow and unfurl them; it did not scrutinize them in order to control and coerce, but snuggled up to them and warmed them. It did not command, but appealed to the sentiments. Here, we encounter another of those rare instances where 'discourses' may sensibly be said to be substantially and directly influential in constructing subjectivity.[69]

The development in fiction and sensitivity ties in with many other social changes. This includes the emergence among the ruling classes of a femininity which took empathy and feelings as its essence and the emotional well-being of the family as its responsibility; and the parallel development of a masculinity, the thrust of which was to ensure the family's economic survival, and the most essential traits of which were resolutely determined action and chilly calculation in dealing with others. Tendentially, then, the man suppresses any emotion and becomes sheer smooth surface, while the woman becomes pure emotion without any protective surface. So it was that they were thrown on each other, and thrown back to constant conflict with each other.

To those men who for some reason refused to be identified with this masculinity, a special role of artist or author was open (the existence of which, in turn, is related to a multitude of other factors in the development of the institutions of art). These men entered into a kind of coalition with women, to the effect of developing sensitivity. Thus, on the one hand, it was often women's emotional life that they made the subject of empathetic descriptions or identified with their own in a kind of 'literary transvestism' (their own emotions, after all, were their 'female side', since women had a monopoly on feelings). And on the other hand it was women, above all, who made up their readership. Even in our day, fiction is read particularly by women; if women are still sensitive and sensitivity is still womanly, it is not least for this reason. However, fiction was not the only art form to foster sensitivity. The concurrent development of music also brought out feelings. Opera represents the junction and the culmination of these developments; here music and literature, colour and form, light and movement synthesized, making the opera house a space of concentrated emotions. Obviously these art forms and emotional spaces were the prerogative of certain classes and strata. In the course of time, however, they gained greater ground, partly through the diffusion of lengthier education and partly by entering into symbioses with popular forms of culture. In this way, the modern cultivation of sensitivity became widespread.

Even though sensitivity is not especially homosexual, the homosexual has special reasons for developing it. It is not his actually having to renounce feelings which is decisive here – after all, he has that in common with so many others. It is primarily the fact that he has feelings which – for whatever reason – he refuses to renounce, even if required. This draws his attention to these emotions, and to the rapport between emotions and surface; and at the same time it gives rise to a profusion of other feelings (wrongness, uneasiness, loneliness, etc.). The swell of emotions and the attention paid to them enter into mutual reinforcement processes with the elements of high culture and education that he cannot help but encounter (for many reasons; not simply because he has turned into a snob in an attempt to compensate for his feelings of inferiority and wrongness). Thus, the homosexual reads *belles-lettres* and cultivates art and culture because he is so sensitive; and the more he cultivates them, the more sensitive he becomes. It takes more than reading in the manuals of medicine that the homosexual is sensitive actually to *become* a sensitive homosexual;

going to the opera is certainly conducive. And the very accentuation of the surface which so much else in his existence invites (the city, the meetings, etc.) intensifies the sense for feeling in the sensitive homosexual: precisely because he lives to such a large extent in a world of surfaces (and is also generally sensitive), he is alive to what is beneath the surface, what it suppresses. Moreover, the scope of his sensitivity, as well as his persistence in cultivating it, is bound up with his particular position in relation to the modern formations of gender.

17 Masculine – feminine

Modern life involves *being gender* and gender *role* at one and the same time.

On the one hand, it is impossible *not* to be a man or a woman; one always already is. Not merely in the trivial sense of being equipped with certain sex organs and bodily potentialities from the start. There is no way of being born and bred in modern Western societies without becoming provided with and providing oneself with certain of the characteristics linked in these societies with one's biological sex – certain expectations, mannerisms, sensations; and without having learned to appreciate at least some of the realities and possibilities that come with this and having associated certain pleasures with them and a certain fear of losing them. A person has been *oriented towards* being a 'man' or a 'woman'. (The transsexual is the exception that – partly – proves the rule.)

On the other hand, it is impossible to *be* a man or a woman. The term 'sex role' is an expression of the fact that gender is problematic; the very spread of the term indicates that the feeling is widespread; and there is no reason to believe that the uncertainty stops with those who are sociologically tainted. It is altogether impossible not to sense that it is problematic to be a man or woman today; it is no longer something one just is.[70]

Let us look at the matter from the man's angle. The background to his uncertainty is well known: the evolution of production technology and the labour market; the democratization of education and politics; the development of contraceptive techniques and of social institutions for child care; sexualization and the demands of fashion for innovation. As a result, the individual man runs the risk of meeting, and *knows* that he risks meeting, a woman who is better than him in practically all areas – even those that should otherwise be the domains of his manhood: more articulate and better at repartee, better at thinking logically, consistently and at mastering the situation, better at elbowing her way up the hierarchy, better at driving a car and at fixing it, at operating a computer and at juggling with mathematical models.

On the one hand, then, he can hardly not (want to) be a man; on the other hand, it is impossible for him to be entirely sure of what it actually entails and if he really is one. There are fewer and fewer areas left where it is possible to satisfy himself of his special quality as a man; manliness has been 'drained of its functions', you might say. There is almost nothing left but *sport* – the domain of the sheer physical performances of his 'naked' body – where, so to speak, he can *be himself* as a man (and this is undoubtedly one of the reasons for the extreme popularity of sport in modern societies – amongst men). But even here, he risks meeting a woman who is better; and even if he has trained to become world champion in putting the shot, he risks meeting a woman who can outrun him.

Yet, there is one thing she does not have and one thing of which she is not capable. As other areas lose their importance as distinctive marks of virility, this thing and its capability (rising, penetrating and thrusting up into, exploding and firing off) assume all the more importance. The male sex organ and its abilities, and the symbolism to which it gives rise, have no doubt always had their part in enabling a man to be a man. But in 'Sambia', for example, the whole world was sexually segregated and a man was a man because he was associated with all dominant and life-imparting forces and substances (trees, stones, fluids, etc.) in the cosmic whole. And in ancient Athens, a man was a man because he dominated not only in bed but in the house and in the city as well.[71] In modern societies, however, there is no gender in the cosmos on which to pin a handle, nor is there really any in society any longer; here, a man is only a man because he has a penis. Gender narrows down to biological sex: sex organs; the rest takes on the appearance of superstructures that might – you never really know quite how far – be different. Psychoanalysis is the perfect ideological expression of this situation.

A consequence of women advancing into all areas is thus that the man's sex organ, for him, is isolated and elevated into the exclusive centre of manhood. There is a further corollary to this outcome. The male sex organ and what it can do represents, as it were, only the *possibility* of his being a man; some *proof* must be provided: a manhood test.

Undoubtedly, manliness has always involved having to prove one's manhood. (There are no *womanhood tests*, surely; woman is something one is supposed to become, passively; it *comes to* one, by nature or by a man.) With the advance of women, however, this mandatory production of evidence changes on a number of scores. Once, the test could be passed in so many fields (hunting, war, politics, etc.); but now, the venue for the evidence becomes the sheer 'naked' relationship to the woman: on the one hand, she is trespassing into one field after another, making it impossible for him to demonstrate there his special quality as a man; on the other hand, she is encroaching, making it plain that the relationship with her is the venue where the test is to be performed. Moreover, there is a change in the 'legal body': it is now the woman, who, if not the supreme judge, is at any rate the key witness; it is to *her* that he must prove his manliness, as much as or more than to other men. And finally, a change in the 'burden of proof' occurs: above all, it is now a matter of proving one's masculinity as a *difference* from femininity (and not just as equality with other men).

The evidence that a man is a man, therefore, must now be proof that he is not a woman, and it must be presented in relation to her. We have already seen what options are open to him in this respect; the proof of his being a man is that he does it. Sex becomes sex act; the uniting of the sexes a corroboration of their difference.

This reduction of gender to sex organ and sex act is only a *trend*, however. The advance of women has queried the essence of masculinity, as well as shifted the nature of the legal body, the conclusive evidence and the venue for its presentation. But it has not succeeded in making masculinity *disappear* to the point where nothing was left but penis. The cultural man-images are still there, and there are plenty of enterprises to keep them alive; furthermore, they keep themselves alive, so to speak, by clinging to the living male body, as an extension of it and a schema for it at one and the same time.

In this situation, then, where the man's masculinity has become uncertain yet nevertheless forms his point of origin and orientation, the individual man must relate to how he will manage to be something he cannot be, yet cannot avoid being. Gender turns into a project, into a question of choice and strategies. The whole gamut of possibilities is open, in principle: he may wish to become one with being a man, running like a bat out of hell to live up to it; he may be and want to be it with a distance; or he can attempt to dismantle greater or smaller parts of traditional masculinity and assume certain traditionally feminine traits.

But the field is open more in principle than in reality. Having become a man is his starting point and that towards which he is always already directed, that which his expectations and desires are bound up with. No longer being considered a man arouses anxiety, ever more so the closer it approaches what appears to be the centre of his gender. Defence and attack start. Gender switches to a battle of the sexes.[72]

Into this electric field the homosexual is born. (One may well wonder whether he could ever have entered the world at all and grown to adulthood without this healthy climate. But as mentioned, the task is not to write the history of the origin of the species.) He is not simply forced, like any other man, to relate to himself as a man and decide how and how much he wishes to be so. He, more than any other man, is bound to do so. Regardless of whatever compelling causes, *idées fixes* or chance desires have caused an individual to become 'homosexual', he is thus forced to enter into an explicit relation to his masculinity – by very definition, as it were; since he, more than any other man, is defined as a *man who is not a man*.

I am not thinking here particularly of the fact that the homosexual (or 'Urning') was defined already by Ulrichs back in the middle of the nineteenth century using the formula 'a woman's soul in a man's body', nor of the fact that this definition was dragged into, and came to leave a considerable imprint on, the medical definition.[73] I am thinking of the social background for definitions such as these to become prevalent. This background is first and foremost the gender situation I have just outlined. To an increasing extent, a man is only a man insofar as he is *not* a woman, and in practice that means insofar as he does to her that which she cannot do to him: penetrate with his erect member, thrust up, and fire off. And seen from his point of view, she is the one it is *being done to*; so he is not to *be done to*, for then he is not a man.

The homosexual, however, is characterized precisely by *not defining himself like that*: he is not a real man because he does not prove his relationship to the woman in that way. Moreover, he may even allow himself to have done to him the thing that makes her a woman; but *what* he does with another man is secondary in modern societies; decisive is what he does *not do* with women. However much he may have climbed trees as a boy and shot with bow and arrow, however much his face is boorishly butch and his prick the size of a forearm, however much he is brusque and bragging and watches every single football match on TV: *in society's terms he is not a real man* – and to that extent he is, under these circumstances, *a woman*; and he cannot help but know.

Thus, in a different and more profound sense than other men, the homosexual is forced to relate to his masculinity. You might say that while other men are forced to decide how much of a man they intend to be, he has to decide how much of a woman he intends to be. It is possible that he finds waving his hands and flitting a shawl highly amusing, or that he will eventually relish such womanly delights; it is also possible that he will not have the faintest desire to do so; but he cannot avoid relating to it, taking a stand, making a choice. And however little or much he chooses to be masculine or feminine – with the starting point and resources he happens to have (desires, fear, risks, physical wherewithal, etc.), he has the certainty of being so with *distance*. (Of course, I am not claiming that there are not men with, say, feminine facial features; anyone can see that, so let us occupy ourselves with something more interesting.)

There is also another reason why the homosexual – regardless of how his individual background may otherwise be – has to come close to femininity. It is impossible for him not to enter into it to some extent, since the fictional products (film, theatre, etc.) – and reality – of the modern world primarily have women where he would like to be, i.e. in the sexual or erotic relation to a man. But he can never become one with this identification; just as his non-masculinity prevents him from merging completely with being a man, his masculinity prevents him from merging completely with being a woman.

For the homosexual cannot – any more than other men – shirk being a man: that is his starting point and what he is always – more or less – directed towards; he too experiences the benefits of masculinity and feels the pleasures of the male body and is hit by the alluring radiance of the cultural male images. This masculinity of his constitutes one of the conditions for his existence, on a par with the city, scientific practice and the tense rapport with others. And his particular form of existence can only be understood by taking this condition into consideration as well.[74]

It is instructive to draw a comparison with *lesbians* here. Indeed, they too are squeezed out of the family, are the object of scientific analysis, sense the uneasiness in their role, etc. One might wonder, therefore, why they have not developed the same form of existence as the male homosexuals: with brief encounters, sexualization, sense of style and staging, of images, camp and so on.

Of course, they have too, to some extent. But there is also a difference, and this is precisely to do with the fact that they have *femininity* as a starting point. Hence, for one thing, a kind of 'time-lag': the lesbian *species* has existed only for seventy or eighty years, whereas the male homosexual has been around for more than a hundred. So they have not lived with 'the conditions of modern life' *for as long*.[75]

In addition, they are subject to the economically and socially unequal opportunities that pertain to being a woman as opposed to being a man (the 'double suppression' of the lesbians) and have thus had a barrier particularly in relation to the city and the staging of semi-public spaces. As a woman on her own, it was not so easy to walk around a dark park at night or even just sit on a bench in full daylight (that is, unless the point was to establish contact with a *man*). And generally speaking, they have not enjoyed equal economic and social opportunities for realizing extravagant aesthetic fantasies as to how the world should look (though some have). So they have not lived *as close* to 'the conditions of modern life'.

And thirdly, their femininity has functioned not only as a condition preventing the lesbians from living as long with and as close to the other conditions of modern life, making their form of existence a kind of stunted version of that of the male homosexuals. (This fits nicely into the classic wisdom of sexology otherwise: of the lesbians it must be said, above all, that there is *less of* them, in every respect.) But this femininity, *and* its problematization, was in itself a modern condition of life, instrumental in lesbians developing a *different* form of existence – it has created a different imprint and pointed to a different answer.[76]

The masculinity of the male homosexual, then, is an important factor among the conditions of life that make up the background to his form of existence. It works, for instance, by bringing him particularly close to some of these other conditions – among them, not least the world of the city, owing to the traditional affinity between masculinity and the public, urban sphere. From this proximity springs his easiness and delight in brief sexualized encounters with strangers. Rather than being the expression of a shameful defect inherent in masculinity, his promiscuity is, from this point of view, an adequate answer to the possibilities of the modern, urbanized world.[77]

18 Oppression

> I oppose the established order because I regard it as a state of injustice . . . My fight is a fight for freedom . . . We demand [it] as our clear right. We, too, were born to freedom. You have no right to oppress, persecute and deride us.
>
> Carl Heinrich Ulrichs,
> *The Riddle of Man–Manly Love* (1865)
> (translation adapted)

The homosexual is unthinkable without the simultaneous claim for his emancipation. Not merely because from the outset he grew up in a world where the ideas of freedom and equality, oppression, struggle, rights and emancipation were on the agenda, so that it would be odd if he did not end up interpreting his situation in the light of them and attempting to exploit them; but also because the very proclaimed identity of 'homosexual' is to a certain extent *calculated to* get the maximum mileage intrinsic in the modern concepts of rights, oppression and emancipation. Admittedly, on a number of points, the discourse on the homosexual person tallies well with experiences and sensations that are part of this special form of existence, but it is unlikely that so many would adopt the discourse so readily and make of it their own identity, were it not that such benefits were intrinsic to it. Seen from this angle, 'the homosexual' is a tactical design that can provide the desire for other men with an access to the field where the game is played and destinies decided.

Let us take a closer look at the lines of argument with which this desire has asserted its demand for rights. Throughout the period from the latter half of the nineteenth century to the present day, there are a few arguments that recur and can be found even in the meekest and most self-abhorrent.

1 *It's our nature.* We were born that way, or at least we became that way so early on that it is as good as nature. We are and must be thus; so the question of when we found out about it is a meaningful and interesting one which we readily go into. And not only have the homosexuals always been thus, there have always been homosexuals; not only is it integral to the nature of the homosexual that he must be so eternally, but eternal nature itself has willed the existence of homosexuals. Ergo, we can't help it, can't be blamed for it, and

have a right to be so. Houmark: '*we* too have a right to be and to live', for we 'did not create ourselves' – the right 'to be the one nature decreed us to be'.[78] Here we see how the idea of the homosexual person is put forward in order to justify sexual desires and actions. These are not haphazard or self-elected; on the contrary, they are *ineluctable expressions and results of a deep-seated inner 'nature'* which is engrained like *fate* in a *special group* of people.

2 *We are useful and do no harm.* All those lists of famous 'homosexuals' – artists, military commanders, etc. – that figure in the homosexuals' apologias from the mid-nineteenth century onwards are, of course, also designed to show what outstanding and useful members of society many homosexuals have been. And the rest had better be so, too: it is 'through our work, our aptitude, our assiduity and our respect for our vocation' that we 'defend' 'our right to be' (Houmark).[79] Best of all, of course, would be to show that the homosexual cannot only be useful despite his homosexuality but is so precisely because of it. Here, the idea of the homosexual person is again profitable: the homosexual's homosexuality is a nucleus that lies within him and is not merely manifested in peculiar sexual acts and desires but altogether in a series of personality traits, such as social sentiment, educational flair, artistic talent and an ability to negotiate between the sexes. Besides, we do no harm, as again we can prove with the aid of the idea about the homosexual person. We are non-contagious, as homosexuality is either within a person or else it is not there. By the same token, we do not seduce anyone; if the young man concedes, it must be because it is within him, for such things come from within. Finally, we do not give public offence or undermine social institutions, since we are, precisely, outstandingly social creatures or at any rate ought to be so and have the best qualifications for it.

The thing that got 'homophiles' into a rage against the new gay movement in about 1970 was precisely the fact that it systematically destroyed this line of defence, by proclaiming the irreconcilability of homosexuality with the existing morality and social order. Altogether the gay movement emerges as a leveller of old arguments, switching from a defensive to an offensive strategy. In the process, the reference to 'the homosexual person' declined in importance, for it was now a matter not of justifying homosexual interests but of attacking the circumstances that prevented them from unfolding freely. On the other hand, however, the gay movement carried on along the old lines of argument. It did not abandon the reference to usefulness, but simply gave it a future setting: we are useful for establishing a liberated society and do no more harm than that necessitates. And our potential in this respect consists precisely in 'being' a special kind of person whose desires and self-expression do not allow themselves to be hedged in by the ruling forms. And within the talk of having to come out, be oneself, be allowed to 'be who we are', surely there still lurks a reference to a 'natural' inner being.[80]

All in all, then, the idea of the homosexual person figures largely as a tactical device in these arguments in favour of the desire for other men. By couching the desire in this idea it is possible to present it as natural and useful and thus seek access to the field in which rights can be asserted, oppression cited and emancipation demanded.[81]

But this construction is fragile. In order to be effective, the argument needs to be connected to norms and conceptions beyond its control. It is interesting to note exactly what normative authorities are appealed to and are thus presumed to wield the power of persuasion: *usefulness* and *nature*. As for usefulness, it is not so strange, since it appears to enjoy a general trust in modern societies (as opposed to abandonment, for example, or remembrance of the Lord). But it may be surprising that anybody is able to believe he can justify his existence through reference to nature, considering what 'nature' has primarily become in modern societies: an object to be worked up for utility if not considered sufficiently useful as it is. Nature, therefore, is a problematic category of defence for the homosexual, as indeed has been proved in full by the practice of the natural sciences. That they were not able to pinpoint the nature of the homosexual did not prevent them seeking to eradicate it with every possible expedient.

How is it, then, that the right for same-sex lovers to exist, the complaint about oppression and the cry for emancipation are still being coupled to 'nature', the inner essence, that which one 'is and must be'? What is it that makes them cling to this identity, continuing to all appearances to *expect* that being the way they were 'decreed' to be should give them the right to be so? There are surely a number of reasons. Let us look at two.

1 Natural science has succeeded neither in pinpointing nor in

eradicating the 'nature' of the homosexual. Consequently, this has acquired a particularly staunch, lofty, primordially legitimate air; if anyone might have doubted its very existence, it now appears elevated above and beyond any doubts, precisely because of its evasiveness. It was also this combination of triumphant 'nature' and impotent natural science that *actually* formed the basis for the strongest argument in favour of improving at any rate the legal situation of the homosexuals: *since* it is their nature, *since* they consequently cannot harm others by it, and finally *since* science happens to be unable to alter it, there is no legitimate rationale for criminalizing it.

2 'Nature' then *could* not be eradicated. Nor, perhaps, *should* it. In modern societies, 'nature' also doubles as a name for the antipole and presupposition of the man-made: the wonderfully given, genuine and primordial, which should be honoured and allowed to exist. Thus, 'nature' – including that of the human and of the sexes – still retains something of its aura, or rather it is repeatedly reimbued with it, as a reaction or an alternative to what it has primarily become. It is also still able, therefore, to demand not to be repressed. Nature *ought to* be reason enough. The homosexual is a hopeful creation.

Modern existence *is* not without hope. It always has as its background the certainty that there is history, that progress in material welfare can be achieved, that suffering need not be unavoidable and that it is possible, in principle, for people to exert an influence on the social conditions of their own lives. Modern existence is not without unrest, longing, expectations; not without the certainty that things may be different, and better. It is from the outset located within the electrical field between oppression and emancipation; the right to be better off and not feel forced to put up with anything is always already a part of what it understands itself to be, its forms of identity: wage-earner, youth, dole client, person of independent means, woman, pensioner, consumer.

At the same time, modern existence is obliged to *justify* that it has a right not to be oppressed, to be better off. Modern societies – its background – are arguing ones, as appears from the typical institutions: science, law, parliament and public sphere. One must 'assert' one's rights; i.e. *speak about* them as well as prove by way of *rational grounds* that one has them. Arguments may not always matter very much; yet one is forced to use them, even in dealings with oneself.[82]

Thus arises the problem of the criteria for what has the right to develop; since, clearly, not anything and everything can rightly claim that it is oppressed, demand liberty and equality. Here, in general, 'nature' appears in an ambivalent light: on the one hand, it is still possible to endow actions and wishes with a certain legitimacy if they can be passed off as natural; on the other, nature is often precisely what must be changed in the evolution towards the other and better – *it*, too, could be different. If the homosexual appears to be especially entangled in these contradictions, it is not just because his suffering is so insistent, but also because he has so insistingly committed himself to a particular form of reasoning from the start by virtue of his proclaimed identity.

19 Sex, friendship, love and life

The really remarkable thing about gay lifestyle, writes Edmund White, is that it has succeeded in *separating* sexuality, friendship and love. They are no longer chained to each other in a prison of marriage. Thus, sex can be more playful and artistic, pursuing the eccentric and capricious motions of desire. Friendship – often with former sex-partners – is like an elaborate root system, providing emotional and social continuity. And love, thus relieved, can take the form of consciously open relationships, built on mutual esteem and respect for the other's freedom and responsibility.[83]

But if sex, friendship and love are separated in this manner, for the individual they are nevertheless part of one and the same life. They must therefore be *combined*, and that seems to create certain difficulties. One's friends may not like one's lover, and vice versa; couples are often a bore to be with, levelling each other and communication to a mealy-mouthed common denominator; sex outside the relationship makes imminent the dangers of jealousy and losing. Besides, each of the elements listed by White as being separated may well contain difficulties of their own: not all sex – though some, however brief – implies a wish for love forever; friendship networks may burst or let one fall through; love does not always cope well with the freedom of the other. Then would it not be better, after all, to concentrate on the *one-to-one*, restricting sex to it and giving it absolute priority over other relationships?

At any rate, the couple and its relation to sex and to friendship networks seem to hold out the most tricky problems. So let us take a closer look at what characterizes homosexual men's couples. Even from their starting point, these are typified by a number of special circumstances. They are in a certain sense *free*: no societal norms stipulate that two men must live in a one-to-one relationship, nor is it dictated by financial necessity or demands to safeguard succession and continue the lineage. The partners are also from the outset *equal* in a specific sense, i.e. in terms of gender. No financial disparity has been brought into the relationship on the grounds of gender difference, nor any socially prescribed role allocation regarding the scope or nature of work in or outside the home, or concerning emotional and sexual give-and-take. Finally, the partners are not merely of the same sex and gender but are of the *male* one. Of course, this is not tantamount to saying there are no individual preferences regarding tasks and performance. The conditions of 'liberty, equality and maleness' may also be counteracted by desires of conforming to presumed standards: e.g. that people ought to maintain a one-to-one; that love implies fidelity; that one partner must play the husband, the other the wife. Such standards may indeed be specially articulated and imposed by certain groups of homosexuals. On the other hand, they do not enjoy universal backing among homosexuals: awareness of alternative ways and valuations is widespread, and with it a degree of debate and reflexivity on such matters.[84] To some extent, this is also reinforced by the norms of society at large, since these are not unequivocal with regard to homosexual couples. In addition, as we have seen, there is always a *distance* present in the homosexual concerning both his social relationships and his gender performance.[85]

All in all, there is a 'setting free' from surrounding society's general (i.e. heterosexual, male–female) starting points for one-to-ones. Accordingly, it is not unreasonable to expect a homosexual men's one-to-one to be essentially (even if not wholly) 'entered into for its own sake, for what can be derived by each person from a sustained association with another' and 'continued only in so far as it is thought by both partners to deliver enough satisfaction for each individual to stay within it'.[86]

What from one point of view is a setting free from usual starting points for one-to-ones simply constitutes *other* conditions from another point of view. The lack of social prescriptions as well as the gender equality generate tasks of working out who should do what, how and why; and the fact that both partners are men may imply special difficulties associated with the borderline games I mentioned earlier on (cf. chapter III, section 20). It may be argued, though, that such problems are no worse than the games and tensions thriving in couples with gender difference (even if they are not identical with them).[87] Indisputably worse, however, are the effects of the negative outlook on the part of the surroundings and the lack of sanctioning on the part of society; this may be destructive to the point of preventing partners finding a place to live or even be together on their own. However, in the following discussion I shall disregard this, by no means because it is unimportant, but in order better to be able to investigate another question in connection with one-to-ones that start out from the conditions of relative freedom and equality.

What, under such conditions, does it take for a relationship to *succeed* (by which, initially at least, we will understand that it is of a fair duration and experienced as fairly satisfactory by both partners)? Some factors appear with reasonable clarity to be promotive. First of all, a mutual liking, but also mutual care and respect (including respect for the other's personal growth), as well as trust in the other's determination and capacity for continued liking, care and respect.[88] There must also be a division, fungible and acceptable to either party, of tasks and performances – not necessarily an equality, though the recognition that things might be done otherwise and a readiness to change would undoubtedly not go amiss (and such qualities are, as we have seen, basically present in the homosexual).

I have less credence in the often recommended qualities of *knowledge of one's self*, unearthing one's 'real', 'true', 'deepest' traits and motives: of *disclosing oneself to the other*, revealing and rendering accessible these traits and motives; and of *communication* – especially *verbal* communication – *oriented towards a common understanding* of these 'innermost' traits and motives, as well as of their legitimacy (that good reasons can be given for them, or that they should be changed).

My objection is not the oft-adduced one that such values are middle-class and feminine (i.e. happen to converge with what has been construed as feminine values).[89] It may be that the middle class, and women, have better prerequisites for successful one-to-ones and that, if anything, these conditions should be provided for others as well. Rather, the basic problem, as I see it, is that the position is scarcely tenable. It presupposes the existence of a fixed reference point, a *true self* with a dual structure: on one pole, a dimension that can be (a) made transparently accessible, (b) divulged, (c) communicated, negotiated and readjusted; on the other pole, a dimension that – though perhaps not entirely unaided – can and will make accessible etc., and that accordingly possesses the quality of *sincerity*.

Such a relation of self essentially has the character of a *narrative*, i.e. a story with a series of special features: it must contain a hidden and essential meaning; it must be 'tellable' within fairly commonly known conventions of story-telling; and it must be understandable, in the triple sense that it is possible to arrive at its 'real' but concealed meaning through interpretation, to render it accessible to others, and to make it available for evaluation and modification in the light of higher evaluation criteria – i.e. available for 'reworking' or 'rewriting'.

Now, if this narrative could be boundlessly and arbitrarily rewritten, it would not serve its purpose of providing relatively firm ground for one-to-ones. Obviously, versions conditioned by the individual, group, class, etc. must be possible, just as the narrative must be modifiable in connection with changes in life. But there must also be a fixed and incontrovertible matrix – otherwise the narrative falls flat: then there is no 'real self' to be found, communicated and adjusted. Basically, two such nuclei for the narrative of self have been at issue in modern times: one referring to body (biology, nature), the other to childhood developments.[90] For these narrative matrices to be absolutely certain, they need an authority capable of guaranteeing them. As we all know, such authorities are in supply and such authorized matrices consequently in circulation. Here is one of them.

What the homosexual is seeking in his relationship with the other man is *really* union with the mother and at the same time separation from her. From infancy, the mother is the great, powerful figure in his life: he loves her and wants to be united with her, yet at the same time is afraid she'll engulf him so that he loses his masculine autonomy. Therefore he also wants to be separated from her and to confirm his masculinity in a relation to another woman; but he's afraid of that as well, for then he risks arousing his mother's jealousy and losing her love. What does he do now? He finds another man instead of another woman; for then he can at the same time remain faithful to his mother and have his independence (=gender difference) reinforced in relation to her, through a jab of masculinity from his intercourse with the other man; and into the bargain perhaps even be symbolically united with the maternal breast by means of *fellatio*. Yet he is so unsure of himself that while he is entirely reliant on others for affirmation, nonetheless he can never truly be affirmed by them, for he cannot bond with them and cannot tolerate them bonding with him, since he is afraid of losing himself and is incapable of taking an interest in anyone other than himself anyway. Therefore, he constantly has to replace them and try to bolster himself with new jabs of masculinity.[91]

The basic problem with this narrative matrix is not its sinister prognosis for homosexual couples, nor that it is outrageously insulting. Psychoanalytic therapy *might* be a necessary remedy for the first; as for the second, the narrative contains its own explanatory device: if Tom and Harry cannot associate it with their bicycle trips and fresh scones in bed on Sunday morning, it is because the real meaning of their activities is *unconscious*. Nor is the problem that this narrative folio of childhood may seem horrendously arbitrary, as indeed there are countless varieties of it circulating on the story market (although it certainly must weaken the authority of either).[92] The problem concerns the fundamental claim that, on principle, it is possible to find a true matrix for the narrative of the development of self and relatings from childhood. No sure basis for such folios exists, nor can one be found: the childhood 'experiences' constitutive of them are, in principle, non-verifiable; the borderline separating childhood fantasy and reality cannot be drawn; the narrative, of necessity, turns into *fiction*. It is no use substituting body (biology, nature) for childhood – it, too, when implored, largely gives nothing but equivocal answers concerning the very points that are crucial in constituting a life story.[93]

Life narratives, therefore, should be evaluated in the light of broader criteria for *stories connected with life*, e.g. in relation to the impact they make on conducting one's life. Narratives intended to disclose the 'true self', as grounded in childhood, have implications that may appear quite adverse: the chronic monitoring, vigilance and suspiciousness with regard to actions and wishes ('What do they *basically* express'? 'Is it *really* something else I want?'); the unending search for 'authentic' wishes; the retrogradation; the condemnation to repeat the same thing eternally or spend the rest of one's life 'working over' it. It is often claimed that such pursuits are a necessity for anyone wishing to be set free for a happier life. This may work for some; and obviously there are dimensions of life that seem to lend themselves to reasonable interpretation through such narratives of the self, its relations and its constitution. However, I think they overlook or underestimate a number of important aspects and hence give a problematic weighting.

Foucault's distinction between the *hermeneutics of self* and the *aesthetics of existence* may serve as a navigating indicator. The 'hermeneutics of self' refers precisely to unearthing, disclosure and communication of a supposedly real and authentic self, whereas the 'aesthetics of existence' concerns the art of conducting one's life.[94] Applied to the workings of couples, the differences may perhaps be illustrated by way of the following buzz-word list: rather sensitivity than understanding; rather tact than pressure; rather distance than adhesiveness; rather bear with than bear down on; rather be reasonable than ask for reasons; rather camp than cramp; rather go on than go on about; rather face-work than soul-tunnelling; rather hug than talk; rather laugh off than carp on; rather television than inspection; rather be a couch potato than spill one's beans. And, most certainly, rather *ad hoc* than *ad nauseam*.[95]

There are further dimensions to life – and to life stories – which I think are underrated, not merely by Freudian self-hermeneutics but also by Foucaultian existential aesthetics.[96] On the one hand there is the languor of life – routine, habit, fatigue, world-weariness, indolence, enmeshment, weight; the perpetual being dragged down and swallowed by the unleavenable heaviness of being. And on the other, there are leaps and coincidence, as well as incompatible urges and idiosyncratic foibles.[97] Both the dimension of inertia and that of incalculability involve holes – black holes or plainly gaping voids – in terms of the possibility of a reflexive construction of personal integrity by way of a coherent narrative. Consequently, deciding to live in a long-term one-to-one relationship does indeed imply the courage to 'gamble upon the capacity of the individual actually to act with integrity'[98] and his capacity of continued liking, caring and trusting.

Similar considerations apply to the question of sexuality outside the couple. The question is unavoidable and must be tackled in one way or another. Male homosexual existence is, as we saw, sexualized existence, rooted essentially in the city as its basic life space. Herein lies the fickleness and whimsical eccentricity that White speaks of; in both respects, desire is severely disinclined to be reasoned with. Indeed, urban sexuality, always already beyond the politically correct, is only partly open to understanding and reasoning.[99] It can, of course, be explained in relation to its background, and its symbolic aspects can be analysed in terms of their inner hidden meanings; but it has a particular quality transcending this – a certain excitement and pleasure – which cannot be apprehended by way of explanation and interpretation.[100]

The capacity for tact and acceptance, the ability to tolerate torpor and gamble with chance are important factors in a steady relationship if it is to succeed, as well as in deciding whether it should include sexual fidelity or indeed should involve sexuality as a necessary element.[101] But such abilities are also important in assessing whether there must be a steady relationship in a life for it to succeed.[102] The sustained one-to-one has much to commend it. The experience of a continued and shared history of good times and crises coped with, of mutual liking, caring and trust, as well as the *security* connected with this can be difficult to find elsewhere, let alone the experience of love, of the joy in the other and in the relationship.[103]

However, individuals' points of departure, resources and capabilities are highly diverse. Further, there are traditions of many different ways of life in the homosexual world: apart from long-term monogamous couples, there are e.g. serial monogamies; couples with institutionalized infidelity; marriages of convenience; organized *ménage-à-trois* set-ups; close, steady, non-sexual two-person friendships; ways of life that centre around the social life of organizations, friendship networks or pub environments; intense intercourse with pornography; and combinations of these.[104] The ideal of the steady, monogamous loving couple easily turns tyrannical (owing to the groundswell of cultural norms bearing upon it) and generates an amount of guilt in the ways of life that differ. Instead of maintaining one particular ideal, it might be more reasonable to reconcile ideology with the reality of the *de facto* varieties of relationship in the homosexual world, i.e. look for the qualities that exist in such various relationships, or at least promote a moral-aesthetic discussion that considers their virtues and shortcomings in a comparatively unprejudiced manner – for instance those of the lifestyle that cultivates the relationships of watching pornography. An adequate morality and criteria for a good life can only be developed by realistically facing existing conditions of life and relating both to the limits they impose and to the possibilities they provide – including those of the particular traditions and the institutions for non-commital sex that have evolved in the homosexual world, founded as it is in the facticity of the city.[105] Finally, it is quite possible that different ways of life will be adequate for different phases of life – in individually varying sequences, transitions and combinations. The homosexual's characteristic mobility – change, break-up, restlessness – is not necessarily an expression of narcissistic character disorders or puberty fixations, nor is it always of evil.[106] The absence of sure communities and fixed identities sets free to change, and the masses and potentialities of urban life favour it. Experimenting and compromising are relevant answers to these conditions of life.

20 Another country

> It seems to me I would always be better off where I was not and this question of moving is one I discuss incessantly with my soul.
>
> Finally my soul explodes, and wisely cries to me: Anywhere! Anywhere! Only let it be out of this world.
>
> Baudelaire, 'Anywhere out of the world' (1867)

Baudelaire's poem might well be claimed to express a yearning which is less peculiar to the homosexual than it is general to modernity – or one that was to become general and reach fruition in modern mass tourism. Seen in relation to the latter, however, the homosexuals were from the outset an avant-garde ('Most homosexuals travel widely', notes Herman Bang, 'if they are well-to-do');[107] in addition, they had special reasons to wish for another country. As a sheer lamenting of the lack of a place to be, as an abstract desire for another country, or as fantasies and recollections of specific places: from Bang's *Those Without a Nation* to Baldwin's *Another Country*, from Stoddard's *South Sea Idyls* to the *Spartacus Guide*, the wish was always there.[108]

But where was that other country, if indeed it could be pinpointed? Let us consider which areas might possibly qualify.

1 It must be a *place to be*, a world where homosexual relationships can be realized, without guilt and without shame, in full daylight; a place, then, where other norms prevail, or at least a morality that is not overly restrictive and an authority that is not excessively interfering. In other words, a place outside the dominant civilization with its inhibitions and prohibitions.
2 It must be a place that provides a suitable setting and suitable means for the development of this love that wishes to cast off the yoke of civilization, a place appropriate to pleasure and play, where it is possible to be naked and in direct contact with nature,

where there is simplicity and abundance: sun and warmth, shade and freshness, beaches and springs, trees, fruit and flowers.

3 Moreover, it must be accessible from the civilized world (i.e. north-west Europe and North America), located in a none too remote radius, also in case there should be a return.

4 Finally, there must be reasonable order and security there as well as reasonable comfort. Some individuals may have ventured still further afield in their dreams and in reality, but it should not be forgotten that the homosexuals are civilized people capable of forfeiting the benefits of civilization only with difficulty. It must be warm but not beyond what is tolerable; at the end of the afternoon one needs to sit in a chair and have decent tea served; if there must be nature, then without too many snakes and scorpions.

It is surely the combination of these factors that explains why certain areas did not become popular in this special homosexual geography – India, Japan, Black Africa, the Eskimo regions, eastern Europe – whereas others did: the Pacific islands and coastal regions of Central America for the North Americans, the Arab countries and, in general, countries along the Mediterranean for the Europeans.[109]

But these areas represent only the externally uncivilized; *within* civilization, too, there were as yet uncivilized areas (or areas that could appear uncivilized), as yet untouched forest and mountain landscapes with their populations of powerfully calved peasants and glum woodcutters. Or civilization itself produced its own special 'un-civilization', the simultaneously lawless and supervised zones of the city: the crowds, the parks, the botanical gardens, the proletariat, the public lavatories where culture finally had to give in to nature. It is interesting to see how a series of innovations and re-sitings take place in the space of the city – concurrent with the formation of the homosexual – in the period of the great urbanizations during the latter half of the nineteenth century, often in the now demolished precincts of the big cities: railway stations, zoological gardens, botanical gardens, parks and natural history museums. The city was to be brought into the country, and nature into the city, all at the same time. The 'countryside' which formed the setting of the fictitious world in which homosexuality could be consummated was often precisely the country of the city, projected beyond the city: the elaborate grounds and exotic vegetation of the botanical gardens, with acacias and murmuring fountains.[110]

The very distance sometimes sufficed to render another country attractive: for the Americans, Europe; for the Europeans, America. (And in some instances, it was in fact simply a matter of escaping, and in a hurry, to a place where one could be as unknown as possible.) Or the attraction of distance could be combined with the specially exotic aura surrounding certain countries: Hungary, for example, because of its geographical and ethnic proximity to the Asiatic hordes, the chivalrous and the savage, the flashing eyes and the flashing rapiers.[111] On one single occasion, an entirely new Realm of Hope arose, a post-civilization or a higher societal form: the new Soviet Union, which abolished all laws against homosexuality. 'There was one country, after all, where utopia was in the process of becoming reality', was André Gide's hope.[112] But the realization may always have been uncertain, and was anyway short-lived, as Gide himself was to find during his visit in 1936.[113]

From the start, contradictions were built into these journeys to or dreams of another country. Not merely between the wish for the anti-civilizatory fulfilment of homosexuality and the homosexual's need for the benefits of civilization, but also between this unadulterated natural setting and the need for *subculture*, which could only be satisfied in the big cities. In the artificially uncivilized areas of the cities, surveillance and detention threaten; in the externally uncivilized areas, nature threatens and – worse still – boredom.

There seemed to be no solution to these dilemmas. Yet at one point a kind of escape opened up, concurrent with the gay liberation of the 1970s. Homosexuality, it seemed, could be realized in the 'liberated zones' at the centre of the largest cities of the civilized world. It was possible to travel *to them*, try to live one's life in these ghettos, 'communities', or at least go there for a weekend. The country that is not was there after all; it was called Castro in San Francisco, Greenwich Village in New York, the Marais in Paris or the city centre of Amsterdam. The tension between reality and fantasy was levelled; uncompromising utopia transformed into *Realpolitik*. The dominant world became the best of all; whatever else was missing could be made up on holidays to Ibiza, Mykonos and Haiti. The wish for a place to be became the wish for change, escapism from the world turned into gay tourism. The contemporary gay man is ideal-typically 'on the go' as well, on the hunt for *more* places. The regular travel reports in the international gay press witness to this indefatigable eagerness; even the remotest and most hopeless regions must be reconnoitred, be it China, where no one has yet heard of a live homosexual, or be it on bicycle.[114] If there is still another country, it is there to be conquered.

In this world, however, utopia resurrected in a new form: as the wish for a country without homosexuals.

21 The homosexual form of existence

We have now reached the point where it seems appropriate to sum up the results of the preceding reconnaissances in relation to the problematics outlined early in this chapter (section 3) concerning the 'nature' of the homosexual.

1 *Being homosexual* is not, as might seem at first sight, something which by law of nature accompanies an *erotic preference* for other men; it is not an *essence* implanted in certain individuals from birth or from early childhood, forcing them to live in a particular way and providing them with the characteristic attributes of the homosexual.[115]

This can be seen even from the fact that the erotic preference has not been invariably and ubiquitously connected with these attributes. However much Socrates, Alexander the Great, Leonardo da Vinci or Shakespeare may have been interested in other men, they were not homosexuals, in the sense set out in the preceding sections.

2 Nor is the homosexual form of existence merely a result of social *oppression* that has prevented men with an erotic preference for other men from living like the majority and developing characteristics like them, thus compelling deviant lifestyles and deviant personality traits.[116] For why *these particular* ways of life and these traits, this form of existence? It is not just a deficiency and an absence, it is also a *something*.

3 Nor is the homosexual form of existence simply the result of a social *discourse* (label, role, category, etc.) which for some reason or other certain individuals come to appropriate and mould into their *identity* and further, into a corresponding *subculture*.[117]

It is correct that a social complex of attitudes does exist with regard to eroticism between men (as I have described in section 2 of this chapter). Further, it is true that a number of individuals adopt these as their own attitudes to themselves (as we saw in section 3, there is close concordance between the homosexual self-conception and the social discourse or role). It is also correct that role and identity are mutually reproductive: the attitude of the surroundings is of essential importance to the individual homosexual's attitude to himself – and this in turn becomes confirmatory for the attitude of the surroundings. Examples: The mother cries because homosexuality is considered a tragedy, and it becomes a tragedy because the mother cries. Homosexuals are sent to psychiatrists because they are assumed to be sick, and they are regarded as sick because they go to a psychiatrist. Or there is a case of interaction between discourse, identity and the homosexual subculture: homosexuals are considered different, so people give them a wide berth, so they develop their own spaces and ways of social life, and that makes them different.

The 'homosexual *role*' or '*discourse*' thus has considerable bearing on the forging of the homosexual *identity* and *subculture* (and to that extent, on the homosexual form of existence); it can with some reasonableness be said that these three factors intermesh in a system which, once set in motion, tends to reproduce itself, the discourse or role being the driving force. Taking a closer look at the homosexual form of existence, however, as we have done in the preceding chapters, it transpires that a number of *other* factors are also of crucial importance. They are instrumental in providing the special script for this role. Further, they make up the background and supply the input that keeps this only partially self-reproducing system afloat and operating; for, from examining the discourse or the role itself, there is no way of comprehending in all respects how some can 'appropriate' it and turn it into an identity, how the word can transubstantiate into flesh. It may be written into the homosexual's script, for instance, that he is sensitive, but how indeed is it possible for someone to *become* sensitive? Moreover, the totality of the factors we have elucidated in this section make up the background for a number of features of the homosexual form of existence that are not included in the script at all. Thus the common conception of the homosexual – and correspondingly, often the homosexuals' proclaimed self-conception – partly gives a distorted picture of this form of existence, not merely because homosexuals individually differ greatly, but also because their common features, their 'species characteristics' as homosexuals, are not captured by this discourse and the self-conception of the corresponding identity. These are, in part, illusory; one cannot, therefore, confine oneself to analysing the homosexual from the angle of discourse (role, label, category, etc.).

4 Being homosexual, as has emerged from the preceding chapters, is not primarily a matter of discourse and identity, but a way of *being*, a *form of existence*. As such, it comprises a number of particular characteristics. These, we have seen, include certain basic '*tunings*' and *recognitions* – e.g. of existential uneasiness and freedom, of injury and feeling watched, as well as of a certain distance from one's own masculinity and potential femininity. There are also particular ways of *experiencing* – such as aestheticization, sexualization, camp and sensitivity; particular *dreams* and *longings* – e.g. of another country; and particular *forms of conduct* and *expression* – such as stylings and stagings, travels and breaks, signals and gaze. Further, there are specific forms of *social relation* – including brief encounters, changing relationships with partners, couples with institutionalized infidelity, as well as organization and friendship networks.

Viewed in this context, the concept of *identity* assumes a dual significance, as I have developed it in the preceding chapters. On the one hand, the homosexual identity is *the confirmation of the discourse* (the role, category, label, etc.): a more or less public, in part strategically determined affirmation of a given and confined framework of meaning. This is what I call *proclaimed* identity; it may not be a direct affirmation of the role and discourse, but is often more or less of a modifying compromise.[118] On the other hand, the homosexual identity is the *confirmation of the form of existence*, its accepting self-reflection. These two versions of identity represent the extremes of a continuum – or discontinuum – along which the modern homosexual is stretched and in which any individual homosexual has to manoeuvre around. In no instance, however, is the homosexual identity *identical to* the homosexual form of existence; it remains a certain, unquestionably important, though limited, part of it.

The term *form of existence* was chosen because this made it possible to link up with and exploit inspiration from the continental European tradition of phenomenology and existentialism, particularly that of the early Heidegger.[119] The choice is not a dogmatic one; life – 'homosexual' or not – can hardly be subsumed under a specific and limited series of terms. But the choice may advance a vision of the world – and of human being – perhaps more adequate for a comprehensive study of the phenomenon of the modern homosexual. Further, it may help turn increased attention towards the particular *conditions of life* that make up the essential background to this form of existence.

As a particular, historically and socially specific form of existence, the homosexual is not merely the product of the forces of preference, oppression or discourse and the powers underlying these. He is first and foremost a *defile for the problematic of modern life.* The modern conditions of life – the city, the collapse of norms, the absence of safe and secure communities and identities, the struggle of the sexes, the images and the stagings, the institutions of art, the theory and practice of liberal democracy, the external surveillance of the police and the internal analysing of science – form the background to his life-world, presenting themselves at the same time to the individual homosexual as a problem area in which he is always already placed and in relation to which he cannot escape placing himself. The homosexual form of existence is what it is because it concurrently bears the immediate *imprint* of these conditions and problems, is an *answer* to them, and to a certain extent *follows the answer guidelines* contained in them. His particular *erotic preference*, *the oppression* and *the discourse* act primarily as reinforcing factors in this context; they help to push him closer to these conditions of life (though he is not just pushed towards them, they also pull at him); further, the oppression and the discourse (and perhaps indeed the preference) are themselves to a large extent expressions of these conditions (cf. chapter V).[120]

Regardless of the causes, motives, etc. that induce an individual in any single instance to enter on the homosexual form of existence – and I have no desire to interfere in this – he becomes in the process a defile for the problematics of modern life. The peculiar thing about him, his unique character as a homosexual, is due to the very fact that he has a particularly close affinity to this problematic and is thus a particularly open or exposed defile.[121]

22 A world

The homosexual form of existence is, as we have seen above, essentially social: it involves a relation to others one feels one resembles more or less, with whom one interacts, with whom one exchanges experiences and views. Insofar as this aspect is singled out for special consideration, we may speak of the homosexual *social world*.[122]

From one point of view, this world as a whole has the nature of an *imagined community*.[123] It exists in individuals' *sense* of belonging, having in common, being familiar with, receiving and perhaps contributing. The political side of community is the *movement*, always potentially inflammable owing to the homosexual's position in the tension between wrongness and demands of right.[124] Both imagined community and imagined movement may, of course, materialize in various kinds of manifestation.

In yet another sense, however, the homosexual form of existence has the nature of a social world: it is supra-individually present. It changes, of course, with time, *inter alia* as a result of individuals' and groups' activities; but it exists, at a given point, ahead of the specific individual, and it exists independently of him: he may disappear, it will still be there. It is also superior to him: he must love it or leave it, or at any rate find some way to accommodate. The encounter with this world can often have the nature of a culture shock, and living in it can require a good deal of socialization.

This supra-individual presence of the homosexual world – just like its existence as imagined or manifested community or movement – is largely related to its being objectively present or *sedimentated*. Its particular moods and recognitions, ways of experiencing and dreams, forms of conduct and expression, social relations and interactions have been precipitated in or linked to substance that in some sense or other may be termed material. Among these 'material' carriers or foundations of the homosexual world is, obviously, its population; as well as its special venues and institutions; designs of spaces, things and persons; times, events and festivals; rituals and customs governing contacts and relations; jargon and communication media, texts and discourses, sounds and images. It is further upheld by various forms of vested interest: commercial, political or identity-cultivating. This materially present character of the homosexual world is also the reason why a homosexual is always able to find it (or ascertain its absence), wherever he travels in the modern West, and feel at home there.

The homosexual is not the only one who has a 'world'. It would seem that a good deal of others, under the conditions of modern urban life, develop or participate in those kinds of social life; especially those people who are temporarily or more permanently outside the family. Such 'worlds' are essentially urban: they are largely worlds of strangers and not just of personal acquaintances;

they depend in part upon the non-personal, urban free flow of signs and information, as well as upon the pool of strangers, for recruitment and reproduction; they occupy time-space slices of the city and need urban stages to be enacted on. They are one of the ways in which communality is created in modern societies when not given. The homosexual world, however, as the preceding chapters show, has its special features, attributable to the homosexual's particular closeness to the modern conditions of existence and his particular answers to them. It is also quite encompassing and mandatory, since the social life of the homosexual *as* a homosexual remains situated primarily outside the family; for the same reason, it is comparatively old and well established. It thus functions as an environment providing him on the one hand with opportunities for conducting a life, and on the other hand contributing by virtue of its special forms and content to producing or reproducing him as a homosexual. Furthermore, it is particularly through the material sedimentatedness of this world that homosexual existence acquires a certain coherence and completion. In other words, this is what establishes a substantial part of the background for making it reasonable to talk of a homosexual *form* of existence.

23 Refusing to be homosexual

Those who *refuse to be homosexual* claim, as we saw, that there is nothing the slightest bit 'homosexual' about them besides a particular erotic preference: this is not associated with special character traits or ways of life, other than those artificially and unreasonably cultivated; it entails no distance unless one engenders it oneself with one's demonstrations and diatribes; there is no problem unless one makes it into a problem. Analogously, though mostly from a completely different context, postmodernist or deconstructionist views have claimed the homosexual to be little more than an illusory though rather successful device of power, a 'master narrative' beneath which nevertheless thrives almost infinite difference.[125]

Under the conditions of modern life, however, having an erotic preference for other men *is*, as we have seen, synonymous with problem, distance and differentness, special traits of character and specific ways of life; in short, a particular form of existence. 'Homosexual' is not just a conceptual abstraction that does violence to reality by cutting away the real multiplicity and diversity of the individuals so that it can lump them together in the same basket. It is not merely a formal abstraction but a *real abstraction*: the abstraction from diversity expressed by the category is present in reality as a *trend towards uniformity*.[126] Reality is – to a certain extent – homogenized; and if this implies violence, reality itself is the one to have committed it; even though the category may have been an important aid to the process.

As stated earlier, the idea of the homosexual form of existence as a real abstraction does not, of course, imply the assertion that all actual homosexuals are identical and have been so since the end of the nineteenth century. However, in realizing certain erotic preferences – wherever they come from – one cannot avoid becoming involved in this form of existence to some extent, irrespective of one's background and affiliations in terms of class, race, etc. This is partly because such a realization brings one into close contact with the very same conditions of which the homosexual form of life is a result and to which it is an answer. Further, this form of existence will be encountered as something which is already there since, as a matter of fact, it *has* become established and *materially sedimentated* as the dominant pattern for living – the dominant *world* – under such circumstances (cf. section 22). Accordingly, the homosexual world exerts a gravitational pull on individuals. Sometimes, this occasions a certain choice or change of occupation to facilitate living in this world; in any case, it necessitates some degree of adaptation to times, places, mores etc. – i.e. of uniforming.[127] And the basic features of the modern conditions that make up the background to the homosexual form of existence – including those of the materialized social world of this existence – have persisted largely unchanged since the latter part of the nineteenth century.[128]

Yet even under these circumstances, homosexuals are different: classwise, racewise, ethnically, regionally, individually. So why emphasize the similar and identical rather than the diverse and manifold?

It is clearly important to stress the differences, as *against* prejudices and group pressure, and when dealing with the lives of individual 'homosexuals' or the interactions and external relations of various contingents of 'homosexuals' (or other varieties of same-sex lovers).[129] But it is also important to draw attention to the similarities and the common features

1 because it may be enlightening or enjoyable to spot them or look

them in the face or reflect in them (as we have done in this section);

2 because these features endow the homosexual with a special role to play in maintaining modern society as a whole (cf. chapter V); and

3 because, with them, a series of factors is stated of importance to historical developments (cf. chapter VI).

Under the circumstances of modernity, refusing to be homosexual is either a special kind of *Realpolitik*, an effort to contain the impact on one's existence which, under the circumstances, strong erotic interests in other men cannot help but produce – which is realistic only to a certain extent. Or else it is a utopian wish: that more or fewer of the modern conditions of life were different and/or that homosexuals were not the only ones to come so close to them.

24 Railway stations

From the latter half of the nineteenth century the large railway stations appear in the cityscape at the same time as the homosexual. They have no doubt played a part in producing this modern creature, not merely being places through which he was conveyed into the city, but also providing by virtue of their peculiar ingredients and atmosphere a fertile soil for this particular form of existence and perhaps even this erotic interest.

They are among the places he likes to roam,[130] and have been so from the very outset; thus in 1914, Hirschfeld mentions in his enumeration of 'open' venues the area around long-distance main-line and underground stations on a par with the heavily trafficked streets of the centre, certain squares and public urinals, the roads skirting large parks, and the pavements outside certain pubs, baths and theatres.[131] (From the start of the twentieth century, even *trains* on urban subway networks also ranked among those especially favoured roaming grounds, as Hirschfeld reports from Berlin, and Comstock from New York. 'I know of a number of homosexuals in Berlin whose love life is enacted almost exclusively on the city rail transport system; often, they ride around several times, circling the city until chance brings them a suitable and willing object in a compartment free of fellow passengers.' 'I am informed by an expert in nervous diseases, that in New York, upon the elevated railroad, these perverts travel and frequently meet others of the same sex, and leave the cars in order to be in each other's company.')[132]

What is it about the railway stations that draws the homosexual? First and foremost, that they *concentrate the city*. All the elements are there, compacted and condensed within a delimited space: the crowd, the constant flux of new people, the mutual strangeness and indifference; the feeling of motion, options, sexual excitement, potential danger and surveillance; the possibilities for moving and following, for using gaze, sending signals, disappearing in the crowd, etc. In addition, the presence of *facilities* – public urinals, cafés, display windows – for variation, recreation and a little more stationary contact. Here, the homosexual can feel at home.

The railway station is thus a concentration point for a number of dimensions in the homosexual form of existence, one of the spaces that collects, reflects and amplifies within it essential features of his life-world; on a par with the discotheque, the consulting room and the opera. The special thing about the station is that it is also a *travel space*, a place for departures and arrivals. Hence additional moods that vibrate with those of the homosexual: of breaking up, of something fluid, less complete and clear-cut, of chronic transit from one point of life to another. And yearnings, dreams, of going away, of experiences and adventures, of another country. We leave him there, absorbed in what is and with the dream that it might be different.

V

Homosexuality and Society

1 The consequences of homosexuality

Since 'homosexuality' (however absent) and 'homosexuals' exist in modern societies, the thought occurs that these phenomena do not merely result from conditions in such societies but, conversely, must also influence them – and moreover, that they can only continue being there by virtue of that influence. Even if the homosexuals were an out-and-out waste product, they would have a significance for society all the same; garbage, too, puts a strain on competitiveness and the balance of payments. In other words, it is not enough to regard them merely as products and outcomes; we must consider how they integrate into the overall reproduction of society and what role they play in its development.

For a long time, of course – just as long as the modern phenomena 'homosexuality' and 'homosexuals' have existed – it has been argued that they exerted an influence on the surrounding society in various ways. Homosexuals often make outstanding commanders and great educators, it has been claimed, or else they corrupt infantry and infants alike. And homosexuality undermines society; or conversely, it is what keeps it together.[1] I shall discuss below some of these theories; my overall view, however, in accordance with my general approach, is slightly different from the customary one. If 'homosexuality' and 'homosexuals' exist *only* in modern societies, then it is worth considering whether these phenomena might not play a special role in the maintenance and development of the special phenomena that characterize precisely that type of society.

The following reconnaissances present no comprehensive and exhaustive answer to this question. The topic has never been treated on a broader scale, nor has relevant material been systematically collected. What I adduce is primarily hypotheses, without any secure empirical shoring, yet nonetheless sufficiently buttressed to make them worth presenting, in the manner of a series of essays.

The relations between homosexuality and the surrounding society have developed over the years, of course; this is a topic to which I shall revert in chapter VI. For the time being, I will concentrate on a series of basic features that have remained largely the same from the infancy of homosexuality in the nineteenth century to the present day.

2 Self-analysis

For anyone wishing to find out what functions the homosexual performs in modern societies, it is surely only natural to start by consulting the scholarly literature. As the reader will know, this is preponderantly of a biological, medical, psychiatric and psychological nature. An examination shows that, above all, four overarching issues have been dealt with:

1 What investigative procedures can be used to identify the homosexual?
2 What physical and mental traits characterize the homosexual?
3 What is the reason for some people becoming homosexual?
4 How can the homosexual be cured, and how can people be prevented from becoming homosexual?[2]

Even if this literature completely ignores the question of what use has been made of the homosexual in a societal context, it nevertheless tells us about its own use of him. An initial answer to the question regarding the homosexual's societal function is, then, that he has been *the object of extensive scientific literature* of this type, the object of theories of identification, characteristics, causes, prevention and cure.

These scholarly theories, however, point to an extensive *practical* apparatus. They are not the result of desk-bound philosophizing and do not hover in thin air; they build on *sound empirical research*: measurements, tests, experiments. Since the end of the nineteenth century, countless homosexuals have had their physical stature, the size of their testicles and the shape of their anuses measured; had tissue curetted from their oral cavities, their urine analysed for hormones and their semen microscoped, their glands X-rayed and their brains ECG'ed; they have reported on their mother's age when they were born, their place in the sibling sequence, the number of brothers and sisters, male cousins and female cousins, uncles and aunts; described their relationship with their father and their relationship with their mother; told of childhood games and adolescent experiences, and related their dreams and fantasies; they have completed questionnaires, crossed off multiple-choice charts, made statements about Rorschach figures, drawn a person of the opposite sex or a house, a tree and a person; have been shown moving or still pictures and had the reaction of their pupils, their sweat secretion and penile enlargement measured; they have been prescribed LSD, male sex hormones, female sex hormones, anti-depressants and sedatives, sexual inhibitors and emetics; have ingested nicotine acid and inhaled carbon dioxide; have been hypnotized, electroshocked, lobotomized and castrated.[3]

One should notice that this scientific practice has a *material* aspect as well. Not only are scientists and homosexuals involved, and not only paper and pencil, but also a sizeable machinery of nurses and carers, technologists and secretaries, buildings and beds, equipment and appliances, flasks and chemicals, linen and canvas, medicaments and electricity.

All in all, then, during the past hundred years or so a comprehensive apparatus of analysis has built up around the homosexual. It encompasses even parts of the judicial system, although here this is confined to playing the role of the subsupplier. Thus, a second answer to the question of the use to which the homosexual has been put in modern societies is that he has been *the object of this extensive theoretical-practical-material machinery of analysis*, intended to identify him, ascertain his characteristic features, explain him causally, prevent him and cure him.

What is noteworthy, however, is that this prodigious machinery has failed to work as intended: it has been incapable of solving any one of the four tasks it set itself. Yet functioned it has. What results has it produced through its working, and what role has the homosexual played here?

1 This apparatus of analysis has been essential in reproducing the homosexual. He has entered it with a more or less vague awareness

that he was a *homosexual*: wrong, decisively different from other people, a victim of remote disturbances or mistakes, and subject to secretive and dangerous inner forces that take on peculiar physical and mental manifestations, referred to the analysing and controlling help of experts. And once inside the apparatus, he has been observed, had his body and his conduct examined, been interrogated about his parents and his childhood, has had the interior of his body transilluminated and the innermost reaches of his soul exposed, has become the object of all conceivable efforts at treatment. If he was not 'homosexual' when he entered at one end, he was certainly well on the way to becoming so by the time he exited at the other.

This effect, of course, is not limited to the many individual homosexuals who have come into direct contact with the apparatus. It has spread, through dissemination of the scientific literature, through popularization by educators and the media, until it became common wisdom and everyday practice. From the middle of the twentieth century, at the latest, it was hardly possible to nurture strong erotic interests in another man without becoming 'homosexual'. Thus, an effect of this apparatus of analysis has been to contribute to the reproduction of the homosexual species. And if we view the matter from the individual 'homosexual's' angle and ask what use has been made of him in this context, the answer is that he has functioned as *raw material in the production process through which 'the homosexual' was continually reproduced.*

2 At the same time, however, this apparatus for analysing the homosexual was obviously unable to exist without the homosexual. This is a very simple and trivial inference: if he really had been successfully eliminated, there would no longer have been any basis for an apparatus to analyse him. The homosexual has thus functioned as the *nutrient that kept this apparatus alive*: as raw material and justification for its functioning, and hence also as the fund-raiser.[4]

3 However, this mechanism through which the homosexual and the homosexuality-analysing apparatus mutually reproduce is, for its part, just a piece of a more extensive complex. The homosexual is only one of the figures who has to worry about his sexuality; ultimately, every modern person is instilled with such worries. Similarly, the apparatus developing around the analysis of the homosexual is only a part of the larger apparatus set up to analyse

sexuality in general. Further still, sexuality is only one part, albeit a particularly pithy part, of that *self* that modern people worry about; just as the sexuality-analysing apparatus is only one part of the larger apparatus that is directed towards analysing the self. In sum, an extensive complex with two poles, a complex for self-supervision, self-analysis and self-control.[5]

In this complex, *the homosexual* has been a protagonist. Not only was he an ideal-type of the modern person's self and its structure and surrender;[6] he has also functioned as a reminder of the justification and necessity for this constant self-supervision, self-analysis, self-control and self-surrender. Precisely because the inner forces hide themselves, no one can feel sure. The homosexual has been *one of the vital links between the two poles in this complex, one of the crucial conveyor belts by means of which it has reproduced itself.* The modern self, and the modern concern with it – with what it *really* is a person wants, with whether one is *oneself* – has developed and kept itself alive not least with the aid of 'the homosexual'.[7]

3 Surfaces

In the city, individuals are deposited among 'the crowd'. Every day they encounter masses of other people whom they don't know and never *can* get to now – if only because there are too many people to get to know them all. One does not, therefore, meet them as Fred Bloggs, married to Doris, wending their way to the fields, etc.; instead, it is as *that which can be seen, in passing*. In other words: one encounters them *as surfaces*; by the same token each individual becomes aware that he or she is a surface for the others. Existence in the city, therefore, implies that a surface breaks loose from people, or rather it is *constituted* – established, developed; it was not there before.

But what about the remainder of the person? At the same time as a surface is formed, an inner, a depth, an essence develops – a *self*. This is partly a kind of residuum of what was before and what otherwise is and cannot get absorbed in the surface: being Fred Bloggs, siring his children, boozing away his pay, and so on. For that reason alone, the self is already an entity set in a certain opposition to the surface. Yet a number of other factors are also active in producing this 'self' and have, in fact, been so for many centuries. We have already looked at essential ingredients in what became the result: the 'inner' or 'psychic self' that urges and must supervise and analyse itself; the 'sensitive self' that suffers and savours; the 'empty self' that can never really wholeheartedly get absorbed in anything.

What we now have, then, is a person who has fallen into two parts: an inner self on the one hand, and a surface on the other. The way is thus opened for exploiting this surface in various ways. It can, and must, be modelled. This *design of surfaces* I term *aestheticization*. The more detailed implications of the word will become apparent as I proceed to examine some of the forms of surface design.

Signal One way of designing one's surface is to make it into a signal. For instance, when a man puts on a leather jacket, it may be because he wishes to express, to signal that he is a rocker. Something similar applies to all attire.

The signal function of the surface provides the basis for a *signal aesthetics*. This accentuates the correlation between the self and the surface, inner and outer, content and form. The content must be expressed in the form; the form must signal the content, the way it is supposed to be or would like to be. The aesthetic criterion applied to judge whether such design is successful or not, therefore, is the *congruence* between form and content: only those elements of the form that best express the content must be there, and precisely those must be there.

There is something idyllic about the surface as a signal, something anti-alienative that must delight any old Hegelian Marxist or existentialist. If the inner suffuses the outer, the surface is no longer something detached, rendered autonomous and alienated, for it is regained by becoming one's own consciously intended product. But even among the signal functions of the surface dangers are lurking, waiting to rear their party-pooping head: what if the surface refuses to express the inner? If it expresses something contrary? If it sends out conflicting signals? Think of *punk*, or think of *drag*. Surely, the point here is not that the surface is supposed to plainly express an inner. Once a surface has detached itself, a number of possibilities are available that enable it to turn or to be turned against the self so as not simply to express it but to comment on it in some way or other. We may call the aesthetics attaching to this form of surface a *conflicting-signal aesthetics*. The criterion on which evaluation is based is then *incongruence*: the surface marks its detachment from the self; on the other hand, no more so than still allows it to maintain a commenting relationship to it.

Symbol Irrespective of whether the surface is designed to signal the self directly or send conflicting signals, it must make use of symbols. Take a leather jacket, for instance; classic *Marlon Brando style*. Even before a person puts it on, it symbolizes something – a greater context of particular types of person ('rockers'), a particular universe of interaction and interplay: violence, sex, booze-ups, motorbikes, recklessness, etc. This particular symbolic function of the leather jacket has been considerably blurred over recent years; but it is still quite generally sensed. Similarly so with all other dress: only because it symbolizes something – an affiliation with a particular social universe with specific norms, activities, etc. – can a person try to give expression to his or her self by wearing it. The aesthetic criterion at work here is that the symbol must as precisely as possible *concentrate* or *crystallize* the greater context of signification to which it refers.

Those wanting to signal who they are, therefore, are forced to make use of symbols. But it may also happen that the symbol is detached from this function. For example: it is possible to put on a leather jacket without wishing to be a rocker. In such cases, the symbol has only its symbol function left: to represent the semantic universe belonging to a leather jacket. In this detachment process, several things happen at once. Firstly, the surface detaches itself from *the self*. Whether it is Tom, Dick or Harry who is wearing this leather jacket makes absolutely no difference; it is the leather jacket and what it symbolizes that is significant. The individual is reduced to a carrier machine for the surface. Secondly, the surface also detaches itself from any real-term attachment to the semantic context it symbolizes. This person *is* not a rocker with all the associations that entails; of significance is that he *symbolizes* a rocker. The independence of the surface is taken at its word and exploited. What is of interest, sexually for instance, is to take part symbolically – *purely symbolically* – in this universe. Such detachment processes are widespread in both women's and men's outfits. They are undoubtedly made easy by the fact that the semantic universes to which symbols refer are already largely fictitious, in two ways: as products of professional make-believe (films, pornography, fashion magazines, etc.) and as results of projected feelings (dread, horror, lust, etc.).

When the surface as a symbol is detached, the basis exists for a pure symbol aesthetics. An example: Marlene Dietrich. Her surface is first and foremost a symbol. This was made explicit in Maximilian Schell's 1984 film about her.[8] The director wanted to penetrate beyond the image, the surface, and Marlene put up fierce resistance. She wanted to *be* her surface – as a symbol – the great star, the celebrated diva, the chanteuse, the great dedicated actress, the Woman (with a capital W), *femme fatale*, and so on. It was irrelevant whether she had been given milk or gruel as a baby in Berlin, or how she now looked in her old age. (Nor did she wish to be filmed now; only her voice was heard.) The thing of importance was the glittering surface: *Marlene Dietrich* – as she made her entrance in her trailing mink cape, 'falling in love again'.

A further development of the surface as a pure symbol will attempt to have the surface, while rubbing shoulders as closely as possible with its semantic context, still mark *per se* that it refers neither to a self nor to a real world – in other words, that it is purely symbolic. That could scarcely be the case with Marlene Dietrich; more so with Mae West who, to my eyes, always embodies a distance in her *femme fatale* figure.

Pure surface The surface can also be designed in a third basic way, however. It is possible to relate to it as completely detached, not merely from the self, not merely from any real-term attachment to a semantic context, but from any semantic context whatsoever. Of course, it is impossible to create a design that does not *also* signal and symbolize something, but the emphasis can be very differently distributed. If it is on the surface as pure surface, the basis exists for a form of design which I will call pure-aesthetic. This is a kind of *l'art pour l'art*: the surface is designed for the sake of framing it and framing it *as* a pure surface. Examples of this aesthetics may be combinations of leather jacket and silk tie. Or Balmain's dresses.

Criteria for the success of this form of aesthetics abound. Were they to be collected under one heading, it might be *the un-seen*, the hitherto unseen. But there are many different possibilities for creating this, many different subcriteria: the grotesque, bizarre, monstrous, oversized, extravagant, vulgar, scandalous; the contradictory, garish, mannered, gaudy, flamboyant; the simple, matching; the ornamental, elaborate, artificial, unnatural. Further, the surface that can be framed is not merely that of the attire or of the hair, but of the body itself – for instance in bodybuilding. When ordinary men do a little weight-training, their intentions are no doubt mostly signal-aesthetic in nature: they wish to signal they are real men. But in bodybuilding proper, the purely aesthetic has taken over: the body's surface is designed for its own sake. If Arnold Schwarzenegger died now, he would surely be embalmed and exhibited at the Museum of Modern Art, alongside Yves Saint-Laurent's sartorial creations.

In the modern world it is not only on persons that a surface is constituted but also on *things*. They – or at least those of the great majority – used once perhaps to be designed in keeping with 'primordial' patterns handed down; with industrialization and the capitalist mode of production, that is no longer on. A surface now detaches itself, both for reasons of production – concerning the most efficient operating sequence or the development of new products – and for reasons of circulation, i.e. regard for the market, for competition. The surface must now be framed in a consciously costed and calculated way – *industrial design* arises, and with it a new specialist worker: the industrial designer.

To a large extent, the same aesthetic possibilities exist for designing the surfaces of things as for those of people. I shall illustrate this with a few examples of industrial design. In *Victorian* or *Wilhelminian* (also known as historicist) design, the symbol-aesthetic outweighs the signal-aesthetic and the pure-aesthetic. A lamp, for example, brimming with ornament and borne by a winged female figure, is not intended first and foremost to provide light. It is intended to adorn, i.e. to provide certain symbolic gains connoting luxury and idleness. Industrially mass-produced goods like this must crystallize a fantasy world of feudal splendour. However, this does not involve the object attempting in itself to mark that it is only or primarily a symbol. On the contrary, it presents itself as if its surface were the purest expression of its very fibre: this is what a real lamp looks like. *Functionalism*, on the other hand, is signal-aesthetic in its self-knowledge: the form of things, the design of their surfaces, is allegedly intended to express and signal their utilitarian functions, not bog them down with all manner of symbolism. Notwithstanding, the pure-aesthetic often dominates and terrorizes the functions, as can be seen in both furniture and architecture. In some 'postmodernist' design, the pure-aesthetic has taken over, and done so self-consciously. Things are first and foremost surface – never mind whether they have any use. Thus, pure-aesthetic criteria govern this design: the shocking, vulgar, meaningless. Chairs with a bicycle saddle on a wooden elephant, tables with snapped-off corners and under-lighting.

A third kind of surface production and surface sensibility is related to the emergence of modern *visual media*: photography, film and television. With them, it becomes possible *literally* to detach surfaces from persons, things and interactions, and hence, to design these surfaces, aestheticize them. A photo, for instance, is completely defenceless; it can be cropped, shaded, retouched, etc. And such handling becomes imperative for production and market reasons. Other factors as well make this aesthetic design necessary: including the experience that no single picture provides adequate coverage of any one phenomenon. These necessities, in turn, have repercussions on the actual recording process: since the picture sees only the surface, the surface must be designed even before the picture is taken.

Again, the same basic possibilities exist for the design of pictures as for other detached surfaces. The signal-aesthetic element may predominate, as with portrait photos of politicians radiating firmness of principle, resolve, breadth of view and foresight – this whole strength of character being produced, not least, by a splendid interplay of lighting, retouching, shading, cropping, camera angle. Or the symbol-aesthetic may dominate, as in tourist postcards intended to represent the quintessence of a nation or region. Finally, the pure-aesthetic may preponderate. An example is the picture of the exploding American space ship *Challenger*. Seven people are in the process of burning up; but no one can tell that from the picture; it has to be explained by accompanying words. *In itself*, the picture signals nothing, symbolizes nothing. But it looks imposing. Although, here again, it would certainly not be as interesting if it did not have this macabre backdrop to signal, and this great discharge to symbolize. It is this marriage of pure aesthetics and latent semantic aesthetics that seduced all the world's male editors to feature it on their front pages.

There is yet a fourth factor of crucial importance in the modern development of surfaces: the emergence of *the homosexual*. In the previous section, I have detailed how this new type of person is and must be particularly sensitive to surfaces; and the background to this: city life, role awareness, the need to signal and so on. With such qualities, the homosexual becomes an essential carrier and accelerator in the processes leading to the formation of surfaces and of a sense of surface. It is he who settles down into the pores of industrial design – and who *else* should it be, one might well ask; in their own individual ways, the gender positions largely exclude both men and women from it.[9]

Homosexuals, then, become designers of clothes, person-surfaces and things; and they populate the worlds of photography, film and television. I am not claiming, of course, that no one other than homosexuals has designed clothes and taken pictures (even though one can occasionally have one's doubts). I am claiming that there are *many* homosexuals in these occupations, not least among the aesthetic avant-garde setting the trend for others.

Such a thesis is, by the nature of the case, difficult to argue empirically. Even among the avant-garde, indeed even among the celebrities, it would be hard in many cases to pierce the mystery-mongering that envelops homosexuality. But the thesis is theoretically plausible, and is not *prima facie* out of sync with the empirical material, as anyone – or anyone in the know – will be able to ascertain from leafing through photographic books or fashion magazines.[10]

In the modern world, then, a detachment of surfaces occurs, and a sense of surface is developed. So far, we have focused particularly on one aspect of this sense, related to the design of surfaces. The other aspect concerns *the experience* of them. It now becomes possible to experience surfaces as signals, but also to experience them as conflicting signals, as purely symbolic and as pure-aesthetic – in other words, to experience them *as* surfaces. This, by the way, also increases the possibility of experiencing them in ways other than those envisaged by a designer.

As I wrote in chapter IV, it has become common – at any rate in certain circles – to designate a number of the forms of experience that see the surface *as* surface by the word *camp*. 'Camp sees everything in quotation marks', as Susan Sontag says.[11] The word is thus used in the broad sense. But, as mentioned, it can also be used in a narrow sense, referring to the experience of a particular form of mismatch between the surface as a signal and the content: they are at one and the same time grotesquely and pathetically out of proportion to one another. *Kitsch* is another term for the experience of superficiality. It cannot be neatly distinguished from 'camp', and like the latter it can be used quite broadly; but it can also be reserved for specific experiences: of mock homeliness and remade originality, of extreme extravaganza and no content whatsoever.[12]

Aestheticization, then, is the name for a process in which surfaces come into existence as surfaces and are designed and experienced according to the aesthetic standards of the eye: beautiful or boring, unsuccessful or adequate. Aestheticization is closely related to *sexualization*: they merge and must always appear in some blend or other, since both are largely founded in the worlds of the city, commodities and visual media; moreover, both are furthered by the homosexuals as urban beings and producers of design and images.[13]

Of course, it can be maintained that the detachment of surfaces and the sense of surface are not a specifically modern phenomenon. And obviously, analogous phenomena or earlier forms can be found in previous and other cultures than the modern West. Here, however, a series of operative factors develop which are either new or act with hitherto unseen efficacy from the end of the eighteenth century and through the nineteenth: large-scale urbanization, industrialization, modern visual media and the homosexual person-type; and here this series of factors congregate and reinforce one another. For example, the sense of surface developed in the city is strengthened through the visual media, and vice versa. At the same time, the spread of television not only brings the detachment of picture surfaces but also the urban reality and its forms of experience out into the remotest recesses of the country: every evening, those worthy farmers and fishermen who populate the brains of community researchers, live in the city, in *the crowd*, frequenting countless other people they do not know, in a constant stream, encountering them as mere surface. In this way, aestheticization and sexualization become constantly expanding and tendentially accelerating features of everyday life. In modern societies, we increasingly inhabit a world of surfaces that have detached themselves more and more from the inner, the self, the use value; which are consciously, or at any rate intentionally, designed on the basis of a perception of their being surfaces; and which are experienced *as* surfaces. In the process, the emphasis is also shifted from the signal-aesthetic, coming increasingly to be located in the conflictingly signal-aesthetic, the purely symbolic-aesthetic and the pure-aesthetic.[14]

4 Destruction

There have long been rumours circulating that the homosexuals undermine culture. Not only because each and every one of them mocks decency and defies morality; but because as a group, through the creations of cultural life (novels, theory, plays, etc.), they operate an overall campaign to erode the very foundations of culture. A homosexual clique, a conspiracy, a *mafia*, sits there orchestrating cultural life; from theatres and publishing houses, as authors and critics, actors and directors, it sows its subversive seed.

The thing is – so these rumours would have it – that the homosexual culture producers wish to conceal they're homosexual and, moreover, are rancorous towards the world of 'ordinary people'. This, it is sometimes conceded, may be explainable in terms of the prejudiced attitude of those around them and the discrimination of society. The result, however – we are told – is disastrous. Because the homosexual artists dare not express their experiences directly, they conceal them in heterosexual figures and relations, which thus appear distorted. And because the homosexuals are jealous and vindictive towards the heterosexual world, it is not merely distorted but also disparaged and ridiculed. Above all, this applies to the sexes and the relationship between them: women are portrayed as dumb or calculating, vengeful or alcoholic, cannibalistic or monstrous; men as oafish or egocentric, ruttish or spineless, *beaux-esprits* or beasts; marriage as a disaster.

These artists, the rumours go on, are moreover in league with the homosexual critics, of which there is a whole gaggle. These, too, wish to disguise what they really are and likewise suffer from vengefulness and jealousy of the heterosexuals' world. Thus, in their reviews, they distort the actual nature of homosexuals' plays or novels and promote their dissemination by way of all too uncritical acceptance. Add to this, we are admonished, the swarms of homosexual producers, directors, composers, stage designers, choreographers and media opinion-formers. In a nutshell: plot, mind-policing, destructive attacks on the common values of society – on 'the normal world', on 'human life' and 'the driving forces behind it'.[15]

The rumours, of course, have uttered the truth. Perhaps not as regards a homosexual conspiracy, for many reasons; as Michael Bronski observes: 'Imagine Tennessee Williams, Cole Porter, Lorenz Hart, Marcel Proust, Jean Genet, and Liberace getting together to plot the overthrow of Western morality!'[16] But as regards destructivity. Large proportions of the literature, theory, film, theatre and so on produced by homosexuals contain attacks on existing conventions, norms, rules. But the destructive is not *merely* an expression of a more or less justified homosexual aggression against the suppression by surrounding society. What is being overlooked here is what comes forth in the destruction itself, what it and only it permits to emerge: that which takes place *beneath* the surface, beneath the common conventions, norms and rules, beneath the established forms of self-expression available to content. Only when these are dismantled does the sequestered, the suppressed, the suffering emerge. And the portrayal of this suppression in connection with women, heterosexual men and man–woman relationships is not *just* an expression of a 'literary transvestitism', in which the homosexual, being unable to write openly about his own experiences, dresses them in the garb of 'ordinary people' while in the final analysis it is merely himself and his own feelings he is really depicting.[17] It is also an expression of the *empathy with the suffering* – homosexual or heterosexual, male or female – and the *capacity for compassion* with which the homosexual is imbued by dint of his 'privileged' access to suffering, gender and sensitivity.[18]

Only through the destruction of prevalent surfaces and common norms can the excluded and the suppressed emerge; and only *in* this process of decomposition can it emerge, for it never exists as a positive something behind the suppression, only pervaded by it. Regarding the suppressed, one can be positive only by being destructive.[19]

Now and then, therefore, the homosexual culture producer is even more destructive than he is rumoured to be. Bang's 'By The Wayside' is not the tragic idyll as which it is often read, with the meek, sensitive woman suffering at the hands of her rough, unsympathetic husband, and pining away in the shadow of the lilac trees as the trains pass by.[20] When Katinka Bai in torpid vegetativeness waxes sentimental over the platonic lover's sun in Sorrento and is repulsed by the sight of her fleshly husband cutting his toe-nails in the bedroom, she is ludicrous. Yet at the same time she is also poignant, because there is compassionate pain in the portrayal of a life reduced to vague dreams. And when, after Katinka's death, Mr Bai vainly seeks consolation and satisfaction with the capital's women of easy virtue, he is not merely primitive and brutish, and his defeat not merely well-earned punishment for his shameless besmirching of his wife's memory; he is also a victim of her lack of *flesh*, or more broadly speaking of the hopeless norms which at once called for eternal union and rendered it impossible. Bang's method is exemplary: he simply displays, displaying the destruction and the destroyed in one and the same movement.

Thus, precisely through his radical destructivity, the homosexual has been instrumental in enhancing the modern world's sympathy, its feeling for those suffering, and in developing its notion of suppression. There are bound to be statements averring that this is not specific to the homosexuals' production of culture, but that 'it is true of all good art'. So much the better.[21]

5 Avant-garde in itself

That the homosexuals are an avant-garde is an idea only the homosexuals could come up with. Others may have stressed, occasionally and as a kind of attenuating circumstance, how cultivated and ethically superior they often are (tending swiftly, however, to add that this is far from the case for all of them)[22] – but avant-garde! Nonetheless, such notions are relatively widespread among homosexuals themselves, and it is all too easy to reject them out of hand as pure and simple justification and compensation.[23] Many diverse ideas are at play; I shall outline a few principal forms here.

The vaguest of these are the notions of 'the list of kings', an endless succession of homosexual celebrities from 'Jonathan to Gide' through Socrates, Alexander the Great and Shakespeare. This idea crops up countless times in the lifetime of the homosexual, even as the subject matter of whole books.[24] It serves an out-and-out defensive purpose, of course: 'If it's OK for notabilities to be that way, it can't be wrong for me'; but it also has more or less offensive overtones: 'The more notabilities who are that way and the further back they go, the more respectable it is'; and, essentially: 'Their being great is *due to* their being homosexual'. The idea is thus intended to convince by virtue of its *glorious venerability*. The inherent problem is that there was no distinct homosexual species before the late nineteenth century, which may cast some doubt on its venerability. Moreover, it often leaves a disappointingly vapid impression: were there really no more? – and, is the inclusion of all those inferior Austrian generals and Hungarian lieutenants really necessary to give it the appearance of something even halfway impressive? This sheds doubt on its gloriousness.

The idea of the 'homosexual list of kings' may be said to concern an elite rather than an avant-garde proper. A more precise idea – or series of such ideas – about homosexuals as an avant-garde has notions of *androgyny* at its core.

A 'feminist-socialist' version of this emphasizes the homosexuals' feminine traits: intuition, emotionalism, mildness as well as a sense of nature and intimacy, as opposed to the man's abstract and calculating intellect, aggression, destructiveness and imperiousness. The homosexuals can thus show the way for a new type of man, thereby not merely spearheading – together with women – the emancipation of women (and of men – from their traditional masculinity), but also that of society, since these male traits and values perfuse and sustain the existing, suppressive, exploitative and belligerent society.

Another version of this idea stresses not particularly the homosexual's feminine aspects but his *unification of traits from both genders*: this places him above the constraints of each gender and thus in a position to accomplish things within the grasp of neither the woman nor the man (such as various kinds of 'arts': healing, prophecy, intermediation between the sexes, etc.); perhaps he is even above the constraints of *nature* and connected with the supernatural. This 'spiritualistic-superhuman' version thus draws material for its avant-garde notion from figures in other and earlier cultures (berdaches, shamans).

The two versions frequently merge and are difficult to keep distinct, though the first has surely predominated. They crop up at different points in the history of the homosexual, particularly in times of ferment; as with Carpenter in England and Freimark in Germany around the turn of the century, and in Denmark with Fogedgaard, one of the founders of the Danish homophile movement of 1948. They achieved an international boom with 'gay feminism' in connection with the gay liberation of the 1970s.[25]

The problem – for me – with the superhuman-spiritualistic version of this idea is that it is cocooned in a cosmic view which I do not share. As to the 'feminist-socialist' variant, I am a little more doubtful. The fundamental notion, as we have seen, is that homosexuals *are* androgynous, uniting female and male characteristics. Insofar as 'are' seeks justification by reference to *nature* (that's how they are 'by nature', 'biologically', 'from birth'), this must be said to be anything but certain. Insofar as it is justified with reference to being the way they just 'happen to be' – whatever the reason – my first objection is that they are obviously not all like that. Nevertheless, some surely are, and with others it may be clandestine, or indeed be engendered by this very talk of feminine aspects. This cannot be dismissed out of hand, of course, even though I have my doubts; my next objection, however, is that there lurks a contradiction in this version of the avant-garde idea: how can the homosexuals be avant-garde in a 'struggle' supposed to produce more 'feminine' men when these are often not the ones they fantasize about or desire in practice? Actual constraints are one thing, fundamental potentialities another, you might object. I am not altogether convinced, but will break off the discussion here and return to it in chapter VI.

Yet it is also possible to conceive of the homosexual as avant-garde by virtue not of his femininity but of his *masculinity*. The point of departure here is precisely that the homosexual is a man who is interested in other men and who therefore cultivates virile values. This turns into an avant-garde idea when coupled with notions that masculine traits, and relationships between men, are of importance not only to the homosexuals but are rightly, or ought to be, dominant aspects of society as a whole.

These ideas, too, are found in different variants, which may more or less fuse in practice. The emphasis can be on the equal, the mutual, the sharing and the emotive in man-to-man relationships, seeing in them a basis for solidarity and democracy and a safeguard against materialism, competition and domination; or the aggressive and dominating aspects of masculinity can be accentuated, with their alleged importance in maintaining the existence of society outwardly and its order inwardly (Sparta – or ancient Japan – being the ideal). Moreover, the difference in age and the educational aspect of man-to-man relationships can be stressed; or the relationship between peers.

Ideas such as these enjoyed their heyday in Germany during the early decades of the twentieth century, as with the circle round the magazine *Der Eigene* (Friedländer, Brand, von Kupffer) and with people who enjoyed some affiliation to the German youth movement (Blüher, Wyneken).[26] The more totalitarian variants (like Friedländer's and Blüher's, in particular) were largely rendered impossible by their – spiritual more than practical – affinity with Nazism, although they may still crop up sporadically. Nor does a more democratic version seem to have been significant in recent years: the new gay movement grew up in a climate that virtually predetermined it for 'feminist-socialist' avant-garde notions; and even though tendencies to emphasize male traits and values were soon to make their impact among the broad masses of homosexuals, this 'masculinization' was not associated with avant-garde claims.

Yet another avant-garde idea attaches to *sexuality*. The homosexual is the one that refuses to allow his lusts and pleasures to be contained within the ways dictated by society, and therefore he is particularly hard hit by society's oppression. He thus incarnates 'the oppressed' and 'a promise of happiness', all at the same time and particularly so, thereby becoming as well the rebel *par excellence*: the very person to spearhead the struggle destined to lead to the emancipation of lust and pleasure for everyone. Ideas such as these are theoretically left-Freudian in inspiration (Marcuse, etc.) and enjoyed their heyday in the gay liberation movements of the early 1970s, often in combination with 'feminist-socialist' views.[27]

One may have misgivings about the Freudian overtones in these notions: about the inner drive that urges and seeks to escape, that underlies and is the cause of all possible things – all possible evil if suppressed, all possible good if liberated. Yet though the rhetoric is more or less left-Freudian, the idea need not be so in its substance; the way I have portrayed it above, it might just as well derive its inspiration from the critics of left-Freudianism.[28]

Rather, the problem is that it is difficult to imagine the homosexual playing the role of vanguard for those who may perhaps wish to have their sexual, but by no means their homosexual, desires liberated. And even if this special resistance to the homosexual could be overcome, why should they derive the stuff of their ideas for the future from him rather than all kinds of other sources? These are serious questions which we need to investigate more closely.

There are, altogether, a great many conditions that must be met before it is reasonable to speak of an avant-garde in this context. Firstly, the direction in which the avant-garde is allegedly ahead of the others must be desirable, or at least tolerable. You would hardly call Hitler's storm troopers from the 1920s avant-garde, although they were forerunners of what was to come. Secondly, those one calls avant-garde must actually and demonstrably be 'ahead', in the sense that they represent something new and extraordinary and cannot just as well be claimed to be self-obstructing or moving backwards. Thirdly, it must be possible to show that the others – those the avant-garde is ahead of – are capable of moving in the direction of the avant-garde. Fourthly, the avant-garde must demonstrably be capable of affecting others in its direction. There are three sub-conditions here. (a) What the avant-garde represents – its 'message' – must be such that it can affect the others; at least, it must not arouse animosity in them or cause them to strive in a different direction. (b) The others must be motivated (or motivatable) to 'listen to' the people who make up the avant-garde, or at least it must be possible to bypass any communication blocks. (c) There must be channels or media of communication, so that the 'message' of the avant-garde can reach the others. – Of course, one could very well speak of 'avant-garde' in as much as one group is ahead of the others and they, unaffected by it, nevertheless end up moving in its direction; but in that case it is an *avant-garde in and for itself* and not for the others.

The notions of a homosexual avant-garde discussed above are problematic on one or more of these points: either the direction is unacceptable to the majority; or it is doubtful whether the homosexuals are actually 'ahead' in the direction stated; or there is no reason to believe that the others will move that way; or it is hard to imagine any form of transport between the homosexuals and the others. The latter is a recurring problem.

The exposition of the homosexual and his relationship with society that I have presented in chapter IV and in the preceding sections of this chapter sets the stage for a different notion of the avant-garde, however. Central here is the thought that homosexuals have developed special characteristics and manners, a special form of existence which is an answer to such modern living conditions as city, normlessness, images, generalized and impersonal surveillance, science, gender problematic, absence of matter-of-course identities and communities. This they have done *before* others and *more* than others, in a mixture of desire and distress: in part they were pressured towards these living conditions, not least as a result of oppression; and in part they enjoyed the options inherent in them. Thus they lived, earlier and more persistently than others, close to these modern conditions of life, exploiting the possibilities and tackling the contradictions; the others had to get home to the family. But as the usual 'buffers' against the conditions of modern life also crumble for others in step with general developments, these conditions become a reality for them as well. In short: the homosexuals have lived with and responded to the conditions of the modern world for a hundred years, the 'heterosexuals' are increasingly beginning to do so; in that sense, the homosexuals are 'avant-garde'.

Let us examine more closely whether it is reasonable to speak of an avant-garde here, based on the premises we have just posited. It is possible that the perspective outlined by the homosexuals' form of existence, this direction, does not appear enticing and that, in addition, many will consider it so frightening that they will put up a struggle. I should like to place that question in parentheses and return to it in chapter VI. As regards the next two premises, it is certain that the homosexual form of existence has a series of characteristics which are historically new and extraordinary, and that it is not impossible to envisage the others moving in that direction – indeed, much indicates that things are heading that way. But will they be influenced by the homosexuals here? Precisely in this version of avant-garde ideas – unlike so many other versions – the character of the avant-garde 'message' is such that in principle it can resonate with the interest of the others. If the homosexuals here are avant-garde, it is because they have for a long time lived closer to the conditions of modern life, and it is these same conditions that the others also live under and are increasingly coming close to. The homosexuals are not, as it were, standing yelling to the 'heterosexuals' from another world.

In itself, then, the background exists for the homosexuals to be an avant-garde influencing the others. However, there is reason to believe that the more explicit it appears from the avant-garde message that the 'sender' is homosexual, the less hearing it will receive.[29] In other words, there is a motivation block; as far as I can tell, there are in principle only two ways of surmounting this. Either the conditions of modern life must make themselves felt to a degree and in a way as to make the erotic preference eventually appear rather inconsequential, thus cancelling out the block;[30] or else the block must be bypassable. That involves avoiding the unequivocal articulation of the erotic preference, so that no hint of the sender's homosexuality emerges, or at any rate it remains in the twilight that generally shrouds homosexuality in modern societies: is–is not; will–will not; knows of–does not know. Hence also certain requirements regarding the communication media: an influence can only take place via those media which are not particularly homosexual, that is common media with a common content. Two routes, in particular, are significant in this connection. The homosexual can make his mark on products which are circulating in the general commodities trade (clothes, postcards, etc.) and/or are accessible among the 'cultural public' (theatre, reviews, literature, etc.). Therefore, it is through his occupational function in particular that the homosexual exerts influence, and through this that he links up with the existing powers, such as capital and the intellectual and artistic public. And, breaking it down roughly, his stamp can be left on the semantic content of the product or the stylistic design.

In the preceding sections, we have already seen two examples of how these channels of influence function, so that homosexuals really have been avant-garde here. By influencing the production of style, they have been instrumental in creating self-contained, detached surfaces and in developing the sense of surfaces as surfaces. And by influencing the generation of cultural products with a semantic content (drama, painting, theory, etc.), they have been instrumental in developing the modern world's criticism of norms, its notions of suppression and its feeling for suffering.

To the extent that homosexuals can function as a real avant-garde in other aspects as well, the influence must surely flow along the same channels. Undoubtedly, some such influence has already taken effect as to certain features of the homosexual form of existence, such as sexualization and restlessness. And surely it is conveyed primarily through the stylistic design of cultural products, and less so through their semantic content. But many other features of the homosexual form of existence – at any rate, so far – have hardly found common channels of communication, such as urban pleasures and network life, indeed the creation of social life altogether. These features cannot so easily entrench themselves in the stylistic design of things and objects, of clothes and pictures (although it is possible to a certain degree). To the extent that the homosexuals have been avant-garde here, they have surely been so mostly *in and for themselves*, not for the others.[31]

In conclusion, I would ask the reader to recall that in my discussion on the homosexuals as an avant-garde I have left aside the question of whether this influence is desirable or not. In no way have I claimed that it is necessarily intentional. Nevertheless, this version of the avant-garde idea will surely irritate homosexuals and heterosexuals alike. It will annoy those homosexuals who refuse-to-be-homosexuals, precisely because it presupposes that there is such a thing as 'homosexuals'; and it may annoy those who are willing or even happy to be homosexuals, because they will not think it so nice to be linked with characteristics such as superficiality and restlessness. And the heterosexuals will be upset because it always annoys them to hear that the homosexuals are avant-garde in anything but an unambivalently negative sense. Let us make a concession: if homosexuals are an avant-garde by virtue of their particular relationship with the living conditions of the modern world, they are not the only ones to be so. Other groups, too, have lived close to and responded to these conditions, in the same direction as the homosexuals, or more or less differently: artists, journalists, students, bohemians, poets. Obviously, there are quite some overlaps.

6 Evil

It has often been stressed that the homosexual serves as a scapegoat and bogeyman. But the fact that he can do so is due to his being *evil incarnate*.[32]

Evil – even in modern societies – lurks everywhere. The Queen can be shot, the grass can turn radioactive, the 'Chinese' or the 'Moslems' can attack, passing men can rip open their overcoats and flash their privates. Evil thus has any number of variants, but they can be divided up with certain reasonableness as follows. Evil is what threatens or actually undermines

1 the individual's life and well-being;
2 the group's biological ability to reproduce;
3 the external material conditions for the group's existence (food, soil, etc.);
4 the group's norms, values, institutions, forms of power;
5 the group's identity or the symbolic representative of this (e.g. the People, the Queen, the Nation, etc.);
6 the cosmic order.

This classification differentiates between various kinds of evil on the basis of the various main dimensions of life and society that evil can affect; it makes reasonable sense for a modern, scientifically influenced outlook and is not devoid of a certain connection with the horse-sense of the common life-world. There is, after all, a difference whether it is oneself that is sick or one's potatoes, or the Queen.

That evil can threaten and actually undermine life and society is an expression of it having – or being – *power*. Again, there are manifold and sinister forces at play, though these as well can be divided up with a certain reasonableness on the basis of the six dimensions listed. And in order to achieve its aims, evil takes on different *shapes*, corresponding with the different powers. It incarnates itself, not only but also in human form.

Modern-day notions of evil are further characterized by a special duplicity. Two conceptual universes merge: a more recent one, influenced by a natural-science mentality that explains evil on the basis of bacteria, genes, pressure factors in the earth's crust, etc.; and an older, or at any rate different, one that derives its explanations from other quarters. The two can exist alongside each other, one can prevail over the other, and they can combine to form the oddest combinations.

In this universe of evil, the homosexual plays a leading role. I will illustrate this by means of a few examples.[33]

The threat to the individual's life and well-being In the final analysis, the power at work here is death; it can manifest itself in various guises, but also as the *contagiously diseased.*

There are a number of disease concepts at work in the symbolic universe of modern societies. One is moral, perhaps religious: illness is in some way or other self-inflicted; if a man gets sick, it is because his behaviour has dictated that this should be the outcome, or perhaps it is God's punishment for such conduct, an irresponsible action for which one should be held responsible, as the homosexual is assumed to be for his 'illness'. 'To contaminate' here is to act irresponsibly and inflict the 'disease' on others and/or expose oneself to it.[34]

The other main, modern view of illness is one of science – medical, psychiatric. That the homosexual is ill in that sense has been the subject of little doubt – practically the entire 'scientific' literature on homosexuality since the mid-nineteenth century would be absurd, were he not so. And during the twentieth century, these ways of thinking have become general.[35]

But can the homosexual also contaminate? Here, the impact of science seems to preclude it, for this 'disease' is not caused by virus, bacteria, fungi or parasites, but is regarded as being due to flaws either in the genetic material or in upbringing. This embarrassment has generated a good deal of resourcefulness, giving rise to a number of theories on how a transfer could nevertheless be envisaged: homosexual genetic material may have stowed away in otherwise completely normal parents' genetic equipment and in this way be passed on degenerately from great-uncles, cousins and second cousins; some homosexuals may be irresponsible enough to bring children into the world and in that way perpetuate the perverted heredity; if the homosexual lays a hand on a boy during puberty, the boy may be seduced and impaired for the rest of his life; the mere *presence* of a homosexual may suffice to 'pollute a government office';[36] indeed, a mere *knowledge* of the existence of homosexuals may be sufficient to contaminate.[37]

But the homosexual not only seems to embody the special disease of homosexuality, he also incarnates an unspecified, possibly unlimited series of other diseases. I have already hinted at this in connection with the notions of degeneration: mystically impaired genes, resulting now in one, now in another morbid outcome, transferred from one generation to another in an accelerating process of deterioration until the lineage finally perishes from them.[38] Or if his 'disease' is considered mentally conditioned, it is seen to be ineluctably bound up with a string of other psychological disorders; homosexuality is 'a neurotic distortion of the total personality'.[39]

In short: the homosexual is ill, and his illness is contagious, or at least transmissible. He is a cancerous tumour, an abscess, a plague. And if he has one illness, then he also has the other; one blends into the other or entails it; here, as throughout the realm of evil, no clear-cut dividing lines exist.

The threat to the group's biological reproduction It is possible that the dread of this threat often stems from other sources, and that it therefore involves rationalizations of other forms of dread. At any rate, there is pronounced disquiet about the survival of the lineage (the 'nation', 'race', 'people', 'kin', etc.). Again, the power looming is, of course, death; but the crucial thing here is not the individual's death but the extinction of the group. The symptoms are not the disease undermining the individual; rather, it is a lack of vitality, a weakness or 'softness', an inability to assert oneself, powerlessness, impotence, spinelessness and limpness. Its typical incarnations are the weakling, the coward, the impotent, the childless, the degenerate. And, not surprisingly after that list, the homosexual.

The homosexual, indeed, may be imagined to endanger the perpetuation of the group in many ways: partly, as we have seen, by seducing and corrupting those who are supposed to carry on the lineage; also by means of degeneration, the transmission of weak heredity factors; and finally, in the most enlightened form of horror: by simply having no children. This may seem reasonably innocent, but it is not; by way of an example, let us listen to Himmler's rational costings:

> We have here in Germany . . . about twenty million sexually mature and procreative men, i.e. men over sixteen . . . If I assume there are

> one to two million homosexuals, then this implies that about 7, 8 or 10 per cent of the men in Germany are homosexual. This means, if it remains so, that our people will perish as a result of this plague. A people cannot, in the long run, endure the equilibrium of its gender household is upset in this way . . . A people which has many children can count on global power and mastery of the world. A people of good race but with few children holds a one-way ticket to the grave, to insignificance in fifty or a hundred years, to extinction in 200 or 500 years.[40]

Logically enough, then, Himmler's advice is not to exterminate the homosexuals, which would not solve the population problem, but instead to prevent them from coming into existence (by avoiding an *overly* exaggerated cult of maleness and male sociality).

The threat to the external material conditions for the group's existence Whatever dark powers may once have been fancied to have masterminded droughts, flood, famines and so on, they seem to have been definitively and scientifically defined in modern times: these are *natural forces* (geological, climatic, zoological). In the process, the basis has also disappeared for these powers to incarnate in human form, e.g. as homosexuals. We *know*, after all, that the homosexual does not – as may have been imagined of his predecessor, the sodomite – cast spells on cattle and poison the wells.[41]

Yet, in this scientized world, there may remain one villain – the scientist. It is he (and male he is) who through his experiments causes a shift in the balance of life conditions; and it is he who puts hazardous substances into the hands of unscrupulous people such as the CIA, the Russians, the capitalists. Little wonder if these scientists are also homosexual (as little wonder that wizards and warlocks were also sodomites); and in fact, this is almost certainly the case with the mad scientist in the James Bond film we have looked at.[42]

The threat to the group's norms, values, institutions, forms of power What is it that poses a threat here? Some may be inclined to say it is the *disorderly*: something not being where it should be, defying classification in the great divisions. But that is not enough: not only is it not in its rightful position, but it is also elusive: it is the *slippery and slimy*, that which slip-slides away, constantly escaping. Even that is not enough, though: not merely is it not where it should be, and not merely can it not be pinned down – it also spreads: it is the *excessive, unbridled, debauched, dissolute* and *dissipated.*

However, these characterizations can also be used to varying degrees of the other evils; if something is particularly associated with the threat to the group's norms, values, institutions and forms of power, it must be sought elsewhere. Indeed, the very words no doubt point in the right direction already. What is threatening is not only disorder, slipperiness and debauchery but that which feels *lust* at disorder, slipperiness and debauchery. In other words, the power that poses a threat here is *lasciviousness* – whether it is regarded as the passions, the flesh, sexuality, the drive, desire or covetousness. Which is why it can also *tempt*, making it all the more perilous. Lust is what makes things tick here; its result is this combination of disorder, slipperiness, debauchery and lasciviousness; in a word: *filth.*

Depending on the norms, values, institutions and forms of power more specifically threatened by this filthy lust, it may be incarnated in a host of varied figures: e.g. the felon, the drug addict, the alcoholic, the sex-maniac, the effeminate, the child-molester. In any case, it may just as well be the homosexual, it seems. If being homosexual is not criminal in itself, the homosexual at any rate is of necessity given over to crime, both scientists and laymen have reasoned.[43] Another standard topic of scientific research has been whether homosexuality *per se* involved alcoholism or this was merely a secondary effect, or whether it was possibly alcoholism that led to homosexuality.[44] A similar discussion can be found on drug addiction.[45] As for the sex-maniac, the effeminate and the child-molester, the association with the homosexual is self-evident, for scientific literature and popular belief alike.[46]

The threat to the group's identity or its symbolic representative This identity and its symbolic representatives vary from group to group, from country to country, from one period to another: it may be the People, the King, the Army, the Race, Liberty, Socialism, the Fatherland, Honour or the local or national football team. The power that threatens here is *the foreigners*, possibly in the shape of *the enemy* and his minions, *the traitor*, *the spy*, *the agent.*

Here, too, the link with the homosexual is obvious, it would appear. To the communists, the fascists are homosexuals; to the fascists, the communists; to the democrats, both. If nothing else, the indigenous homosexuals are potential *security risks*: either *con amore* or else out of moral debility, or because they are forced to be so by the intimidation of disclosure.[47]

The threat to the cosmic order If one envisages God as engineering the cosmic order, it goes without saying that the power posing the threat is *the devil* (or the *chaos* that is at the bottom of both God and the Devil). Satan can appear in many manifestations; the homosexual, we are repeatedly assured, is one of them.

But in the modern symbolic universe, God has increasingly been succeeded by another cosmic principle: *nature*, in the sense of natural science. The threat to cosmic order, then, is the *unnatural.* Which brings us back to the paradoxes of rationalized thought, for if 'nature' is the principle governing cosmic order and at the same time dictates the regularities to which all things conform, how can anything unnatural arise? Notwithstanding, 'un-nature' apparently does exist: it appears for example as 'defects' in genes or 'disturbances' in hormones. Here again, as is repeatedly asserted, the homosexual is one of the figures in which this threat to nature can manifest itself.

As will be clear by now, a large number of contemporary notions about evil can reasonably be grouped in one or other of the six dimensions listed earlier. Other ideas are diffuse and do not pinpoint their emphasis specifically: notions of smut, depravity, rottenness, the disgusting, the furtive, the dark. Even those ideas whose prime focus is in a particular category do not lend themselves to being delimited to such. 'Ill', 'sick' and 'unnatural', for instance, may refer to any evil whatsoever. The various evils coalesce, collude, concoct and conspire.[48] It is this interconnectedness that makes it possible to speak of Evil as a unity.

It further transpires that there is no evil which the homosexual cannot embody. And since the whole point of the above explication was to illustrate this, I have drawn my examples and references relatively at random, singling out some of the more distinctive ones. Yet the ideas about the homosexual as the incarnation of evil are hardly random and sporadic. There is much to indicate that a *notional schema* concerning evil, with these six dimensions and with the homosexual as its incarnation, has been present whenever and wherever the homosexual has been known – i.e. in Western societies from the second half of the nineteenth century. Furthermore, there are good reasons to expect that once such a conceptual universe has been established, it will be kept alive. Not simply because various powers – primarily the self-analysis complex, but also the judicial system and the church – have an interest in maintaining it; but also because the homosexual seems to fit in extremely well with this schema, and because he has a particularly intimate connection with the forces that can activate it.

1 The homosexual, as we have seen from the examples, can actually (that is: symbolically) function as the incarnation of evil in *all* its dimensions. In varying degrees, however, this applies equally to a number of other figures; but there are particular reasons that make the homosexual *better suited* than them.
2 The homosexual, in contrast to e.g. the drug addict, carries around a particularly heavy historical legacy attaching him to evil. For at least six hundred years, his predecessor the sodomite was associated with disease, evasion from reproduction, witchcraft, debauchery, treachery and heresy.[49]
3 There *are* actually homosexuals who possess the dubious character traits ascribed to them. For one thing, there are homosexuals everywhere, so it would be strange if some of them were not sick, unscrupulous, spies, alcoholics or criminals. For another, it inheres in the logic of labelling and oppression procedures that, through various channels, those concerned may end up conforming to the attitudes others have towards them: that is, some homosexuals become or make themselves sick, sex-maniacs, spies, criminals, etc.[50] Unlike Pakistani or Arab immigrants, for instance, who are not perceived as being sick or effeminate, nor do they become so. Moreover, the homosexuals have a *special* affinity to some of these qualities for other reasons as well (see below, point 8).
4 The homosexual – unlike the black man, for instance – can hide, and indeed often does so. You never quite know where you have him; he can be lying in wait anywhere – just like evil.
5 The homosexual, as the incarnation of evil, is 'current' in all circles. He can be used by capitalists and communists, democrats and fascists, women and men, vicars and doctors. The only group for which he cannot incarnate evil would seem to be the homosexuals. Though that has not stopped him doing so for them, too: they have wished they were not homosexuals and found other homosexuals abhorrent.[51]
6 The homosexual, for the others, is associated with a more intimate dread, insofar as homosexuality is a disavowed desire of their own.[52] Contrary to this, an ordinary Dane may be quite certain that he is not a Greenlander.
7 The homosexual, to a lesser degree than other figures, is available for scientific rationalization of evil – having been turned into evil not least by way of science. In contrast, it is household knowledge

these days that the immigrant, for instance, should not be thought of as representing evil, nor the criminal of threatening the cosmic order. But when it comes to the homosexual, science itself has guaranteed that he is sick and unnatural.

8 The homosexual, as we have seen in chapter IV, is *particularly* associated with a series of factors that take on an especially precarious nature in *modern* societies: the norms, values, institutions and power relations connected to interpersonal relationships (gender performances, marriage, family relations, general intercourse with acquaintances and strangers). Being homosexual is identical to living in some way other than that prescribed by these forms and norms of social life. This special status of the homosexual is related to his special proximity to the particular conditions of modern life: the city, gender problematization, the self-analysis apparatus, the uncertainty of identity, etc., which constitute temptations and dangers for everyone. This makes him a figure especially apt to be experienced and represented as the *incarnation of the threats of modernity*. In contrast to e.g. neo-Nazis or Jehovah's Witnesses, whatever your feelings about them happen to be, at least there is no suspicion of their wishing to undermine the family or the gender order.

The homosexual, then, is one of the great figures of the modern world, and one of its most usable. He is *the universal equivalent of modern evil*: that which can represent and substitute any evil whatsoever. In fact, there is only one other figure seriously worthy of being entertained as his rival: *the Jew*. After the Second World War, however, the homosexual ousted the Jew, just as gold supplanted silver as universal money.[53] And there is reason to believe that this was not due just to Auschwitz, which for a time at least caused the Jew to change status from the incarnation of evil for the modern world to the incarnation of its bad conscience. The privileged position of the homosexual *vis-à-vis* the Jew may have to do as well with the feeling that his *use-value* as an incarnation of evil is also greater: to a greater extent than the Jew, he is capable of hiding; he is associated with a more intimate dread (after all, comparatively few people have 'Jewish blood in their veins'); as scientifically proven to be sick and unnatural, he is less accessible to scientific rationalization; and, above all, *he has a closer connection with the particularly precarious norms, values and forms of power of modern societies*. The accusations made against the homosexual may often appear so vague or absurd as to sound like pure nonsense, but in fact it is important to pay close attention to their wording. This betrays what is feared; and one will find that it very often relates to the specific aspects of socio-cultural modernity, in the sense explicated above. And it is surely because of this high use-value that the general public forgot that the homosexual was *also* victimized in the concentration camps; society, so to speak, could not afford for him too to be purified by them.[54]

As one of the great incarnations of evil, the homosexual performs various functions in modern societies.

He acts as a *bogeyman* and thus as a *disciplinary element*. The homosexual symbolizes evil: that which threatens existing life and society on one or more scores. That is to be shunned. Instead, one must seek the good, i.e. stick to whatever there already is. A kind of diffusion effect is certainly possible here: if one is afraid of a particular evil incarnated by the homosexual, this conjures up – via the homosexual – the other evils one is also best off fearing, since he incarnates not only that particular evil, but all possible evils. One had better, therefore, cling to existing conditions in every respect. For example, with regard to the fear for one's own life and well-being: if the homosexual is a threat here (*qua* the contagiously diseased), it is best to avoid anything reminiscent of him – like untraditional moral, political or religious viewpoints. Evil thus functions as a conservative factor, precisely through its threat to undermine.

The homosexual, moreover, acts as a *scapegoat* and thus as a *conductor for rechannelling aggression*. Evil is considered the homosexual's *fault*: he incarnates evil not only in the sense that he represents it; he becomes identical to it and evokes it. Which, of course, is why he must be fought down. And as the culprit of all possible evil, he can become the object of all possible aggression. The attempt is made to annihilate the homosexual instead of changing the existing conditions – or oneself. As a symbol, he thus acts as a conservative factor, however avant-garde he may be in the flesh.

Yet, even though the homosexual *is* there in the place of evil and can always be used, it is not always that he *is* used; after all, the modern world does not live in a chronic state of acute panic *vis-à-vis* homosexuals. In the century and more since the birth of the homosexual, there have surely always been individuals and small groups who have needed him as an incarnation of one or more evils;

and most people will no doubt have been haunted by these notions when chancing upon him in the media or in real life (and indeed, as we have seen, he seems to have been ubiquitously present as a ghost). But apparently it takes more to galvanize large groups or whole societies into action and work them up into a state of explicit *moral panic* directed against homosexuals.

A prototypical case of such collective hysteria was enacted in Denmark during the years 1906–11. This period was characterized by the arrest and interrogation of a sizeable number of individuals; parliamentary activity; legal clamp-downs; increased medical surveillance and production of scientific literature; broad media coverage and popular mobilization. In a substantial number of cities throughout the country, civic meetings were held, arranged by the local MP, mayor and the like, and attended by hundreds of specially invited 'men of importance'. Speeches were delivered by famous names from Copenhagen and local men of standing (priests, teachers, etc.); and by way of conclusion, a resolution was adopted, calling for more rigorous enforcement as well as the tightening-up of laws against the 'spread' of homosexuality.[55] Another major homosexual panic occurred in Denmark in the 1950s and early 1960s; here, in the age of radio, movies and television, popular mobilization adopted a somewhat different character, as the new mass media largely supplanted the old public meetings.[56]

Taking a closer look at these events and comparing them with corresponding phenomena in other countries, it may be possible to identify some general determinants needed to produce a situation of moral panic targeted at homosexuals.[57]

Firstly, at least one evil (real or imagined) must be so topically prominent and at the same time strike or threaten across such a broad range that it can be feared by very large groups (in Denmark in 1906–11, the threat to the gender pattern seems to have been particularly important; in the 1950s, problems of authority within the family, combined with a fear of the dangers and allurements of the city). Alternatively, several groups must individually and simultaneously feel the threat of their own serious evil.

Secondly, the homosexual must be linked or 'linkable' with the evil or evils in question. This condition is fulfilled insofar as a notional schema exists in the general symbolic universe with the homosexual as the incarnation of all conceivable evils.

It is hardly necessary, however, for the homosexual to be particularly to the fore of public consciousness in advance or that there is already a pronounced link between the homosexual and the evil or evils feared. It undoubtedly has an extremely conducive effect; but the accentuation of the homosexual and the coupling with evil can also take place in the situation itself. There is some leeway here, which can be padded out or exploited by sheer chance, or by fanatics and cynics (like McCarthy in the USA of the 1950s).

Providing these conditions are met, the following sequence of events can be imagined: a strong and widespread fear of some evil is linked – either directly or through coincidence or manipulation – with the homosexual, thus bringing to the fore the old notional schema in which the homosexual embodies any evil whatever. This schema is thus awoken from its torpor and becomes present in its entirety. Consequently, it is capable of functioning as an explanatory key to all manner of evils and as a signpost for all possible aggression – that is, towards the homosexual.

A cardinal point, then, for cranking this mechanism into action is the existence of something widely felt to be a grave evil. This experience is often dependent on additional prerequisites. Such is the case with the 'threats' from socio-cultural modernity which the homosexual has so often been imagined to incarnate (e.g. 'threats' to the family from the city, or to masculinity from women). In this context, economic and political factors undoubtedly play an essential part. A high degree, and an equal distribution, of financial resources and state-provided social security may further a comparatively relaxed, open and experimental approach to the conditions and possibilities of modernity. Conversely, the more that resources and social security remain scarce or unequally distributed, the greater the risk that modernity is perceived as threatening and that the homosexual is called upon to exercise his functions as a privileged incarnation of modernity's evil.

7 Hotchpotch

The homosexual is an important figure in modern societies. He supplies raw material for science and fund-raises for it; he provides significant contributions to the generation of the psychic self and the sensitive self, and of modern superficiality, hence also of the modern schism between self and surface; he creates art and entertainment, style and images, enjoyments and sensitivity; he performs vital functions in the modern economy, ensures the circulation of capital and sets capitalists' wives' hair and creates their dresses; he incarnates evil and helps to keep up the gender system and the nuclear family. 'Society has a duty to get the best and the most possible out of its individuals', including 'these lunatics', the Danish author and Nobel prizewinner Johs. V. Jensen stated in 1906: 'Confine them, I say, and give them some needlework to do!' 'They also lend themselves well to library erudition; confine a few there!' was his advice.[58] Reality far outdoes his pious wishes; each and every part of the homosexual is exploited: his manpower, his creativity, his symbolic value and his body; and he is part of society's reproduction at all levels: the symbolic and the material; the economic, the juridical and the ideological; the social and the cultural; or however else you choose to break it down. The phenomena typical of modern society can barely be imagined to have grown strong without him, just as he could surely not have existed without them. Finally, he sheds light – or shadow – on the non-homosexuals' interest in other men, being instrumental in developing 'absent homosexuality' and endowing it with its special form of (non-)existence. And as we have seen, this is co-productive of such important social matters as police and sport, science and violence, seeing and spacing, heterosexualization and bi-genderization.

In sum, the specifically modern phenomena of 'absent homosexuality' and 'homosexuals' enter into intimate reciprocal reproductive and developmental relations with the other special institutions, ways of social life, norms etc. of modern societies. In the pages above, however, we have studied only a number of these interrelations and only, as I announced in the introduction, in the manner of sketches and essays. All in all, it may appear to be slightly haphazard why some things were included and others not. This most certainly has to do with the fact that there is not so much research to draw on. In addition, however, the nature of modern societies is generally not such as to render a strictly systematic account possible. If it could once be believed that they were kept together by a single principle, a single overarching power, this has proved to be an illusion. If anything, modern societies are a hotchpotch of diverse factors and phenomena that concur for a time and reinforce one another, merge into one another, undermine one another, transform and generate new factors and phenomena. In this complex, homosexuality in its two forms plays an essential part: as cause and effect, as conveyor belt and defile, and as prism and mirror, concentrating and reflecting a large number of the other factors and connections. It is not unreasonable, therefore, to assert, as I have done at the start of this book, that modern societies are societies in which homosexuality is found.[59]

The complex of socio-cultural modernity and its individual components are in a process of constant change. That applies equally to homosexuality, as a link in the complex; on the one hand, it has a relatively independent existence and a relatively autonomous significance for the development of the whole; on the other, it is itself a complex, joined and permeated by the greater wholeness, and dependent on what happens to this and the other components. To a certain extent, we have so far abstracted from this development. In the last chapter we shall therefore focus our attention directly on these changes and thus impart more movement to the somewhat static picture developed by the preceding chapters.

VI

The Disappearance of the Modern Homosexual

1 The homosexual problem

Homosexuality and the homosexual came into being as a problem. With regard to 'absent homosexuality' among the heterosexuals, it is manifested in repudiations, evasions, denials: *is–is not*; *wants–rejects*; *knows–knows nothing*. As for the homosexuals, there could be disagreement as to the crux of the problem: whether it lay in the attitudes of society or the nature of the homosexual. However, there can be no doubt that being homosexual was and is a problem; even those who proclaim how good it is to be gay reveal it by having to legitimate themselves in this way.

The problem, therefore, requires a solution. Once again, there could be disagreement as to what this might be: whether society's attitudes should be changed or the homosexual eliminated. The latter notion, as we have seen, was common among the heterosexuals, to whom it seemed likely that the possible instances of homosexuality among the non-homosexuals ultimately derived from the homosexuals. But it was also, as we have suggested, a common notion among these: from the self-hating homosexuals who wish they had never been born like that, to the cultured conservatives who 'refuse to be homosexuals', to the radical intellectuals who want to do away with all oppressive social classifications. The most diversified of contingents among the homosexuals, then, can find one another in the wish that the homosexual problem should be solved by eliminating the homosexual, although they have quite different views regarding the alternative: a life sanitized of homosexuality; a society with 'decent' behaviour and a general hush-hush; or one in which everyone is bisexual, or where sex among men simply isn't a problem.

Is there hope for the unhappy, the worried, the troubled, the wronged, the victimized, the timid, the horrified and the revolutionary? *Is* there a final solution to the homosexual problem?

2 Dissolution

The homosexual is a kind of time bomb, encoded with its own explosion. Or perhaps rather its own discreet disappearance. The very circumstances which form the background of his existence also act towards eliminating him; at the same time, he himself helps along. This has been the case ever since he was a boy at the end of the last century; but it has become all the more clear over the years. There are two distinctive tendencies.[1]

Socio-cultural homosexualization There is a tendency for the particular cultural and social traits of the homosexual – his special ways of living, experiences and expressions – to spread and become universal. The conditions of modern life affect an ever-growing number of people and become increasingly more urgent, or they appeal more and more. The former buffers – above all, marriage and the family – are in a process of steady dissolution. Living in the city – in 'a world of strangers' – has become a reality for more and more people and opens up new possibilities for social life and personal development. 'The heterosexuals', too, know that the family is not an eternal institution into which they have entered once and for all: they may divorce, establish another family, live outside the family, use the world of strangers as a resource, a place where one can go and find other people to build up new kinds of relationships. They, too, experience promiscuity, broken relationships and serial monogamy, and they establish networks of friends rather than relatives. Further, urban structures as well as visual media and everyday design permeate life, suggesting such modes of behaviour and experience as aestheticization, sexualization, staging, camp and kitsch. For most, not much seems to be preordained or eternally secure and stable in relation to work, social intercourse and personal identity – even gender has generally grown into a role and a problem, or an opportunity. The institutions of high art, transformed, supplemented and democratized as film, video and rock music, help promote sensitivity in everyone. The theory and practice of liberal democracy increasingly become a lived reality as each identity is conceived from the outset in terms of relative oppression and the right to improvement. With changes in life space, direct social control from family and neighbours gives way to anonymous, potential supervision and control for everyone, along with the corresponding attention and awareness of the possibility of being watched. The ideologies and institutions of self-analysis are ever-expanding, leaving practically none without some idea that they have an inner self and sexuality, precious but hidden and dangerous, always in potential need of therapy. In this way, the conditions of life which formerly belonged to homosexuals in particular are now increasingly becoming common to all. To a certain degree, these conditions are also changing; but the changes often imply a reinforcement or a further development of conditions and ways that were already customary for the homosexual. One example is the spread of television; with it, an urban world – a world of strangers and all that comes with it – penetrates directly into the secluded life space of the home and the family. Further, the homosexuals themselves operate a kind of socio-cultural export enterprise: by virtue of their participation in the commercial production of style and in the cultural arena, they are instrumental in spreading, as we have seen, ways of life and forms of culture (cor)responding to the modern conditions of life. In general, the processes are most advanced in societies with a certain degree and distribution of economic wealth and state-provided social welfare. Only then can individuals really use the conditions of modern life to create workable and satisfying ways of life, and only then do they achieve the necessary security to do so.[2]

Thus, what was 'specifically homosexual' disappears, in that the universal becomes just like it. In this sense, a 'homosexualization' takes place, which does not however involve erotic preference to the same degree.[3]

Scientific devaluation As described in chapter V, a complex of self-analysis has developed in modern societies, comprising two poles: the self at one end and the apparatus of analysis at the other. The homosexual, as we saw, has played a major part in sustaining this complex: he is the embodiment of the lurking and impending dangers that necessitate and validate constant self-monitoring, self-analysis, self-control and self-exposure. Behind this seemingly innocent movement of the hand may be hidden the deepest abyss, and that's how bad you can end up if you don't watch out.

However, the homosexual's role as the whip for self-analysis gradually tends to be downplayed. In the first place, it is obviously more difficult to use him as a bogeyman the less his lifestyle and personality traits differ from others'. Yet there are also reasons founded in the more internal workings of the self-analysis complex. This has not in fact been able to eliminate the homosexual; consequently, as time goes on, it loses credibility to the extent that the battle against the homosexual serves as its legitimation. Another important factor in this scientific devaluation of the particular danger of disease associated with the homosexual is the spread of notions of oppression and emancipation, liberty, equality and happiness. It would perhaps be *best* if one could help the homosexuals get rid of their homosexuality; but since this isn't possible, it is difficult to justify why exactly that group of people should be subjected to special suffering, due to a stigma of disease and danger, and hindered in pursuing happiness on equal terms. All the more so as these notions of oppression and emancipation are part of the arsenal of justification promulgated by the self-analysis complex itself; and as the implicated – the homosexuals – actively know how to make use of them (and, as we have seen, also help to spread them in other ways).

In this manner, the homosexual as the ominous icon of disease is increasingly turning into a hindrance to the continued reproduction of the self-analysis complex. In addition, he is ever more unnecessary in this role. The stronger the complex has grown, the better it is able to reproduce itself via self-analysis alone. Not only because this has become habit and matter-of-course, but also because it offers a bonus in itself: the quest for hidden inner meanings and causes is just as fascinating as expeditions to distant places, and even more so, in that it is with itself that the self is concerned. The analysis becomes its own motivation and legitimation.

On the other hand, it is difficult for the self-analysis complex entirely to drop the homosexual as a reminder of the danger and the necessity of control. Consequently, it would seem that the notion of the homosexual as sick must be kept alive *and* given up, all at the same time. The logical 'solution' to this dilemma is obviously a *devaluation* of the homosexual's 'sickness'. This trend is evident in much of the scientific literature from recent decades. A number of variations are possible.

1 *Maceration of the disease*: all, even the heterosexuals, have homosexual tendencies, hence from that angle it isn't so pathological; but the homosexual has repressed his heterosexual tendencies, and therefore *he* is sick just the same.[4]
2 *Generalization of disease*: it isn't just the homosexual who is ill, but the heterosexual as well; in other words, it isn't *that* bad, but it is nonetheless bad enough.[5]
3 *Displacement of the disease*: it is perhaps not a sickness in itself to be homosexual; but there is a great likelihood – because of circumstances in fetal development or in early childhood that have led to or resulted from a homosexual inclination – that it is related to *other* serious mental illnesses, accompanied by neuroses and character disorders, a cover-up for psychoses and borderline pathology.[6]
4 *Splitting of the disease*: it may not be a sickness in itself to be homosexual, but if a person displays homosexual inclinations they may nevertheless be pathological.[7]

In sum, there is a devaluation of the homosexuals' particular 'sickliness'. And at the same time a revaluation of the sickliness of others: the sexuality of those who are 'normal' is just as suspect, their selves just as disturbed. In the upshot, the homosexual is still regarded as ill or susceptible to disease, but not (much) more than so many others.

What is particular about the homosexual, then, tends to disappear; and with it, the background for making him embody evil.[8] With 'socio-cultural homosexualization', nothing remains of him, so to speak, except his special sexual preference; but that, too, in the same process loses much of its dramatic significance by way of the general sexualization (glances, signals, meetings, experiments, surfaces, etc.) and the general acknowledgement of the collapse of norms, along with the non-given of identities and ways of life. All must now decide for themselves and their given or chosen surroundings the best way to shape their lives. And at the same time, the pathologizing agencies are removing the severity of the alleged sickliness of this special sexual preference.

Hence, increasingly the only difference left is preference, and this is no worse than other minor differences. An indifference surfaces which may perhaps even turn into equal value and universal possibility. What characterizes the phenomena of 'absent homosexuality' among the heterosexuals is the ever-increasing incitement to homosexuality – all the while it is rejected. But as the sexual interest for other men loses its association with particular danger and unfathomable consequences, the foundation for these monotonous rejections is undermined. One *could* perhaps try it oneself, now that it is everywhere anyway.[9]

This trend towards a disappearance of the modern homosexual is evident in conjunction with the introduction of 'registered partnerships' for homosexuals in Denmark. The public debate surrounding the introduction of the bill is indicative.[10] Not surprisingly, many of the arguments were familiar ones, well rehearsed in countless controversies over homosexuality and society. There were, however, some significant shifts in emphasis, and some of the old assertions were absent, or nearly so. The changes were most distinctive among those in favour of better opportunities for same-sex love and pleasure. In such circles, certain types of argument have traditionally predominated. I have discussed these in other contexts; to facilitate the reader's overview, I shall briefly repeat them here.

First, there is the reference to the *essentially or naturally homosexual type of person.* According to this argument, same-sex desire and pleasure is neither accidental nor deliberately chosen. It is instead the inescapable expression and result of a deep-seated inner nature belonging to a certain group of people. This core may be of a biological origin, or it may be the result of early childhood experiences; in any case it is something fundamental and essential. And precisely because same-sex desire is the expression of this inner nature, one cannot be blamed for it or expected to suppress it.[11] Consequently, the homosexuals should have the same rights and opportunities as those enjoyed by others. This argument was already presented in full detail (as well as in all its inner contradictions) in Ulrichs's writings in the 1860s, at the very dawn of modern homosexuality. It may be termed *the* classic legitimating figure of same-sex love and pleasure – whether in the complaining, pity-begging version of the 'defective' and 'misshapen' homosexual creature, or in the more defiant, acceptance-oriented version of the unique and beneficial homosexual character contributing vitally to society. Even today, such figures of legitimation are common in the everyday usage of homosexuals as well as among their advocates in the sciences. As an example, I shall quote Whitam and Mathy: 'The formulation of a homosexual orientation as biologically derived and therefore immutable, appearing in all societies at about the same rate, characterized by similar elements in different societies, and serving as the basis for significant contributions to society, is not only more scientifically accurate, it is also far more politically promising for homosexual rights than other contemporary formulations.'[12]

Another classic figure of legitimation refers to *respectability*. In themselves, it argues, homosexuals are fully as respectable as are heterosexuals. The great majority of the homosexuals live in stable couples or have no higher wish than to do so. Whatever deviations may occur from this norm – such as promiscuity, serial monogamy or sex in parks and public lavatories – are the result of legal and social discrimination, persecution or oppression. Precisely because the homosexuals lack the acknowledgement of society, they are forced to meet in dark and dubious places and live out their need for love in alienated, reified, fetishized and instrumentalized forms. Accordingly, this would disappear if the homosexuals were granted the same rights as the heterosexuals. This type of argument, which of course is easily associated with that of the essentially homosexual person, was a favourite in the 'homophile' movement during the 1950s and early 1960s in Scandinavia, the Netherlands, France and the US.[13] But it hasn't gone entirely out of fashion. It has the advantage of being usable by conservative and radical moralism alike; and even today it is often wielded in debates on the prevention of AIDS and HIV.

A third argument among the classic justifications of same-sex love and pleasure is characterized by *not* demanding the same rights for homosexuals as those which exist for heterosexuals. According to this view, the homosexuals are distinguished by not confining their lives and pleasures within the limitations demanded by society. Because of this, they are particularly hard-hit by societal regulation and oppression. And consequently, they are the symbolic or real incarnation of the oppressed and of the alternatives, as well as of refusal, resistance and liberation. If, however, they are given the same rights as the heterosexuals, they will merely become integrated, disciplined and bourgeoisified, and lose their oppositional or revolutionary power. This type of argument was very popular in the heyday of gay and lesbian liberation during the 1970s.[14] But it is still widespread today, also among heterosexual leftist intellectuals. Indeed, it is quite popular in many countries as an argument *against* registered partnerships; besides, it keeps popping up in a number of other contexts, for instance clad in the languages of postmodernism, multiculturalism or queerness.

Justifications like the ones mentioned form an integral part of *being homosexual.* As we have seen, the modern homosexual is essentially a *legitimating* creature (ch. chapter IV, section 19). In the Danish debate surrounding the introduction of 'registered partnerships', however, these justifications were absent, or all but absent. Consequently we seem to be witnessing here the disappearance of an essential part of the modern homosexual. And if we look at the content of the justifications, we shall be able to see further aspects of this disappearance. One major reason why the usual arguments were missing was no doubt that they'd lost credibility. It was simply no longer convincing to refer to the essentially and naturally different personality type of the homosexuals, or to their being inherently and particularly respectable *or* alternative – when the non-homosexuals are increasingly exhibiting the same personality traits and becoming equally 'respectable' or unrespectable and 'alternative'.

The trend towards a disappearance of the modern homosexual is also manifested in connection with the arguments of the opponents. Not that these contained any surprises in themselves: there was ample reiteration of traditional arguments. One such line of argumentation referred to the authority of the Bible or Nature: homosexuality was sin and heathenism, inborn defect or perversity. Another line centred on notions of the dissolution of marriage, family, morality, culture and society: marriage would be devalued and ridiculed, families broken, children harmed, and youngsters bewildered; homosexuality would spread, as would crime, drugs and disease in its wake; and the gates would be opened for further decay: child adoption by homosexuals, church weddings for homosexuals, bigamy. For these reasons, homosexual relations should not be officially recognized by society. What was new, then, was neither the content of the opponents' arguments, nor the zeal with which they were advanced by certain groups. However, the result – the actual introduction of registered partnership – showed that they had lost their power of persuasion. 'Nature' and 'God', as well as 'the Family' and 'Society' have a difficult time authorizing one particular way of life when most people in fact choose to live otherwise or at least would not deny they might consider it.[15]

The trend towards a disappearance of the modern homosexual is further evidenced by the arguments prevailing among the supporters. Above all, these arguments centred on the principle of *equality*: homosexuals would now gain (with a few exceptions) the *right to equal freedom of choice* as had heterosexuals in relation to the privileges and obligations of forming couples. Among the gains mentioned was the opportunity for a greater emotional and financial security in relationships, as well as a higher degree of commitment and responsibility in feelings and actions. Generally, however, the various possible benefits of registered partnerships were not a main theme. The emphasis lay on the *principles* of equality, freedom and justice. The realization of these principles was often presented as a value in itself, not least in relation to the situation of minorities. Moreover, it was frequently added, legal equality implied an official, societal acknowledgement of the *equal value* of homosexual and heterosexual relations.[16] This would have a positive impact on the attitudes of homosexuals towards themselves, as well as on the attitudes and reactions of others in relation to them. Equality and equal value, then, were the main arguments of the supporters of 'registered partnership', and as it turned out, the ones that won the battle. This was in line with the views of the majority of Danes, according to opinion polls in 1988 and 1989, where questions were posed in terms of equal rights.[17]

The background for this state of debates and events is obviously to be found in the broader equalizing of differences between the homosexuals and 'the others' sketched above, as well as in the fact that this equalizing moves in a homosexual direction, so to speak. In short, any feature of the modern homosexual that you might want to emphasize as particularly characteristic or alternative is becoming increasingly – *common*. It is therefore no longer obvious why 'the homosexuals' shouldn't have precisely the same legal and social rights (and injustices) as others. This is how the matter may also appear to those homosexuals who have no desire to make use of such rights themselves, e.g. the right of 'marriage'. In fact, it seems that the majority of both gays and lesbians simply considered it an extension of their possibilities of choice and social acceptance.[18] Therefore they saw no reason to argue against registered partnerships, even if they themselves had no plans to give up their own particular way of life in favour of it. This conclusion is further corroborated by the fact that relatively few have actually entered a registered partnership, even though very little opposition to the new law was voiced by homosexuals.

Thus, the introduction of registered partnerships in Denmark should not be misinterpreted as a 'normalization' or 'bourgeoisification' or 'straightification' of the homosexual. On the contrary, 'homosexual marriage' has become possible only on the basis of the decline in prestige and importance of marriage and the family. Indeed, the decline of those institutions is a crucial aspect of the processes related to the disappearance of the modern homosexual and the basic *homo*-genization of ways of life.

Insofar as the modern homosexual is disappearing, we might speak of a *postmodernization* of same-sex love and pleasure. And in fact, it is easy to summarize the particular features of the Danish debate on registered partnership in the rhetorical terms of postmodernism: *post* Nature, *post* Respectability, *post* the Alternative – as well as *post* God, *post* the Family. Moreover, a consummate homo-genization would seem to imply yet another 'post' (although for some this may appear as the ultimate negation of postmodernity): *post difference*! Well, well. First: a disappearance of the modern homosexual does not necessarily imply that all differences will disappear (cf. section 4 below). Second: the disappearance of the modern homosexual is a phenomenon that, even in those areas where the homosexual exists, is merely a *tendency*, far from having been fully developed. To use the Danish debate on registered partnerships as an example once again: true, the old type of justification was not very pronounced. But the arguments were still made on the basis of and in relation to 'the homosexual', i.e. explicitly or implicitly it was contended that they are of a kind that should be entitled to freedom, equality and justice. And that is also a sort of justification. Moreover, the fact that the majority of Danes did support the introduction of registered partnerships need not imply that they considered homosexuals to be of *equal value* to heterosexuals – or even that they didn't consider them 'unnatural' or the like. All that can be safely concluded is that they thought homosexuals should be given (more of) the same *rights* that heterosexuals had. One might interject that, by accepting legal equality, the majority must have accepted by implication a societal acknowledgement of equal value as well. Insofar as this is the case, it does not necessarily indicate that they considered homosexuals to be of equal value. Indeed, it is more likely that they merely thought homosexuals should be treated *as if* of equal value – precisely because they did not consider them to be so. The source may just as well have been a sense of pity as of respect. The fact that homosexuals were not given full marriage rights points toward this interpretation, which is also supported by other available evidence. The introduction of registered partnerships in Denmark, then, testifies to a society not particularly advanced, but somewhere in the middle of the kind of transformation sketched above in relation to ways of life as well as to the end of the homosexual.[19]

In most other parts of the world it is rather absurd to speak of a disappearance of the homosexual, since he doesn't even exist. In some countries he is in the process of being brought into existence, which in these contexts seems to be quite an appropriate procedure and practice. For instance, in eastern Europe where gays and lesbians are organizing and trying to manifest an identity and a lifestyle in the public sphere, it would not only be absurd but also obstructive to speak in such terms.[20] Even where the homosexual has been well established for decades, it doesn't always make sense to speak of a trend towards his disappearance. In most (north-) western societies, the era of the 'classical' modern homosexual can be dated from the later nineteenth century and into the 1970s. What happens after this, however, takes different forms in different national socio-cultural contexts. In the US, for example, the changes do not have the character of a disappearance of the modern homosexual. They are of another sort, expressed by the phenomena of 'queerness': the use of the word 'queer' as a self-applied label, 'queer nation', 'queer theory'. The US is characterized by an immense inequality in the distribution of wealth and social benefits due to the lack of a genuine welfare state. These are factors which tend to make the experience of modernity a potentially unpleasurable one for very many people. Therefore, instead of making use of the possibilities of the particularly modern conditions of life, people tend to rely on the family or other so-called 'primary' groups that can support them in a world which may otherwise be dangerous and annihilating. Thus, clinging to the family, and to a fairly archaic ideal of family life, is pronounced in the US. And, as we have seen, the more the ideology of the family is emphasized, the less favourable are the conditions for the homosexuals, since their lives as homosexuals are by definition, so to speak, situated outside the family, and thus they may easily become targets of projection for the fears associated with modernity. The rise of the 'queer' in the US is related to the fact that the family, with its patterns of gender and authority, is still widely considered to be the secure haven against the threats of modernity, and that modernity, for the majority of the population, is still considered threatening. However, the recent phenomenon of the queer is not a mere continuation of the 'classical' modern homosexual. After all, it is post-1970s; and it is nourished by the sense of disbelief and anger generated by the gap between the existence of huge, openly gay worlds on the one hand, and the harshly anti-homosexual outside world on the other. Still, this situation – at least in some versions of queer ideology, and particularly in the ideas of a queer nation – gives occasion for a restating of ideas and rhetorics from the radical liberation movements of the late 1960s and early 1970s: *We're radically different from the rest of them, we're better than them, we're more liberated than them, we are besieged by them, they want to annihilate us, we are at war with them, we contain the seeds of their liberation . . .*[21]

The situation is fairly similar in Great Britain. In other parts of (north-)western Europe, this rhetoric and movement of queer radicalism is hardly possible any more. Yet even here the changes *after* the classical modern homosexual do not necessarily or simply take the form of a trend towards his disappearance. Holland is a particular case. The relaxing of traditional ideologies, the level and distribution of wealth and social welfare, as well as the changes of lifestyles, are hardly less advanced than in Denmark.[22] And they are, undoubtedly, accompanied by a trend towards the disappearance of the modern homosexual. This, however, is counteracted by another trend: a restaging of the (post)modern homosexual, at the ideological level at least, as the avant-garde and signpost of changes in the socio-cultural life of society. This phenomenon is no doubt related to the strength of the Dutch homosexual movement and subculture – which in turn is perhaps related, partially at least, to the circumstance that Holland, owing to its geographical location and traditions of tolerance, receives a huge and continuous influx of 'homosexuals' from countries far less advanced, bringing with them their experiences of being 'different' as well as their sheer numbers. The ideology appropriate for these circumstances is hardly one of a 'disappearance', but neither is it one of brutal oppression, total war and radical difference. What remains is the idea of a socio-cultural avant-garde, leading the way for a population that is a little bit slow.[23]

The (north-)western part of continental Europe is but a tiny part of the globe. Moreover, the world of the future will no doubt bring together increasing numbers of people of various ethnic and cultural backgrounds, and one may wonder to what extent such globalization will also bring with it a perpetuation of *radically* different values and ways of life. However, it seems very unlikely that the modern conditions of life won't become close and constant realities for more and more people. In this way, the world is no doubt becoming increasingly modernized, and modernization is becoming increasingly global. And consequently, these universally shared conditions of life will present an impetus towards a homogenization of lifestyles, i.e. towards making them share the basic traits of the modern homosexual's form of existence. Now, if differences in the amount and distribution of wealth and social welfare are severe in the future, it can be expected that many people will cling defensively to their own particular traditional values and ways of life. In that case, the homosexual may well come to be perceived, once again, as the incarnation of the threats of modernity. If, however, a high degree of equality in economic and social opportunities is realized, modernization will likely bring with it a gradual and rather relaxed homo-genization of life-styles and a concomitant *happy end* of the homosexual.[24]

3 Death of the homosexual

Beneath this discussion of the extinction of the species, the other death is imposing itself: that of individuals, grotesque, unsavoury, unreal or real. Some of us are dying, many know they are infected, some know or think they aren't, the rest do not want to know, but we live with it now. It is outrageously absurd that it had to happen just as things were better than ever.

But in a way this death is not so alien to us. There is something terribly intimate about it. We always seemed to belong to medicine. The body must now be monitored for purple blemishes as well, the sweat on the upper lip interpreted; surveillance is doubled, the exterior is not only a sign of homosexuality but also of death. The fear, again doubled, is about the consequences, unfathomable, annihilating. Our lives are from now on even more choice, even more a calculation between the predictable and the unpredictable, even more project. We must consider how safe sex is, what we want to do with the rest of our lives if or when we find that we have AIDS, and whether we want to die slowly and hideously or take our own lives in order to will some kind of dignity. The anonymously inspected, scientifically monitored, semi-public death; or among friends provided they care enough, or with *the* friend provided one exists and he stays on. The lonely death, Herman Bang on the train across the American continent, alone and nervous and uneasy and mannered. *(He fairly gave the impression of being ill. He clung to them and never stopped thanking them for coming. 'I've been in constant terror over how things would go once I arrived in Chicago', he said; 'I can't speak a word of English and I'm not the least accustomed to travelling alone – and in this foreign country where no one understands me, and I understand no one. All along I've had the feeling something will happen to me on this journey, and now I hear that the "Cleveland", which I was to take from San Francisco, has had a collision with an American cruiser near Honolulu. That, you have to admit, must be a warning.' Before leaving that evening on the train, he was able to rest a while at the University Club, where he was to join a small dinner party. Having slept, he livened up, became cheerful, and once again told his stories and laughed. But each time his laughter was stilled by violent coughing bouts. It was not without anxiety that they drove him back to the station to take his coach in the Overland Ltd, the fastest express train on the Pacific Line.*[25]*)* The *justified* death, for being so wrong and guilty of so much evil. *One reaps what one sows*, at least it's easier to feel that way than not.

Regardless of how the individual responds to this death, it is impossible to be homosexual without it being present now and making itself felt everywhere. Parts of the homosexual community have reacted rationally by taking up the struggle: through visitors' and help programs for the ill, encounter groups and support groups for those who have the antibodies, information and counselling for all; as well as public and political activity in order to increase government efforts in combating the disease. Here the community shows the dogged stamina and resistance it has built up over the past decades.

Just as AIDS threatens the life of the individual homosexual, it attacks that of the species as well. In the first place, of course, because so many of us die. Moreover, because AIDS can threaten the fundamental institutions of the homosexual form of existence. From the one-to-one we fall, or let ourselves fall towards the association and the friendship network, and from them towards the city. It is the city – with its meetings and meeting places – which ultimately bears us; in any case, it is one of the pillars. The very quickness and mass character or urban sexual relations made them dangerous for a while until safe sex was learnt.

If indeed AIDS hacks away at certain conditions for the homosexual's life, it lends support in others. It is capable of giving artificial respiration to the feeble theories on the particular sickliness of the homosexuals. It can invest a tinge of good credit standing to the crisis-ridden homosexuality-cause-seeking industry, and once again grant it respite in fulfilling its obligations. It reactivates the slumbering imagery of sickness and extinction, destruction and filth, aliens and the unnatural, and again lets the homosexual embody evil. It draws the line once more. We thereby arrive at the unsavoury paradox that the very disease which kills the homosexual as individual helps to keep him alive as species.

If one wishes to discuss utopia in these circumstances, it must be done to a certain degree *in spite*. However, although AIDS and the public campaigns against its spread may have slowed down developments towards the disappearance of the modern homosexual, they have not, generally, increased negative reactions against homosexuals.[26] Safer sex is being learnt and knowledge of same-sex relations is being heightened.

4 Taste and the alien

If the homosexual disappears, what can one imagine will come about instead? *Universal bisexuality*, was the answer from parts of the Gay Liberation movement in the 1970s.[27] Yet on the face of it, there is something unseemly about this answer. If the experiences of the homosexuals give occasion for a distinct ethic, this can certainly not be one that prescribes rules for how people should find pleasure so long as they don't harm anyone. Rather, it should emphasize the right to abandon oneself to a certain preference, to make a life out of it if one wishes.

What the gay liberationists meant, though, was no doubt often precisely this: that people should do as they please, without harm, no matter if it is with a man or a woman; and they should at least recognize that they themselves have or could have erotic or sexual interests in their own sex as well. As mentioned (section 2) the trend already seems to be moving in this direction, in some countries at least. Whether a man wants another man is becoming a matter of prefer-ence, of *taste*, wherever it comes from, and of getting the most out of the kind of life which one taste or the other makes possible. In this way, a certain utopia is becoming real:

> In remote parts of the country, among certain groups, an explanation is still considered requisite if someone is vegetarian. In ever wider circles, explaining is no longer necessary even though the majority of people surely still eat meat. If someone came up with the idea that vegetarians are a special group, fundamentally different from the rest of humanity, with a particular life story (something about mother's nipple?) and a particular personality, that it is wrong (disgusting, sickly), a problem for themselves and for society which required the investigating and regulating intervention of medical

> science – no one would bother to listen. It is not being a vegetarian, but having this attitude towards vegetarians that would be considered strange, perhaps requiring an explanation.
>
> Being vegetarian is not a question of radical difference, wrongness, life history and personality type, it is a matter of preference, taste; at best perhaps of art: some vegetarians take their preference to unimaginable heights of gastronomical delight for themselves and others; at worst – for those who insist on meat for dinner every day and *refuse* to eat vegetarian – a matter of *eccentricity, foolishness, a whim*: that woman has a thing, you see, but that's her business (just as *their* perpetual demand for meat can seem ridiculous the other way around). 'Each to her own taste', 'there is no accounting for tastes'; it is possible to talk about them, i.e. *depict* their qualities, attempt to *persuade*, but it is senseless to try to *prove* that liver pâté tastes better than lentil pâté.[28]

So, too, with men's desire for men: nothing that makes radically different, wrong, radiates a particular personality or demands monitoring and explanation – but a taste; a huge *de-dramatization*. The idea of taste thus implies a complete change of attitude towards same-sex sexuality, eroticism and love. Another set of questions can be raised: not where it comes from, but what you can get out of it.

The cultivation of this taste will no doubt carve out or create its special spaces, institutions, times, ways – which will differ more or less from those developed by *aficionados* of e.g. vegetarianism, bridge or opera.[29] Socially, however, they might not be experienced very differently from these.

How large will such groups of impassioned cultivators of same-sex taste be? The question is perhaps not all that innocent. While the notion of a common bisexual praxis may seem a megalomanic projection of wishful fantasy aimed at eradicating, once and for all, any distinction between a 'homosexual minority' and a 'heterosexual majority', the idea of a community of taste may imply another latent presupposition. At least in its typical exemplifications (such as opera or bridge), it seems to proceed from the assumption that these groups would be *small*, and perhaps also vulnerable, and thus it re-establishes a form of minority–majority conception.

Obviously, one might choose other cases for comparison: aficionados of soccer, for example, or of roast veal.[30] But there remains an important and interesting dimension regarding the question of size: how do we imagine *most men* will live with respect to sexual or erotic relations with other men? Further, we can use the fear that is perhaps concealed in the size question as an incentive to ask with renewed energy: is it truly realistic to believe that a utopia of taste could come close to becoming a reality? Granted, the processes of socio-cultural homosexualization and scientific devaluation will remove a great deal of aversion to same-sex eroticism, but won't there still be a more 'fundamental' dislike among most men?

Upon reviewing the results of the analysis, we may be certain that there is no biological or other non-historically determined aversion among men to sexuality with other men (cf. chapters II and III). With respect to modern societies we have furthermore been led to assume a *universal* readiness for such relations – otherwise the phenomena of absent homosexuality could not come about.[31] But is there perhaps a dislike which isn't merely, as I put it at the end of chapter III, a reflection or shadow cast from the homosexual, but rather something founded in the *modern societal conditions themselves* in which and against the background of which absent homosexuality exists? And if so, this aversion would, if anything, become more widespread with the spread of these conditions of life to ever larger groups.

Rather the opposite, I shall argue. The life spaces of most people are increasingly those of a telemediated social world of strangers – in other words of a *telecity*.[32] This involves an emphasis on distance, gaze and surfaces which in itself implies *aestheticization* as well as *sexualization*, all the while the contrast of masculinity to femininity is accentuated – precisely, as an aestheticized and sexualized contrast. Consequently, the male body and its cultural attire become sexualized for men. It has been argued that the man or men in the picture resist sexualization by being active and averting their eyes from the viewer.[33] But this is no longer always true, not even when the pictures move: the close-ups and slow motions of the male body in porn videos or televised sports partially neutralize the activity, making the man static enough to be an object of sexualized spectation.[34] More fundamentally, the objection contradicts itself: it presupposes that men can be sexualized only if they assume the same position in the picture as that which, in modernity, has traditionally been assigned to *women* – although, in fact, the sexualization of men as *men* would seem to require that they retain a fair amount of their culturally defined masculinity and be, for example, active and sullen (once in a while, at least).

The various forms of *aestheticized sexualization* of men for men are becoming increasingly explicit. For instance, the picture surfaces in a number of today's most popular advertisements for masculinity products are already nearly indistinguishable from the gay soft porn of the 1950s.[35] Along with the growing public debate on sexual matters, this will imply a greater general acknowledgement of the eroticism and sexuality in the attractions between men, as no shadow can fall any more from the already vanished homosexual. The result amounts to a form of sexualized or erotic relation between men which is *post* homosexualization, absent of absent homosexuality.

Conceivable, then, as one possibility, is a continuum between a comparatively small group of aficionados of same-sex tastes and a large group of part-time telemedia enjoyers. The difference, however, is not as great as it might seem, since even the impassioned cultivators of same-sex taste increasingly live in a telemediated world of sexualized, non-orgasmic relations to strangers. This is one reason why the traditional type of surveys on the prevalence of 'homosexuality' are already in danger of becoming antiquated even before they are carried out: the questions asked are partially irrelevant; sexuality is not what it used to be.

But surely there will be larger or smaller groups that, for one reason or another, have developed an aversion or estrangement regarding this taste. Perhaps they will write lengthy speeches merely pretending to discuss the pros and cons, or plainly derogating this alien taste, as was the case at times during antiquity and the Middle Ages; it could be quite entertaining.[36] If they aren't content with venomous comments and personal dissociation, but also wish to eradicate this taste and its impassioned cultivators in practice, they must be forced to let be. A modern rationality should not allow annihilating assaults on difference which doesn't harm anyone even though it may be alien.

In any case, however, it is difficult to imagine that a certain amount of justification would not be necessary and tempting for the impassioned practitioners of same-sex taste. In modern societies it seems altogether inconceivable that identities, ways of life or even just preferences could exist without a certain amount of legitimizing. As stated earlier, this stems not only from the Enlightenment experience that given circumstances can be changed and that hence, there are always possibilities for creating better opportunities for particular differences and interests. It is also related to the fact that modern societies are largely argumentative in their basic structure, as is apparent in their typical institutions such as science, the judicial system and parliament.[37] What one might wish for same-sex love and sexuality is, however, that the *excess* of justification still adhering to it might be eradicated. In this connection, one could propose the rule that the more legal equality there is, the less there is to legitimize. This is supported by the fact that shortly after the introduction of registered partnerships, the Danish debate over this right nearly subsided even among its opponents.[38]

Utopia might be somewhere where you wouldn't have to justify your desires for other men but could simply live them in peace with society and your neighbour. In *Negative Dialectics*, Adorno comments on an expression by Eichendorf about 'beautiful strangeness' in the following manner: 'The state of reconciliation would not annect the strange and alien with philosophical imperialism, but be happy that this remained, in the proximity granted, the distant and different, beyond the opposite and same.' Such a state would not imply any justification of one's little idiosyncrasies or immense joyful ecstasies. But it's utopian.[39]

5 Playing

Modern life-worlds are increasingly marked by the severance of surfaces from content – that is, by *superficiality*, *fetishism*, *fragmentation* and whatever terms are commonly used to convey the idea that things are in a sorry state. Are they?

Here are two comments.

First, we cannot just pretend that it isn't the case, or simply hope that it will stop one day. It is no doubt true that *capital* has been a party to the development of this superficiality, but the latter cannot be reduced to a simple expression of the operations of capital. It is also the result of a number of other factors we can scarcely imagine not existing. Indeed, *the homosexual* we can do without – even though of course it would be with sadness that we took leave of him, and only on condition that society and culture have been expressly and fully homosexualized, as in fact they will have had to be in this case. The homosexual would then have accomplished his historical mission, one could say. But other factors at work are harder to imagine ourselves doing without: urbanization, mass production, visual media. The Cambodian experiment of moving the city to the countryside has lost its appeal; moreover, it is unlikely that the global billions of people can survive in a world without an industrialized economy. Nor is it likely that visual-media technology will be demolished, or that we should decide to introduce old taboos against making images. Hence, one cannot hope oneself out of a fetishized life-world.[40]

Moreover, modern superficiality has its advantages. A number of games between surface and interior are made possible. On the one hand, for example, you can long to shed the surface and just *be yourself*, on the other, the autonomy of the surface may constitute a kind of liberation from subjectivity. It can be quite fatiguing to be yourself all the time. Superficiality makes possible new forms of pleasure, a new aesthetic creativity and new forms of experience. To take a single one of these: camp. This is a way of experiencing which penetrates the alleged concordance between expression and interior; as such, it is critical. At the same time it is humane: granted, it stresses the grotesque in the disparity between form and content, but also that which is touching in the content's intentions. Finally, it makes possible retrieving a heap of junk from the dustbin of history, to achieve a new aesthetic pleasure from the rubbish. That is what you'd call an *achievement of civilization*.

I know the objections well. *Children* cannot live with all this ambiguity and artificiality and play-acting, they need security, guidelines and genuine feelings. Children aren't thought of in the universe you've unfolded, they don't exist in your book at all and there's no place for them either; what's more, their absence is the perfect expression of the homosexual interest's raving overestimation of itself, the final ontological proof of what is its lack. I – almost – haven't the strength to repeat what everyone already knows, that so many homosexuals love children (not just boys), that many are in child-related professions, that many have children and even more wish to have them. It is important above all to take a closer look at the objection that children cannot be in a world where grown-ups' surfaces do not immediately or primarily express their eternally innermost selves. It is true that children love to lean on you and sense that you feel the friendliness you show them. What's cruel about them is that after a while they get tired of it, shamelessly they go off on their own or take to jumping on you and being impossible; or that's what is wonderful about them, the cat-like as opposed to the dog-like. They are fickle and gamesome, playful. Of course it would never occur to me to regard 'childhood' as pure nature. Either their playfulness is a product of culture, or they just happen to have it; at any rate it's there, even if it were as bad as Soviet pedagogy hoped: that they play because they aren't allowed to work. They'll play-act security and sincerity for a while, but when they tire of it they stop; conversely, they sometimes keep on even when we're no longer amused. They are annoying. They pretend, they're calculating (has anyone ever met a non-strategic child?), they are conniving bastards, as we say, a bunch of nasty little pranksters. Here, too, we perhaps project our own culturally produced fantasies of unity and clarity onto the tiny ones when we want to perceive this as their true essence, once again they are the innocent, the unbesmirched, those who can heal that one who has fallen apart, into inner and outer, surface and self. Children should of course be treated decently, just as other people; instead of perpetual demands for authenticity, they need perhaps more a fellow player. I'm not saying there isn't any difference between children and grown-ups, or that the playing is simply the same here as there; but what's surprising is not any incompatibility; rather it's the similarities.

6 The cultural wardrobe

It always seemed a ridiculous notion to me that the erotic or sexual interest in men is focused in particular on their cocks. Nevertheless, this is what many a non-homosexual scientist has maintained. From this it would follow that they ascribe their own heterosexuality to a special interest in the genitals of the opposite sex, but they must speak for themselves. Thinking back, I wasn't particularly interested in the other man's cock, although I got used to appreciating it as well. One of the guys I was in love with in high school I loved for his beautiful body, his red lips and blue eyes, and because he was so brilliant; the other for his critical eye and his sense of humour. When the leather angels flew by on their bikes along the country roads below, it was their wildness and vehemence and tight jeans and black leather that enraptured me; if, in my teens, I was at home alone and made myself a guy by stuffing quilts and blankets and pillows into a pair of jeans, it was the ass I took extra care in shaping to a bulge so I could rub the uneven surface of my groin against it; and at the age of fourteen, when I saw a guy a bit older carrying fruit crates into the house, it was his legs with hair made golden by the sun that brought me to the verge of fainting. In sum, their *masculinity*; that is what it's all about.[41]

It would in fact be strange if the sexual or erotic interest in other men didn't have something to do with their masculinity, whatever that is and wherever it comes from. It's a false abstraction that it's 'the person' that counts; the desire for men is not directed at their general human qualities, and in no way their feminine sides; it embraces them as men. It's a lie that we in reality desire the androgynous; that is a disavowal of the qualities of lust in the homosexual imagination and experience. If his femininity is of interest, it is because *as a man* he has the capacity to perform as a woman *as well*, but not because he *is* one. The desire is not directed at 'the whole person', it wants the total man.

Masculinity comes to us covered with cultural images, they exist before the individual man appears in reality and the fantasy of him. The potentialities of his body are always shaped beforehand and entwined in the cultural masculinity. History, fiction, photography and film have established an archive whose pictures reappear and mix with the living typology: the rocker, the cop, the footballer, the Turk, the soldier, the truck driver, the kid, etc., who play their parts on the appropriate/d fields, grounds and arenas. Masculinity is hedged by matrices; the cruelty, the shows of strength, the impudent eyes, the wry smile, the tough repartee, the masculine insecurity and vulnerability and his special way of tackling it, it has all been seen before, from leather cross-strap and boots to Sean Connery and James Dean. (I limit myself to the *dazzling* images, precisely because they are the ones that seduce us.) The body is pre-shaped as male body; only its odour escapes the pictures and yet it doesn't, it is visible as streaks and shadows on the T-shirt and socks. In this fantastic world the individual guy or man appears, his smile reiterates and departs from that of the cultural male images.

It's impossible to ascertain exactly where culture stops and nature begins in this masculinity, and perhaps it isn't so interesting. The fantastic thing about it is precisely its blending of style and body, reality and unreality. What once was or still remains of nature has been culturally enriched. This gives it its immense richness, the lure of the images, the diversity, the magnitude. It is at least larger than the cock, even though this can be pumped up pornographically so as to dominate. Those who are born after me and in more sophisticated areas than the countryside, and therefore raised on pornography, can hardly avoid knowing straight away the significance to be attributed to the cock, but even for them, it would be foolish to reduce masculinity to cock. Masculine pictures are everywhere, different and falling into categories that move and turn into each other. The individual man chooses and fixates, without reason, at random, grotesquely. When they bore him he may join the turning to others, or they become boring because other pictures begin to appeal.

Masculinity is totally fetishistic. The pictures are all-powerful; surfaces have detached themselves and become autonomous, absorbing desire. Fantastically staged figures and forms stage the individual man and the fantasy. The masculine pictures themselves pump life into the reality whose life they live off.

It can be complicated enough, for example, to be in bed with a guy under these circumstances since you are also in bed with your fantasies and his, both of your stagings, besides bodies, selves, and whatever else comes with it. His body and his outfit are projection screens for fantasies; if the projection doesn't fit the screen, irregularities and dislocations occur to which one can perhaps shut one's eyes, otherwise they can be disturbing; if it fits perfectly the experience becomes double-dimensional, one image on top of the other, identical without melting together, you can relish being in bed with a perfect surface. It is strange to touch your fantasy with your hands. It can be so intense; why not avoid being with him again, why not simply cultivate the illusion well aware it is an illusion, rather than having it spoiled by some accidental incongruency? Conversely, that which in him departs from the picture can suddenly gain intensity, because it spreads or without reason. His particular variant can be made into image, or it makes you carve a new selection from the body of cultural images, which you at least in retrospect can interpret from your having found a new type to look for. The images are replaced. Momentarily something deposits itself against them; that which isn't identical to the image breaks through and becomes fantastic itself, depth or love, it's strange that he *is there*, next to me, with the heat of his body, his hopes and his unpredictability. In any case, the autonomous surfaces and fetishized images have come to stay, and they *civilize* by making possible new aesthetic pleasures; whatever shortcomings they previously might have due to their restrictedness and limited number are now assuaged by a steadily growing production; modern media have given us a gigantic repertoire of image for masculinity, pictures in motion at that. The fetishizing of surfaces also civilizes by loosening the bond of nature, it *rationalizes*, at least just as much as the spread of democratic language with its built-in reference to achieve a consensus. We haven't yet reached the point where the detachment of surfaces cannot, once again, turn into a longing for what is to be the genuine and authentic: Blut und Boden; Kinder, Kirche, Küche; *a strong man*. But the more the surfaces are detached and become autonomous, the more the roles are severed from nature, the more accessible they become for staging and pleasure, the more they can be treated *as* surfaces, *as* roles, *as* images. In this way we can free ourselves from the narrow-minded pornography of psychoanalysis, or at any rate place it on a level with other things. We can transcend the 'active/passive' phantasm, historically perhaps the most common blockage of sexual relations between men, when masculinity no longer rises and falls with the cock and where it is placed when it has its orgasm, when the cock's place within masculinity can be determined and varied through the game. We can finally reach the point at which the dangerous in masculinity is maintained all the while it's suspended, the violence, the domination, the power display; it can stop when it isn't fun any more. Emancipation *from* masculinity *to* masculinity. It exists at the junction between culture and nature, where it can come into being and yet can let be.

Notes

References to the literature are generally given in alphabetical order, though this may be transgressed in order to represent geographical spread and/or chronological development (of events or research) when these are thematically important.

I Introduction

1 Katz 1976: 209–79. Later Katz himself problematized this terminology for being latently sexist, and instead suggested 'crossing women' (Katz 1983: 682 n. 10). I think both words could be accused of carrying problematic connotations – but indeed, the phenomena referred to were not without problems for the women involved; and I think 'passing' is the better term.

2 Brown 1975. Brown's description concerns a bath house in New York in 1975. It might as well have been Amsterdam, Berlin, Toronto, Copenhagen, Sydney or Paris in 1975 – or today.

3 Whenever 'homosexuality' and 'homosexual' are used without further specification they refer to men and relations between men. Obviously, the meaning, delimitation and adequacy of concepts such as homosexuality, sexuality, masculinity, modernity, etc. will be discussed in the course of the exposition; at first, I shall use them in an unspecified 'everyday', 'colloquial' sense (assuming, for a while and not totally without reason, that such a sense does exist). A particular problem concerns the term 'desire'. In most contexts, I would have preferred to avoid it because of its psychoanalytic connotations. However, English does not have a word directly corresponding to the Danish 'lyst' which can be used rather unspecifiedly and positively. Sometimes 'passion' would be adequate (cf. Sinfield 1994: 11); in other instances

it would simply be too 'passionate', and in any case it would leave us without a corresponding verb; so mostly I have used 'desire'.

4 Among the pioneering works were those of Dennis Altman (1971; 1982), Michel Foucault (1976), Gilbert Herdt (1981), Guy Hocquenghem (1972), Mary McIntosh (1968), Maureen Mileski and Donald Black (1972), Jonathan Katz (1983), Ken Plummer (1975), William Simon and John Gagnon (1967; Gagnon and Simon 1973), Randolph Trumbach (1977), Carrol A. B. Warren (1974); Jeffrey Weeks (1977); they were followed by numerous others. (Of those mentioned, the anticipatory work of Mileski and Black may be said to belong among the unjustly forgotten classics of homosexuality studies.) It should be noted that 'radical' constructionism, denying any biological or early childhood determination of same-sex *preference*, was much less widespread even among the founders of constructionism than assumed by its adversaries. See e.g. Foucault 1982–3; Plummer 1975: 102, 124, 130, 135; Weeks 1981: 108ff.

5 Thus Sedgwick 1990: 40ff; Herdt and Boxer 1992: 3 (cf. Herdt 1992: ix); Butler 1993: 4ff; Seidman 1993: 105f.

6 The discussion and critique of 'constructionism' will, of course, be detailed in the course of the exposition. Merely for purposes of an introductory illustration of *one* of the trends I have in mind: the theoretical framework of 'discourses construct identity by way of power' is, I think, exemplified brilliantly by the works of Judith Butler (1990; 1993), notwithstanding her criticism of 'discursive' or 'linguistic monism' (1993: 6, 192; cf. Bech 1995). It is important to keep in mind that I am criticizing a *trend* which, however widespread, is rarely encountered in pure cultivation; sometimes it is present as mere rhetoric, though quite often it constitutes a bit of a straitjacket for the exposition of the richness in the actual analyses conducted.

7 The comparatively detailed nature of this discussion seems appropriate since the book differs considerably from the canons of conventional social science, particularly in the Anglo-Saxon world.

8 In other words, I have attempted to make the main text of the book accessible also to non-academic readers, whereas the footnotes contain discussions on more specialized theoretical and methodological issues.

9 Cf. Marx 1857–8: 253, 320, 459–61, 619. Obviously, Marx did not speak of homosexuality here, but of capital.

10 Again, I think that some distinctions made in Marx's analysis of capital (and in some of its interpretations) are instructive: those between the 'general, systematic analysis' ('allgemeine Analyse') and the historical one. The more precise elucidation of these levels of Marx's method was anticipated by Zelený (1962), but, I think, most clearly elaborated in the German and Danish receptions known as 'Kapitallogik' (of which the Danish one is, occasionally, less Hegelian and metaphysical than the German. – 'Kapitallogik' is associated with the names of e.g. H.-J. Krahl, A. Sohn-Rethel, A. Schmidt, H.

Reichelt, H.-J. Schanz). In fact, Marx not only made a distinction between historical and general analysis, he prioritized the latter as the necessary prerequisite for the former: '. . . our method indicates the points where historical investigation must enter in, or where bourgeois economy as a merely historical form of the production process points beyond itself to earlier historical modes of production. In order to develop the laws of bourgeois economy, therefore, it is not necessary to write the *real history of the relations of production*. But the correct observation and deduction of these laws, as having themselves become in history [als selbst historisch gewordene Verhältnisse], always leads to primary equations – like the empirical numbers e.g. in natural science – which point towards a past lying behind this system. These indications [Andeutungen], together with a correct grasp of the present, then also offer the key to the understanding of the past – a work in its own right . . . This correct view likewise leads at the same time to the points at which the suspension of the present form of production relations gives signs of its becoming – foreshadowings of the future. Just as, on one side the pre-bourgeois phases appear as *merely historical*, i.e. suspended presuppositions, so do the contemporary conditions of production likewise appear as engaged in *suspending themselves* and hence in positing the *historic presuppositions* for a new state of society' (Marx 1857–8: 460f [I have added the first German insertion in the quote and corrected the other one], cf. 105, 320, 463). I have quoted this long passage since it represents, in a paradigmatic form, some of the metatheoretical guidelines of the analysis in the present book – focusing, that is, on *modern homosexuality*, and not on 'bourgeois economy'. However, I don't agree with the prioritizing of 'general, systematic' analysis; but I do think that historical and structural analysis are interdependent, and that a focus (such as in the present book) on the 'structural' analysis can offer particular insights.

11 A further method of significance for this revised edition is the qualitative life-history interviews that I conducted in 1988 (see Bech 1989a).

12 Or, in the German phrase: 'zu den Sachen selbst', 'getting to the things themselves'. There have, of course, been quite some efforts over the years to make use of inspirations from phenomenology and existentialism in the study of homosexuality. There is, for example, a tradition in the German *Kulturraum* – one may recall the works of Oswald Schwarz, Helmut Schelsky, Hans Giese, Medard Boss – though this is a tradition, I think, with rather disastrous results, transforming early and mid-twentieth-century norms of normality into an ontology of existence. (Cf. Schwarz 1931; 1935: 249–62; Schelsky 1955; Giese 1958; Boss 1966: 108–30). There is also some influence from existentialism and phenomenology in the American sociology of homosexuality – the work of Carrol A. B. Warren (1974; cf. also Warren and Johnson 1972; Warren and Ponse 1977) springs to mind as excellent; however, it is

conducted in a tradition somewhat different from what I am attempting (her work being along the lines of Sartre rather than Heidegger, of Goffman rather than Kracauer or Benjamin – to put it fairly schematically).

13 For example, for erotic or sexual pleasure to become an object of medical and psychiatric procedures such as symptomatological examination, diagnostic analysis and manipulative treatment, pleasure would have to be apprehended as consisting of determinable surface manifestations as well as a hidden but identifiable meaning and cause. Cf. Foucault 1976: parts II and III.

14 Cf. Adorno 1966: 183ff; 1962.

15 This has, of course, been noticed by others as well (e.g. Cohen 1991), although often in a half-hearted fashion (e.g. Laqueur 1990: 11–14 vs 23).

16 I am referring here to Heidegger's concept of the fundamental *Gestimmtheit* – i.e. 'being tuned' of being-in-the-world. (Although Heidegger preferred another term at the ontological level: *Befindlichkeit*. Cf. Heidegger 1927: sections 29–30, 40. – A note on terminology: I use the English terms 'attunedness', 'tuning' and 'mood' for the German *Befindlichkeit*, *Gestimmtsein* and *Stimmung*. This is somewhat different from Macquarrie and Robinson's English translation, see nn. 2 and 3 to p. 172 of the English edition). Some implications of Heidegger's ideas on this point were elaborated by Binswanger (1932) and Bollnow (1941/56), but nothing of this seems to have had much influence in phenomenological sociology. The tradition which gained prominence here was that of Husserl as further developed by Schutz – a tradition which, in regard to the role of tunings and emotions, has been characterized as marked by a cognitivistic or intellectual bias (Eberle 1984: 182f, 433, 511; cf. also Douglas 1977). – It should be noted that the concepts of 'tuning', 'mood' and 'attunedness' are not identical to widespread notions of 'feeling' or 'emotion'. For one thing, tunings (etc.) are more fundamental, diffuse, all-embracing, colouring than emotions/feelings. (Cf. the discussion in Bollnow 1941/56: ch. II.) Moreover, 'tuning' refers to a philosophical anthropology and a world view totally different from that of, e.g., psychoanalysis or symbolic interactionism: tunings are not situated on the level of the individual, they are not reducible to 'meanings' or 'significations', nor are they inter- or transactional – they cut across the distinctions of subject and object, me and others. This makes it possible to conceive of 'social' or 'collective' tunings, e.g. attached to life spaces, as I shall do later in the book. Cf. Bollnow 1963: ch. IV, 4; see also Bech 1996.

17 A detailed discussion of the phenomenological concept of 'life-world' and its vicissitudes, as well as those of 'phenomenological method', is outside the scope of this book. The following treatments are useful and illuminating: Welter 1986; Eberle 1984. I find – as do no doubt most 'phenomenologists' – the application of the method, i.e. the actual

analyses, much more instructive of the details and tenor of 'phenomenological method' than are abstract discussions of its principles. There is, however, an excellent and electrifying discussion of Kracauer's method in Mülder 1985: 68–125 (see also Frisby 1985: 109–86); and Heidegger's brief discussion of his method in *Being and Time* (1927: section 7) is exemplarily clear and instructive. Among the works that I consider paradigmatic in demonstrating the method-in-use are those listed in n. 18 below (whether or not the authors would like the label 'phenomenological'). Accordingly, the comments on 'life-world' and 'method' presented in this introduction are in an emphatic sense introductory and preliminary; the precise substance and implication of both can appear only in the course of the analyses.

18 Cf., respectively, Heidegger 1927; Benjamin [1927–40]; Sartre 1943; Kracauer 1926 and 1930.

19 Accordingly, the guiding questions of this book may be phrased in the following manner: what is it to be a homosexual man – and what is it to be a man not-being-homosexual? Further: what characterizes the human mode(s) of being in the world, when being-homosexual and being-not-homosexual is possible?

20 In this respect, the masters of phenomenological life-world analysis are not Husserl or Schutz but Kracauer and Benjamin.

21 I should like to stress the empirical side of this. Because of the fairly unconventional style of the book, some readers may be inclined to think that it is not 'empirical' enough. However, the theory presented is, during the course of its development in the book, 'tested' against a considerable body of empirical work, others' as well as my own.

22 For reasons of space, references have been restricted to works that have been particularly innovative or highly influential; moreover to works that are representative of or compile results from a number of scholarly efforts, or which exemplify a phenomenon in a particularly illuminating way.

23 See e.g. Atkinson 1992.

24 See the discussion and references in Mülder 1985: 106ff. Much of Kracauer's work, as well as much of Benjamin's, is exemplary in this respect. The controversy between those two authors on the one hand and Adorno on the other is illuminating here. One cannot paste the concrete things into the texts, lectured Adorno (1966: 11ff (I have changed the translation); cf. Adorno 1964; Adorno: letter to Benjamin (10 October 1938) in Lonitz (ed.) 1994: 364ff; and the discussion in Jay 1978). But somehow they managed to, thereby making the reading of their texts such a different experience from that of reading Adorno. From another point of view, the discussion is one of whether these works of Kracauer and Benjamin should be relegated to the (dubious) realms of 'philosophy', 'essayism' and 'journalism', or can be considered part of the social sciences; I think it would imply a great loss for the latter if they aren't.

25 Adorno 1957; cf. also Adorno and Horkheimer 1947; Adorno 1966; Foucault 1971.
26 The phenomenological focus of the book may also produce the objection that it underestimates the 'material', i.e. the impact from capitalist economy and the state. On this, see my comments in ch. III, section 21; ch. IV, sections 22–3; ch. V, section 7; ch. VI, sections 2, 5.

II Homosexualities Out of Date

1 Herdt 1981.
2 Herdt 1984 contains a comprehensive discussion of older and more recent literature on a large number of Melanesian societies in which sexual relations between men are universal. In some of these societies the intercourse is not oral but anal (ibid.: 17, 21, 23, 25, etc.); and in some societies the older man may very well continue sexual relations with boys even after his marriage (ibid.: 17, 27, 29; Baal 1984).
3 Cf. Herdt 1981: 2–3, 232–9, 252, 282.
4 Cf. also Kulick 1985: 30–6.
5 Herdt 1981: 282, 319.
6 Plato: Charmides 154C–D. I have made minor changes in the English translation by W. R. M. Lamb; the most controversial one being my change of 'lovers' (Greek: *ἐρασταί*) to 'wooers' (to avoid misunderstanding).
7 Foucault 1984a: 62–73, 273–7. For some reservations on the 'freedom' of Greek ethics see Cantarella 1992: 215ff.
8 Dover 1978/89: 84–7, 171; Buffière 1980: 605–7; Foucault 1984a: 214–16, 219–22.
9 Dover 1978/89: ch. IIB and C; 1988; Foucault 1984a: ch. IV; Halperin 1990: ch. 3. For some reservations about the 'intercrural' position see Dover 1978/89: 204; Boswell 1994: 53. – Patzer (1982: esp. 104–23) interprets the pederasty of the 'classical period' as being primarily a consequence of two factors: on the one hand, the handing down of religiously oriented initiation rites, and on the other hand the emergence of a new, broad and not especially sexual celebration of beauty. Both aspects are in contrast to the views of Dover, Foucault and Halperin, who place more weight on the secular and directly lascivious, and whose reading I find more convincing. (Cf. also Patzer's own modifications, ibid.: 124f). Halperin (1990: ch. 3) makes the point for Greece that Herdt makes for Sambia, in stressing the erotic, desirous and pleasurable nature of men's sexual relationships with each other; in contrast to the efforts of much scholarship (Patzer's included) at explaining this away.
10 Dover 1978/89: 86f; Foucault 1984a: 214–16.
11 Quoted from Katz 1976: 285, 292.

12 Devereux 1937.
13 Ibid.: 502, 510f, 514, 516, 518.
14 Callender and Kochems 1983: 453; cf. also Roscoe 1991.
15 Devereux 1937: 513–16.
16 In an insightful article, Anishnawbe (1988) has stressed the importance of paying attention to the differences among berdache figures, related to differences in economic, social, gender etc. organization of each tribe. See also Gutiérrez 1989.
17 Hill 1935: 273–6. Other interesting cases are reported in Bowers 1965: 166–8; Boscana *c.*1822: 54. – For general overviews and discussions of the anthropological material on men-women among North American Indians, see Callender and Cochems 1983; Roscoe 1987; Roscoe 1991; Whitehead 1981; Williams 1986. Almost all of the texts containing original material offer only very sparse information. Of the somewhat more extensive presentations of originally collected material, two especially give information on the question of interest in the present context (i.e. the question of the existence and prevalence of sexual relations between men): the articles by Devereux (1937) on the Mohaves, and by Hill (1935) on the Navahos (which is why I have concentrated on these cases). Both texts distort their material to some extent by projecting modern concepts of 'homosexuals' and 'homosexuality' on it; I have discreetly removed this straitjacket in my summaries of their results.
18 Williams 1985. Cf. the discussions in Williams (1986) and Roscoe (1991) on the modified survival or reinvigoration of the man-woman figures among American Indians.

III Absent Homosexuality

1 Wellings et al. 1994: 183, 185, 190. The percentages given in the quotes are not directly comparable, since they derive from two different sets of questionnaires and since the study does not always present comparable calculations even where they could be made. Cf. n. 12 below.
2 The reader is reminded that the aim is here to produce an overview of forms of male–male sexuality which are indubitably universal and universally acknowledged within given societies, not an overview of all the forms of male–male sexuality that have existed in various societies around the globe.
3 Although we should be *very* clear about it, e.g. also about the implications of the criteria used for making this main distinction. Indeed, a major result of this study is the problematizing of some of the criteria often used in macro-historical overviews of male–male sexual relationships. Cf. ch. IV, n. 74.
4 Cf. e.g. the references in Herdt 1984: 17, 47; Adam 1985a: 21, 30f.

5 Very helpful discussions and overviews are presented in Greenberg 1988: chs 2–6; Murray (ed.) 1992; Murray (ed.) 1995.

6 More specifically, it has been argued that far into the twentieth century there existed a conception and practice of male–male sexual relations which did not focus on the fact that both partners were of the same biological sex, but instead on the assumed, polarized gender identities of the partners (masculine vs feminine). Accordingly, a 'real man' could very well have sex with another man as long as the latter was perceived to be feminine and 'passive'.

7 Kinsey et al. 1948: 623, 650 (their emphasis removed).

8 It is above all Kinsey's empiricism that makes his work so advanced even today. This empiricism is in fact a 'sticking to the phenomena', both in the collecting of the material and in the analysis of it, through systematically disregarding the usual theoretical and everyday preconceptions of 'homosexuals' and 'heterosexuals'.

9 Kinsey et al. 1948: 650 (their emphasis removed).

10 Kinsey did not use probability sampling and presumably recruited too high percentages of respondents from prisons and reform schools, as well as from urban homosexual networks (Laumann et al. 1994: 289).

11 Kinsey conducted his interviews from 1938 to 1947, i.e. around the Second World War, a period characterized by a huge upheaval in family and gender relations, with many men coming to big cities and/or entering gender-segregated ways of life (cf. Berube 1990; D'Emilio 1983: ch. 2). Further, the distinction between 'homosexuals' and 'heterosexuals' which was later to become common to the point of appearing natural, was not as pronounced and widespread then, especially not outside the educated classes, with the effect that sexual relations between men were perhaps more widespread (Chauncey 1982–3; 1985; 1994).

12 A recent major American study arrives at a maximum of 9 per cent of men reporting that they have engaged in any physical contact of a sexual nature with another man since puberty, a percentage which exceeds the 7.7 per cent reporting 'one or the other form of same-gender sexual attraction or interest' (Laumann et al. 1994: 294ff). A recent major British study arrives at a maximum of 6.1 per cent reporting any (physical) homosexual experience since thirteen, a percentage which exceeds the 5.5 per cent of men reporting any homosexual attraction (Wellings et al. 1994: 181ff). However, it seems that both studies – because of their methods – underreport the percentage of men attracted to sexuality between men, when compared to the percentage of those with physical homosexual experience. Concerning attraction/interest, the American study asks its questions in the present tense, whereas concerning experience, questions are asked in relation to life since puberty. The British study does ask questions concerning attraction in relation to life since thirteen, but does so only in the face-to-face interview and not in the accompanying

self-completion booklet. However, concerning experience there is in fact a marked difference in the percentage who report this in the face-to-face interview when compared to the self-completion booklet (5.2 vs 6.1 per cent). Nevertheless, although the percentage of men with any sexual interests in other men during their lifetime since puberty would perhaps exceed the US 7.7 per cent and the UK 5.5 (or even the US 9 per cent and the UK 6.1), had the studies used a more consequent (or indeed a more in-depth) methodology, the result would undoubtedly still be a far cry from Kinsey's 50 per cent.

13 The estimates of the number of inmates involved in homosexual relations range from a few to 90 per cent. Buffum, examining the American material up to 1970, states that 'most' estimates are around 30–45 per cent (Buffum 1972: 12f; cf. also Propper 1981: 10).

14 E.g. Kirkham 1971; Ibrahim 1974; cf. also Wooden and Parker 1982: 15, 37; Tewksbury 1989.

15 E.g. Gagnon and Simon 1968 (the quotes are from p. 29 of this article); Buffum 1972.

16 Cf. Lockwood 1980: 31–3, 104–12 (the quote is from p. 32 of this book); Nacci and Kane 1983: 35f; Nacci and Kane 1984: 47f.

17 Cf. the Maryland prisoner's account to Money and Bohmer (1980: 262–5).

18 Sagarin 1976: 250; Johnson 1971: 90.

19 Kirkham 1971: 339; Sagarin 1976: 252; Tucker 1982: 64–7, 72, 76; Rideau and Sinclair 1979: 28; cf. Propper 1981: 69–71.

20 Cf. Kirkham 1971: 332–46; Tucker 1982: 66; Wooden and Parker 1982.

21 Cf. Richmond 1978; Coggeshall 1988.

22 Cf. Kirkham 1971: 333–5; Johnson 1971: 92–3.

23 Cf. Kirkham 1971: 338; Tucker 1982: 66; Wooden and Parker 1982: 108. Consequently, although the punk is, so to speak definitionally, not-Man (with a capital M) this is not identical to his being not-man. This is a crucial distinction and one to which I shall return at various points throughout the book.

24 Carroll 1977: 432; Sagarin 1976: 251; Davis 1968: 13; Kirkham 1971: 336; Wooden and Parker 1982: 75, 76, 103, 110.

25 Kirkham 1971: 348; Scacco 1975: 304, 305; Rideau and Sinclair 1979: 23; Johnson 1971: 84; Davis 1968: 14; Tucker 1982: 69.

26 Johnson 1971: 93; Gagnon and Simon 1968: 26; Kirkham 1971: 346; Tucker 1982: 66, 70, 75; Rideau and Sinclair 1979: 22, 27; Wooden and Parker 1982: 76ff; Nacci and Kane 1983: 35; Nacci and Kane 1984: 46f.

27 In the discussion, I have exclusively used literature on US conditions (apart from one more general text: Richmond 1978), since this literature is the most extensive. Obviously, it is not possible to generalize without further ado from an American context to prison conditions in all countries in the modern West. In this respect the literature is not representative; however, this is irrelevant insofar as the

aim is to investigate whether 'otherwise heterosexual' men under certain circumstances may entertain homosexual interests and relations, and whether a man's sex appeal as a man plays a part in this homosexuality. But prison homosexuality involving 'non-homosexual' prisoners is in any case not an unknown phenomenon in the rest of the Western world (for some references, see Bech 1987: 326). Another possible objection concerning representativeness is the following: It might be argued that the phenomena of prison sexuality belong not to 'modern homosexuality' but to an earlier (and/or different: class or ethnically specific) formation of male–male sexual relations, organized not in terms of the sex of the partner, but in terms of the gender identities assumed by the participating men ('male' vs more 'female' identities). However, I have only made use of literature from the 1960s and on (although some of it does also refer to earlier literature). It might be interjected that an older/different culture has been able to survive in the extraordinary context of prisons. Although there is undoubtedly some truth in this, I believe the argument is far too simplistic. Most of the prisoners – not to mention the researchers and prison authorities – no doubt come from a social world in which the formations of modern homosexuality prevail; accordingly, their main sexual 'identity' is largely modern, defined within the binary opposition of 'homosexuals' and 'heterosexuals'. – Of course, there are more works on the subject than the ones used in this analysis; but nothing suggests that the literature employed is not representative for the attitudes characteristic of such prison investigations in general. It should be mentioned, though, that Wooden and Parker (1982) do not consider prison homosexuality a problem in itself. – That 'otherwise heterosexual' men behave 'homosexually' is well known from other contexts as well, such as those of prostitution and public lavatories (e.g. Reiss 1961; Klein 1989; Humphries 1970; Desroches 1990). I have chosen the prison context because it is less problematic in a discussion of the prevalence of homosexuality. It is always possible to claim that men become prostitutes or participate in tea-room trade because of their *special* homosexual interests; whereas mostly, it is not for this reason that men land in prison.

28 Freud 1905: 145, note of 1915; cf. 1920: 171; 1940: 155f.

29 Freud's views on homosexuality are not gathered in one particular work, and the statements that can be found in various places throughout his works must, as I have done here, be read in their context as well as in the overall context of the entire psychoanalytic theory and its developments. Only then can one try to piece them together to a more comprehensive 'Freudian' theory of homosexuality. The reader is also reminded that the following discussions do not deal with the question of why some people 'become homosexual', but with the quite different one of a possible *universal* homosexuality in all men in modern societies.

30 Freud 1905: 141–7; cf. also 1920: 154; 1930: 105f n. 3.
31 Freud 1912–13: 141–3.
32 Freud 1905: 222f; 1914: 87–90; cf. also 1905: 229f; 1921: 103.
33 Freud 1913: 60f; 1914: 87–90; 1918: 27f; cf. 1908: 215f; 1909: 109; 1922: 230f.
34 Freud 1914: 90, 101.
35 Freud 1920: 159 n. 1; 1922: 231f; 1923b: 37.
36 Freud 1910: 98–101; 1921; 108f.
37 Freud 1905: 146 note of 1915; 1913: 332.
38 Freud 1923b: 33; 1923c: 90f; 1925: 250; 1918: 46f; 1937: 250.
39 Indeed, Freud himself speaks of the possibility of a 'dissolution' and 'demolition' (1923b: 32–4; 1924: 177).
40 For instance, Lacanian or object-relations-theory versions of psychoanalysis offer similar possibilities for arguing in favour of a universal homosexuality – and similar weaknesses.
41 E.g. Bieber et al. 1962: 274; Ovesey 1969: 16–22; cf. Lewes 1988: 166ff.
42 It was never a main interest of Freud's to uncover possible homosexual components underlying universal phenomena. The indications which can nevertheless be found must be read, as I have, in the context of the entire psychoanalytic theory and its development in order to determine their full significance. For example, Freud's various statements concerning a 'father complex' and the like e.g. in 'Totem and Taboo' (Freud 1912–13) must be read in connection with the paper on 'The Ego and the Id' (1923b). For the same reason, a detailed discussion of the various arguments would carry us much too far.
43 Freud 1923b: 31–8; 1912–13 and 1939 are giant variations on this theme.
44 Freud 1923b: 28–39; cf. also 1914: 93–102.
45 Freud 1911: 61; 1921: 103; 1922: 231f; 1923b: 37; cf. also 1921: 141.
46 Freud 1922: 223.
47 Cf. e.g. Freud 1912–13: ch. IV.
48 Hocquenghem 1972: ch. 2. I shall return to Hocquenghem's analysis in another context (section 11).
49 No doubt, Hocquenghem was well aware of the 'unprovability' of his analysis and considered this to be part of the game. – On the problems in psychoanalytic theories positing repressed/sublimated homosexuality as the basis of culture and society, see also Owen's (1987) brilliant critique of the homophobic elements in some feminist versions of this.
50 *Din nabos søn*, directed by Jørgen Flindt Pedersen and Erik Stephensen; Denmark 1981.
51 The Greek word is *poustis*. Cf. also Schildt 1976: 185f.
52 Altman 1971: 84–92; 1982: x, 40, 60–5, 70f; Hocquenghem 1972: 41–7, 89–92, 96–8 and passim; Mieli 1977: 122–45, 153–8 and passim; cf. Freud 1905: 237f; 1911: 59–73; 1922: 227, 232; 1923a: 256; 1933: 97f; cf. also Ferenczi 1914.
53 Freud himself discusses the possibility of different types of repression

mechanism before reserving in 1926 the word to cover one particular defence operation. Cf. Freud 1911: 66–8; 1915a: 146–58; 1915b: 180–5; 1916–17: 294–8; 1923a: 246; 1923b: 14f, 16 n. 1; 1926: 163f; 1933: 89–92. As for sublimation, Freud tries to distinguish it from repression in various ways: sublimation allows some, though modified release (1922: 227); it is socially valuable and useful (1905: 156, 237f; 1911: 61; 1916–17: 345; 1918: 70f; 1923a: 256; 1930: 79f); it is less violently and abruptly enforced (1910: 79f; 1922: 227; cf. also the interpretations of Marcuse 1955: ch. 10); it is more successful and pleasurable (1910: 135f; 1912: 232; 1916–17: 345f; 1930: 79f). In any case, the distinction remains unclear and/or dubiously valorized.

54 This conception has been variously termed the 'drive reduction', 'hydraulic', 'male' or 'phallocratic' model of sexuality. Cf. e.g. Gagnon and Simon 1973: 11; Bailey 1990: 148f.

55 To state that homosexual wishes may arise in a given situation is not identical to claiming that such homosexuality is 'situational' in the traditional sense of this phrase: i.e. reducible to being merely an emergency measure. Cf. section 3 above; and the remaining sections of this chapter.

56 Stangerup 1966: 265. Herman Bang (1857–1912) is broadly acknowledged as one of the greatest writers in Danish literature (although most would also agree that *Mikaël* is not one of his best novels from the point of view of literary technique). For a general discussion of Bang's work, life and sexuality, as well as the attitudes of the secondary literature, see Bjørby 1986; Rosen 1993: 628–54.

57 On the film versions see e.g. Theis 1984: 103f; Finch 1987; Dyer 1990: 24f.

58 Bang 1904: 35, 186.

59 Ibid.: 41.

60 For references to the secondary literature see Bech 1987: 330.

61 Bang 1904: 13, 168.

62 Ibid.: 17; cf. Secher 1973: 304f; and Lane 1836 (vol. II): 100–2 (a 'classic' of orientalism, reprinted several times, e.g. also 1890). Cf. also Sedgwick 1985: 192f.

63 Bang 1904: 138, 57.

64 Ibid.: 23.

65 Ibid.: 37, 117, 166, 192f. Obviously, I am not implying that Bang knew T. E. Lawrence in 1904. But for later readers – 'homosexual' or not – he is an integral part of the (homo-)mythology of 'Arab' countries.

66 Bang 1904: 11, 12, 20, 53, 65, 85, 135, 136, 137, 201, 211, 212.

67 Ibid.: 17, 42, 54. On the Tuileries Gardens as a sexual meeting place for men, from the eighteenth century and on, see Coward 1980: 238, 243; Barbedette and Carassou 1981: 37f.

68 The unspecified 'the reader' = 'we' = 'he or she' of this section (indeed of this book) is to indicate that there is in principle no gender limit to sensing the presence, however absent, of sexual interests between men

in modernity. For instance, Sedgwick (1985; 1990) has amply demonstrated in practice that 'the woman' *can* know. But obviously, different reading positions offer different advantages in this respect (for women, e.g. the power related to the fact that it 'is always open to women to know something [i.e. the desire of men for other men] that it is much more dangerous for any nonhomosexual-identified man to know' – Sedgwick 1990: 209f). Accordingly, it is far too simple to claim that women's relation – in reading or in real life – to the phenomena of male homosexuality is one of being excluded; it is as much a matter of, among many other things, being turned on or identifying. – Cf. also Moore 1988; and notes to ch. III, section 16.

69 Obviously, I do not claim that no one else has identified or made use of such analytic guidelines. Indeed, they belong to the tool kit indispensable for studying the relations between homosexuality, textuality, and life. Cf. e.g. Austen 1977; Clum 1992; Craft 1994; Dollimore 1991; Fone 1995; Keilson-Lauritz 1987; 1991; Koestenbaum 1989; Martin 1979; Miller 1988; Moon 1991; Sedgwick 1985, 1990; Sinfield 1991; 1994a: ch. 3; Summers 1990; Yingling 1990. I do not imply, of course, that the identification of 'homosexuality' 'hidden in' or 'behind' the texts is the main objective of all these authors. However, in the contexts of their diverse analyses, they must pursue this question as well.

70 This will be the theme of ch. V, section 6.

71 Ferenczi 1911: 144.

72 Ibid.: 149.

73 Ferenczi 1914; Freud 1923b: 43.

74 Hocquenghem 1972: 41.

75 I am referring here to material cited by Hocquenghem as well as to other relevant material; cf. discussions in and notes to ch. IV, section 7; ch. V, sections 2, 4, and 6.

76 Cf. Hocquenghem 1972: ch. 2.

77 Greenberg has pointed to an additional factor which may be productive of homosexual paranoia at the level of social institutions. From the last third of the nineteenth century there was a marked increase in state and economic bureaucracies, favouring the development of a 'bureaucratic' – rational and unemotional – personality among the men employed, which in turn implied a fear of (homosexual) intimacy among men and the necessity of repudiation. Cf. Greenberg 1988: ch. 10; cf. also Sedgwick 1990: 182–8.

78 Hocquenghem 1972 (French edition): 36 (the passage is missing from the English edition).

79 From *Kontext* (Copenhagen), 45 (1983), 58–9.

80 From *Seksualpolitik* (Copenhagen), 1 (1984), 8.

81 Cf. Mieli 1977: 124; Dundes 1978; Simpson 1994: 80. But indeed, if we think we must make an interpretation by way of sexual symbolism, how would we know it is not *hetero*sexual? – as, indeed, often assumed (e.g. Stokes 1956).

82 As appears, I consider 'life-spaces' to be of particular importance among the conditions forming the 'background' to the phenomena of modern homosexuality. The topic of spatiality has gained increasing attention among scholars in recent years, and produced some interesting affinities between a number of cultural and sociological studies and developments in geography. Again, my own approach is influenced by existential phenomenology – at least in a broad sense of this term, and not so much by the tradition from Heidegger or Bollnow, always on the verge of transforming 'space' into *Boden* and Bavarian *Bauernhof*. Rather, my work has similarities to that of Kracauer and Benjamin, attempting to delineate the lived spaces of modernity and doing so in non-nostalgic ways. Cf. Bech 1992b; 1996; Bech, forthcoming (b).

83 Plum and Simonsen 1984: 21.

84 For some references see Bech 1987: 331 n. 5. The international football association (FIFA) has in fact gradually strengthened its rules regarding the proper behaviour of players, although an explicitly specified prohibition against kissing, 'gang groping' and the like is still – absent (personal communication from a World Cup referee). On kisses, see also Harper 1994: 124ff.

85 See Øllgaard 1984 (on ice-hockey); Simpson 1994: 78, 82 (on football); cf. also Dunning 1986: 274f (on rugby).

86 There are many rumours concerning the relation between homosexuality and sport, but very few investigations. Even among the Freudian left there are usually merely a few remarks *en passant* (e.g. Siegert 1970: 854; Vinnai 1970: 61–5; Altman 1971: 85; 1982: 61f; Mieli 1977: 123f; Vinnai 1977: 102–4; Hoch 1979: 81). Cf. also Dundes 1978; Oates 1987: 30–2; Simpson 1994: 69–93. There is an interesting empirical study in Garner and Smith 1977; judging from this, fairly many men in team sports do not stop at 'sublimations' or 'repressions' of homosexual interests. But the sample is small. Cf. also the case material presented in Pronger 1990; and the 'auto'-biography of the American football-star David Kopay (Kopay and Young 1977).

87 The relation of constitution between male interest and male spaces is not unidirectional (in the sense that male interest is constitutive of male spaces and not the other way round). Whether or not spaces have been constituted by male interest – or by other interests, by nature, or by chance – once they become populated by men they are co-constitutive of male interest.

88 Reading the English rendering of this question I am reminded of a similar question posed by Margaret Morse in relation to the use of slow motion in the representation of male figures in televised sports: 'What is the significance of the slowness of their motion?' (Morse 1983: 55). This wonderful phrasing is indeed, like my own, a phenomenological one (although Morse is, I think, too quick in applying psychoanalysis to answer the question).

89 As we have seen already (section 13), there are other spaces where

looking is mandatory (such as the soccer stadium). This underlines the importance of the particular structure or form of various kinds of space, a point to which I shall return repeatedly in the following chapters.

90 The empirical material for the analysis of these male relations derives from the author's field work at a gym in Copenhagen at various intervals from 1984 to 1994. ('Taurus' is a cover name.) In this analysis of 'absent homosexuality' I have of course concentrated on 'non-homosexual' men, i.e. tacitly 'subtracted' the 'homosexuals' who also appear at Taurus. One may ask how this is possible; but there are ways (cf. ch. IV, sections 9 and 10). Besides, the 'homosexuals' hardly make up more than one-fifth of the entire clientele. I have been told that male relations are different in the gyms where the pumping of giant muscles is essential. There, the interest in other men is much more direct; and there is much more explicit gazing, posing, fingering and commenting. This somewhat different situation does not affect what is fundamental in the present analysis: that in the very decision to become a man is included an interested relation to other men, and that this relation is materialized in the structure of space.

91 'Classic' studies concerning socio-cultural differences in men's ways of carrying themselves are Mauss 1950; Bourdieu 1977, 1990.

92 Cf. Sartre 1943.

93 I am not, of course, implying that such 'identifications' are 'total' in the sense that an individual becomes one with this 'male identity'.

94 Or, in psychoanalytic terms, that there is a difference between identification and cathexis. Yet Freud himself was not always quite certain. His comments in fact revolve mostly on the connections and transitions between them, entangling him in contradictions as well. Cf. Freud 1921: 105–8; 1923b: 29–32.

95 In this section and the preceding one, then, I have attempted a particular kind of 'transcendental phenomenology', exploring the conditions of possibility for the constitution of homosexuality among 'non-homosexual' men. A guiding question has been this: given that absent homosexuality is pervasive among men, what then must characterize masculinity (as a way of being-in-the-world) for this to be possible? – I should like to emphasize that the analysis and its results do not imply any essentializing of specific forms of masculinity. Firstly, the extent to which 'male interest' – interest from men to other men – prevails is dependent upon the degree of accentuation of masculinity (since male interest is an implication of masculinity); and obviously, this is historically variable. However, I do believe that there is a transhistorical dimension to it as well, but I do not think that this is very problematic in itself. This leads to the second point: masculinity and male interest should be distinguished from their particular *forms*, which are certainly not always very agreeable, either to women or to men. At this more concrete level, the particular forms of masculinity

may be profitably analysed by incorporating the power/structure/praxis framework of 'hegemonic masculinity' suggested by Carrigan et al. 1985.

96 I saw the cinema version of the film twice in 1989/90 and made notes of the dialogue. I have not been able to recheck the remark about 'wanking'; in the video version available via the market this is – absent.

97 Cf. Garde 1964; Rowse 1977; Greif 1982.

98 Forster [1914]/1971 and [1922–58]/1972. Cf. the discussions in Altman 1977; Meyers 1977: 90–113; Martin 1983.

99 Cf. the discussion in Meyers 1977: ch. VII.

100 Readers today, notes Halperin, 'are, if anything, rather too well informed about the dreary details of Forster's personal life' (1990: 75).

101 Cf. Altman 1982: ch. 5.

102 This, I believe, is also the reason behind the change in intensity or tone noticed by Dyer: namely that the film 'plays down' the sexual feeling between the two men, in the sense that there 'is certainly no development of the undertow of gay feeling that you get in the book' (Dyer 1985: 138).

103 Cf. Heede 1985.

104 Cf. Russo 1981: 54 (on *Diamonds are Forever*); 154f (on *From Russia with Love*; *Goldfinger*); 253 (on *Live and Let Die*).

105 Boswell 1980: chs 10–11; Bray 1982: ch. 1.

106 The films referred to above are *St Elmo's Fire* (director: Joel Schumacher; USA 1985); *Dead Poets Society* (director: Peter Weir; USA 1989); *A Chorus Line* (director: Richard Attenborough; USA 1985); *A Passage to India* (director: David Lean; England 1984); *Code of Silence* (director: Andy Davis; USA 1985); *A View to a Kill* (director: John Glen; England 1985); *Cop au Vin* (director: Claude Chabrol; France 1985); *King Solomon's Mines* (director: J. Lee Thompson; USA 1985); *The Shooting Party* (director: Alan Bridges; England 1984).

107 In commenting upon my analysis of *A Passage to India*, Angvik (1989: 290–7) has implied that I conceive of reading as a simple, passive and fundamentally uncreative process of identifying an essential meaning and message implanted in the text by the author's intentions. An attentive reading (!) of my text should make clear that my views and analytic practices concerning such matters are a bit more complex.

108 The representation of homosexuality in films has, in many countries and for long periods, been subject to censorship exerted by the state or self-censorship exerted by the film industry itself (cf. Russo 1981: 31, 33, 118–22; Theis 1984: 102–13; Wotherspoon 1991: 52). However, presenting homosexuality in ways so that its presence can be denied is precisely a characteristic of absent homosexuality – so from

this point of view formalized censorship constitutes no problem for representation. And indeed, it is reasonable to believe that absent homosexuality has been widespread from the start and all the way through; not even the cute little mice in Walt Disney's *Cinderella* go scot-free (cf. Russo 1981: 75). But there are also substantial reasons to assume that primarily after the Second World War, and especially from the 1970s, it became virtually impossible to produce films without homosexuality (cf. ch. III, section 22). For general surveys, discussions and lists of films and homosexuality see Russo 1981; Mellen 1977; Philbert 1984; Theis 1984; Dyer (ed.) 1977/84; Dyer 1993; Stewart 1993. The length of such lists notwithstanding, they leave out most of the films that would be of interest from our present point of view, since they focus on more explicit representations of homosexuality, and in particular on films in which one of the *characters* may be identified as a homosexual. In most films, however, the existence of absent homosexuality can only be 'demonstrated' by being construed rather laboriously through fairly extensive writing. This is also the reason why it makes no sense to present a simple list of films with absent homosexuality. – We should not forget, of course, to mention that there is also a – comparatively tiny although increasing – number of films in which homosexuality is neither missing nor 'absent', but positively present. For some references see Dyer 1990; Stewart 1993; Murray 1994.

109 *Batman* (director Tim Burton; USA 1989). Cf. Bech 1989b.

110 In consequence, there is ultimately no *empirical* way of falsifying the theory of a universal absent homosexuality in films. It can merely be proved inadequate, or *no longer* adequate, by *another comprehensive theory*, founded upon a different mass of socio-cultural material – as indeed I shall try to develop it in ch. VI when discussing the *disappearance* of the phenomena of modern homosexuality, including 'absent homosexuality'.

111 Russo 1981: 261f. – The pattern I have identified above bears some resemblance to the one identified by Gross (who, however, focuses on homosexual characters): sometimes, 'gay people' are visible in the media, but then almost invariably as either victims – of violence or ridicule – or villains; mostly, however, they are ignored or denied – 'symbolically annihilated' (Gross 1991: 26–7). I would stress the 'symbolic' aspect of the 'annihilation', i.e. the presence of the absence produced by it. See also section 18 below.

112 Russo 1981: xi–xii.

113 To recycle a phrase by Eve Sedgwick (1990: 248), although now in a changed, 'materially' socio-spatial rather than epistemological context. Sedgwick's work (*Epistemology of the Closet* as well as *Between Men*) abounds in spatial metaphors ('closet' is one of them, 'between' is another, 'triangle' a third, 'spectacle' a fourth, etc.); this chapter combines inspiration from her work with my own explora-

tions of sociality and spatiality, as presented in the preceding and following sections. Other highly inspiring works are Bailey 1990 and Edelman 1992. Cf.: also Bech 1992b; 1993; 1996.

114 Cf. Morse 1983 (on slow motion and replay); Poynton and Hartley 1990 (on commentators); Bech 1992b.

115 Dollimore 1991: chs 16 and 17. From a psychoanalytic point of view, homophobia is the fear (and the concomitant actions) resulting from the repression of the self's homosexual desires. From a 'materialist' or 'cultural' point of view, homophobia is, according to Dollimore, a strategy of social control, a means of securing an identity formation conforming to the heterosexual masculine norm by way of an excluding, displacing and marginalizing construction of the 'other' (in terms of sexuality, gender, culture, race, class, nationality). The strategy, then, works by demarcating the boundaries of the normal by way of positing an object of fear, hatred, rage and persecution. Dollimore also points to the alliances into which the two forms of homophobia may enter.

116 Sedgwick uses 'homophobia' to denote a 'mechanism for regulating the behavior of the many by the specific oppression of the few'; the strategy works by exploiting 'homosexual panic', the latter being 'a structural residue of terrorist potential, of *blackmailability*, of Western maleness' (Sedgwick 1985: 88f; 1990: 20f).

117 There is even quite some degree of terminological concurrence between their work and my own (I am referring also to the Danish edition of the present book – Bech 1987). I take this to be an expression of a commonly felt need to theorize a field left comparatively untheorized by constructionism until the mid-1980s – the field of 'non-homosexual' men's relations to homosexuality – and to do so while avoiding the pitfalls of an overly facile psychoanalytic reductionism.

118 Other differences or divergences would concern the confidence placed (after all) in the analytic and theoretical tenets of psychoanalysis (cf. e.g. Sedgwick 1990: 211f), as well as the weight attached to the phenomena of 'identity'. Thus, the difference between 'absent homosexuality' and what I shall term 'the homosexual form of existence' is not one of a homophobic male identity vs a homosexual identity. Apart from other criticisms that may be directed at the theoretical emphasis on 'identity' (cf. my discussion in ch. IV), it also seems to me that ideas of a masculine homophobic identity may tend to suggest an intrapsychic 'depth' or 'essentialness' that differs from my conception of a societal machinery or logic overdetermining and subjugating a universal male interest and potential erotic.

119 Sedgwick 1990: 33f; cf. n. 116 above.

120 Foucault's wording about 'King Sex' is known from Foucault 1977, and has been recycled by a number of other authors (e.g. Weeks 1980: 20). Similar critical ideas have been widespread in feminism since the

early 1970s (e.g. Smith-Rosenberg 1975, cf. Smith-Rosenberg 1993). And of course, they can be found in other contexts even before: e.g. Marcuse 1955.

121 And perhaps the literature of 'non-homosexual' authors needs a rereading, explicitly focusing on such 'positive' aspects rather than on the 'negative' ones?

122 For an informative discussion of a number of examples, see Edwards 1994: chs 2 and 4.

123 In other words: 'male interest' and its potential turning into 'male erotics' and, further, into physical-orgasmic sex is a transhistorical implication of any masculinity. 'Absent homosexuality' is the typical form that this interest assumes in modern societies. 'Homophobia' may perhaps most adequately be used to designate a particular aspect of absent homosexuality, emphasizing the negative pole as well as the dimension of passion. In this specific sense, important dimensions of homophobia have been elaborated by Herek (e.g. 1987). Cf. section 14 above.

124 In other words, the book aims at an analysis which is *neither* gynephobic (or 'mysogynic') *nor* homophobic *nor* male-phobic.

125 To use, metaphorically, the metaphors of psychoanalysis: take away the phallus, and there is very little left. Cf. also Bersani 1995 – who, however, seems to be using the metaphors of psychoanalysis less metaphorically than I would.

126 This has implications for the exploration of 'pre-homosexual', i.e. pre-modern male–male sexual relationships as well. In such analyses can often be found formulations like 'What mattered [to the Greeks, the Romans, the Arabs, early twentieth-century working class] was not the sex of the object, but whether or not the partners implied were active or passive, penetrating or penetrated.' If not clearly qualified, such assertions carry the danger of blurring the fact that, generally, it does and did matter to men whether the objects of their erotic and sexual interest and intercourse are men or women. Thus, in a review of Halperin's and Winkler's books on ancient Greece, we are told that 'the gender of a man's sexual partner was largely irrelevant' (Hoffman 1991: 89). However, the asterisked footnotes in Halperin (1990: 33f) precisely dissociate his analyses from such possible misunderstandings. Moreover, assertions like the ones mentioned tend to obliterate the *pleasures related to the maleness* of male–male erotic relationships. On the possible ethnocentric, or modernity-centric, background for such notions see ch. IV, esp. section 17.

127 In this form, 'friendship' is a modern phenomenon (cf. Giddens 1992), 'freed' from economic, political and kinship bonds of clientelism, etc. as well as from group solidarity and loyalties. However, it is not merely a modern phenomenon, as such forms of friendship were also cultivated in other periods (cf. below). It might be argued, though, that in these forms (or at least in some of them) friendship between

two men was subordinated to (or considered to be subordinated to) wider religious ends and arrangements.

128 Empirical studies of friendship corroborate this (cf. Wellman 1992; Cohen 1992; Rubin 1986: ch. 7). Some researchers, however, have pointed to a possible renaissance of friendship, concomitant with changes in gender and family relations of late modernity. But such friendships have not yet been documented outside the very small circles of 'men's movements' or apart from a few individual cases.

129 Cf. Boswell 1980: chs 8 and 9; Kon 1979: 13–73; Martin 1989; Rasch 1936; Rosen 1980; 1993: 323–73; Rotundo 1989.

130 See also Spangler's discussion of male friendships on US television since the 1950s (Spangler 1992).

131 Although it can be rendered likely: e.g. Rubin 1986: 103ff.

132 Cf. e.g. Herzer 1982: 216; Baumgardt 1984c: 38f; Janssen (ed.) 1984: 16, 25, 26, 29, 32, 35, 38, 40–1, 44: Barbedette and Carassou 1981: 151; Katz 1976: 389; Axgil and Fogedgaard 1985: 57.

133 The topic of friendship may serve as an illustrative case for some of the tasks confronting an analytic approach which tries to avoid certain pitfalls in the theories of psychoanalysis or 'homophobia'. First, we cannot take for granted that there is a desire for friendship in modern societies, since we have found no universal 'homosexual drive' which must seek expression in friendship or buddy relations. Only because certain phenomena are present in the materialized dreams of popular culture may we infer the existence of a widespread wish for friendship in modern societies. As for the question of why this modern desire is denied precisely in the manner of *avoidance*, and nevertheless allowed some existence in public fantasy, I have attempted to interpret this in the light of the framework established in the preceding chapters on 'absent homosexuality', including the relation of this to the social spatiality of (spectatorial) closets. And again, I have avoided any reference to 'homophobia' or similar notions because of their latent 'male-phobic' implications. An example may elucidate this further: Mellen (1977) analyses the buddy relations in American cinema as steaming with half-smothered homosexuality. However, in her view these relations are primarily expressions of a *fear of women*: otherwise it is unimaginable that men might entertain more – or even as much – interest in each other as in women. That is, unless they are *homosexuals*, in which case forgiveness may be granted, provided they admit it. Such an analysis testifies to the overly facile intercircularity of the ideas of gynephobia and homophobia (whether or not they are named by these terms) as well as their intimate connection to male-phobia within certain circles. A similar instructive example is Mieli 1977: 125–8.

134 Cf. the discussions in Nardi 1982; Israelstam and Lambert 1983; Lemle and Mishkind 1989.

135 Vinterberg 1987.

136 On such domains in other societies, see e.g. the articles in Ardener (ed.) 1981; and Spain 1992.

137 See Hergé 1963: 36, 42; 1954: 30; 1953: 39.

138 See e.g. Sedgwick 1985.

139 These criteria are in line with the ones elaborated by a number of feminists during the 'porn wars' and similar battles within feminism, e.g. by Rubin 1984/93; Califia 1979–94.

140 Please note that I write 'appears as'. Obviously, the 'natural' masculinity (including its distinction from femininity) celebrated in male sports, is a cultural product – although it does have a 'natural' or 'material' base in the body and its capacities. And indeed, the sports celebrated by men are precisely those privileging the capacities of the male body. Cf. ch. IV, section 17; Bech 1991a; K. Dyer 1982.

141 Please note that this view is not equivalent to Freudian notions of an ever-present (or 'latent') drive or energy. But it does, phenomenologically, accept the energy-like aspects of some sexual excitement.

142 The example given as an introduction to the discussion of absent homosexuality – the film on torture under the Greek junta dictatorship – occupies a particular place in relation to the question of the historicity of violence and inter-male sexuality. On the one hand, the torture training and profession applies a 'premodern' category of same-sex sexual relations (that of 'poustis'); on the other hand, it is being used in relation to a period of ambivalent modernization in Greece; and finally, the film is produced with the explicit view of presenting it to modern Western audiences.

143 Since violence is such a sensitive issue I should like to stress some aspects of the discussion above. First: the section does not intend to present a comprehensive analysis of violence. It focuses solely on the relations between 'male interest', male–male sexuality and male–male violence. Second: a major purpose of the section is to avoid any reductionist analysis of these relations by distinguishing between a number of different forms, amalgams and functions of violence. Third: the section does not aim at any 'naturalization' (or indeed any celebration) of male–male violence. However, it does indicate that *certain forms* of violence seem to be an inescapable possibility in all relations between men, since they are connected to the existential problematics and potentialities of identification, learning and play which are inherent in 'male interest' (as well as to bodily capacities of pleasure). On the historicity of 'male interest' see ch. III, n. 95 to section 14; on its possible transformation in late or postmodern societies see ch. VI.

144 Again, I am referring particularly to Marx as interpreted by the tradition of 'Kapitallogik'. Cf. n. 10 to ch. I. – To avoid misunderstanding, I should like to stress the historical and conglomerate-like character of this dialectical machinery (analogous to that of capital).

It is composed of various factors and phenomena, each with differential histories, though increasingly combined and reinforcing each other from the latter half of the nineteenth century (though not in any linearly unbroken way). However, it remains labile and changeable, exposed to influences from the surroundings, as well as containing in itself some seeds for its dissolution (cf. ch. VI).

145 Analogous to value and valorization in Marx's analysis of capital.

146 Although, given the ubiquity of absent homosexuality it is, in a way, so very easy to 'verify', and any reader should by now be able to discern it: go to the cinema, switch on the television, go out on the town, and it is (not) there.

147 The concept of 'real abstraction' has been developed especially in the tradition from Marx via Adorno to the versions of 'Kapitallogik' mentioned in chapter I (n. 10). A paradigmatic point of reference has been the considerations in Marx 1857–8: 105ff. – Continental European stereotyping will have it that such conceptual entities are annoying foreign elements to the Anglo-Saxon mind, allegedly concerned with the particular and the singular ('who precisely is doing exactly what under which particular conditions'). As stated in chapter I, however, the aim of this book is to identify, 'as far as possible', basic features which have remained constant over the years; and here, I believe, we have found some such features.

148 Thus, the characteristic features of absent homosexuality will become further illuminated when seen in the light of their relation to the particularly modern configurations of masculinity–femininity–the homosexual and masculinity–the homosexual–the apparatus of self-analysis. Moreover, these factors are crucial for the explanation of why absent homosexuality exists.

IV The Homosexual Form of Existence

1 All quotations in this section are from Pontoppidan 1891. The exhibition referred to is the 'Great Nordic Industrial, Agricultural and Art Exhibition' of 1888, in effect a 'world exhibition'.

2 The term 'contrary-sexual' was introduced by Westphal (1869).

3 On the term 'homosexual' and its competitors, cf. Courouve 1985; Herzer 1985; Féray and Herzer 1990, and the discussions and the literature referenced in section 3.

4 The above is an attempt to elaborate, as differentiatedly and concisely as possible, the basic features of 'scientific' and general-public views on 'the homosexuals' (the 'contrary-sexuals', 'uranians', etc.) in the Western world during the last 100 or 130 years. I have presented what I believe is the prevailing form of this, but as stated, at a more fundamental level it should be read as indicating a *problématique* (in the sense of the French 'épistémologie' of Canguilhem, Bachelard,

Althusser, Foucault): a series of underlying and interrelated assumptions that govern which types of questions and answers can at all be brought up. I use 'homosexual' as the general term to cover the entirety of this 'problematic'. I do not claim that, during this period in the West, there have been no *other* public conceptions of men's erotic interests in men than the notion of the 'homosexual' – I claim that it has been the predominant one among the articulated notions (cf. references below as well as notes to section 3). One aspect deserves particular comment. It has been argued that the late nineteenth-century medico-psychiatric conceptions of the homosexual (or the 'invert') did not consider the sex of the object for sexual interest to be the essential and determining factor in making distinctions, but instead the ascribed gender status of a person; in other words, decisive was not whether a man had sex with another male but whether he was experienced as a 'man' or 'woman' in the relationship (Marshall 1981; Katz 1983: 139–47; Chauncey 1982–3; 1985; 1994: 47–9. I shall term this the idea of 'gender inversion'). There is much in favour of this; however, the case history of the grocer – focusing on the sex drive object and emphasizing the masculinity of the case subject – may serve as an indication that things are perhaps more complicated. It is useful to distinguish four levels in modern concepts of same-sex sexuality: (a) the phenomenon serving as point of departure for discussion (or in medical terms: for diagnosis); (b) what is considered the underlying 'essence' of this phenomenon; (c) phenomena considered necessary concomitants of the essence; (d) ideas of the developmental causes (or in medical terms: the aetiology). Only if gender inversion is *the* defining characteristic on all of these four levels would it be reasonable to speak of a full-blown idea of gender inversion. A survey of the international literature from the 1870s to the 1910s seems to suggest that this is rarely the case. The phenomenon attracting attention is almost invariably the sexual drive and its object. The 'essence' of this phenomenon is far from always considered to be gender inversion. In some cases, femininity ('physical' or 'mental') is considered to be a necessary *concomitant* of the essence; often, however, it is seen as a phenomenon which may or may not accompany, *or* it is explicitly denied that there should be any relation between the two. As for the developmental cause, it seems rather uncommon to view this as being essentially and basically a matter of gender inversion. The – admittedly very influential, and internationally so – tradition coming closest to our ideal-type of gender inversion is the German–Austrian line of Ulrichs, Westphal, Krafft-Ebing, Hirschfeld and their ideas of 'not sufficiently' sex-differentiated embryonic developments, leaving the persons afflicted with various degrees of physical or mental traits of the 'opposite' sex. One should be aware, though, that such views were explicitly contested in Germany and Austria; furthermore, quite a number of medical writers seem to have *de facto* concentrated on the sexual drive and the sex of its object and paid little attention, if any, to questions of gender inversion (cf. the discussions in Egger 1993; Herzer 1992; Hohmann 1987; Hutter 1992: 88–103; Jones 1990: 66–9; Oosterhuis's introductions in Oosterhuis (ed.) 1991). Moreover, even within the tradition from Ulrichs there are quite a number of tensions and contradictions, as witnessed e.g. in the ever more elaborate differentiations of 'types', 'varieties' and 'intermediate stages', including from 1910 Hirschfeld's category of non-homosexual transvestites (Hirschfeld 1910). Indeed, the complications can be found virtually from the start. In Ulrichs's first paper, the 'Urning' is unequivocally defined by his gender inversion, just as Ulrichs can only imagine that an 'Urning' is attracted to a 'Dioning', i.e. a real man (1864a: sections 7–11, 51–3; 1864b: section 38). In the following writings this becomes increasingly problematized by an ever more elaborate typology of 'Urnings', including very masculine ones; there is also a growing recognition that 'Urnings' may feel attracted to other 'Urnings', and indeed that 'Dionings' may have feminine components of their sex drive (Ulrichs 1865b: sections 80–3, 114–19; 1868: sections 1–40, 122–3; 1870: section 24; 1879: section 126). By 1904, the number of varieties had reached 403, in the calculations of one scholar within this tradition (cf. Lieshout 1993). In France (*the* other major site for production of medical discourses on same-sex sexuality in the late nineteenth century – cf. Courouve 1981), ideas of a 'psychic hermaphroditism' as an essential or accompanying feature played some role; but again, they were also explicitly contested, and they had to compete with altogether different concepts (e.g. the concept of 'fetishism' in the influential tradition from Binet). Indeed, the French debate in the late nineteenth and early twentieth centuries seems to have concentrated on the *lack in masculinity* among the men afflicted by 'inversion' rather than on their 'femininity' (a crucial though often ignored distinction to which I shall return). (Cf. the discussions in Copley 1989: 135–54; Hahn 1979: 26–85; Nye 1989.) In Britain, there was comparatively little 'scientific' literature on the subject. Ellis, *the* medical authority, was very reticent in applying ideas of gender inversion on any of the four levels – when writing on *men* (cf. Weeks 1977: 57–67; 1980–1). Indeed, notions and theories concerning women were often rather different from those concerning men – a trend, I think, confirmed by the American literature. Chauncey (1982–3) notes this difference; nevertheless, he argues that gender inversion was the predominant idea in the American literature before 1900. A review of the literature he references up to 1900 (and partially re-references in Chauncey 1994: 386 n. 5), however, shows that ideas of gender inversion as underlying essence, as necessary concomitant or as cause did not reign supreme in the literature concerning *men*, and in some cases they are, implicitly at least, rejected. Nor does other American medical literature from the period seem to testify to any overwhelming impact of such ideas before 1900 (Katz 1983: 179–303; Hansen 1989: 95). (For other countries, cf. discussions in Dalsgaard 1984: 27–32; Rosen 1993: 667–94; Hekma 1987. I should add that in many cases I base my view on the material discussed by the authors referenced throughout this note rather than on their interpretation of it.) Finally – and this applies to all of the regions mentioned – ideas of gender inversion as the essence, as a necessary concomitant or as the cause of men's sexual interest in other men *continued throughout the modern period.* Accordingly, it seems to me that even in the late nineteenth century we find a *problématique* – a field of discussion as to whether gender inversion or sex drive object is the essential and decisive factor – rather than a settled account in favour of the priority of gender inversion. And consequently, I am not convinced that we find the radical though gradual change in medico-psychiatric conceptions during the early part of the twentieth century hypothesized by Chauncey, Marshall, Katz, and others. Rather, it was a matter of a fairly superficial change in terminology. We are touching here upon one of this book's main theoretical points, and I shall briefly and preliminarily state it here: *before* the modern homosexual, men's same-sex attraction was *not* inescapably, and perhaps not even generally, conceptualized in terms of femininity (although in some cases, it was in fact conceptualized in such terms). *After* the establishment of the modern homosexual, as well as *in the process of this establishing* in the late nineteenth century, femininity is an inescapable and important but not *the* determining element in the conceptual *problématique* of homosexuality. These crucial distinctions may have been blurred by the relative underdevelopment of studies of men, masculinity and the maleness of male sexual relations, and the concomitant import of ideas developed in feminist studies of women (a problem also noticed by Chauncey 1982–3). Obviously, I am here merely pointing to a divergence; I shall return to details as well as background and some further implications in the following sections (esp. 3 and 17). As for the question of change in the ideas on the homosexual during most recent decades, cf. ch. VI, section 2.

5 Cf. notes to section 2 above. This is not the place to enter into a detailed discussion of the relative contributions, made by medicine and those immediately concerned, to the historical construction of the concept of the modern homosexual. But it might be noted that, although Ulrichs was not a doctor, his ideas are obviously dependent upon those of the biology and medicine of his time.

6 For some overviews of the self-conception (or 'identity') of the homosexuals in various countries and periods within modernity, see the socio-historical works of Weeks 1977; Hahn 1979; Barbedette and Carassou 1981; Girard 1981; Kennedy 1988; Baumgardt 1984a, 1984b, 1984c; Janssen (ed.) 1984; Katz 1983: part II; Kinsman 1987; Rosen 1993: chs 11–12; Mikkelsen 1984. The self-conception 'homosexual'

seems to have spread first among the educated classes (and it is precisely their ideas that gained expression in the public sphere); further, it is likely that this self-conception does not really gain ground in all groups of the population till round the middle of the twentieth century (cf. Chauncey 1994; D'Emilio 1983b; Marshall 1981; Sinfield 1994; Wotherspoon 1991; Carbery 1992; Rifkin 1993: ch. 4; Hekma 1992; Nilsson 1994; Löfström 1994; Bech 1989a). However, there are differences here between the various regions in the modern West, Germany being ahead of other countries. Until late in the twentieth century, there existed other forms of self-experience and to some extent also other forms of social identities for men cultivating erotic interests in other men, particularly in the countryside and in the groups of the urban population that did not enter into contact with middle-class education and values. Thus, in English-speaking countries, there are identities such as 'bachelor', 'wolf', 'punk', 'lamb', 'trade' (cf. Chauncey 1994). These are not the subject of this book, which is only concerned with the phenomena of 'modern homosexuality'. However, I would like to point out that, as far as I can see, such alternative – 'non-homosexual' – conceptualizations *did not generally and primarily* centre on ideas of gender inversion or of an opposition between masculinity and femininity. I shall return to the premises of this view as well as detail it in section 17.

7 Cf. the extracts from the correspondence between Whitman and Symonds in Katz 1976: 340–51. On Whitman's inspiration from the contemporary 'science' of phrenology, see Lynch 1985.

8 The attempt took place among people with some affinity to the organization 'Gemeinschaft der Eigenen' and/or the German youth movement. For more details see ch. V, section 5 (including the references in n. 26 there). The late nineteenth-century British cult of aestheticism and Hellenism may be viewed as another attempt at formulating a different framework of understanding (cf. Dellamora 1990; Dowling 1994). In Denmark, Hans Christian Andersen's fairytales 'The Little Mermaid' and 'The Dung Beetle' can be seen as early experiments in formulating a framework of understanding – although this time in poetic language and without the classicist scholarship of the British or the quasi-medical scientism of the Germans. See Rosen 1980; 1993: ch. 7; Bech forthcoming (a).

9 Instructive examples are Schofield 1965; Hoffman 1968.

10 Obviously, the choice of term (discourse *or* label *or* role *or* script) is, in some cases, indicative of differences in theoretical stance and analytical approach. But there are also strong and significant common features: all of the terms refer to linguistically structured prescriptions and expectations concerning behaviour, and this is decisive in relation to the general problematic I wish to discuss here. – The model *roles/scripts/categories/labels/discourses construct identities* is easily identified in the classics of constructionism from the 1960s and 1970s

(Gagnon and Simon, McIntosh, Plummer, Weeks), and it is still far from extinct. The frequent occurrence in the literature of the term 'identity' to designate what being homosexual 'is all about' is indicative. To endow the mechanics of construction with additional motion and power a driving force is frequently added. In the 1970s and early 1980s this would often be *capital* (or *patriarchy*, or combinations of both); during the 1980s and 1990s it has increasingly been supplanted by a force seemingly a bit attenuated but perhaps all the more pervasive: *power*, simply. Cf. e.g. Butler 1993.

11 The illusory character of 'identity' was an important theme already in the classics of constructionism; I am merely pointing to what may be a change of focus (concomitant, no doubt, with the prioritizing of the terms 'discourse' and 'counter-discourse'). Again, the influential works of Judith Butler (1990; 1993) may serve as an instructive example.

12 It is beyond the scope of this book to write a history of the ideas concerning the varieties of modern 'homosexuality'. The point is to identify, in an ideal-typical way, the *major trends* of the debate. Accordingly, I do not claim that no other approaches exist than those outlined; nor do I claim that the theories and analyses of specific works – e.g. within the 'constructionist' tradition – can be reduced to the ideal-type of 'constructionism' presented above. That this is not the case should become sufficiently clear from the references given in the following chapters.

13 Houmark [1926]/1950: 25, 53f. Christian Houmark (1868–1950) was a writer and journalist (although certainly not a major figure in Danish literature). In this chapter I have referred to him – and his posthumously published *Naar jeg er død* ('When I am Dead') – as a kind of principal witness of what it is to be homosexual. This is primarily because I am fascinated by the force with which he wields the scourge. Obviously, I do not think that his statements can be taken without qualification to represent every 'homosexual's' situation and experience during this period; I shall twist and turn and make use of them for various purposes, as will appear.

14 This section is the first of four dealing with moods or 'tunings' (all marked by the suffix '-ness'). The analytical and theoretical point of this is related to the phased introduction and elaboration of a particular, alternative frame of reference for the study of the modern homosexual: above all a Heidegger-inspired notion of *existence*, prioritizing 'tunings' (*Stimmungen*) – in contrast, I believe, to all other frameworks. The briefness and 'lightness' of this chapter corresponds with my conviction that wrongness, although an important and pervasive component of 'being homosexual', is not the most important one. For more detailed – as well as academically more orthodox – descriptions of homosexuals' experience of wrongness and their reactions to this see e.g. the excellent classics of Adam 1978: chs III

and IV; Plummer 1975: 141–7, 188–93. Stating that, in the period since the last part of the nineteenth century, 'the others' have generally disapproved of the homosexuals can hardly cause heated debate. Indeed, no investigations point in any other direction. As for developments during most recent years, see ch. VI, section 2.

15 It is certainly not difficult to find expressions of this in homosexuals' writings. (For some Danish examples see Bech 1987: 337 n. 2.) Please note that the 'uneasiness' I am writing about is an existential one, a basic 'tuning' not to be confused with insistent feelings of depression or despair. Accordingly, the existence of such uneasiness is neither verified or falsified by the assurances of older 'scientific' literature that the homosexuals feel awful, or by those of more recent literature that they feel great. As for the phenomenological, interpretative method used in these chapters on tunings, see my discussion in chapter I.

16 Houmark [1926]/1950: 24f.

17 Cf. e.g. Wittman 1970: 31, 39; Hodges and Hutter 1974; Mieli 1977: 227f; and the discussions in Weeks 1977: 190–2; Girard 1981: 92 and 95f; D'Emilio 1983b: 235–6.

18 For an example, see Hannon 1975.

19 As appears, I use the term 'role' here not merely in its usual sociological sense, denoting a set of expectations or prescriptions of behaviour, but also in its Goffmanian, 'dramaturgical' sense, referring to the tasks and possibilities of play-acting and performing.

20 Obviously, I am not arguing that homosexuals should not 'come out' (quite the contrary, in fact). – As noted above, discussions of the internal insecurities and multiplicities of 'identity', never absent from the classics of constructionism, gained momentum in the 1980s and 1990s. Often, however, these debates have a psychoanalytic outlook that I do not share (cf. ch. III, sections 4 and 8; ch. IV, section 19). I should like instead to refer to an excellent 'existentialist' (and perhaps rather 'forgotten') classic: Warren and Ponse 1977.

21 Respectively, Houmark [1926]/1950: 27; and Bell and Weinberg 1978: 175, 179.

22 In describing the characteristics of *urban life* – a pervasive theme in this chapter – my inspiration derives from the following older and more recent classics: Simmel 1903; Kracauer [1925–33]; 1937; Benjamin [1927–40]; [1937–40]; Wirth 1938; Goffman 1963; 1971; Sennett 1977; 1990; Lofland 1973; Hannerz 1980; Berman 1982; Walkowitz 1992; cf. Bech 1992b; 1993; 1996. As for the relation between the city and the homosexual, it seems to me that the debate has been dominated by three analytically distinguishable approaches. (a) The *quantitive model*: the larger the city, the more homosexuals will live there; consequently, there will also be more institutions (bars etc.) and forms of social life for homosexuals; and in further consequence, also more diversified institutions and social forms. (b) The *dissolution-of-community model* focuses on the absence of the forms of social life and

organization characteristic (or supposed to be characteristic) of the village, the neighbourhood, kin and family. This allows for several versions, depending on the appraisal of the homosexual and of the city. (i) Social attitudes force homosexuals to live under these inhuman circumstances. (ii) Homosexuals, due to their inherent immoral impulses, can hardly wait to wallow in the mud. (iii) Homosexuals are now able to escape social control and achieve some fulfilment of desire and pleasure. (c) The *community model*, in contrast, argues that the homosexuals' life in the city is far from asocial and disorganized. On the contrary, in the city is created a highly complex homosexual order (often denoted by the terms of homosexual 'subculture' or 'community'). Of course, these various approaches have affinities to general debates in the study of urbanization and urbanism (see the excellent overviews in Wellman and Leighton 1979; Lofland 1983). In some contrast to these approaches, my own focuses on the extent to which homosexual existence is a phenomenon *of* the city and not just something occurring *in* the city (to use the distinction of Hannerz 1980: 3, 248). Obviously, such concerns have not been totally absent from the literature. Firstly, in accounts of the life of the modern homosexual, the features of the city and of urban life often enter as a kind of 'self-evident' background. Secondly, a number of writers have, in exploring the forms of 'public sex', in fact been studying modes of urban life (e.g. Humphries 1970; Delph 1978; Lee 1978). A more explicit, comprehensive and reflexive focus on the relations of homosexuals and the city has come to the fore in some outstanding works of the 1990s: Bell et al. 1994; Binnie 1995; Chauncey 1994; Duyves 1995; Hekma 1992; Maynard 1994; Mort 1995; Nilsson 1994. I do, however, still think it is important to keep in mind Hannerz's distinction and study homosexual 'identity', 'behaviour', 'subculture' and 'community' (or broader: *existence*) as phenomena *of* the city and not merely *in* the city – as I shall endeavour to do throughout this chapter. See also the wonderful essay by Rifkin (1995).

23 Police surveillance of homosexuals is abundantly documented in the literature. Indeed, the establishment of modern police forces occurs in the same period as the birth of the modern homosexual. Some early expressions of the relationship are the writings of the Parisian heads of police: Canler in 1862, Carlier in 1887 and 1889, Macé in 1889 (cf. Hahn 1979: 73ff; Copley 1989). For some more recent examples see references in Bech 1987: 338 n. 1 to ch. IV, 8. There is an instructive example and a wonderful discussion of police surveillance in Maynard 1994.

24 Cf. ch. III.

25 Cf. Humphries 1970: ch. 4; Delph 1978: chs 3–5; Corzine and Kirby 1977; Lee 1978: 75.

26 Cf. ch. IV, section 2; ch. V, section 2.

27 The medical literature abounds with case histories sent to doctors by

homosexuals themselves. Cf. the discussions in Müller 1991: part II; and in Plummer 1995.

28 Cf. ch. V, section 2; ch. VI, section 2.

29 Much of the inspiration for this chapter, of course, derives from Foucault. All too often, his work has been read as if he prioritized – or in fact talked of nothing but – the role of discourses in the construction of the homosexual. (This is a view repeated again and again, even in quite recent literature, e.g. Butler 1993: 192; Evans 1993: 11). Indeed, Foucault's wording in the chapter on the 'implantation perverse' (Foucault 1976: ch. II.1) does come close to the idea of the construction of the modern homosexual by way of discourses and nothing but discourses. However, when read in the context of the entire *History of Sexuality* (Foucault 1976, 1984a, 1984b) things appear in a different light. In the first volume Foucault stresses three factors as pertaining to the 'dispositif de la sexualité': discourses, practices and institutions (apart from power and agencies). And in the introduction to the second volume he introduces, in commenting upon the analyses of the first, the term *expérience*. You might say that what he describes in the first volume as a *dispositif* (a machinery, device, or 'deployment' of sexuality), is now described from another (I would say phenomenological) point of view as an 'experience'.

30 For instance, an individual's way of 'being homosexual' is obviously mediated by his class, race, ethnic, regional, generational background and affiliations. Moreover, such factors may prevent him from developing and joining a homosexual form of existence, and instead make him participate in other modes of experience and conduct, other identities and ways of life. However, as stated earlier, this book concentrates on the phenomena of 'homosexuality'. Cf. also sections 21–3 below.

31 An overview in Adam 1987.

32 The importance of gaze and cruising in the homosexual form of existence appears from numerous accounts and analyses covering the entire period of the homosexual, and indeed goes further back since it belongs to the eroticism of the city (cf. also Bech 1993; 1996). For some examples see Casper 1863: 38; Mayne 1908: 42f; Hirschfeld 1914: 629f; Barbedette and Carassou 1981: 38; Dalsgaard 1984: 84f; Cory 1951: 116–19; Hooker 1961: 48f; Hoffman 1968: 46–8, 56–8; Dannecker and Reiche 1974: 83–6; Ponte 1974; Lee 1978: 53–8; Read 1980: 12f, 90f. The exposition is based also on the author's field work around the Western world. In real life, things are even more complicated – or exciting – than described in this chapter, because there are national and local variations in the rules for the uses of the gaze.

33 Himmler, translated from Stümke and Finkler 1981: 435.

34 Bang [1909]/1922: 19f. The 'mysterious mutual recognition' belongs to the mythology – and reality – of the homosexual species. Other early examples are found in the works of G. A. Blumer (1882: 'able to

recognize each other') and T. G. Comstock (1892: 'a mysterious bond of psychological sympathy') (both quoted from Katz 1983: 183, 227); as well as Carlier (1887: 'reconnaissent entre eux'; quoted from Hahn 1979: 77). On the theme of signs and recognitions see also e.g. Moll 1902; Hirschfeld 1914: 693f; Katz 1983: 367, 573, 579; Weeks 1977: 163; *Vennen* (Denmark) (1950), 2.4: 86; (1950), 2.6: 134; Wotherspoon 1991: 53f; Chauncey 1994: 187ff; cf. also Beaver 1981.

35 On homosexuals' meetings and meeting places see e.g. Hahn 1979: 144–50; Barbedette and Carassou 1981: 25–38; Hirschfeld 1905: 37–64; 1914: 682–99; Weeks 1977: 37–9; Dalsgaard 1984: 84f; Wotherspoon 1991: 57ff; Carbery 1992; Hekma 1992; Garber 1992; Chauncey 1994: chs 6–8; Newton 1993: 180ff; Maynard 1994; Nilsson 1994; Duyves 1995. Sociological classics are Humphries 1970; Delph 1978; Lee 1978.

36 E.g. Cory 1951: 136f and 139f; Hoffman 1968: 174–9; Bon and d'Arc 1974: 311; Greenberg 1988: 359 n. 19; Gagnon 1990: 199.

37 E.g. Cory 1951: 137f; Bieber et al. 1962: 253; Hoffman 1968: 171–4; Dannecker 1978: ch. 13; Stubrin 1994: 123ff; Dannecker 1996. Seidman (1991: ch. 6) points to a further, 'discoursive-constructionist' aspect, arguing that casual sex was cultivated in the 1970s because it was fuelled by discourses imbuing it with personal and social significance.

38 Although perhaps the instability is not to be explained in the terms of psychoanalysis, as is generally the case, e.g. by the authors mentioned in note 37 (apart from Seidman). I shall return to this topic in ch. IV, section 19.

39 E.g. Hooker 1961: 47–51; Dannecker and Reiche 1974: 78–82; Vinnai 1977: 38.

40 Delph 1978: 105–6.

41 Weinberg and Williams 1975: 175–6.

42 Information on homosexuals' associations – extent, structure, purposes and effects – can be found in the historical expositions of homosexuals' lives, e.g. Weeks 1977; Katz 1976; 1983; Licata 1978; D'Emilio 1983b; Duberman 1993; Lauritsen and Thorstad 1974; Steakley 1975; Baumgardt 1984b; 1984c; Stümke and Finkler 1981; Girard 1981; Mikkelsen 1984; Axgil and Fogedgaard 1985. There is a fairly extensive overview in Adam 1987.

43 On homosexual neighbourhood space see Castells 1983: ch. 14; Knopp 1992; cf. Bell 1991. In commenting upon a conference paper of mine (Bech 1993), Veldboer has accused me of remaining ignorant of the development and importance of homosexual spatial 'niches' (Veldboer 1994: 106f). How could one? But I *would* like to point to some potential risks involved in stressing the importance of neighbourhood space: the ideological, nostalgic dangers often connected with notions of 'community', 'home' and 'place'. Cf. also n. 22 above.

44 On homosexuals' friendship networks and the functions of these see e.g. Hirschfeld 1914: 678–81; Leznoff and Westley 1956; Westwood

1960: 184f; Hooker 1961: 54f; Sonenschein 1968; Dannecker and Reiche 1974: 109–17; Warren 1974: 49–55, 76–93; Bell and Weinberg 1978: 171–5, 178f; Håkansson 1984: 440–6.

45 The idea of the friendship network as a substitute family is aired e.g. in Bell and Weinberg 1978: 173, 178. Indeed, it seems that many authors on homosexual networks (e.g. the ones mentioned in the preceding note) tend to ignore other structural differences between friendship networks and nuclear family than the quantitative one (that there are *more* people in the network). Weston (1991) discusses 'chosen families' as a type of relationship different from friendship networks ('gay families differed from networks to the extent that they quite consciously incorporated symbolic demonstrations of love, shared history, material or emotional assistance, and other signs of enduring solidarity' – ibid.: 109). And obviously, parts of what I call 'friendship networks' are more densely knit than other parts. The ideology of gay or lesbian 'families', however, seems to me a rather culturally specific one: more appropriate to the USA than to the rest of the Western world; more appropriate to the USA of the late twentieth century than to earlier periods; and more appropriate to women's relations than to men's. I would agree with Weeks's statement: 'The broadening of the term "family" to embrace a variety of both domestic arrangements and types of relationships (and it is important to stress that these are not necessarily the same) must be seen as a political response to diversity rather than a useful sociological categorisation. In effect it takes for granted the discourse of family life . . . [T]here exists a plurality of relational forms which are regarded by many as both legitimate and desirable and which are different from any recognizable familial pattern' (Weeks 1991: 150). Obviously, in cases involving parenting or co-parenting the term 'family' can be more appropriate (at least for social reasons). Cf. also Nardi 1992b; Altman 1982: 189f; Henriksson 1995.

46 Cf. Henslin 1971.

47 I have discussed the particulars of modern urban sexuality, as well as the 'inevitable' connections of city and sexuality in greater detail in Bech 1993 (cf. also Bech 1996). Some of these particulars may, in one way or another, characterize non-urban, non-modern sexuality as well; but that falls outside the scope of this book.

48 I have touched upon this in Bech 1993, and shall elaborate it further in Bech (forthcoming (b)). The point is not merely that partners in urban sex are – by definition, so to speak – strangers. Rather, distance and strangeness are radically *constitutive* of urban (and consequently, of modern) sexuality. The importance of gaze and fetishism (in a non-clinical sense) is indicative of this.

49 Baldwin 1962: 226.

50 In many people's minds, the world is supposed to be divided into two spheres: public and private; and insofar as sexuality is even mentioned,

this is a matter of the private sphere and its spaces, i.e. of the *home*. The description above, however, points to the existence of a particular *intimacy of the city*, however difficult it may appear to conceive of such a phenomenon, and however appalling it may seem to some. It is sometimes argued that the critical discussion of the invectives of alienation, reification, instrumentalization and the like is outdated since no one thinks in such terms any more. I do, however, have an inkling that these are precisely the categories that automatically spring to most readers' minds *vis-à-vis* my descriptions of urban (gay) sex.

51 Cf. ch. IV, sections 2 and 7.

52 But such 'bumping into' is in fact a chronic condition, as we have seen in ch. III on the omnipresence of absent homosexuality. In using the expression that 'the heterosexual' is a reflection of 'the homosexual' I am alluding also to the notion of reflexive concepts in Hegel's sense. One category does not exist outside the reflective relation to the other; in this case, moreover, the determining pole is the homosexual, the spot is on him. Obviously, this is a structural determination (a partial one at that) of the phenomenon of 'the heterosexual', not a historical exposition of his coming into being. For details of various aspects of this process see Katz 1990; 1995; Chauncey 1994: ch. 4; cf. also the analyses in ch. III, section 19 above and ch. IV, section 17 below.

53 The sexualization of the homosexual is further connected with his position in relation to modern genders and the processes through which these are produced. Moreover, modern masculinity constitutes a condition favourable to urban sexualization (see section 17).

54 On the production and presentation of a 'masculine' self in the disco environment see Chesebro and Klenk 1981.

55 The description of the gay disco is based on my participant observation studies from most parts of the western world during the 1980s and 1990s. Recently, there has been much rumouring about the death of the disco. No doubt, other forms of dance sociality have evolved; but the disco still seems to be thriving (although obviously, the modes of lighting and sound as well as the outfits of its patrons are changing – though to my eyes not radically). See also the very different and wonderful articles by Bredbeck and by Burston on disco survival/revival (Bredbeck 1996; Burston 1995: 174–9). Changes in social life spaces and ways of life will be a topic of ch. VI.

56 On balls: e.g. Barbedette and Carassou 1981: 16–19, 45; Krafft-Ebing 1886: 434f; Méténier 1904: 84, 86–7, 114–16; Hirschfeld 1914; Theis and Sternweiler 1984: 60f, 65f; Fraenkel 1908: 72–4. On the manners of Oscar Wilde: e.g. Jullian 1968; Hyde 1976.

57 On von Gloeden: e.g. Leslie 1977 (there are numerous books in all major languages discussing and presenting von Gloedens photos). – On 'mid-century dream texts', see e.g. 'Wolf' 1952; Vidal 1948: ch. 3; cf. the discussion in Austen 1977: 116–28, 159; Sarotte 1975: 251, 258.

58 Cf. Chesebro and Klenk 1981: 92.

59 Thus, on TV viewers' distance to royal weddings, see e.g. Adorno 1969.
60 Bang 1904: 39. Cf. also the discussion of the novel in ch. III, section 9.
61 Watching, during a repeat of a German TV recording from the 1960s, *Adorno*, legs crossed several times, piously babbling about *Tauschwert* in a group of obsequious intellectuals, might even bring one close to the experience of *kitsch*.
62 Cf. Benjamin (1935) on the 'Verfall' of aura; see also Bech 1992b.
63 *Aficionados/as* may wish to consult the Danish edition on this.
64 My favourite text on camp remains Sontag's sophisticated article from 1964. Since then, quite a number of treatments of the topic have appeared, often highly illuminating and, in addition, most entertaining (e.g. Newton 1972: 104–11; Babuscio 1977; Dyer 1977; Booth 1983; Core 1984; Ross 1989: 135–70). None of the treatments, however, corresponds to the one given by me in this section. Often 'camp' is used as a term for a very broad spectrum of forms of experience; or the emphasis is placed on the detached: that the surface loses any connection with an inner and is not to be taken the slightest bit seriously, whereby what I call camp proper – the unity of the grotesque and the moving, of the sympathetic and the distanced – vanishes from the field of vision. And sometimes camp is related to forms of experience and expression which apply only to homosexuals (or 'queers' or other special, minor groups) and are not linked to broader social developments (urbanization, etc.). These comments serve primarily to specify my own use of the word 'camp' in relation to others; it is not my intention to intimate that there would be any point in cramming a phenomenon like camp into a rigid definition. There is a broad spectrum of coherent forms of expression and experience that can only be separated analytically, and different definitions and treatments are suitable for highlighting different aspects of this continuum. Perhaps I should add that reading the article by Meyer (1994) has not made me change my mind on this, although I've enjoyed it greatly. See also ch. V, section 3.
65 Cf. Both 1981: 30–41.
66 The contributions in Bergman (ed.) (1993) and in Meyer (ed.) (1994) highlight the potentials and problems of various sorts of camp used as a political strategy for homosexuals (or for 'queers').
67 On the sensitivity and/or hypersensitivity of the homosexual, see e.g. Ulrichs 1864a: 26; Geill 1893: 476; Mayne 1908: 82f, 279f; Hirschfeld 1914: 175–8; Greenspan and Campbell 1945: 684–6; Bergler 1956: 16. Cf. also the numerous empirical investigations of homosexuals' 'femininity', including their sensitivity (e.g. by means of the Minnesota Multiple Personality Inventory) (cf. references in Weinberg and Bell (eds) 1972, and in Riess 1980: 307).
68 On the development of and the relation between fiction, sensitivity and modern gender: classics are Watt 1957: chs 5 and 6; Habermas 1962:

sections 4–6; Stone 1977: part IV. On literary 'transvestitism' see Taylor 1981.

69 Miller (1988) has pointed out the 'policing' functions of the novel in relation to feelings, but I do think this policing is rather different from the one executed by psychoanalysis.

70 An objection to such views is exemplified by Coleman 1990. Most of the time there is, he argues (in relation to ideas of impression management concerning masculinity), simply no problematic of being a man like the one postulated by social constructionists: people simply *do what they do*, without considering whether or not they are making a satisfactory presentation of themselves. This objection is, I think, partially begging the point, since no one would really deny that such 'spontaneity' and 'naturalness' is predominant in many instances. The question is whether there is, nevertheless, an insecurity at a more fundamental level; and my argument is that this must be the case *precisely in modern societies* because these are not merely sociologized and urbanized, but also gender-problematized and homosexualized, thereby making such problematics more than just an occasional exception. My focus on male 'insecurity' in this section is not to deny that masculinity is embedded in institutions and reproduced by social practices (cf. Carrigan et al. 1985). Notwithstanding, there is also an *experiential* side to 'being a man' – in fact a pivotal site for the constitution and reproduction of masculinity – and this is what I am concentrating on here.

71 Cf. ch. II, sections 1 and 2.

72 As should be clear by now, the gender analysis suggested here from a structural and modernity-oriented perspective, centres on two factors: whether or not social spheres/spaces and social tasks/functions are generally and radically gender-segregated. It is a constitutive feature of modernity that they are not. More precisely, modern societies are *gender-problematized*, in the sense that, although generally not gender-separated, spheres are *not* generally populated or tasks generally performed by men and women to an equal extent or without some amount of fairly deep-seated barriers to 'free flow'.

From this main condition of gender problematizing derive a number of other characteristic features of modern genders. As for masculinity: being a man is now essentially a matter of staging a bodily difference from, and in active opposition to, women (as well as of restaging the differential features of cultural wardrobe traditionally associated – or retrospectively associable – with male gender). Gender problematizing, then, is *the* constitutive characteristic of modern genders. Obviously, in terms of historical development there is no single and comprehensive rupture. Gender problematizing – due primarily to women's activities and 'intrusion' – has been a developing trend in the West since the eighteenth century (in some countries – France and England – earlier than in others); but the latter part of the nineteenth century witnessed a significant upsurge. Nor should it be forgotten that, although the active staging and demonstration of body difference now becomes a crucial component of masculinity, it is not the *only* important one. First, each gender is still significantly determined (and internally differentiated) by the spaces and functions it *mostly* occupies, and the power differential connected to these. (On the historical construction of modern masculinity, see e.g. Cohen 1993; Crosset 1990; Kimmel 1987; 1990b; Selzer 1990; and the contributions in Mangan and Walwin (eds) 1987.) Moreover, the constitution of both genders is increasingly influenced by the entirety of the conditions specific to modern life, such as the city, the apparatus of self-analysis, the changes in the institutions of art, the development of rational language and the parliamentary complex (cf. elsewhere in this chapter).

The contention that masculinity is constituted in a bodily and active relation and opposition to femininity, and that this is specifically modern, implies that male gender construction in previous and other forms of society did *not* proceed in this way. Indeed, claiming that it did implies an ethnocentric or rather, modernity-centric projection. Obviously, this is not tantamount to maintaining that some sort of socio-culturally constituted opposition of masculinity in relation to femininity may not have played an important part, but merely that it was not identical to the bodily centred, actively oppositional demarcation from femininity. Further, in a climate of a (socio-culturally constituted) 'obviousness' concerning gender segregation of spaces and functions in premodern societies, the practice of being a man was probably primarily a matter of a relation *between men* and not between man and woman. Important indications of this (and an important issue for further study) are the invectives used to men in exhorting them to become real men (or blaming them for failing). It seems that these invectives were not primarily related to femininity; such terms were sometimes used, but others seem to have been more important: those referring to 'not man', 'not man enough', 'child', 'incompetent', 'useless'. Cf. Gilmore 1990: 32, 43, 73, 75, 90, 92, 104, 112, 115, 127, 132f, 140f. And conversely, the practice of being a woman was *not* mainly one of a particular relation to men.

An objection to the above might refer to the rise of greater gender equality related to the development of affective individuality, companionate marriage and the domesticated family among the upper classes during the eighteenth century (Trumbach 1978; 1989a; 1989b; Stone 1977). However, it is not clear how widespread this trend was; further, the 'equality' referred to was certainly an equality of what was perceived to be radically *different* genders. Moreover, I think that the problem of gender differentiation in this context should be distinguished, conceptually and in its social and historical effects, from what I have termed 'gender problematizing'. The latter is, above all, a result of the 'intrusion' of women into 'male' spheres and tasks, whereas the former is due to a 'domestication' of the male. In real life, the two may overlap and interact; however, unless analytically separating them, one runs the risk of overemphasizing continuity in gender developments. I think this may be the case also with Laqueur's theory of the development of the 'modern' two-sex model since the eighteenth century (Laqueur 1990: chs 5 and 6). Perhaps there are *two* 'modern' two-sex models competing with the older one-sex model and with each other, and increasingly so since the nineteenth century?

It may be an advantage of structural modes of analyses to identify such basic distinctions at a high level of abstraction, distinctions which may then prove useful search-lights in historical and socio-cultural investigations. I shall specify some further implications of this below (n. 74). I have dealt more extensively with the problematics of gender and modernity in Bech 1991a; 1992b; 1994; 1995.

73 Cf. ch. IV, section 2.

74 In the preceding chapters, I have repeatedly commented on the relations between modern homosexuality and modern gender formation. The theoretical aspect of this has now been formulated in more comprehensive and elaborate terms, and I should like to spell out a few implications for empirical research.

1 As for the analysis of *modern* male homosexuality, it is important to investigate the extent to which different varieties of this are influenced by the specific, active and oppositional construction of modern genders, particularly masculinity, vs the extent to which they are produced by their situatedness in particular spheres, *or* by the general conditions of modern life (the self-analysis complex, etc.).

2 As for the study of *non-modern* 'sexual' or 'erotic' relations between men, it should be explored how far they are influenced by the practices and performances of a masculinity *not* primarily constituting itself in an active and bodily opposition to femininity. To the extent that such non-modern sexual relations between men are, notwithstanding, associated with some sort of socio-culturally specific femininity, this can*not* be explained simply by making reference to the 'rigid' polarity of masculinity and femininity in these societies (*à la*: since people are conceived of in terms of gender and gender polarity, a man's sexual attraction to another man 'must' make him a kind of woman. The alleged necessity of this conclusion belongs entirely to a *modern* logic, not applicable to any other era).

3 Consequently, historical investigations of the *development* of modern male homosexuality deal with the problematics of a transition from male–male sexual relations that are only indirectly and secondarily related to a male–female opposition.

This, I think may add rather important dimensions to the empirical study of men's sexual relations in different periods and regions, and help unravel some difficulties. Four examples may illustrate this. In

Chauncey's otherwise magnificent study of *Gay New York* (1994), the following types of claims are made in relation to notions of same-sex desire and gender in the working class at the turn of the century. On the one hand: 'Sexual desire for men was held to be inescapably a woman's desire' (p. 48; cf. pp. 100, 103, 104). On the other hand, Chauncey states that 'Even evidence of persistent and exclusive interest in sexual relations with another man did not necessarily put a man in the same category as his partner' (p. 96; cf. p. 65). Further: on the one hand, Chauncey implies that penetration/penetratedness was a crucial axis in determining a person's gender status. Accordingly, being penetrated by another man was equivalent to being feminized (pp. 66, 81, 84, 124). On the other hand, Chauncey lists a large number of incidents (indeed, several *types* of relationships) in which being penetrated does not imply feminization (pp. 86ff). I believe that these contradictions reflect tensions between theory and empirical material. Theory posits a transformation from a cultural system where 'gender governed the interpretation of sexual practices' (p. 127) to a system of modern homosexuality – whereas the empirical material indicates that this is not what was happening. Indeed, the transformation is rather one from a system where gender (that is, oppositional gender differentiation) did *not* govern the interpretation of sexual practices to one where it did (or more precisely, was an inescapable component of interpretations). There can be no doubt, though, that some of the men sexually attracted to other men – but, to all appearance, only minor groups of them – did in fact see themselves (and were seen by others) in terms of femininity. These, however, were exceptions to the rule; and accordingly, they are phenomena demanding *additional* explanation. The obvious objection would refer to the 'Mollies' of eighteenth-century London (cf. Trumbach 1977; 1989a; 1989b; Bray 1982: ch. 4). However, even with this case there has recently been much debate about the particular qualities, scope, social effect and historical continuity of Molly 'effeminacy' (cf. Bristow 1995; Cohen 1993; Fout 1992; Hekma 1994b; Norton 1992; Sinfield 1994b). In fact, I think that the conceptual problems noted by me in relation to the historical development have much affinity to the problematics motivating many of these authors' investigations.

This leads to my second example. Provided the points made in my first example are accepted it might still be argued that, at the turn of the century (and perhaps even into the 1960s), a feminine identification was the predominant element in the constitution of identity among the men with strong erotic interests in other men. But again I think this may be a kind of slanting projection, mistaking an important and pervasive factor for a predominant one. Indeed, Chauncey repeatedly states that non-feminine (in their own conception at least) identities like 'queer' or 'gay' were the most widespread ones in early twentieth-century New York (Chauncey 1994: e.g. 101; cf. ibid.: 14–23).

My third example concerns the elaboration, at the most general transhistorical and transcultural level, of conceptual schemes to facilitate overview and study of the varieties of same-sex sexuality (e.g. Adam 1985a; 1985b; Herdt 1990; Murray 1992b: xiii–xxxiii; Trumbach 1977). The researchers stress the heuristic character of such schemes; however, this does not raise the distinctions above discussions of their *adequacy* as tools for overview and analysis. Usually only three or four patterns of same-sex sexuality are distinguished at this overall level; invariably, 'gender-defined', 'gender-structured', 'gender-stratified', 'gender-reversed' or 'transgenderist' organization of homosexuality is one of them. Again, I would warn against the potential modernity-centrism of such systematizing: is 'gender defining' really a relevant main category *at the most general level* of world history and world cultures? That some male–male sexual relations were conceived of in terms of gender difference is beyond doubt; but is it not possible that these should rather be treated as exceptions to or modifications of *more adequate* overall classificatory schemes? Indeed, Murray states (1992b: xxii) that 'There is no question that a *pasivo* is a "kind of man," definitely not "a kind of woman" in Mesoamerica.' But if so, what sense does it make to place him under the *main* distinguishing category of 'gender-defined' organization of homosexuality – and, by implication at least, to use him as part of the legitimation for the appropriateness of this as a main category? (cf. ibid.: pp. xiv–xvii). Even to the extent that one of the partners in an inter-male sexual relationship does indubitably perform as a woman according to the culture's standards – e.g. by wearing women's clothes – we should be very careful in using this as a 'prototypical' example which may in turn help to 'prove' the legitimacy of a major category of 'gender-defined' homosexuality. Such a procedure may well come dangerously close to arguing in a circle. Why, for instance, should we not take the Navaho *nadle* as a point of departure for categorizing endeavours – instead of the Mohave *alyha*? (cf. ch. II, section 3, and n. 3 to ch. III, section 1). Cf. also my critique of Prieur's otherwise brilliant analyses of the *jotos/vestidas* of Neza, Mexico City (Prieur 1994; Bech 1994).

My fourth example concerns the widespread idea that, in pre-modern societies, penetrating/penetratedness was a constitutive nucleus of gender difference. The theory I have outlined above implies another approach. Generally, one should be on the lookout for a possible *huge variety* of meanings, reasons and pleasures associated with being penetrated: experimentation, prodigality, joy, submission, ecstasy, dirt, sociality, love, and so on. Mostly, 'being penetrated by another man' is probably to be conceived in terms of *male–male* meanings, not of male–female meanings. And in the cases where penetrating/penetratedness is indeed a major constituent of a perceived difference in gender status, this cannot simply be explained by making reference to the gender polarities of these societies (apparently a recurrent feature of *all* pre-modern societies, with the debatable exception of the Tahitians) but needs *additional* explanation. Obviously, the picture may become rather complicated by the integration, 'transfer' or 'spill-over' of a number of meanings and pleasures in each instance (including meanings related to male–female distinctions). In fact, imperial Rome might prove to be a more instructive case for generalizations and typifications than the much more well-researched one of classical Greece.

75 This is disputed and calls for qualification. Indeed, most of the various factors and phenomena necessary for the constitution of a modern lesbian species were present as early as those of the modern male homosexual (e.g. the interventions of medical sciences and practices; the existence of urban networks; gender problematizing). However, it seems that the lesbian species did not, by then, develop to the same extent and with the same propelling energies as did the male homosexual one. This has to do with conditions I shall turn to in a moment, as well as with the existence of certain *other possibilities* for developing close relationships, identity and ways of life among women (Faderman 1981; Smith-Rosenberg 1975; Vicinus 1984; 1985). So from this point of view there is some reason in speaking of a 'time-lag', in a descriptive and non-normative sense.

76 It is not the aim of this book to enter into a more detailed discussion of this theme. Some classics in the field are Faderman 1981; Hacker 1987; Kokula 1981; Lützen 1986.

77 On this important point I disagree with e.g. Blachford 1981; Edwards 1994: ch. 5; Evans 1993: ch. 4; Kimmel 1990a; Levine 1992. For a critique of feminist fears of gay men see also Bristow 1989.

78 Houmark [1926]/1950: 25, 55.

79 Ibid.: 45.

80 The American Gay Liberation Front's Statement of Purpose, 31 July 1969 (quoted from D'Emilio 1983b: 234). Indeed: 'We reject Society's attempt to impose sexual roles and definitions of our nature' (ibid.).

81 The connection between the concept of 'the homosexual' and the ideas of oppression and liberation appears clearly from numerous homosexual defence writings. This complex of ideas is constitutive for extensive bodies of work such as those of Ulrichs and Hirschfeld; and altogether it has demarcated the horizon for the reflections and arguments of the majority of individual homosexual writers as well as movement representatives (as recognized e.g. by Foucault 1976; Weeks 1977; cf also Silverstolpe 1987).

82 The extent to which modern societies – including language, cultural understandings, social institutions and individual personalities – have been permeated by 'rational arguments' has perhaps been most comprehensively – and most affirmatively – elaborated by Habermas (1981) (I should like to introduce the term 'parliamentary complex' for

the cohering entirety of these phenomena.) Criticism of the dangers and/or the merely conventional, tactical and outward nature of such 'rationalizing' is presented e.g. by Sennett (1977), as well as by much 'postmodernist' writing.

83 White 1983.

84 In the interviews I conducted in 1988 with twenty men (Bech 1989a) selected on the basis of their *difference* in terms of age, residence, class, etc., such reflexivity was a recurrent feature overall.

85 Cf. ch. IV, sections 5 and 17.

86 To quote Anthony Giddens' characterization of the ideal types of 'pure relationship', 'confluent love' and modern 'intimacy' (Giddens 1992: 58). As for Giddens on homosexuals as having a specially favourable point of departure for developing such relationships, see ibid.: 15, 28, 123, 135, 144. Giddens, however, puts the main emphasis on women's relationships; in the context of the present book, my emphasis is on men's relationships.

87 Cf. ch. III, section 20; ch. IV, sections 16 and 17.

88 The qualities of care, respect and trust are related to the pre-social or pre-socialized (indeed 'pre-ontological') moral impulse that Bauman speaks of (1993: ch. 4), even if they may encompass other aspects as well.

89 There is an informative discussion on the (alleged) femininity of such values, in Swain 1989.

90 On the nature of such matrices (or 'folios' or 'general interpretations'), see Habermas 1968: ch. 11.

91 Cf. Socarides 1968: 58–72; 1978: 63–87; 1990: 14; Dannecker 1978: ch. 13; Vinnai 1977: 32–46; Ovesey and Woods 1980: 332. Other psychoanalytic authors share the view that the homosexuals are inherently inhibited in their ability to form stable relationships because of 'narcissistic' disturbances developed during childhood, but they explain this somewhat differently: e.g. Bychowsky 1961 (fixation to a stage of ambivalent pre-ego object relations); Kernberg 1975: 227–37, 239f (oral frustrations). And some authors change their mind on homosexuals' 'narcissistic' disturbances, yet remain convinced of their intrapsychically disturbed abilities of forming stable relationships (thus Dannecker 1996).

92 There is an extensive – though far from exhaustive – survey of varieties in Lewes 1988.

93 For instance, from the fact that women give birth to children does not follow how they should treat the children (or indeed, that the 'biological' mother should take care of the child). The lack of a sure foundation and a factual verification concerning narrative matrices of 'childhood' or 'body' cannot be remedied by way of therapy. The starting point of the search for such matrices is a problematizing of the 'evidence' nature regarding the experience of feelings and motives. However, if evidence of experiences can, on principle, be problema-

tized, this is also the case with the 'evidence' of experiencing that particular narrative folios of childhood or body are 'true' in relation to one's life. Stating – as Freud did (1937), and much psychology-inspired thought since him – that the narrative can be verified by a person's *future* doings and experiences is begging the question. First, adducing a narrative may influence future activities and partially make of it a self-fulfilling prophecy; moreover, a life story must always, to some extent at least, be written *in retrospect*, making a sure fixing of its totality (and even of the basic features of this totality) impossible in advance.

94 Foucault 1984a; 1984b.

95 Obviously, this is not Foucault's list, but mine. First, as far as I can see, Foucault's writings on the art of existence centre on the relation of the individual to himself (and indeed: to *him*self), rather than on the problems of couples. Besides, Foucault does not deal with such devices as television (cf. n. 96 below). Moreover, I have composed the list with a view to the following points on the 'languor' of life, thereby also injecting a dose of everyday indolence into the quite strenuous work ethos that may appear to be associated with Foucaultian aesthetics of existence. – It is interesting to note how many of the words that seem adequate in delineating an aesthetics of existence relevant to being-together are metaphors from the language of the senses and sensitivity, or more specifically, from the language of various forms of 'playing', such as gambling, joking or music (e.g., flair, attunement, sympathetic, perceptiveness, ear, *Fingerspitzengefühl*).

96 It should be noted that the aesthetics of existence which Foucault did elaborate in some detail were those of particular groups in antiquity (Foucault 1984a; 1984b). Obviously, he was aware that these were not the only possible ones. Cf. Foucault 1984a: 10f; 1983; and various interviews during the 1980s, e.g. 1981; 1982.

97 This is not the place to go into detail on these matters. Put in very broad terms: I prefer the stories (or *parts* of the stories) of Kierkegaard, Heidegger and Simmel to those of Freud.

98 Giddens 1992: 138.

99 This is no doubt true of all 'sexuality', though not in transhistorically identical forms.

100 Metatheoretically, I would relate this to Heidegger's concept of the fundamental *Gestimmtheit* – i.e. 'being tuned' of being-in-the-world (see ch. I n. 16). More specifically, the particular excitement of sexualization is a fundamental 'tuning' of *modern* being-in-the-world, i.e. of being-in-the-city. This 'meaning-less' dimension of sexual excitement is an essential aspect of what might be called its aesthetics; and scholarship and science have to accept and respect that it is simply there, beyond the realms of interpretation or explanation, and can only try to re-present it adequately (cf. Bech 1993).

101 Investigations on homosexual men's couples have found that sex

outside the relationship is widespread and often treated not as a breach of faith but as a matter to be accepted or accommodated. Cf. e.g. Blumstein and Schwartz 1983; Bryant and Demian 1994; Harry 1984; Kurdek and Schmitt 1986; McWhirter and Mattison 1984; Plummer 1978.

102 Such abilities and qualities are undoubtedly practised daily by plenty of women and men alike. I can't really imagine how else any 'intimate' relationship could possibly last for any length of time. – Interestingly, Julien (1993: 64) reports from his study of forty-one male homosexual couples in Montreal that, apparently, psychological health and partnership satisfaction had nothing to do with *verbal* communication among the partners, although it was related to good communication in terms of common *activities*. Cf. the analogous result in Pingel and Trautvetter 1987: 56f.

103 Cf. ch. IV, section 12 on the breakable nature of networks.

104 Cf. Bech 1989a.

105 Indeed, it is tiring that the discussion on homosexual one-to-ones – or the lack of them – is often conducted in 'objective', 'scientific' terms rather than coming out as what it primarily is: a discussion about morals and the art of conducting a life. Only secondarily – in the form of reference to existing conditions of life – do 'scientific' arguments come into play with any substantial gravity. Inasmuch as my exposition in this chapter bears the character of a homily (or is 'appealing' rather than descriptive), it is in accordance with this point of departure: the comprehension and abilities that may be necessary for a good life may not be widespread in homosexual (or other) life, but they may perhaps be helped along by being appealed to.

106 On the psychoanalytic notions of 'narcissistic' disturbances see nn. 37–8 above. Ideas of puberty fixation and mental immaturity have been articulated in e.g. Sullivan 1953: 258; Friedenberg 1959: 121–5; Bychowsky 1961: 257f; Menninger 1963; Fine 1987.

107 Bang [1909]/1922: 20.

108 Bang 1906 (the English translation of the novel has the title: *Denied a Country*); Baldwin 1962; Stoddard 1873; *Spartacus Guide* 1970 (and subsequent editions).

109 In addition, the choice of destination was often influenced by the opportunities or borders set up by the colonialist divisions of the globe (cf. Bleys 1993: 167). It should be added that the homosexual geography also included destinations and 'homelands' displaced in time: above all, ancient Greece. The homosexual's dream of, journey to or flight to another country is known from fiction (cf. Austen 1977: 11–15, 79, 108, 174, 186, 191, 210, 211; Sarotte 1975: 925f, 940, 943; Jones 1990: 119, 136, 139f, 195f, 215, 256f, 259f, 271f, 276f; examples in Sutherland and Anderson (eds) 1961: 389–410). See also the discussion in Aldrich 1993. Besides, it is known from travel accounts by and biographical information on homosexuals, well-known ones

(such as Krupp, Carpenter, Wilde, Gide, Isherwood, Forster, Peyrefitte, Burroughs; cf. also the list in Bleys 1993: 176), or unknown ones (cf. e.g. the letters and descriptions quoted in Hirschfeld 1914: chs 26–8). Finally, it is known from travel guides for homosexuals, ranging from fairly random lists in magazines to systematically elaborated books (like the *Spartacus Guide*). – An initial – and original – inspiration for this chapter is the article by DeVall (1980) – perhaps another of those 'forgotten classics' of homosexuality studies. Cf. also the excellent article by Bleys (1993) on the relations between homosexual wishes and imperialist scripting of otherness.

110 On the (civilized) homosexual's attractedness to men from the more 'natural' classes or races see Weeks 1977: 40f, 52, 125f; Weeks 1980–1: 55ff; Hyde 1976: 187f; Chauncey 1994: 108ff; Hirschfeld 1914: 639f, 643f; Limpricht 1991; Austen 1977: 15; Barbedette and Carassou 1981: 46–8; Rifkin 1993: ch. 4; P. Sedgwick 1982–3. It should be emphasized, though, that the lines of attraction undoubtedly ran the other way as well. – On the theme of city vs country in homosexuals' imagination see Austen 1977: 171f; Martin 1979: 22. Fone (1983) primarily views the topos of rural idyll as an expression of a particular homosexual 'arcadian' tradition with roots that go back to Vergil, whereas in the present context we are dealing with the particularly modern background for its spread and elaborations.

111 Mayne (ed.) 1906: 42f, 149f, 165f, 203.

112 Gide 1936: 15 (Gide does not speak particularly of homosexuality in this context).

113 Gide 1936: 63 n. 1; cf. Herbart 1937: 21f. See also Pollard 1995.

114 See Nelson 1984.

115 Cf. sections 2 and 3 above.

116 Cf. section 3 above, and ch. VI, section 2, n. 13.

117 Cf. section 3 above. The reader is reminded that the positions discussed here are ideal-typical constructions, intended to represent major *trends* of the debate and not specific works.

118 See sections 12 and 18 above.

119 Heidegger 1927. Cf. my discussion in ch. I.

120 I do not reject the possibility of 'biological' or 'early childhood' influences on the constitution of same-sex sexual preference. The present analysis, however, shows that – if existing – they are of insignificant importance for the problematics considered in this book. Accordingly, one is tempted to quote Foucault: 'On this question I have only an opinion; since this is only an opinion it is without interest.' (Foucault 1982–3: 11). (Occasionally, however, it may be relevant to offer an opinion: Bech 1989c.)

121 As should be clear from the references to the preceding chapters, I am far from claiming no one else has discussed the various aspects of the modern homosexual that I have been dealing with. The contribution I hope to have made, on the theoretical and conceptual

level, in this chapter of the book may be summarized in the following points. (a) The introduction of a framework for perceiving the 'nature' of the modern homosexual – the framework of a *homosexual form of existence* – which may be more adequate than the widespread one of a homosexual *identity*. Further, the introduction of a distinction between two dimensions or poles of 'identity' in relation to form of existence. (b) The integration of 'discourses' (roles, scripts, etc.) within a more comprehensive range of *modern conditions of life*. More specifically, I have pointed to the importance of the *urban* in the constitution of the modern homosexual – and notably, the importance of studying him as an existence *of* the city and not merely as someone existing *in* the city. Thus, as we have seen, the urban permeates practically *all* dimensions of his existence. Further, I have emphasized the overall importance of spatiality, i.e. of *life spaces*, as a background for the homosexual form of existence. Moreover, I have pointed to the significance of modern genders in the constitution of the modern homosexual – and notably, the importance of the specifically modern forms of *masculinity*, as well as of the particular relations between masculinity and the other conditions of modern life – such as the urban. (c) I have delineated *various modes and dimensions of 'construction'* (within the horizon of a life-world) between modern conditions of life and the homosexual (on the general level: 'impact', 'answer', 'guided answer'). The reciprocity of construction between the homosexual and modern society will be explored in ch. V. (d) In sum, I have identified the homosexual as being *absolutely modern* (to paraphrase Baudelaire), a concentration and crystallization point for the particulars and problems of modernity. Connected to this is an anticipatory indication (to be elaborated in ch. VI) of the developing and suspending dialectics of specifically homosexual and generally modern.

122 There are a number of reasons why I have chosen 'world' as the chief and most comprehensive concept in relation to the social aspects of the homosexual form of existence. First, there is a tradition for this term in studies of homosexuality – and indeed, in studies conducted from a perspective that is not anti-homosexual (at any rate, when judged by the standards of the time they were written). Examples are Hooker 1965; Hoffman 1968; Warren 1974. My other main reason for choosing the term is the wish to connect to the phenomenological tradition of 'life-world' theory, though this is not a dogmatic choice and should not be understood in any 'reductionally culturalist' sense as merely a question of symbolic universes, normative expectations and interpretative horizons. In addition, the choice has been made in a dialogue with and delimitation from other possible terms. 'Ghetto' (cf. Levine 1979) implies a 'residential concentration' and to this extent it is synonymous with what is nowadays more often termed 'neighbourhood'; consequently, it is too restricted for the range of

phenomena discussed here. Besides, it connotes an excessive stress on the dimensions of oppression and oppressedness. 'Community' or 'subculture' may, of course, be used to cover a wide range, or even the entirety, of the field I have termed 'world' (cf. Warren 1974: chs 2–5; Lee 1978; Murray 1980; 1992a; Dannecker and Reiche 1974: 67–144; Plummer 1975: ch. 8). The very word 'community', however, connotes (to my ears at least) feelings or manifestations of togetherness and solidarity, for which reason I have preferred to use it for designating a certain aspect or mode of world. As for 'subculture', the term has often been used in analyses focusing on 'culturalist' dimensions of 'culture'. Alternatively, it sometimes (over)focuses on the dependence of the 'sub-' on the 'main' or 'mother' culture. And sometimes it is inserted, in constructionist analyses, as a sort of remedy or expedient when a lack is felt in (or after) the 'discourses/roles/categories construct identities' approach. 'Movement' is an important aspect or mode of world but not coextensive with it. Indeed, parts of the homosexual world are mostly very immobile or at least do not move in the sense of a movement. 'Way of life' or 'lifestyle' would seem to be more relevant as denotations not of the social and materialized dimensions of the homosexual form of existence, but as alternative terms for 'form of existence'. In the preceding sections I have detailed why I prefer the latter. Moreover, the terms 'homosexual way of life' or 'homosexual lifestyle' are often highly unspecified *or* – and this may be the most common usage – used simply as synonymous with the enacting of a particular sexual preference (perhaps as a tool in the linguistic cosmetics designed to present a more favourable image of this). 'Tribe' (or 'tribe of taste') in the sense of Maffesoli (1988; 1993) may easily connote an uncritical celebration of difference and a nostalgic anti-modernist impulse. Insofar as this is not the case, it connotes a nomadism, a degree of fluidity, change and diffuseness not adequate in relation to the social and material aspects of the modern homosexual world. Indeed, it may be more appropriate in relation to the *disappearance* of the modern homosexual and what comes after (or *post*) him (see also Mendès-Leite 1993: 26; and cf. ch. VI below). This is also the case with 'scene' in the sense of Irwin (1977) or 'community of affect' in the sense of Hebdige (1989); cf. Turner 1969. Yet another possibility is 'status group' (Evans 1993: 44ff, 84ff), but this refers to a different, 'external' perspective than the phenomenological one implied in 'world'. (On the relation of my analysis to dimensions of economic and political spheres see ch. V, section 7, n. 59.

123 Cf. Anderson 1983.

124 'Movement', of course, may also be used as a term for a more formalized political association; cf. section 12 above.

125 Cf. section 3 above.

126 On 'real abstraction', see also ch. III, section 21, n. 147. On the

historical and conglomerate-like character of the formations of modern homosexuality – including that of the homosexual form of existence – see also ch. III, section 21, n. 144.

127 Such accommodation is facilitated by the fact that the homosexual world is predominantly a *leisure* world. When it is also an individual's place of work, he is even more immersed in it.

128 As previously mentioned, the changes of the most recent decades have been abstracted for consideration in ch. VI.

129 As mentioned earlier, I myself have conducted an interview study particularly designed to elucidate class, age, ethnic, regional and lifestyle, as well as individual, differences among 'homosexuals' (Bech 1989a).

130 Cf. information on meeting places in travel guides for homosexuals, such as the *Spartacus Guide*.

131 Hirschfeld 1914: 696. Cf. also Chauncey 1994: 196ff, 420f nn. 32 and 35.

132 Hirschfeld 1914: 698f; and T. G. Comstock, quoted from Katz 1983: 227.

V Homosexuality and Society

1 On homosexuals as great educators and commanders: see e.g. Hirschfeld 1914: 517f, 657, 638f. See also notes to ch. V, section 5 below. On homosexuals as the cement of society: see e.g. Friedländer 1904: esp. p. 211–16; Freud (cf. the discussion in ch. III, section 5 above). On the homosexuals as corruptive and destructive, see ch. V, sections 4 and 6.

2 Cf. e.g. the discussions in Hooker 1965: 83f; Simon and Gagnon 1967: 177f; Weinberg and Bell 1972; Lautmann 1977: 126–37; Bayer 1981: ch. 1; cf. also notes to ch. IV, section 2.

3 Cf. e.g. the reports in Weinberg and Bell 1972; Katz 1976: part II; Albæk and Hansen 1981: 33–40; Schmidt 1985; Hertoft 1986; Graugaard 1993.

4 E.g. Szasz 1970: 174–6; Lautmann 1977: 126–37.

5 On the emergence, characteristics and expansion of this complex see Foucault 1963/72; Foucault 1976. Another inspiring line of investigation is the Anglo-Saxon tradition of psychiatry critique; among its classics are Goffman 1961; Scheff 1966; Szasz 1970.

6 See ch. IV, section 7.

7 As for recent developments in research see ch. VI, section 2. One should, however, not imagine that the kind of science depicted here is extinct. For some examples see the articles by Pillard, Gooren, Money or Bancroft in McWhirter et al. (eds) 1990; cf. also the discussion in Paul 1993, as well as the widely publicized works of LeVay (1993) and Hamer (1993).

8 *Marlene* (director: Maximilian Schell; West Germany 1984).
9 This is not equivalent to claiming that there have not also been a number of women engaged in modern professional design right from its start.
10 Cf. also the observations by e.g. Bronski 1984; Chauncey 1994; Dyer 1990.
11 Sontag 1964: 280. Cf. also ch. IV, section 15.
12 Calinescu 1987: 225–62; Booth 1983: 20–2. Cf. also ch. IV, section 15.
13 Cf. ch. IV, section 13; and Bech 1992b; 1993.
14 My discussion of aestheticization and surfaces is inspired by analyses from semiotics, art theory and media studies: among others, the 'classic' works by Barthes 1970; Baudrillard 1973; 1976; Benjamin 1935; Haug 1971; Hebdige 1979; Jameson 1984. During very recent years these topics have, of course, been widely discussed, particularly in connection with the debates over postmodernism. My own contribution concerns the relations between aestheticization and the development of detached and autonomous surfaces; including (a) the specification of the various (logical and in part also historical) stages in the development of these relations; (b) the identification of the structural correspondence and the interrelations between the development of surfaces and aestheticization in, respectively, the city, industrial design and the visual media; (c) the indication of the interrelations of these developments and the existence of the modern homosexual. Some further implications of this will be developed in ch. VI.
15 Kistrup 1985. The rumours are in fact as old as the homosexual. For some American examples see Bronski 1984: 125ff. For some Danish examples see Bech 1987: 261ff.
16 Bronski 1984: 127f.
17 On 'literary transvestitism': see ch. IV, section 16.
18 Cf. ch. IV.
19 Cf. Adorno 1966; 1970.
20 Bang 1886. Cf. the interpretations by Rosenberg 1912: 69–73; Secher 1973: 113–45; Rossel 1982: 37. 'By the Wayside' (the English tradition has chosen the title *Katinka*) is perhaps Bang's best novel, one of the masterpieces of nineteenth-century world literature.
21 The extensive presence of 'homosexuals' and 'closeted homosexuals' among the main writers of modern drama, poetry and fiction is too well documented by now to need elaboration here. See the works mentioned in ch. III, n. 69.
22 Cf. e.g. Freud 1911: 61; 1916–17: 304; Smitt 1951: 16f; Jacobsen 1964: 104–6; Ruitenbek 1967: xvii.
23 Thus Dannecker 1978: 36.
24 Cf. e.g. Kertbeny 1868: 43–5; Hirshfeld 1914: 648–73; Garde 1964; Rowse 1977; Greif 1982.
25 Cf. Carpenter 1914: esp. ch. III; Freimark 1905: 17–19, 20f, 28, 37, 39,

40f; Fogedgaard 1946: esp. 12–18; 'Homophilos' (pseudonym for Fogedgaard) 1949; Third World Gay Revolution (Chicago) and Gay Liberation Front (Chicago) 1971; London Gay Liberation Front's manifesto 1971, quoted in Walter (ed.) 1980: 8; excerpts from *Come Together*, 15 (1973), quoted in Walter (ed.) 1980: 203–10 (cf. also the discussions in Weeks 1977: 196f, 203, 205, and in Walter (ed.) 1980: 39–42); FHAR 1971: esp. 54f, 56 (cf. the discussion in Girard 1981: esp. 93–5); Homosexuelle Aktion West-Berlin 1973: esp. 41, 49; Evans 1978: esp. ch. 10; Fernbach 1981: esp. 197–208; and the discussion in Adam 1987: 75–101. On the continuity of this tradition, see the contributions in Thompson (ed.) 1988: parts II and III.

26 Thus Kupffer 1900: Introduction, esp. pp. 1–12; Friedländer 1904: 255–322; and 1909 (most concisely in 'Sieben Thesen' in the latter work); Blüher 1919: vol. I, pp. 3–9, 137–46, 241–8, and vol. II, pp. 102–10, 217–24; Wyneken 1921: ch. VIII; and the material presented (rather than the interpretation of it) concerning R. Oelbermann and the 'Nerother Wandervogel' in Krolle 1986. Cf. the discussions in Steakley 1975: 42–58; Baumgardt 1984b: 23–6; and the introductions and transcripts in Oosterhuis (ed.) 1991.

27 Cf. e.g. FHAR 1971: 54f; Hocquenghem 1972: esp. 101–21 (cf. the discussion in Girard 1981: 90f); Altman 1971: esp. 232–8; Gay Revolution Party Manifesto (*c.*1971); Ahrens et al. 1974: esp. 107–11; Mieli 1977: esp. 114–21, 228–30; and the discussions in Weeks 1977: 185–206; and in Adam 1987: 75–101.

28 Cf. Foucault 1976: 157–9.

29 See ch. V, section 6 below.

30 I shall return to this possibility in chapter VI.

31 There are some indications that this is changing in very recent years, as the experiences of homosexuals are being utilized e.g. in films addressed to a general audience or in sociological studies by non-homosexuals (see n. 86 to ch. IV, section 19). This would take us *post* the era of 'modern' homosexuality and into that of the trends towards its disappearance (cf. ch. VI).

32 Theories on the homosexual as scapegoat and bogeyman can be found e.g. in functionalist-inspired sociology of deviance and in Marxist analyses; cf. e.g. McIntosh 1968; Lindkvist and Moritz 1975.

33 The theoretical inspiration for this chapter on the relation between evil, modern societies and the homosexual springs from many diverse sources, not least Adorno and Horkheimer 1947; Bauman 1989; Berger and Luckman 1966; Douglas 1966; Foucault 1961, 1975, 1976; Mosse 1985; Sontag 1978; Szasz 1970. My own focus concerns the multidimensionality of modern evil and its relation to the homosexual as a 'privileged incarnation' and 'universal equivalent' of evil.

34 The moral-religious conception of homosexuality as disease is associated with certain cosmological ideas (cf. the subsection on 'The threat to the cosmic order' below), and in modern societies it usually enters

into alloys and alliances with secularized, scientific ideas. Over the past *c*. 125 years of the homosexuals' lifetime, Christian circles have been assiduous in elaborating this kind of opinion; and during recent years, such views have been industriously relaunched in debates over AIDS.

35 Cf. ch. IV, section 2; ch. V, section 2.

36 A US Senate Committee report of 1950, quoted from D'Emilio 1983b: 42.

37 E.g. Bergler 1956: 7f. On the various versions of the ideas concerning the contagiousness of the homosexual: cf. the references in Weinberg and Bell 1972; Katz 1976, 1983; as well as the notes to ch. IV, section 2.

38 Degeneration was a master idea in the discussion of homosexuality until the Second World War. Cf. the notes to ch. IV, section 2.

39 Bergler 1956: 9.

40 Himmler's speech of 18 February 1937 to the SS squad leaders; quoted from the German text in Stümke and Finkler 1981: 220f and 434.

41 Cf. Bray 1982: ch. 1, esp. pp. 21 and 27; Bleibtreu-Ehrenberg 1978: 276f.

42 Cf. ch. III, section 15.

43 Cf. e.g. Schelsky 1955: 81; and references in Weinberg and Bell 1972, and in Hocquenghem 1972: 29–32.

44 Cf. the discussions in Nardi 1982, and in Israelstam and Lambert 1983.

45 Cf. e.g. Samuel Kahn: *Mentality and Homosexuality* (Boston, 1937), referenced in Cory 1951: 94; Houmark [1926]/1950: 29; Kolansky and Moore 1971: 486–91; Smith 1972: 150.

46 Cf. e.g. the references in Weinberg and Bell 1972; and cf. ch. IV, sections 2, 13 and 17; and ch. V, section 2.

47 On the threat to group identity and its representative, cf. e.g. Ostrymiecz 1931; Bley 1931; and the references to examples in Stümke and Finkler 1981: 148–62, 351, 439; D'Emilio 1983b: ch. 3, esp. pp. 48–9; Katz 1976: 91–5; Weeks 1981b: 240f; Hodges 1983: ch. 8, esp. pp. 496–510; Axgil and Fogedgaard 1985: 98f. Cf. also the press coverage in January and February 1984 regarding the dismissal of the German NATO General Kiessling.

48 For instance, in the fears associated with – and co-constitutive of – modern nationalism and racism, the imagined threat to the group's identity or symbolic representative coalesces with the imagined threat to its biological reproduction, and – not least by way of this connection – with the rest of the possible threats.

49 Cf. e.g. Bleibtreu-Ehrenberg 1978: ch. VI; Boswell 1980: chs 10 and 11; Bray 1982: 14–18; Goldberg 1992.

50 Cf. the Anglo-Saxon tradition of deviance analysis and labelling theory (overview and discussion in Plummer 1975; (ed.) 1981).

51 Cf. e.g. Dannecker and Reiche 1974: chs 35–6.

52 Cf. ch. III.

53 Cf. Marx 1867/87: ch. 3.

54 On homosexuals in the concentration camps: cf. Heger 1972; Jellonnek 1990; Lautmann et al. 1977; Lautmann 1990; Plant 1986: 152–81; Stümke and Finkler 1981: 212–339. On the homosexual as the universal equivalent of evil: an example is that of a British 'Black Parents' Action Group' which in 1986 declared that 'homosexuality is a white plot to undermine the black family' (quoted in Halifax 1988: 35). Obviously, some such examples would seem merely bizarre, were it not for the consequences they entail if the proponents have their way. Another example: 'I am firmly convinced that the entire substance of the clergy and of the whole of Christianity is an erotic male bonding [*Männerbund*] aimed at establishing and reproducing this 2,000-year-old Bolshevism' (Heinrich Himmler, 1937, translated from the quotes in Stümke and Finkler 1981: 439). Meve (1990) contains an illuminating examination of the widespread anti-fascist use of the stereotype of the 'homosexual Nazi' (an example: 'There is already a slogan in Germany: "Eradicate the homosexual and fascism will disappear" ' – Maxim Gorki). It is also instructive to pay attention to the aversion in some Western countries in relation to (a) government 'compensation' to homosexuals who had survived incarceration in concentration camps; (b) permission to erect monuments or plaques for these victims; (c) permission to homosexual organizations to participate in commemorations for victims of concentration camps. (On Germany, cf. Stümke 1989: 147ff; on France, cf. Boisson 1988: 206ff.) – My remarks on the Jew or the homosexual as the privileged incarnation of evil should not be misinterpreted to imply any 'competition' as to suffering.

55 Cf. Dalsgaard 1984: 38–73; Rosen 1993: 719–80.

56 Cf. Mikkelsen 1984: 71–115; Ufer 1965; Axgil and Fogedgaard 1985; Bech 1987: 290f.

57 Concerning homosexual panics in various countries since the 1880s, see also Andersson 1985; Chauncey 1993; 1994: ch. 12; D'Emilio 1983b: ch. 3; 1989; Rose 1994: 14ff; Silverstolpe 1980: 144–92; Steakley 1983; Stümke and Finkler 1981: 148–268; Weeks 1977: 14–31, 156–63; Wotherspoon 1991: ch. 3.

58 Jensen 1906.

59 As should be clear, I am not implying that the socio-cultural phenomena of modernity which I have been examining in the preceding sections of chs III, IV and V exist without any interacting and interdependent relation to the modern economic and political formations. (Indeed, I have been referring to these throughout the book. For a more thematic analysis of the impact from capital and the state, important contributions have been made by e.g. Adam 1985b; D'Emilio 1983a; Evans 1993; Greenberg 1988; Kinsman 1987; 1991; Weeks 1980.) But I do think that the phenomena I have been focusing on in this book form a conglomeration of a certain 'material' character as well as of a weight comparable to that of capital or state, and one

often ignored or downplayed by other analyses. See also n. 40 to ch. VI, section 5.

VI The Disappearance of the Modern Homosexual

1 In the real, historically concrete world of late modern societies (or 'contemporary modern societies') the trend towards a disappearance coexists with the persistence of the formations of homosexuality. Accordingly, the fact that I have treated disappearance in a separate and concluding chapter should not occasion the misconception that modern homosexuality does not still exist. Very often, one and the same concrete phenomenon embodies aspects of both persistence and disappearance. But the two can, reasonably and advantageously, be analytically separated.

2 I shall deal more extensively with these changes from modernity to late or postmodernity in my *Modern Life Spaces* (Bech forthcoming (b)). A detailed list of contributions to the debate could go on endlessly. Among the major works – with fairly different emphases, interpretative frames and appraisals of the changes – are Bauman 1991; 1995; Beck and Beck-Gernsheim 1990; Chambers 1986; Chaney 1990; Featherstone 1991; Fischer 1982; Fiske 1987; Gergen 1991; Giddens 1991; 1992; Lash and Urry 1994; Sennett 1990; Shields 1991; Sontag 1964, 1977; Urry 1990; Wellman et al. 1988. See also references on specific aspects throughout the book. – In relation to these changes, and put in the terminology of postmodernism, the homosexual may be said to be 'pre-postmodern', postmodern before the advent of postmodernity. It might be interjected that his identity as homosexual is much too fixed to be termed 'postmodern'. However, as we have seen in ch. IV, this seemingly so fixed identity is inherently problematic, contradictory and on the verge of dissolving into a void; and in this duality of fixed and insecure, of being and nothingness, the homosexual is no doubt foreshadowing a characteristic trend of identity experience in contemporary Western societies.

3 The 'socio-cultural homosexualization' which I speak of here is not synonymous with the 'homosexualization' discussed in ch. III in relation to the processes of expansion of absent homosexuality. – In his pioneering work, Altman (1982) has used the term 'homosexualization' in much the same way that I use 'socio-cultural homosexualization'. I see my own work as a continuation and an elaboration of his on this point. The differences may be summarized in the following manner. I have made a number of specifications, particularly in relation to the concepts of avant-garde in itself vs avant-garde for others, as well as in relation to the living conditions making up the background to the processes of socio-cultural homosexualization. In addition, I do not think that these conditions can be adequately

summarized by a term like 'consumer capitalism'; they are of a broader and, in a way, more fundamental nature, not reducible to consumerism and capitalism although no doubt helped along by them. Further: on the more concrete level of analysis I am, in this book, interested in broader western developments – including, as will be clear from the rest of this chapter, the *differences* from the American case.

4 Thus Vanggaard 1962: 1430–4; Jacobsen 1964: 106f.

5 Thus Dannecker and Reiche 1974: 346–50; Dannecker 1978: 86–100. Cf. also the critique of recent ideas on 'sexual compulsivity' and 'sex addiction' in Levine and Troiden 1988; Irvine 1995.

6 Thus Morgenthaler 1984: 55–104; Isay 1989; and the discussion in Lewes 1988: ch. 10.

7 The deletion of homosexuality as a mental disorder from the American Psychiatry Association's *Diagnostic and Statistical Manual of Psychiatric Disorders* in 1973, and the accompanying (indeed continuing) debate on the introduction of 'ego-dystonic homosexuality' is an example of this. Cf. Bayer 1981; Lewes 1988: ch. 10. – Obviously there are more possible variations than the four described above: examples are Friedman 1988; Dannecker 1996.

8 The case of Denmark (which I shall further detail in a moment) is indicative. Thus, in an opinion poll of 1947, 61 per cent of the respondents rated homosexuality as the worst or second worst 'crime' on the following list: murder, rape of an adult woman, burglary, forgery, drunk driving, hunting outside the hunting season, and homosexuality (reported in Havelin 1968: 73). In an opinion poll of 1985, 50.7 per cent of the respondents found that society in general did not show sufficient understanding of the conditions of the homosexuals.

9 I shall return to the question of the disappearance of 'absent homosexuality' in ch. VI, section 4.

10 The Danish law on 'registered partnerships' was passed on 26 May 1989 and has been in effect since 1 October 1989. In a registered partnership two people of the same sex obtain the same rights and obligations as a man and a woman have in marriage, with the exception of adoption rights, rights of custody of the partner's children, and the option of church weddings. The law further differs from the Danish Marriage Act in that one of the partners must be a Danish citizen and resident of Denmark. The ceremony is carried out by the same officials and (usually) in the same surroundings as those used in civil marriage ceremonies, and with an equivalent wording. Up until the end of 1995, about 2150 registered partnerships have been contracted, approximately a third of them by women. Some of them have subsequently had their partnership blessed by a vicar. I have analysed the debate and other events surrounding the introduction of registered partnerships in greater detail in Bech 1991b; 1992a. In the following, I shall summarize the results of these analyses.

11 Cf. ch. IV, section 18.
12 Whitam and Mathy 1986: 182.
13 Cf. D'Emilio 1983b: 75–125; Mikkelsen 1984: 53–70; Girard 1981: 38–73; Adam 1987: 60–9. A similar argumentation is found among the much smaller and weaker British homophile movement (cf. Grey 1992). It should be noted that the beginnings of the homophile movement were often more radical than what later became their public image.
14 See the references from the 1970s and 1980s in ch. V, section 5, nn. 25 and 27.
15 Interestingly, during the 1980s there seems to have been a minor 'tightening up' of what might be termed the 'relaxed' attitudes of the Danes to the values of 'the family'. This, however, should be seen against the backdrop that Denmark was already the country in the West with far the most relaxed attitudes in this matter. Moreover, practice remains even more 'relaxed'. Further, the changes in attitudes that have indeed occurred seem to be consistent with an increasing emphasis on a certain version of individualistic values – implying, among other things, the view that if you enter the commitments of a family relationship you should stick to it (but on the other hand respecting that others may choose to live differently). In this context it is also interesting that there has been no increased emphasis on religious values – again, Denmark remains the most secularized country in the West. See Bech 1992b; Gundelach and Riis 1992: 11–40, 59–82, 211–18; Ester et al. 1994: chs 3 and 5.
16 'Equal value' (in Danish: *ligeværd*) is a matter of human worth and dignity, whereas 'equality' (Danish: *lighed*) refers to social and legal rights and opportunities.
17 I am not of the opinion that political decision-making is the result of 'pure' discussions in which 'the best argument wins' – especially not when homosexual topics are concerned. Nonetheless, arguments are not without some measure of significance as motivating forces; and even where they aren't crucial to decision-making, they can be used as *justification* for the decisions – which is equally indicative of changes, since major groups of people, at a given time, are not likely to use just any argument to justify their actions. For a more detailed analysis see Bech 1992a.
18 Moreover, for homosexuals it is perhaps not altogether clear why they, as substitutes so to speak, should embody the wishes of leftist intellectuals for an alternative – regardless of the degree to which they may share the desire for social change.
19 Cf. Bech 1989a; Lützen 1988; Fouchard 1994; Gaasholt and Togeby 1995: 37f. An additional piece of evidence is furnished by an anti-discrimination case which occupied the interest of the media shortly after the introduction of registered partnerships: a lawsuit, brought to court by the public prosecutor at the request of the National

Organization for Gays and Lesbians, against the writer of a letter to the editor. Invoking the Bible, the woman in question had described homosexuality as the most loathsome form of adultery and the homosexual as a sort of thief who steals his neighbour's honour, and perhaps his life, by inflicting AIDS upon him. She was sued with reference to the law on anti-discrimination, which since June 1987 includes the provision that a group may not be publicly defamed on the grounds of its sexual orientation. The woman was found guilty but was acquitted on appeal. The case, its background and its results testify to the particular intermediate stage of Danish developments in relation to the disappearance of the modern homosexual.

20 Obviously, the situation differs between (and within) the different countries of eastern Europe, as well as of southern Europe. On Hungary, see Tóth 1995; on Spain, see Smith 1992.

21 Cf. the argument regarding the 'alternativeness' of the homosexuals (the third among the 'classical figures of justification'). – The above is not intended as an exhaustive description or critique of the phenomenon of the queer (for some informative introductions, overviews and discussions, see Abelove 1995; Bérubé and Escoffier 1991; Berlant and Freeman 1992; Browning 1993: ch. 2; Duggan 1992; Lauretis 1991; Penn 1995; Warner 1993). Most 'queers' would no doubt stress the inclusiveness of the term in regard to 'multiple differences' (those of gender, race, ethnicity, age and sexual proclivities, among other things). However, it remains debated whether such inclusiveness does not instead do violence to difference, thus also erasing the specific importance of *same-sex sexual* deviance. In any case, 'queer' derives its meaning from being *oppositional* to 'straight' – indeed radically so: being *confrontational*, definitely not assimilationist. Accordingly, a certain world view is typical of queer thinking: the vision of a monolithically present and massively destructive 'dominant society' allowing only forms of wily resistance or oblique defiance. In fact, this world view is shared (expressly or per implication) by many of the most brilliant contemporary US theorists on same-sex matters, whether or not they sympathize with notions of 'nation' or indeed of 'queer', and however different their strategies and perspectives: be it the theatrical performativity of Butler (1993) or the affective productivity of Sedgwick (1993a; 1993b); be it the Foucaultian existential aesthetics of Halperin (1995) or the Freudian desirous genealogies of Bersani (1995). On the other hand, the very diversity of these strategies and perspectives testifies to the enormous creativity and imagination of American queer (or 'post-gay') undertakings in language, theory, art and actions. Thus, even in those countries where the overall world view does not really make sense any more, it is impossible not to be inspired by the queer – because the homosexual has in fact not disappeared here, either; and to the extent that he has, there is still a life to be lived.

22 However, women's participation in the workforce is low. Furthermore, stating that changes in Holland are hardly less advanced than in Denmark is not the same as claiming they are identical to the latter; for example, religion plays a much more important role in Holland – notably, however, in the form of different religions respecting each other's right to be there.

23 On gay movement and subculture in Holland see Duyves 1995; Duyvendak 1994; Hekma 1994a; Krouwel 1994. I should add that the interpretation given above is my own. – On Germany between the 'fall of gay identity' on the one hand, and segregative 'permissive indifference' and hostility towards gays on the other, see Bochow 1993; Hegener 1993.

24 On a global scale, much will depend on the development of Europe and the European Union.

25 Jacobsen 1966: 211. Herman Bang was found unconscious in his compartment on the train from Chicago to San Francisco, and died the following day, 29 January 1912.

26 In Denmark, the introduction of registered partnerships is indicative of this, as are the polls mentioned in ch. VI, section 2. Cf. also Gundelach and Riis 1992: 214. Even in the US and Britain attitudes towards homosexuals do not, in the long run, seem to have become more negative during the years of AIDS (of course, one may add that they are severely negative anyway). Cf. Wellings et al. 1994: 253ff; Lauman et al. 1994: ch. 14; Smith 1990; Ester et al. 1994: 114. (The figures given in the latter work, seemingly indicating a decrease in acceptance of homosexuals in Denmark during the 1980s, are misleading, cf. the breakdown of the figures in Gundelach and Riis 1992: 214.) – On the dialectic of state and homosexual community reactions to HIV/AIDS, see the excellent work by Altman (1994).

27 Cf. e.g. Wittman 1970: 331; Altman 1971: 229, 233f, 236f; 'Guy' in FHAR 1971: 75f; Homosexuelle Aktion Westberlin 1973: 41.

28 Bech 1983: 60.

29 Plummer (1975: 171f) mentions surfing, medieval dancing and stamp collecting as other imaginable exemplifications – before voting instead for the utopia of universal bisexuality.

30 Interestingly, Kertbeny – who was probably the coiner of the term 'homosexual' – speaks of sexual preference as a taste on a par with the preference for roast lamb or roast veal. Cf. Kertbeny 1868. Obviously, the use of 'taste' to characterize same-sex sexual preference has a long history, particularly prominent in the eighteenth century.

31 Cf. ch. III. Phenomenologically speaking, 'male interest' and its unobstructed transition into sexualization constitutes the transcendental condition of possibility for the phenomena of absent homosexuality.

32 Cf. Bech 1992b.

33 Cf. R. Dyer 1982; Steinman 1992. It has also been argued that if the

man in the picture does not conform to these demands he is 'punished', e.g. by being ridiculed (Neale 1983; Poynton and Hartley 1990).

34 Cf. ch. III, section 16.

35 Cf. Mort 1988; Moore 1988; Henriksson 1989; Bech 1991a. Very delightful examples of the homosexual soft porn of the 1950s can be found in the photographs by Robert Mizer (reprinted in Mizer 1987).

36 Cf. Boswell 1980: chs 9 and 11.

37 Cf. ch. IV, section 18; ch. V, section 2.

38 Cf. Bech 1991b.

39 Adorno 1966: 191 (I have changed the English translation). Adorno himself wanted to capture this alien-ness, the desire for other men, in the clamp of the conceptual apparatus of psychoanalysis, so that man would be freed from it in an emancipated society. Cf. Adorno 1963: 543f. See also Halle 1995.

40 This is an important point and a major reason why I have not given priority to the analysis of capital or state in this book, but instead focused on a different – and in a way more fundamental – 'material', socio-cultural conglomeration and its dynamics. Once established, this conglomeration obtains a logic of its own, and exerts an influence of its own, not reducible to the factors that constituted it historically or continually help to reconstitute it.

41 No, I am *not* implying that 'women' lack humour and astuteness – or cannot have red lips and blue eyes. Masculinity, *desirable masculinity*, is not to be pinpointed in such specifications; its centre – imaginary and not rigidly specifiable – lies in the crossings of a number of dimensions: among others, those of nature/culture, present/future, tradition/distance, body/fantasy.

Bibliography

The date following the author's name is the year of first publication (or, if in square brackets, the year of writing). If two dates are given separated by an oblique the first is the year of first publication (or of writing), and the second the year of publication of the revised version (or the year of publication of a text written earlier). In this case, or if another edition has been used in the present book it is indicated by a separate year later in the reference.

Abelove, H. 1995: 'The Queering of Lesbian/Gay History'. *Radical History Review*, 62, 44–57.

—— Barale, M. and Halperin, D. (eds) 1993: *The Lesbian and Gay Studies Reader*. New York: Routledge.

Adam, B. 1978: *The Survival of Domination: Inferiorization and Everyday Life*. New York: Elsevier.

—— 1985a: 'Age, Structure, and Sexuality: Reflections on the Anthropological Evidence on Homosexual Relations'. *Journal of Homosexuality*, 11(3–4), 19–33.

—— 1985b: 'Structural Foundations of the Gay World'. *Comparative Studies in Society and History*, 27(1), 658–71.

—— 1987: *The Rise of a Gay and Lesbian Movement*. Boston: Twayne.

Adorno, T. 1957: 'Sociology and Empirical Research', tr. G. Bartram. In: Connerton, P. (ed), *Critical Sociology: Selected Readings*. Harmondsworth: Penguin, 1976, 258–76.

—— 1962: 'On the Logic of the Social Sciences'. In: Adorno et al., *The Positivist Dispute in German Sociology*, tr. G. Adey and D. Frisby. London: Heinemann, 1976, 105–22.

—— 1963: 'Sexualtabus und Recht heute'. In: Adorno 1977, 533–54.

—— 1964: 'Der wunderliche Realist'. In: Adorno, *Noten zur Literatur III*. Frankfurt: Suhrkamp, 1965, 83–108.

—— 1966: *Negative Dialectics*, tr. E. Ashton. New York: Routledge, 1990.
—— 1969: 'Freizeit'. In: Adorno 1977, 645–56.
—— 1970: *Aesthetic Theory*. London: RKP, 1984.
—— 1977: *Gesammelte Schriften*, vol. 10.2. Frankfurt: Suhrkamp.
—— and Horkheimer, M. 1947: *Dialectic of Enlightenment*, tr. J. Cumming. New York: Herder & Herder, 1972.
Ahrens, H., Bruns, V., Hedenström, H., Hoffmann, G. and Marvitz, R. 1974: 'Die Homosexualität in uns'. *Kursbuch*, 37: 84–112.
Albæk, E. and Hansen, K. 1981: *Velkommen på prutten – om bøsser, ret og moral*. Aarhus: Grus.
Aldrich, R. 1993: *The Seduction of the Mediterranean: Writing, Art and Homosexual Fantasy*. London: Routledge.
Altman, D. 1971: *Homosexual Oppression and Liberation*. New York: Avon, 1973.
—— 1977: 'The Homosexual Vision of E. M. Forster'. In: Altman, *Coming Out in the Seventies*. Boston: Alyson, 162–71.
—— 1982: *The Homosexualization of America, the Americanization of the Homosexual*. New York: St Martin's Press.
—— 1986: *AIDS and the New Puritanism*. London: Pluto.
—— 1994: *Power and Community: Organizational and Cultural Responses to AIDS*. London: Taylor and Francis.
Anderson, B. 1983: *Imagined Communities*. London: New Left Books.
Andersson, L. 1985: *Homofiljakten – et skådespel i Göteborg på 50-talet och dess intressenter*. Gothenburg: RFSL (Historiegruppens Handlingar, 2).
Angvik, B. 1989: 'Forfattar, tekst, lesar'. *Lambda Nordica*, 3–4, 280–322.
Anishnawbe 1988: 'Sex/Gender Systems in Native North America'. In: Roscoe, W. (ed.), *Living the Spirit: A Gay American Indian Anthology*. New York: St Martin's Press, 32–47.
Ardener, S. (ed.) 1981: *Women and Space: Ground Rules and Social Maps*. London: Helm.
Atkinson, P. 1992: *Understanding Ethnographic Texts*. Newbury Park: Sage.
Austen, R. 1977: *Playing The Game: The Homosexual Novel in America*. Indianapolis: Bobbs-Merrill.
Axgil, A. and Fogedgaard, H. 1985: *Homofile kampår: Bøsseliv gennem tiderne*. Rudkøbing: Grafolio.
Baal, J. 1984: 'The Dialectics of Sex in Marind-Anim Culture'. In: Herdt (ed.) 1984, 167–210.
Babuscio, J. 1977: 'Camp and the Gay Sensibility'. In: Dyer (ed.), 40–57.
Bailey, P. 1990: 'Parasexuality and Glamour: The Victorian Barmaid as Cultural Prototype'. *Gender & History*, 2(2), 148–72.
Baldwin, J. 1962: *Another Country*. New York: Dell, 1963.
Bang, H. 1886: *Ved Vejen*. English: *Katinka*, tr. T. Nunnally. Seattle: Fjord, 1990.

—— 1904: *Mikaël.* Copenhagen: Trondal, 1981.
—— 1906: *De uden Fædreland.* English: *Denied a Country*, tr. M. Busch and A. Chater. New York: Knopf, 1927.
—— [1909]/1922: *Gedanken zum Sexualitätsproblem.* Herausgegeben von Dr Wasbutzki. Bonn: Markus & Weber.
Barbedette, G. and Carassou, M. 1981: *Paris Gay 1925*. Paris: Presses de la Renaissance.
Barthes, R. 1970: 'The Third Meaning'. In: Barthes, *Images, Music, Text: Essays*. London: Fontana, 1977.
Baudelaire, C. 1867: 'Anywhere out of the world' ('N'importe où hors du monde'). In: Baudelaire, *Little Poems in Prose*, tr. A. Crowley. Chicago: Teitan Press, 1993.
Baudrillard, J. 1973. *The Mirror of Production*, tr. M. Poster. St Louis: Telos, 1975.
—— 1976: *Symbolic Exchange and Death*, tr. I. Grant. London: Sage, 1993.
Bauman, Z. 1989: *Modernity and the Holocaust*. Cambridge: Polity Press.
—— 1991: *Modernity and Ambivalence*. Cambridge: Polity Press.
—— 1993: *Postmodern Ethics*. Oxford: Blackwell.
—— 1995: *Life in Fragments: Essays in Postmodern Morality*. Oxford: Blackwell.
Baumgardt, M. 1984a: 'Berlin, ein Zentrum der entstehenden Sexualwissenschaft und die Vorläufer der Homosexuellen-Bewegung'. In: Berlin Museum (ed.), 13–16.
—— 1984b: 'Die Homosexuellen-Bewegung bis zum Ende des ersten Weltkrieges'. In: Berlin Museum (ed.), 17–27.
—— 1984c: 'Das Institut für Sexualwissenschaft und die Homosexuellen-Bewegung in der Weimarer Republik'. In: Berlin Museum (ed.), 31–43.
Bayer, R. 1981: *Homosexuality and American Psychiatry: The Politics of Diagnosis*. New York: Basic.
Beaver, H. 1981: 'Homosexual Signs (In Memory of Roland Barthes)'. *Critical Inquiry*, 8(1), 99–119.
Bech, H. 1983: 'Mellem mænd'. *Kontext*, 45, 53–67.
—— 1987: *Når mænd mødes: Homoseksualiteten og de homoseksuelle.* Copenhagen: Gyldendal.
—— 1989a: *Mellem mænd.* Copenhagen: Tiderne Skifter.
—— 1989b: 'Whatever Happened to Robin The Boy Wonder?' *Lambda Nordica* (Sweden), 3–4, 260–79.
——1989c: ' "Homoseksualitet": En præsentation og diskussion af positionerne i den aktuelle videnskabelige strid: "essentialisme" versus "konstruktionisme" '. *Nordisk Sexologi*, 7(2/3), 129–48.
—— 1991a: 'Mandslængsel: Hankøn i moderne samfund'. *Varia* (Denmark) 1, 83–97.
—— 1991b: 'Recht fertigen: Über die Einführung "homosexueller Ehen" in Dänemark'. *Zeitschrift für Sexualforschung*, 4(3), 213–24.

—— 1992a: 'Report from a Rotten State: "Marriage" and "Homosexuality" in "Denmark" '. In: Plummer (ed.) 1992, 134–47.

——1992b: 'Living Together in the (Post)Modern World'. Paper presented at the European Sociology Conference, 26–9 August, University of Vienna.

—— 1993: 'CITYSEX: Representing Lust in Public'. Paper presented at the International Conference on Sexuality and Space, SISWO, University of Amsterdam, 18–19 June. (German: 'CITYSEX: Die öffentliche Darstellung der Begierden'. *Soziale Welt*, 46(1), 1995, 5–27; revised English version forthcoming in *Theory, Culture & Society*.)

—— 1994: 'Når køn bliver iscenesat'. *Sosiologi i dag* (Norway), 24(2), 23–40.

—— 1995: 'Sexuality, Gender and Sociology'. Review essay. *Acta Sociologica*, 38(2), 187–92.

—— 1996: '(Tele)Urban Eroticisms'. *Parallax*, 2, 89–100.

—— (forthcoming (a)): 'A Dung Beetle in Distress: Hans Christian Andersen Meets Karl Maria Kertbeny, Geneva, 1860'. *Journal of Homosexuality*.

—— (forthcoming (b)): *Modern Life Spaces* (working title). London: Routledge.

Beck, U. and Beck-Gernsheim, E. 1990: *The Normal Chaos of Love*, tr. M. Ritter and J. Wiebel. Cambridge: Polity Press, 1995.

Bell, A. and Weinberg, M. 1978: *Homosexualities: A Study of Diversity among Men and Women*. New York: Simon & Schuster, 1979.

Bell, D. 1991: 'Insignificant Others: Lesbian and Gay Geographies'. *Area*, 23(4), 323–9.

—— Binnie, J., Cream, J. and Valentine, G. 1994: 'All Hyped up and No Place to Go'. *Gender, Place and Culture*, 1, 31–47.

Benjamin, W. [1927–40]: *Das Passagen-Werk*, vols I, II. Frankfurt: Suhrkamp, 1982.

—— 1935: 'The Work of Art in the Age of Mechanical Reproduction'. In: Hanhardt, J. (ed.), *Video Culture: A Critical Investigation*, Layton, UT: Peregrine Smith, 1986, 27–52.

—— [1937–40]: *Charles Baudelaire: A Lyric Poet in the Era of High Capitalism*. London: Verso, 1983.

Berger, P. and Luckmann, T. 1966: *The Social Construction of Reality: A Treatise in the Sociology of Knowledge*. Garden City, NY: Doubleday.

Bergler, E. 1956: *Homosexuality: Disease or Way of Life?* New York: Hill & Wang.

Bergman, D. (ed.) 1993: *Camp Grounds: Style and Homosexuality*. Amherst: University of Massachusetts Press.

Berlant, L. and Freeman, E. 1992: 'Queer Nationality'. In: Warner (ed.), 193–229.

Berlin Museum (ed.) 1984: *Eldorado. Homosexuelle Frauen und Männer in Berlin 1850–1950: Geschichte, Alltag und Kultur*. Berlin: Frölich & Kaufmann.

Berman, M. 1982: *All that is Solid Melts into Air: The Experience of Modernity*. New York: Simon & Schuster.

Bersani, L. 1995: *Homos*. Cambridge, Mass.: Harvard UP.

Bérubé, A. 1990: *Coming Out under Fire: The History of Gay Men and Women in World War Two*. New York: Free Press.

—— and Escoffier, J. 1991: 'Queer/nation'. *Out/Look*, 11.

Bieber, I. et al. 1962: *Homosexuality: A Psychoanalytic Study*. New York: Basic.

Binnie, J. 1995: 'Trading Places: Consumption, Sexuality and the Production of Queer Space'. In: Bell, D. and Valentine, G. (eds), *Mapping Desire: Geographies of Sexualities*. London: Routledge, 182–99.

Binswanger, L. 1932: 'Das Raumproblem in der Psychopathologie'. In: Binswanger, *Ausgewählte Vorträge und Aufsätze*, vol. 2. Berne: Franke, 1955, 174–225.

Bjørby, P. 1986: 'The Prison House of Sexuality: Homosexuality in Herman Bang Scholarship'. *Scandinavian Studies*, 58(3), 223–55.

Blachford, G. 1981: 'Male Dominance and the Gay World'. In: Plummer (ed.) 1981, 184–210.

Bleibtreu-Ehrenberg, G. 1978: *Homosexualität: Die Geschichte eines Vorurteils*. Frankfurt: Fischer.

Bley, W. 1931: 'Spionage und anormale Veranlagung'. In: Lettow-Vorbeck, P. (ed.), *Die Weltkriegsspionage*. Munich: Moser, 378–83.

Bleys, R. 1993: 'Homosexual Exile: The Textuality of the Imaginary Paradise, 1800–1980'. *Journal of Homosexuality*, 25(1/2), 165–82.

Blüher, H. 1919: *Die Rolle der Erotik in der männlichen Gesellschaft: Eine Theorie der menschlichen Staatsbildung nach Wesen und Wert*, 2 vols. Jena: Dietrich.

Blumstein, P. and Schwartz, P. 1983: *American Couples: Money, Work, Sex*. New York: William Morrow.

Bochow, M. 1993: 'Einstellungen und Werthaltungen zu homosexuellen Männern in Ost- und Westdeutschland'. In: Lange, C. (ed.), *AIDS: Eine Forschungsbilanz*. Berlin: Sigma, 115–28.

Boisson, J. 1988: *Le triangle rose: La déportation des homosexuels (1933–1945)*. Paris: Laffont.

Bollnow, O. 1941/56: *Das Wesen der Stimmungen*. Frankfurt: Klostermann, 1956.

—— 1963: *Mensch und Raum*. Stuttgart: Kohlhammer.

Bon, M. and d'Arc, A. 1974: *Rapport sur l'homosexualité de l'homme*. Paris: Encyclopaedie universitaire.

Booth, M. 1983: *Camp*. London: Quartet.

Boscana, G. *c*.1822: *Chinigchinich*. Banning, Calif.: Malki Museum Press, 1978.

Boss, M. 1966: *Sinn und Gehalt der sexuellen Perversionen: Ein daseinsanalytischer Beitrag zur Psychopathologie des Phänomens der Liebe*. Berne: Huber.

Boswell, J. 1980: *Christianity, Social Tolerance, and Homosexuality: Gay People in Western Europe from the Beginning of the Christian Era to the Fourteenth Century*. Chicago: University of Chicago Press.
—— 1994: *Same-sex Unions in Premodern Europe*. New York: Villard.
Bourdieu, P. 1977: 'Remarques provisoires sur la perception sociale du corps'. *Actes de la recherche en sciences sociales*, 14, 51–4.
—— 1990: 'La domination masculine'. *Actes de la recherche en sciences sociales*, 84, 2–31.
Bowers, A. 1982: *Hidatsa Social and Ceremonial Organization* (= Bureau of American Ethnology Bulletin, 194). Washington: US Government Printing Office.
Bray, A. 1982: *Homosexuality in Renaissance England*. London: GMP.
Bredbeck, G. 1996: 'Troping the Light Fantastic: Representing Disco Then and Now'. *GLQ*, 3(1), 77–107.
Bristow, J. 1989: 'Homophobia/Misogyny: Sexual Fears, Sexual Definitions'. In: Shepherd, S. and Wallis, M. (eds), *Coming on Strong: Gay Politics and Culture*, London: Unwin Hyman, 54–75.
—— 1995: *Effeminate England: Homoerotic Writing after 1885*. New York: Columbia UP.
Bronski, M. 1984: *Culture Clash: The Making of Gay Sensibility*. Boston: South End.
Brown, R. M. 1975: 'Queen for a Day: A Stranger in Paradise'. In: Jay, K. and Young, A. (eds), *Lavender Culture*. New York: Jove/HBJ, 1979, 69–76.
Browning, F. 1993: *The Culture of Desire: Paradox and Perversity in Gay Lives Today*. New York: Crown.
Bryant, A. and Demian (1994): 'Relationship Characteristics of American Gay and Lesbian Couples: Findings from a National Survey'. *Journal of Gay and Lesbian Social Services*, 1(2), 101–17.
Buffière, F. 1980: *Éros adolescent*. Paris: Les belles lettres.
Buffum, P. 1972: *Homosexuality in Prisons*. Washington: US Department of Justice.
Burston, P. 1995: *What are You Looking at? Queer Sex, Style and Cinema*. London: Cassell.
Butler, J. 1990: *Gender Trouble: Feminism and the Subversion of Identity*. New York: Routledge.
—— 1993: *Bodies That Matter: On the Discursive Limits of 'Sex'*. New York: Routledge.
Bychowsky, G. 1961: 'The Ego and the Object of the Homosexual'. *International Journal of Psycho-Analysis*, 42(3), 255–9.
Califia, P. 1979–94: *Public Sex: The Culture of Radical Sex*. Pittsburgh: Cleis, 1994.
Calinescu, M. 1987: *Five Faces of Modernity: Modernism, Avant-Garde, Decadence, Kitsch, Postmodernism*. Durham, NC: Duke UP.
Callender, C. and Kochems, L. 1983: 'The North American Berdache'. *Current Anthropology*, 24(4), 443–70.

Cantarella, E. 1992: *Bisexuality in the Ancient World*, tr. C. Cuilleanáin. New Haven: Yale UP.
Carbery, G. 1992: 'Some Melbourne Beats: A "Map" of the Subculture in Adelaide Before World War II'. In: Aldrich, R. and Wotherspoon, G. (eds), *Gay Perspectives: Essays in Australian Gay Culture*. Department of Economic History, University of Sydney, 131–46.
Carpenter, E. 1914: *Intermediate Types among Primitive Folk*. New York: Arno, 1975.
Carrigan, T., Connell, B. and Lee, J. 1985: 'Toward a New Sociology of Masculinity'. *Theory and Society*, 14(5), 551–604.
Carroll, L. 1977: 'Humanitarian Reform and Biracial Sexual Assault in a Maximum Security Prison'. *Urban Life*, 5(4), 417–37.
Casper, J. 1863: *Klinische Novellen zur gerichtlichen Medizin: Nach eigenen Erfahrungen*. Berlin: Hirschwald.
Castells, M. 1983: *The City and the Grassroots: A Cross-cultural Theory of Urban Social Movements*. London: Edward Arnold.
Chambers, I. 1986: *Popular Culture: The Metropolitan Experience*. London: Routledge.
Chaney, D. 1990: 'Subtopia in Gateshead: The MetroCentre as a Cultural Form'. *Theory, Culture & Society*, 7(4), 49–68.
Chauncey, G. 1982–3: 'From Sexual Inversion to Homosexuality: Medicine and the Changing Conceptualization of Female Deviance'. *Salmagundi*, 58, 114–46.
—— 1985: 'Christian Brotherhood or Sexual Perversion? Homosexual Identities and the Construction of Sexual Boundaries in the World War One Era'. *Journal of Social History*, 19, 189–211.
—— 1993: 'The Postwar Sex Crime Panic'. In: Graebner, W. (ed.), *True Stories from the American Past*. New York: McGraw-Hill, 160–78.
—— 1994: *Gay New York: Gender, Urban Culture and the Making of the Gay Male World 1890–1940*. New York: Basic.
Chesebro, J. and Klenk, K. 1981: 'Gay Masculinity in the Gay Disco'. In: Chesebro (ed.), *Gayspeak: Gay Male and Lesbian Communication*. New York: Pilgrim, 87–103.
Clum, J. 1992: *Male Homosexuality in Modern Drama*. New York: Columbia UP.
Coggeshall, J. 1988: ' "Ladies" behind Bars: A Liminal Gender as Cultural Mirror'. *Anthropology Today*, 4(4), 6–8.
Cohen, E. 1991: 'Who are "We"? Gay "Identity" as Political (E)motion'. In: Fuss, D. (ed.), *Lesbian Theories, Gay Theories*. New York: Routledge, 71–92.
—— 1993: *Talk on the Wilde Side: Toward a Genealogy of a Discourse on Male Sexualities*. New York: Routledge.
Cohen, T. 1992: 'Men's Families, Men's Friends: A Structural Analysis of Constraints on Men's Social Ties'. In: Nardi (ed.), 115–31.
Coleman, W. 1990: 'Doing Masculinity/Doing Theory'. In: Hearn and Morgan (eds), 186–99.

Copley, A. 1989: *Sexual Moralities in France, 1780–1980: New Ideas on the Family, Divorce and Homosexuality*. London: Routledge.
Core, P. 1984: *Camp: The Lie that Tells the Truth*. London: Plexus.
Cory D. 1951: *The Homosexual in America: A Subjective Approach*. New York: Greenberg.
Corzine, J. and Kirby, R. 1977: 'Cruising the Truckers: Sexual Encounters in a Highway Rest Area'. *Urban Life*, 6(2), 171–92.
Courouve, C. 1981: *Bibliographie des homosexualités 1882–1924*. Paris: Archives Unisexuelles.
—— 1985: *Vocabulaire de l''homosexualité masculine*. Paris: Payot.
Coward, D. 1980: 'Attitudes to Homosexuality in Eighteenth-century France'. *Journal of European Studies*, 10(4), 231–55.
Craft, C. 1994: *Another Kind of Love: Male Homosexual Desire in English Discourse, 1850–1920*. Berkeley: University of California Press.
Craig, S. (ed.) 1992: *Men, Masculinity, and the Media*. Newbury Park: Sage.
Crosset, T. 1990: 'Masculinity, Sexuality, and the Development of Early Modern Sport'. In: Messner and Sabo (eds), 45–54.
Dalsgaard, J. 1984: *Den homoseksuelle sædelighedsskandale i København 1906–07*. Paper, Department of History, Aarhus University.
Dannecker, M. 1978: *Theories of Homosexuality*, tr. D. Fernbach. London: GMP, 1981.
—— 1996: 'Probleme der männlichen homosexuellen Entwicklung'. In: Sigusch, V. (ed.), *Sexuelle Beziehungen und ihre Behandlung*. Stuttgart: Thieme, 77–91.
—— and Reiche, R. 1974: *Der gewöhnliche Homosexuelle: Eine soziologische Untersuchung über männliche Homosexuelle in der Bundesrepublik*. Frankfurt: Fischer.
Davis, A. 1968: 'Sexual Assaults in the Philadelphia Prison System and Sheriff's Vans'. *Trans-Action*, 6(2), 8–17.
Dellamora, R. 1990: *Masculine Desire: The Sexual Politics of Victorian Aestheticism*. Chapel Hill: University of North Carolina Press.
Delph, E. 1978: *The Silent Community: Public Homosexual Encounters*. Beverly Hills: Sage.
D'Emilio, J. 1983a: 'Capitalism and Gay Identity'. In: Snitow, A., Stansell, C. and Thompson, S. (eds): *Powers of Desire: The Politics of Sexuality*. New York: Monthly Review Press, 100–13.
—— 1983b: *Sexual Politics, Sexual Communities: The Making of a Homosexual Minority in the United States 1940–70*. Chicago: University of Chicago Press.
—— 1989: 'The Homosexual Menace: The Politics of Sexuality in Cold War America'. In: D'Emilio, *Making Trouble: Essays on Gay History, Politics, and the University*. New York: Routledge, 1992, 57–73.
Desroches, F. 1990: 'Tearoom Trade: A Research Update'. *Qualitative Sociology*, 13, 39–61.

DeVall, W. 1980: 'Leisure and Lifestyles among Gay Men: An Exploratory Essay'. In: Harry, J. and Man, S. (eds), 44–60.

Devereux, G. 1937: 'Institutionalized Homosexuality of the Mohave Indians'. *Human Biology*, 9(4), 498–527.

Dollimore, J. 1991: *Sexual Dissidence: Augustine to Wilde, Freud to Foucault*. Oxford: Clarendon.

Douglas, J. 1977: 'Existential Sociology'. In: Douglas and Johnson (eds), 3–74.

—— and Johnson, J. (eds) 1977: *Existential Sociology*. Cambridge: Cambridge UP.

Douglas, M. 1966: *Purity and Danger: An Analysis of Concepts of Pollution and Taboo*. London: RKP.

Dover, K. 1978/89: *Greek Homosexuality* (updated and with a new Postscript). Cambridge, Mass.: Harvard UP, 1989.

Dowling, L. 1994: *Hellenism and Homosexuality in Victorian Oxford.* Ithaca: Cornell UP.

Duberman, M. 1993: *Stonewall.* New York: Dutton.

——, Vicinus, M. and Chauncey, G. (eds) 1989: *Hidden from History: Reclaiming the Gay and Lesbian Past*. New York: New American Library.

Duggan, L. 1992: 'Making it Perfectly Queer'. *Socialist Review*, 22(1), 11–31.

Dundes, A. 1978: 'Into the Endzone for a Touchdown: A Psychoanalytic Consideration of American Football'. *Western Folklore*, XXXVII, 75–88.

Dunning, E. 1986: 'Sport as a Male Preserve: Notes on the Social Sources of Masculine Identity and its Transformations'. In: Elias, N. and Dunning, E., *Quest for Excitement: Sport and Leisure in the Civilizing Process*. Oxford: Blackwell, 267–83.

Duyvendak, J. 1994: *Gay Subculture between Movement and Market*. Paper for the conference 'Organizing Sexuality'. SISWO, Amsterdam.

Duyves, M. 1987: 'The Minitel: The Glittering Future of a New Invention'. *Journal of Homosexuality*, 25(1/2), 1993, 193–204.

—— 1995: 'Framing Preferences, Framing Differences: Inventing Amsterdam as a Gay Capital'. In: Parker, R. and Gagnon, J. (eds), *Conceiving Sexuality: Approaches to Sex Research in a Postmodern World.* London: Routledge, 51–68.

Dyer, K. 1982: *Challenging the Men: The Social Biology of Female Sporting Achievement*. St Lucia/New York: University of Queensland Press.

Dyer, R. 1977: 'It's Being so Camp as Keeps us Going'. *Body Politic*, 36, 11–13.

—— 1982: 'Don't Look Now: The Male Pin-up'. *Screen*, 23(3–4), 61–73.

—— 1985: 'A Passage to India". In: Dyer 1990: 137–49.

—— 1990: *Now you See it: Studies on Lesbian and Gay Film*. London: Routledge.

—— 1993: *The Matter of Images: Essays on Representations*. London: Routledge.
—— (ed.) 1977/84: *Gays and Film*. New York: Zoetrope, 1984.
Eberle, T. 1984: *Sinnkonstitution in Alltag und Wissenschaft: Der Beitrag der Phänomenologie an die Methodologie der Sozialwissenschaften*. Berne: Paul Haupt.
Edelman, L. 1993: 'Tearooms and Sympathy, or The Epistemology of the Water Closet'. In: Abelove et al. (eds), 553–74.
Edwards, T. 1994: *Erotics & Politics: Gay Male Sexuality, Masculinity and Feminism*. London: Routledge.
Egger, B. 1993: 'Iwan Bloch'. In: Lautmann (ed.), 86–90.
Ester, P. et al. (eds) 1994: *The Individualizing Society: Value Change in Europe and North America*. Tilburg: Tilburg UP.
Evans, A. 1978: *Witchcraft and the Gay Counterculture: A Radical View of Western Civilization and Some of the People it has Tried to Destroy*. Boston: Fag Rag.
Evans, D, 1993: *Sexual Citizenship: The Material Construction of Sexualities*. London: Routledge.
Faderman, L. 1981: *Surpassing the Love of Men: Romantic Friendship and Love between Women from the Renaissance to the Present*. New York: William Morrow.
Featherstone, M. 1991: *Consumer Culture and Postmodernism*. London: Sage.
Féray, J.-C. and Herzer, M. 1990: 'Homosexual Studies and Politics in the 19th Century: Karl Maria Kertbeny'. *Journal of Homosexuality*, 19(1), 23–48.
Ferenczi, S. 1911: 'On the Part Played by Homosexuality in the Pathogenesis of Paranoia'. In: Ferenczi 1916, 131–56.
—— 1914: 'The Nosology of Male Homosexuality (Homo-Erotism)'. In: Ferenczi 1916, 250–68.
—— 1916: *Contributions to Psycho-analysis*, tr. E. Jones. London: Stanley Phillips.
Fernbach, D. 1981: *The Spiral Path: A Gay Contribution to Human Survival*. London: GMP.
FHAR (Front Homosexuel d'Action Révolutionnaire) 1971: *Rapport contre la normalité*. Paris: Champ libre.
Finch, M. 1987: 'Mauritz Stiller's *The Wings* and Early Scandinavian Gay Cinema'. *The European Gay Review*, 2, 26–31.
Fine, R. 1987: 'Psychoanalytic Theory'. In: Diamant, L. (ed.), *Male and Female Homosexuality: Psychological Approaches*. New York: Hemisphere, 81–96.
Fischer, C. 1982: *To Dwell among Friends: Personal Networks in Town and City*. Chicago: University of Chicago Press.
Fiske, J. 1987: *Television Culture*. London: Routledge, 1989.
Fogedgaard, H. 1946: *Tilværelsens Mysterium: Livets og Dødens Gaader*

i aandsvidenskabelig Belysning (3rd revised edn). Copenhagen: Okkultismens Forlag.
Fone, B. 1983: 'This Other Eden: Arcadia and the Homosexual Imagination'. *Journal of Homosexuality*, 8(3–4), 13–34.
—— 1995: *A Road to Stonewall: Male Homosexuality and Homophobia in English and American Literature, 1750–1969*. New York: Twayne.
Forster, E. M. [1914]/1971: *Maurice*. Harmondsworth: Penguin, 1972.
—— [1922–58]/1972: *The Life To Come and Other Stories*. London: Edward Arnold.
—— 1924: *A Passage To India*. London: Edward Arnold, 1964.
Foucault, M., tr. R. Howard. 1961: *Madness and Civilization: A History of Insanity in the Age of Reason*. London: Tavistock, 1971.
—— 1963/72: *The Birth of the Clinic: An Archeology of Medical Perception*, tr. A. Smith. New York: Vintage, 1994.
—— 1971: 'The Discourse on Language', tr. R. Swyer. In: Foucault, *The Archeology of Knowledge*. New York: Pantheon, 1972, 215–37.
—— 1975: *Discipline and Punish: The Birth of the Prison*, tr. A. Sheridan. Harmondsworth: Penguin, 1979.
—— 1976: *The History of Sexuality*, vol. 1: *An Introduction*, tr. R. Hurley. New York: Vintage, 1978.
—— 1977: 'Non au sexe roi'. *Le nouvel observateur*, 644, 12 March.
—— 1981: 'De l'amitié comme mode de vie'. *Gai Pied*, 25.
—— 1982: 'Michel Foucault, an Interview: Sex, Power and the Politics of Identity'. *Advocate*, 400.
—— 1982–3: 'Sexual Choice, Sexual Act: An Interview with Michel Foucault'. *Salmagundi*, 58–9, 10–24.
—— 1983: 'What is Enlightenment?' In: Rabinow, P. (ed.) 1984: *The Foucault Reader*. New York: Pantheon, 32–50.
—— 1984a: *The History of Sexuality*, vol. 2: *The Use of Pleasure*, tr. R. Hurley. London: Penguin, 1992.
—— 1984b: *The History of Sexuality*, vol. 3: *The Care of the Self*, tr. R. Hurley. London: Penguin, 1990.
Fouchard, J. 1994: *Seksuel adfærd med risiko for HIV-smitte – blandt mænd i Danmark, der har sex med andre mænd*. Copenhagen: Faculty of Health Sciences.
Fout, J. 1992: 'Sexual Politics in Wilhelmine Germany: The Male Gender Crisis, Moral Purity, and Homophobia'. *Journal of the History of Sexuality*, 2(3), 388–421.
Fraenkel, E. 1908: *De Homosexuelle*. Copenhagen: Frimodt.
Freimark, H. 1905: *Der Sinn des Uranismus*. Leipzig: Uhlig.
Freud, S. 1905: 'Three Essays on the Theory of Sexuality'. *SE VII*, 130–243. (*SE = The Standard Edition of the Complete Psychological Works of Sigmund Freud*, 24 vols. London: Hogarth, 1953–74.)
—— 1908: 'On the Sexual Theories of Children'. *SE IX*, 209–26.
—— 1909: 'Analysis of a Phobia in a Five-year-old Boy'. *SE X*, 5–147.

—— 1910: 'Leonardo da Vinci and a Memory of his Childhood'. *SE XI*, 63–137.
—— 1911: 'Psycho-analytic Notes on an Autobiographical Account of a Case of Paranoia (Dementia Paranoides)'. *SE XII*, 9–79.
—— 1912: 'Types of Onset of Neurosis'. *SE XII*, 231–8.
—— 1912–13: 'Totem and Taboo'. *SE XIII*, 1–161.
—— 1913: 'The Disposition to Obsessional Neurosis'. *SE XII*, 317–26.
—— 1914: 'On Narcissism: An Introduction'. *SE XIV*, 73–102.
—— 1915a: 'Repression'. *SE XIV*, 146–58.
—— 1915b: 'The Unconscious'. *SE XIV*, 166–204.
—— 1916–17: 'Introductory Lectures on Psycho-analysis'. *SE XV* and *XVI*.
—— 1918: 'From the History of an Infantile Neurosis'. *SE XVII*, 7–121.
—— 1920: 'The Psychogenesis of a Case of Homosexuality in a Woman'. *SE XVIII*, 147–72.
—— 1921: 'Group Psychology and the Analysis of the Ego'. *SE XVIII*, 69–143.
—— 1922: 'Some Neurotic Mechanisms in Jealousy, Paranoia and Homosexuality'. *SE XVIII*, 223–32.
—— 1923a: ' "Psycho-Analysis" and "The Libido Theory" '. *SE XVIII*, 235–59.
—— 1923b: 'The Ego and the Id'. *SE XIX*, 12–59.
—— 1923c: 'A Seventeenth-century Demonological Neurosis'. *SE XIX*, 72–105.
—— 1923d: 'The Infantile Genital Organization: An Interpolation into the Theory of Sexuality'. *SE XIX*, 141–5.
—— 1924: 'The Dissolution of the Oedipus Complex', *SE XIX*, 173–82.
—— 1925: 'Some Psychical Consequences of the Anatomical Distinction between the Sexes'. *SE XIX*, 248–58.
—— 1926: 'Inhibitions, Symptoms and Anxiety'. *SE XX*, 87–172.
—— 1930: 'Civilization and its Discontents'. *SE XXI*, 64–145.
—— 1933: 'New Introductory Lectures on Psycho-analysis'. *SE XXII*.
—— 1937: 'Analysis Terminable and Interminable'. *SE XXIII*, 216–52.
—— 1939: 'Moses an Egyptian'. *SE XXIII*, 7–137.
—— 1940: 'An Outline of Psycho-analysis'. *SE XXIII*, 144–207.
Friedenberg, E. Z. 1959: *The Vanishing Adolescent*. Boston: Beacon, 1959.
Friedländer, B. 1904: *Renaissance des Eros Uranaios: Die physiologische Freundschaft, ein normaler Grundtrieb des Menschen und eine Frage der männlichen Gesellungsfreiheit*. New York: Arno, 1975.
—— 1909: *Die Liebe Platons im Lichte der modernen Biologie*. Treptow bei Berlin: Zack.
Friedman, R. 1988: *Male Homosexuality: A Contemporary Psychoanalytic Perspective*. New Haven: Yale UP.
Frisby, D. 1985: *Fragments of Modernity: Theories of Modernity in the Work of Simmel, Kracauer and Benjamin*. Cambridge: Polity Press.

Gaasholt, Ø. and Togeby, L. 1995: *I syv sind: Danskernes holdninger til flygtninge og indvandrere*. Aarhus: Politica.

Gagnon, J. 1990: 'Gender Preference in Erotic Relations: The Kinsey Scale and Sexual Scripts'. In: McWhirter et al. (eds), 177–207.

—— and Simon, W. 1968: 'The Social Meaning of Prison Homosexuality'. *Federal Probation*, 32(1), 23–9.

—— 1973: *Sexual Conduct: The Sources of Human Sexuality*. Chicago: Aldine.

Garber, E. 1989: 'A Spectacle in Colour: The Lesbian and Gay Subculture of Jazz Age Harlem'. In: Duberman et al. (eds), 318–31.

Garde, N. 1964: *Jonathan to Gide: The Homosexual in History*. New York: Vantage.

Garner, B. and Smith, R. 1977: 'Are there Really any Gay Male Athletes? An Empirical Survey'. *Journal of Sex Research*, 13(1), 22–34.

Gay Revolution Party Manifesto (*c*.1971). In: Jay and Young (eds) 1972: 342–5.

Geill, C. 1893: 'Læren om Psychopathia sexualis og dens retsmedicinske betydning'. *Ugeskrift for Læger*, 4, 403–503.

Gergen, K. 1991: *The Saturated Self: Dilemmas of Contemporary Self*. New York: Basic.

Giddens, A. 1991: *Modernity and Self-identity: Self and Society in the Late Modern Age*. Cambridge: Polity Press.

—— 1992: *The Transformation of Intimacy: Sexuality, Love and Eroticism in Modern Societies*. Cambridge: Polity Press.

Gide, A. 1936: *Retour de l'URSS*. Paris: Gallimard.

Giese, H. 1958: *Der homosexuelle Mann in der Welt*. Stuttgart: Enke.

Gilmore, D. 1990: *Manhood in the Making: Cultural Concepts of Masculinity*. New Haven: Yale UP.

Girard, J. 1981: *Le mouvement homosexual en France 1945–1980*. Paris: Syros.

Goffman, E. 1961: *Asylums: Essays on the Social Situation of Mental Patients and Other Inmates*. Garden City, NY: Doubleday.

—— 1963: *Behavior in Public Places: Notes on the Social Organization of Gatherings*. New York: Free Press.

—— 1971: *Relations in Public: Microstudies of the Public Order*. New York: Basic.

Goldberg, J. 1992: *Sodometries: Renaissance Texts, Modern Sexualities*. Stanford, CA: Stanford UP.

Graugaard, C. 1993: *Professor Sands Høns: Om lægevidenskabelig seksualitets-forskning i mellemkrigstidens Danmark*. Paper, Department of Medicine, University of Copenhagen.

Greenberg, D. 1988: *The Construction of Homosexuality*. Chicago: University of Chicago Press.

Greenspan, H. and Campbell, J. 1945: 'The Homosexual Personality Type'. *American Journal of Psychiatry*, 101(5), 682–9.

Greif, M. 1982. *The Gay Book of Days*. London: W. H. Allen, 1985.

Grey, A. 1992. *Quest for Justice: Towards Homosexual Emancipation*. London: Sinclair-Stevenson.

Gross, L. 1991: 'Out of the Mainstream: Sexual Minorities and the Mass Media'. *Journal of Homosexuality*, 21(1/2), 19–47.

Gundelach, P. and Riis, O. 1992: *Danskernes værdier*. Copenhagen: Forlaget Sociologi.

Gutiérrez, R. 1989: 'Must we Deracinate Indians to Find Gay Roots?' *Out/Look*, 4, 61–7.

Habermas, J. 1962: *The Structural Transformation of the Public Sphere: An Inquiry into a Category of Bourgeois Society*, tr. T. Burger and F. Lawrence. Cambridge, Mass.: MIT, 1991.

—— 1968: *Knowledge and Human Interests*, tr. J. Shapiro. Cambridge: Polity Press, 1989.

—— 1981: *The Theory of Communicative Action*, tr. T. McCarthy. Cambridge: Polity Press, 1992.

Hacker, H. 1987: *Frauen und Freundinnen: Studien zur 'weiblichen Homosexualität' am Beispiel Österreich 1870–1938*. Weinheim/Basle: Beltz.

Hahn, P. 1979: *Nos ancêtres les pervers: La vie des homosexuels sous le Second Empire*. Paris: Olivier Orban.

Håkansson, P. 1984: 'Det okända och förbjudna: Undersökningsrapport'. In: *Homosexuella och samhället. Betänkande av utredningen om homosexuelles situation i samhället*. Stockholm: SOU, 331–543.

Halifax, N. 1988: *Out Proud and Fighting: Gay Liberation and the Struggle for Socialism*. London: Socialist Workers Party.

Halle, R. 1995: 'Between Marxism and Psychoanalysis: Antifascism and Antihomosexuality in the Frankfurt School'. *Journal of Homosexuality*, 29(4), 295–317.

Halperin, D. 1990: *One Hundred Years of Homosexuality and Other Essays on Greek Love*. New York/London: Routledge.

—— 1995: *Saint Foucault: Towards a Hagiography*. New York/Oxford: Oxford UP.

Hamer, D. 1993: 'A Linkage between DNS Markers on the X Chromosome and Male Sexual Orientation'. *Science*, 261, 321–7.

Hannerz, U. 1980: *Exploring the City: Inquiries Toward an Urban Anthropology*. New York: Columbia UP.

Hannon, G. 1975: 'Throat-ramming'. In: Jackson, E. and Persky, S. (eds), *Flaunting It! A Decade of Gay Journalism from The Body Politic*. Toronto: Pink Triangle Press, 1982, 8–12.

Hansen, B. 1989: 'American Physicians' Earliest Writings about Homosexuals, 1880–1900'. *The Millbank Quarterly*, 67, Suppl. 1, 92–108.

Harper, P. 1994: 'Private Affairs: Race, Sex, Property, and Persons'. *GLQ*, 1(2), 111–33.

Harry, J. 1984: *Gay Couples*. New York: Praeger.

—— and Man, S. (eds) 1980: *Homosexuality in International Perspective*. New Delhi: Vikas.

Haug, W. 1971: *Critique of Commodity Aesthetics*. Cambridge: Polity Press, 1986.

Havelin, A. 1968: 'Almenhetens holdninger til homofile og homoseksualitet'. *Tidsskrift for samfunnsforskning*, 9(1), 42–74.

Hearn, J. and Morgan, D. (eds) 1990: *Men, Masculinities and Social Theory*. London: Unwin Hyman.

Hebdige, D. 1979: *Subculture: The Meaning of Style*. London: Routledge.

—— 1989: 'After the Masses'. In: Hall, S. and Jacques, M. (eds): *New Times: The Changing Face of Politics in the 1990s*. London: Lawrence & Wishart, 76–93.

Heede, D. 1985: 'Årets bøssegyser'. *Pan*, 32(5), 14.

Hegener, W. 1993: 'Aufstieg und Fall schwuler Identität: Ansätze zur Dekonstruktion der Kategorie Sexualität'. *Zeitschrift für Sexualforschung*, 6(2), 132–50.

Heger, H. 1972: *The Men with the Pink Triangle*, tr. D. Fernbach. Boston: Alyson, 1980.

Heidegger, M. 1927: *Being and Time*, tr. J. Macquarrie and E. Robinson. Oxford: Blackwell, 1962.

Hekma, G. 1987: *Homoseksualiteit, een medische reputatie: De uitdokte ring van de homoseksueel in negentiende-eeuws Nederland*. Amsterdam: SUA.

—— 1992: *The Amsterdam Bar Culture and Changing Gay/Lesbian Identities*. Paper for the conference on 'Sexual Cultures'. SISWO, University of Amsterdam.

—— 1994a: *The Future of the Queer Movement*. Paper for the conference on 'Organizing Sexuality'. SISWO, University of Amsterdam.

—— 1994b: 'The Homosexual, the Queen and Models of Gay History'. *Perversions*, 3, 119–38.

Henriksson, B. 1989: 'Gossarna i reklamen'. *Lambda Nordica*, 3–4, 194–244.

—— 1995: 'Homosexual Men's Families: The Relationship to and the Creation of Family among Homo- and Bisexual Men during this Century'. In: Henriksson, *Risk Factor Love: Homosexuality, Sexual Interaction and HIV-Prevention*. Gothenburg: Göteborgs Universitet, 201–28.

Henslin, J. 1971: 'Sex and Cabbies'. In: Henslin (ed.), 193–223.

—— (ed.) 1971: *Studies in the Sociology of Sex*. New York: Appleton-Century-Crofts.

Herbart, P. 1937: *En U.R.S.S. 1936*. Paris: Gallimard.

Herdt, G. 1981: *Guardians of the Flutes: Idioms of Masculinity*. New York: McGraw-Hill.

—— 1984: 'Ritualized Homosexual Behavior in the Male Cults of Melanesia, 1862–1983. An Introduction'. In: Herdt (ed.) 1984, 1–81, 363–89.

—— 1990: 'Developmental Discontinuities and Sexual Orientation across Cultures'. In: McWhirter et al. (eds), 208–36.

—— 1992: Preface. In: Herdt (ed.) 1984, ix–x.
—— (ed.) 1984: *Ritualized Homosexuality in Melanesia*. Berkeley: University of California Press.
—— (ed.) 1992: *Gay Culture in America: Essays from the Field*. Boston: Beacon.
—— and Boxer, A. 1992: 'Introduction: Culture, History, and Life Course of Gay Men'. In: Herdt (ed.), 1–28.
Herek, G. 1987: 'On Heterosexual Masculinity: Some Psychical Consequences of the Social Construction of Gender and Sexuality'. In: Kimmel, M. (ed.), *Changing Men: New Directions in Research on Men and Masculinity*. Beverly Hills: Sage, 68–82.
Hergé 1953: *The Adventures of Tintin: Destination Moon*. London: Methuen, 1974.
—— 1954: *The Adventures of Tintin: Explorers on the Moon*. London: Methuen, 1992.
—— 1963: *The Adventures of Tintin: The Castafiore Emerald*. London: Methuen, 1963.
Hertoft, P. 1986: 'Om falske homoseksualitetsteoriers fatale konsekvenser'. *Nordisk Sexologi*, 4(2), 50–62.
Herzer, M. 1982: *Bibliographie zur Homosexualität: Verzeichnis des deutschsprachigen nichtbelletristischen Schrifttums zur weiblichen und männlichen Homosexualität aus den Jahren 1466 bis 1975 in chronologischer Reihenfolge zusammengestellt*. Berlin: Rosa Winkel.
—— 1985: 'Kertbeny and the Nameless Love'. *Journal of Homosexuality*, 12(1), 1–26.
—— 1992. 'Zastrow – Ulrichs – Kertbeny: Erfundene Identitäten im 19. Jahrhundert'. In: Lautmann, R. and Taeger, A., *Männerliebe im alten Deutschland: Sozialgeschichtliche Abhandlungen*. Berlin: Rosa Winkel, 61–80.
Hill, W. 1935: 'The Status of the Hermaphrodite in Navaho Culture'. *American Anthropologist*, 37, 272–9.
Hirschfeld, M. 1905: *Berlins drittes Geschlecht*. Grossstadtdokumente, 3. Berlin.
—— 1910: *Die Transvestiten: Eine Untersuchung über den erotischen Verkleidungstrieb*. Berlin: Pulvermacher.
—— 1914: *Die Homosexualität des Mannes und des Weibes*. New York: Arno, 1980.
Hoch, P. 1979: *White Hero, Black Beast: Racism, Sexism, and the the Mask of Masculinity*. London: Pluto.
Hocquenghem, G. 1972: *Homosexual Desire*, tr. D. Dangoor. London: Allison & Busby, 1978. French original: *Le désir homosexuel*. Paris: Éditions Universitaires.
Hodges, A. 1983: *Alan Turing: The Enigma of Intelligence*. London: Unwin.
—— and Hutter, D. 1974: *With Downcast Gays: Aspects of Homosexual Self-oppression*. London: Pomegranate.

Hoffman, M. 1968: *The Gay World: Male Homosexuality and the Creation of Evil*. New York: Basic.
Hoffman, R. 1991: Book review. *Journal of Homosexuality*, 21(3), 87–101.
Hohman, J. 1987: *Geschichte der Sexualwissenschaft in Deutschland 1886–1933*. Berlin: Foerster.
'Homophilos' 1949: 'Hvorfor er vi sådan'. *Vennen*, 1(2–5).
Homosexuelle Aktion Westberlin 1973: *Zur Frage, warum Schwule unterdrückt werden*. West Berlin, stencilled paper.
Hooker, E. 1961: 'The Homosexual Community'. In: Coopersmith, E. (ed.), *Personality Research. Proceedings of the XIV International Congress of Applied Psychology*. Copenhagen: Munksgaard, 1962, 40–59.
—— 1965: 'Male Homosexuals and their "Worlds" '. In: Marmor, J. (ed.), *Sexual Inversion: The Multiple Roots of Homosexuality*. New York: Basic, 83–107.
Houmark, C. [1926]/1950: *Naar jeg er død. Et selvportræt*. Copenhagen: Branner & Korch.
Humphries, L. 1970: *Tearoom Trade: Impersonal Sex in Public Places*. Chicago: Aldine.
Hutter, J. 1992: *Die gesellschaftliche Kontrolle des homosexuellen Begehrens: Medizinische Definitionen und juristische Sanktionen im 19. Jahrhundert*. Frankfurt: Campus.
Hyde, H. M. 1976: *Oscar Wilde: A Biography*. London: Methuen.
Ibrahim, A. 1974: 'Deviant Sexual Behavior in Men's Prisons'. *Crime and Delinquency*, 20(1), 38–44.
Irvine, J. 1995: 'Reinventing Perversion: Sex Addiction and Cultural Anxieties'. *Journal of the History of Sexuality*, 5(3), 429–50.
Irwin, J. 1977: *Scenes*. Beverly Hills: Sage.
Isay, R. 1989: *Being Homosexual: Gay Men and Their Development*. New York: Farrar, Straus & Giroux.
Israelstam, S. and Lambert S. 1983: 'Homosexuality as a Cause of Alcoholism: A Historical Review'. *The International Journal of the Addictions*, 18(8), 1085–1107.
Jacobsen, E. 1964: *Menneskets psykiske sygdomme*. Copenhagen: Berlingske.
Jacobsen, H. 1966: *Den tragiske Herman Bang*. Copenhagen: Hagerup.
Jameson, F. 1984: 'Postmodernism or the Cultural Logic of Late Capitalism'. *New Left Review*, 146, 53–99.
Janssen, V. (ed.) 1984: *Der Weg zur Freundschaft und Toleranz: Männliche Homosexualität in den 50er Jahren*. Berlin: Rosa Winkel.
Jay, K. and Young, A. (eds) 1972: *Out of the Closets: Voices of Gay Liberation*. New York: Jove/HBJ, 1977.
Jay, M. 1978: 'Adorno and Kracauer: Notes on a Troubled Friendship'. *Salmagundi*, 40, 42–66.
Jellonnek, B. 1990: *Homosexuelle unter dem Hakenkreuz: Die Verfolgung von Homosexuellen im Dritten Reich*. Paderborn: Schöningh.
Jensen, J. V. 1906: 'Samfundet og Sædelighedsforbryderen'. *Politiken*, 30 November.

Johnson, E. 1971: 'The Homosexual in Prison'. *Social Theory and Practice*, 1(4), 83–95.
Jones, J. 1990: *'We of the Third Sex': Literary Representations of Homosexuality in Wilhelmine Germany*. New York: Lang.
Julien, D. 1993: *Réseau social et qualité relationnelle du couple homosexuel: Analyse de leurs effets sur l'incidence de conduites sexuelles à risque*. Montreal: University of Quebec at Montreal.
Jullian, P. 1968: *Oscar Wilde*, tr. V. Wyndham. London: Constable, 1969.
Katz, J. 1976: *Gay American History: Lesbians and Gay Men in the U.S.A.* New York: Crowell.
—— 1983: *Gay/Lesbian Almanac: A New Documentary*. New York: Harper.
—— 1990: 'The Invention of Heterosexuality'. *Socialist Review*, 20, 7–34.
—— 1995: *The Invention of Heterosexuality*. New York: Dutton.
Keilson-Lauritz, M. 1987: *Von der Liebe die Freundschaft heisst: Zur Homoerotik im Werke Stefan Georges*. Berlin: Rosa Winkel.
—— 1991: 'Maske und Signal: Textstrategien der Homoerotik'. In: Popp, H. and Kalveram, M. (eds): *Homosexualitäten – literarisch*. Essen: Die blaue Eule, 63–74.
Kennedy, H. 1988: *Ulrichs: The Life and Works of Karl Heinrich Ulrichs, Pioneer of the Modern Gay Movement*. Boston: Alyson.
Kernberg, O. 1975: *Borderline Conditions and Pathological Narcissism*. New York: Aronson.
Kertbeny, K. 1868: 'Brief an Ulrichs 6.5.1868'. In: Herzer, M. 1987: 'Ein Brief von Kertbeny an Ulrichs in Würzburg'. *Capri: Zeitschrift für schwule Geschichte*, 1, 31–5.
Kimmel, M. 1987: 'The Contemporary "Crisis" of Masculinity in Historical Perspective'. In: Brod, H. (ed.), *The Making of Masculinities: The New Men's Studies*. Boston: Allen & Unwin, 121–53.
—— 1990a: 'After Fifteen Years: The Impact of the Sociology of Masculinity on the Masculinity of Sociology'. In: Hearn and Morgan (eds), 93–109.
—— 1990b: 'Baseball and the Reconstitution of American Masculinity, 1880–1920'. In: Messner and Sabo (eds), 55–66.
Kinsey, A., Pomeroy, W. and Martin, C. 1948: *Sexual Behavior in the Human Male*. Philadelphia: Saunders.
Kinsman, G. 1987: *The Regulation of Desire: Sexuality in Canada*. Montreal: Black Rose.
—— 1991: ' "Homosexuality" Historically Reconsidered Challenges Heterosexual Hegemony'. *Journal of Historical Sociology*, 4(2), 91–111.
Kirkham, G. 1971: 'Homosexuality in Prison'. In: Henslin (ed.), 325–49.
Kistrup, J. 1985: 'Hvem tør svare? Spørgsmålet om homoseksualiteten i kunsten – og de private motiver til at stille det'. *Berlingske Tidende*, 21 July.
Klein, A. 1989: 'Managing Deviance: Hustling, Homophobia, and the Bodybuilding Subculture'. *Deviant Behavior*, 10, 11–27.

Knopp, L. 1992: 'Sexuality and the Spatial Dynamics of Capitalism'. *Environment and Planning D: Society and Space*, 10, 651–69.

Koestenbaum, W. 1989: *Double Talk: The Erotics of Male Literary Collaboration*. New York: Routledge.

Kokula, I. 1981: Introduction. In: Kokula (ed.), *Weibliche Homosexualität um 1900 in zeitgenössischen Dokumenten*. Munich: Frauenoffensive, 9–79.

Kolansky, H. and Moore, W. 1971: 'Effects of Marihuana on Adolescents and Young Adults'. *JAMA*, 216(3), 486–92.

Kon, I. 1979: *Freundschaft: Geschichte und Sozialpsychologie der Freundschaft als soziale Institution und individuelle Beziehung*. Hamburg: Rowohlt.

Kopay, D. and Young, P. 1977: *The David Kopay Story: An Extraordinary Self-revelation*. New York: Bantam.

Kracauer, S. [1925–33]: *Strassen in Berlin und anderswo*. Frankfurt: Suhrkamp, 1964.

—— 1926: 'Stehbars im Süden'. In: Kracauer, [1925–33], 66–8.

—— 1930: 'Über Arbeitsnachweise: Konstruktion eines Raumes'. In: Kracauer, [1925–33], 69–78.

—— 1937: *Offenbach and the Paris of his Time*. London: Constable.

Krafft-Ebing, R. 1886/1907: *Psychopathia sexualis mit besonderer Berücksichtigung der konträren Sexualempfindung: Eine medizinisch-gerichtliche Studie für Ärzte und Juristen*, 13th edn. Stuttgart: Enke, 1907.

Krolle, S. 1986: *'Bündische Umtriebe'. Die Geschichte des Nerother Wandersvogels vor und unter dem NS-Staat*. Münster: Lit.

Krouwel, A. 1994: *Towards a General Explanatory Model of Social Movement Success*. Paper for the conference on 'Organizing Sexuality'. SISWO, Amsterdam.

Kulick, D. 1985: 'Homosexual Behavior, Culture and Gender in Papua New Guinea'. *Ethos*, 50(2), 15–39.

Kupffer, E. 1900: *Lieblingsminne und Freundesliebe in der Weltliteratur: Eine Sammlung mit einer ethisch-politischen Einleitung*. Berlin: Brand.

Kurdek, L. and Schmitt, J. 1986: 'Relationship Quality of Gay Men in Closed or Open Relationships'. *Journal of Homosexuality*, 12(2), 85–99.

Lane, E. 1836: *An Account of the Manners and Customs of the Modern Egyptians*. London: Knight.

Laqueur, T. 1990: *Making Sex: Body and Gender from the Greeks to Freud*. Cambridge, Mass.: Harvard UP.

Lash, S. and Urry, J. 1994: *Economies of Signs and Space*. London: Sage.

Laumann, E., Gagnon, J., Michael, R. and Michaels, S. 1994: *The Social Organization of Sexuality: Sexual Practices in the United States*. Chicago: University of Chicago Press.

Lauretis, T. 1991: 'Queer Theory: Lesbian and Gay Sexualities. An Introduction'. *Differences*, 3(2), iii–xviii.

Lauritsen, J. and Thorstad, D. 1974: *The Early Homosexual Rights Movement (1864–1935)*. New York: Times Change.

Lautmann, R. 1977: *Seminar: Gesellschaft und Homosexualität*. Frankfurt: Suhrkamp.

—— 1990: 'Categorization in Concentration Camps as a Collective Fate: A Comparison of Homosexuals, Jehovah's Witnesses and Political Prisoners'. *Journal of Homosexuality*, 19(1), 67–88.

—— (ed.) 1993: *Homosexualität: Handbuch der Theorie- und Forschungsgeschichte*. Frankfurt: Campus.

—— Grikschat, W. and Schmidt, E. 1977: 'Der Rosa Winkel in den Konzentrationslagern'. In: Lautmann 1977, 126–37.

Lee, J. 1978: *Getting Sex: A New Approach: More Fun, Less Guilt*. Ontario: Musson.

Lemle, L. and Mishkind, M. 1989: 'Alcohol and Masculinity'. *Journal of Substance Abuse Treatment*, 6, 213–22.

Leslie, C. 1977: *Wilhelm von Gloeden, Photographer: A Brief Introduction to his Life and Work*. New York: Photographic Publishers.

LeVay S. 1993: *The Sexual Brain*. Cambridge, Mass.: MIT.

Levine, M. 1979: 'Gay Ghetto'. In: Levine (ed.), 182–204.

—— 1992: 'The Life and Death of Gay Clones'. In: Herdt (ed.), 68–86.

—— (ed.) 1979: *Gay Men: The Sociology of Male Homosexuality*. New York: Harper & Row.

—— and Troiden, R. 1988: 'The Myth of Sexual Compulsivity'. *Journal of Sex Research*, 25(3), 347–63.

Lewes, K. 1988: *The Psychoanalytic Theory of Male Homosexuality*. New York: Simon & Schuster.

Leznoff, M. and Westley, W. 1956: 'The Homosexual Community'. In Gagnon, J. and Simon, W. (eds), *Sexual Deviance*. New York: Harper & Row, 1967, 184–96.

Licata, S. 1978: *Gay Power: A History of the American Gay Movement 1908–1974*. Los Angeles: University of Southern California Press.

Lieshout, M. 1993: 'Lucien von Römer'. In: Lautmann (ed.), 141–6.

Limpricht, C. 1991: 'Homosexuelle Bilderwelt: Die dreissiger und vierziger Jahre'. In: Limpricht (ed.), *'Verführte' Männer: Das Leben der Kölner Homosexuellen im Dritten Reich*. Cologne: Volksblatt, 31–45.

Lindkvist, K. and Moritz, K. 1975: 'Förtryck och homosexuell försvarskamp under 1900-tallet'. *Zenit*, 43, 15–33.

Lockwood, D. 1980: *Prison Sexual Violence*. New York: Elsevier.

Lofland, L. 1973: *A World of Strangers: Order and Action in Urban Public Space*. New York: Basic.

—— 1983: 'Understanding Urban Life: The Chicago Legacy'. *Urban Life*, 11(4), 491–511.

Löfström, J. 1994: *The Social Construction of Homosexuality in Finnish Society, from the Late Nineteenth Century to 1950s*. Pd.D. dissertation, Department of Sociology, University of Essex.

Lonitz, H. (ed.) 1994: *Theodor Adorno, Walter Benjamin: Briefwechsel 1928–1940*. Frankfurt: Suhrkamp.

Lützen, K. 1986: *Hvad hjertet begærer: Kvinders kærlighed til kvinder 1825–1985*. Copenhagen: Tiderne Skifter.

—— 1988: *At prøve lykken: 25 lesbiske livshistorier*. Copenhagen: Tiderne Skifter.

Lynch, M. 1985: ' "Here is Adhesiveness": From Friendship to Homosexuality'. *Victorian Studies*, 29, 67–96.

Maffesoli, M. 1988: *The Time of the Tribes: The Decline of Individualism in Mass Society*. London: Sage, 1996.

—— 1993: 'Identification or the Pluralisation of the Person'. *Journal of Homosexuality*, 25(1/2), 31–40.

Mangan, J. and Walwin, J. (eds) 1987: *Manliness and Morality: Middle-class Masculinity in Britain and America 1800–1940*. Manchester: Manchester UP.

Marcuse, H. 1955: *Eros and Civilisation*. London: Sphere, 1969.

Marmor, J. (ed.) 1980: *Homosexual Behavior: A Modern Reappraisal*. New York: Basic.

Marshall, J. 1981: 'Pansies, Perverts and Macho Men: Changing Conceptions of Male Homosexuality'. In: Plummer (ed.), 133–54.

Martin, R. 1979: *The Homosexual Tradition in American Poetry*. Austin: University of Texas Press.

—— 1983: 'Edward Carpenter and the Double Structure of *Maurice*'. *Journal of Homosexuality*, 8(3–4), 35–46.

—— 1989: 'Knights-errant and Gothic Seducers: The Representation of Male Friendship in Mid-nineteenth-century America'. In: Duberman et al. (eds), 169–82.

Marx, K. 1857–8: *Grundrisse: Foundations of the Critique of Political Economy (Rough Draft)*, tr. M. Nicolaus. Harmondsworth: Penguin, 1973.

—— 1867/87: *Capital: A Critical Analysis of Capitalist Production*, vol. I, 3rd edn, tr. S. Moore and E. Aveling. Moscow: Foreign Languages Publishing House (no date).

Mauss, M. 1950: *Sociology and Psychology: Essays*, tr. B. Brewster. London: RKP, 1979.

Maynard, S. 1994: 'Through a Hole in the Lavatory Wall: Homosexual Subcultures, Police Surveillance, and the Dialectics of Discovery, Toronto, 1890–1930'. *Journal of the History of Sexuality*, 5(2), 207–42.

Mayne, X. 1908: *The Intersexes: A History of Similisexualism as a Problem in Social Life*. New York: Arno, 1975.

—— (ed.) 1906: *Imre: A Memorandum*. New York: Arno, 1975.

McIntosh, M. 1968: 'The Homosexual Role'. In: Plummer (ed.), 1981, 30–44.

McWhirter, D. and Mattison, A. 1984: *The Male Couple: How Relationships Develop*. Englewood Cliffs: Prentice-Hall.

—— et al. (eds) 1990: *Homosexuality/Heterosexuality: Concepts of Sexual Orientation*. New York/Oxford: Oxford UP.

Mellen, J. 1977: *Big Bad Wolves: Masculinity in the American Film*. New York: Pantheon.

Mendès-Leite, R. 1993: 'On the Esthetics of Pleasures: Guidelines for a Socio-Anthropology of (Homo)sexualities'. *Journal of Homosexuality*, 25(1/2), 17–30.

Menninger, K. 1963: Introduction. In: *The Wolfenden Report: Report of the Committee on Homosexual Offenses and Prostitution* (authorized American edn). New York: Steinday, 5–7.

Messner, M. and Sabo, D. (eds) 1990: *Sport, Men, and the Gender Order: Critical Feminist Perspectives*. Champagne, Ill.: Human Kinetics.

Méténier, O. 1904: *Vertus et vices allemands*. Paris: Michel.

Meve, J. 1990: *'Homosexuelle Nazis': Ein Stereotyp in Politik und Literatur des Exils*. Hamburg: Männerschwarmskript no. 4.

Meyer, M. 1994: 'Introduction: Reclaiming the Discourse of Camp'. In: Meyer (ed.), 1–22.

—— (ed.) 1994: *The Politics and Poetics of Camp*. London: Routledge.

Meyers, J. 1977: *Homosexuality and Literature 1890–1930*. London: Athlone.

Mieli, M. 1977: *Homosexuality and Liberation: Elements of a Gay Critique*. London: GMP, 1980.

Mikkelsen, H. 1984: *Bundfald: Om den 'homoseksuelle fare' i 50'ernes Danmark*. Paper, Department of Social Sciences and History, Roskilde University.

Mileski, M. and Black, D. 1972: 'The Social Organization of Homosexuality'. *Urban Life and Culture*, 1(2), 187–202.

Miller, D. 1988: *The Novel and the Police*. Berkeley: University of California Press.

Mizer, B. 1987: *Athletic Model Guild*. London: GMP.

Moll, A. 1902: 'Wie erkennen und verständigen sich die Homosexuellen unter einander?' *Archiv für Kriminal-Anthropologie und Kriminalistik*, 9(1), 153–6.

Money, J. and Bohmer, C. 1980: 'Prison Sexology: Two Personal Accounts of Masturbation, Homosexuality, and Rape'. *Journal of Sex Research*, 16(3), 258–66.

Moon, M. 1991: *Disseminating Whitman: Revision and Corporeality in 'Leaves of Grass'*. Cambridge, Mass.: Harvard UP.

Moore, S. 1988: 'Here's Looking at You, Kid!' In: Gamman, L. and Marshment, M. (eds), *The Female Gaze: Women as Viewers of Popular Culture*. London: The Women's Press, 44–59.

Morgenthaler, F. 1984: *Homosexuality, Heterosexuality, Perversion*. Hillsdale, NJ: The Analytic Press, 1988.

Morse, M. 1983: 'Sport on Television: Replay and Display'. In: Kaplan, E. (ed.): *Regarding Television: Critical Approaches*. Los Angeles: American Film Institute/University Publications of America, 44–66.

Mort, F. 1988: 'Boys Own? Masculinity, Style and Popular Culture'. In: Chapman, R. and Rutherford, J. (eds), *Male Order: Unwrapping Masculinity*. London: Lawrence & Wishart, 160–72.

—— 1995: 'Archaeologies of City Life: Commercial Culture, Masculinity, and Spatial Relations in 1980s London'. *Environment and Planning D: Society and Space*, 13, 573–90.

Mosse, G. 1985: *Nationalism and Sexuality: Respectability and Abnormal Sexuality in Modern Europe*. New York: Fertig.

Mülder, I. 1985: *Siegfried Kracauer – Grenzgänger zwischen Theorie und Literatur: Seine frühe Schriften 1913–1933*. Stuttgart: Metzler.

Müller, K. 1991: *Aber in meinem Herzen sprach eine Stimme so laut: Homosexuelle Autobiographien und medizinishe Pathographien im neunzehnten Jahrhundert*. Berlin: Rosa Winkel.

Murray, R. 1994: *Images in the Dark: An Encyclopedia of Gay and Lesbian Film and Video*. Philadelphia: TLA.

Murray, S. 1980: 'The Institutional Elaboration of a Quasi-ethnic Community in Canada'. In: Harry, J. and Man, S. (eds), 31–43.

—— 1992a: 'Components of Gay Community in San Francisco'. In: Herdt (ed.), 107–46.

—— 1992b: 'Introduction: Homosexuality in Cross-Cultural Perspective'. In: Murray (ed.), xiii–xl.

—— (ed.) 1992: *Oceanic Homosexualities*. New York: Garland.

—— (ed.) 1995: *Latin American Male Homosexualities*. Albuquerque: University of New Mexico Press.

Nacci, P. and Kane, T. 1983: 'The Incidence of Sex and Sexual Aggression in Federal Prisons'. *Federal Probation*, 47(4), 31–6.

—— 1984: 'Sex and Sexual Aggression in Federal Prisons: Inmate Involvement and Employee Impact'. *Federal Probation*, 48(1), 46–53.

Nardi, P. 1982: 'Alcoholism and Homosexuality: A Theoretical Perspective'. *Journal of Homosexuality*, 7(4), 9–25.

—— 1992a: 'Sex, Friendship, and Gender Roles among Gay Men'. In: Nardi (ed.), 173–85.

—— 1992b: 'That's what Friends are for: Friends as Family in the Gay and Lesbian Community'. In: Plummer (ed.), 108–20.

—— (ed.) 1992: *Men's Friendships*. Newbury Park: Sage.

Neale, S. 1983: 'Masculinity as Spectacle'. *Screen*, 24(6), 2–16.

Nelson, R. 1984: 'Inside China: A Bicycle Tour'. *The Advocate*, 389.

Newton, E. 1972: *Mother Camp: Female Impersonators in America*. Englewood Cliff, NJ: Prentice-Hall.

—— 1993: *Cherry Grove, Fire Island: Sixty Years in America's First Gay and Lesbian Town*. Boston: Beacon.

Nilsson, A. 1994: ' "Såna" och "riktiga karlar": Om manlig homosexualitet i Göteborg kring andra världskriget'. In: Björnberg, U. et al. (eds): *Janus och Genus: Om kön och social identitet i familj och samhälle*. Gothenburg: Bromberg, 111–40.

Norton, R. 1992: *Mother Clap's Molly House: The Gay Subculture in England 1700–1830*. London: GMP.

Nye, R. 1989: 'Sex Difference and Male Homosexuality in French Medical Discourse, 1830–1930'. *Bulletin of Historical Medicine*, 63, 32–51.

Oates, J. 1987: *On Boxing*. London: Bloomsbury.

Øllgaard, J. 1984: ' "For Schuulz han er homosexuel, homosexuel . . ." '. *Information*, 9 March.

Oosterhuis, H. (ed.) 1991: *Homosexuality and Male Bonding in Pre-Nazi Germany: The Youth Movement, the Gay Movement, and Male Bonding before Hitler's Rise. Original Transcripts from 'Der Eigene', the First Gay Journal in the World.* Translations by H. Kennedy (= *Journal of Homosexuality*, 22(1/2)).

Ostrymiecz, A. 1931: 'Der Fall Redl'. In: Lettow-Vorbeck, P. (ed.), *Die Weltkriegsspionage*. Munich: Moser, 89–98.

Ovesey, L. 1969: *Homosexuality and Pseudohomosexuality*. New York: Science House.

—— and Woods, S. 1980: 'Pseudohomosexuality and Homosexuality in Men: Psychodynamics as a Guide to Treatment'. In: Marmor (ed.).

Owens, C. 1987: 'Outlaws: Gay Men in Feminism'. In: Jardine, A. and Smith, P. (eds), *Men in Feminism*. New York: Methuen, 219–32.

Patzer, H. 1982: 'Die griechische Knabenliebe'. *Sitzungsberichte der Wissenschaftlichen Gesellschaft an der J. W. Goethe-Universität Frankfurt am Main*, 19(1), 1–131.

Paul, J. 1993: 'Childhood Cross-gender Behavior and Adult Homosexuality: The Resurgence of Biological Models of Sexuality'. *Journal of Homosexuality*, 24(3–4), 41–54.

Penn, D. 1995: 'Queer: Theorizing Politics and History'. *Radical History*, 62, 24–43.

Philbert, B. 1984: *L'homosexualité à l'écran*. Paris: Veyrier.

Pingel, R. and Trautvetter, W. 1987: *Homosexuelle Partnerschaften: Eine empirische Untersuchung*. Berlin: Rosa Winkel.

Plant R. 1986: *The Pink Triangle: The Nazi War against Homosexuals*. New York: Holt.

Plato: *Charmides. Alcibiades I and II. Hipparchus. The Lovers. Theages. Minos. Epinomis,* tr. W. Lamb. London: Heinemann, 1964.

Plum, C. and Simonsen, N. 1984: *Emma gad – vi gider ikke. Kogebog*. Copenhagen: Hekla.

Plummer, K. 1975: *Sexual Stigma: An Interactionist Account*. London: RKP.

—— 1978: 'Men In Love: Observations on the Male Homosexual Couple'. In: Corbin, M. (ed.), *The Couple*. London: Penguin, 173–200.

—— 1995: *Telling Sexual Stories: Power, Change and Social Worlds*. London: Routledge.

—— (ed.) 1981: *The Making of the Modern Homosexual*. London: Hutchinson.

—— (ed.) 1992: *Modern Homosexualities: Fragments of Lesbian and Gay Experiences*. London: Routledge.

Pollard, P. 1995: 'Gide in the U.S.S.R.: Some Observations on Comradeship'. *Journal of Homosexuality*, 29(2/3), 179–95.

Ponte, M. 1974: 'Life in a Parking Lot: An Ethnography of a Homosexual Drive-in'. In: Jacobs, J. (ed.), *Deviance: Field Studies and Self-disclosures*. Palo Alto: National, 7–29.

Pontoppidan, K. 1891: 'Pervers Seksualitet'. *Bibliothek for Læger*, 83(7, 2), 507–11.

Poynton, B. and Hartley, J. 1990: 'Male-gazing: Australian Rules Football, Gender and Television'. In: Brown, M. (ed.), *Television and Women's Culture: The Politics of the Popular*. London: Sage, 144–57.

Prieur, A. 1994: *Iscenesettelser av kjønn: Transvestitter og macho-menn i Mexico by*. Oslo: Pax.

Pronger, B. 1990: *The Arena of Masculinity: Sports, Homosexuality, and the Meaning of Sex*. London: GMP.

Propper, A. 1981: *Prison Homosexuality: Myth and Reality*. Lexington, Mass.: Lexington Books.

Rasch, W. 1936: *Freundschaftskult und Freundschaftsdichtung im deutschen Schrifttum des 18. Jahrhunderts von Ausgang des Barock bis zu Klopstock*. Halle: Max Niemeyer.

Read, K. 1980: *Other Voices: The Style of a Male Homosexual Tavern*. Novato, CA.: Chandler & Sharp.

Reiss, A. 1961: 'The Social Integration of Queers and Peers'. *Social Problems*, 9(2), 102–20.

Richmond, K. 1978: 'Fear of Homosexuality and Modes of Rationalisation in Male Prisons'. *Australian and New Zealand Journal of Sociology*, 14(1), 51–7.

Rideau, W. and Sinclair, B. 1979: 'Prison: The Sexual Jungle'. In: Scacco (ed.), 3–29.

Riess, B. 1980: 'Psychological Tests in Homosexuality'. In: Marmor (ed.), 296–311.

Rifkin, A. 1993: *Street Noises: Parisian Pleasure 1900–40*. Manchester: Manchester UP.

——1995: *The Poetics of Space Rewritten: From Renaud Camus to the Gay City Guide*. Paper from the *Theory, Culture & Society* conference, Berlin, 10–14 August.

Roscoe, W. 1987: 'Bibliography of Berdache and Alternative Gender Roles among North American Indians'. *Journal of Homosexuality*, 14(3–4), 81–171.

—— 1991: *The Zuni Man-Woman*. Albuquerque: University of New Mexico Press.

Rose, K. 1994: *Diverse Communities: The Evolution of Lesbian and Gay Politics in Ireland*. Cork: Cork UP.

Rosen, W. 1980: 'Venskabets mysterier: Om H. C. Andersens roman

"O.T.", hans forelskelse i Edvard Collin og "Den lille Havfrue"s forløsning'. *Anderseniana*, 3(3), 167–214.

—— 1993: *Månens Kulør: Studier i dansk bøssehistorie 1628–1912*. Copenhagen: Rhodos.

Rosenberg, P. 1912: *Herman Bang*. Copenhagen: Schönberg.

Ross, A. 1989: *No Respect: Intellectuals and Popular Culture*. London: Routledge.

Rossel, S. 1982: *A History of Scandinavian Literature 1870–1980*, tr. A. Ulmer. Minneapolis: University of Minnesota Press.

Rotundo, A. 1989: 'Romantic Friendship: Male Intimacy and Middle Class Youth in the Northern United States, 1800–1900'. *Journal of Social History*, 23(1), 1–26.

Rowse, A. 1977: *Homosexuals in History: A Study of Ambivalence in Society, Literature and the Arts*. London: Weidenfeld & Nicolson.

Rubin, G. 1984/93: 'Thinking Sex: Notes for a Radical Theory of the Politics of Sexuality'. In: Abelove et al. (eds), 3–44.

Rubin, L. 1986. *Just Friends: The Role of Friendship in Our Lives*. New York: Harper & Row.

Ruitenbek, H. 1967: Introduction. In: Ruitenbek (ed.), *Homosexuality and Creative Genius*. New York: Astor-Honor.

Russo, V. 1981: *The Celluloid Closet: Homosexuality in the Movies*. New York: Harper.

Sagarin, E. 1976: 'Prison Homosexuality and its Effect on Post-prison Sexual Behavior'. *Psychiatry*, 39(3), 245–57.

Sarotte, G.-M. 1975: *Le thème de l'homosexualité masculine dans le roman et le théâtre américain de Herman Melville à James Baldwin*. Lille: University of Lille.

Sartre, J.-P. 1943: *Being and Nothingness: An Essay on Phenomenological Ontology*, tr. H. Barnes. London: Methuen, 1976.

Scacco, A. 1975: 'What All This Means: Can Anything be Done to Affect Change?' In: Scacco (ed.), 298–315.

—— (ed.) 1982: *Male Rape: A Casebook of Sexual Aggression*. New York: AMS.

Scheff, T. 1966: *Being Mentally Ill: A Sociological Theory*. Chicago: Aldine.

Schelsky, H. 1955: *Soziologie der Sexualität: Über die Beziehungen zwischen Geschlecht, Moral und Gesellschaft*. Hamburg: Rowohlt.

Schildt, G. 1976: *Dianas ö*. Stockholm: Wahlström & Widstrand.

Schmidt, G. 1985: 'Allies and Persecutors: Science and Medicine in the Homosexuality Issue'. *Journal of Homosexuality*, 10(3–4), 127–40.

Schofield, M. 1965: *Sociological Aspects of Homosexuality: A Comparative Study of Three Types of Homosexuals*. London: Longman.

Schwarz, O. 1931: *Über Homosexualität: Ein Beitrag zu einer medizinischen Anthropologie*. Leipzig: Thieme.

—— 1935: *Sexualpathologie*. Vienna: Verlag für Medizin.

Secher, K. 1973: *Seksualitet og samfund i Herman Bangs romaner*. Copenhagen: Borgen.

Sedgwick, E. 1985: *Between Men: English Literature and Male Homosexual Desire*. New York: Columbia UP.

—— 1990: *Epistemology of the Closet*. Berkeley/Los Angeles: University of California Press.

—— 1993a: 'Queer Performativity: Henry James's "The Art of the Novel" '. *GLQ*, 1(1), 1–16.

—— 1993b: *Tendencies*. Durham, NC: Duke UP.

Sedgwick, P. 1982–3: 'Out of Hiding: The Comradeships of Daniel Guérin'. *Salmagundi*, 58–9, 197–220.

Seidman, S. 1991: *Romantic Longings: Love in America 1830–1980*. New York: Routledge.

—— 1993: 'Identity and Politics in a "Postmodern" Gay Culture'. In: Warner (ed.), 105–42.

Selzer, M. 1990: 'The Love-Master'. In: Boone, J. and Cadden, M., *Engendering Men: The Question of Male Feminist Criticism*. New York: Routledge, 140–58.

Sennett, R. 1977: *The Fall of Public Man*. New York: Knopf.

—— 1990: *The Conscience of the Eye: The Design and Social Life of Cities*. New York: Knopf.

Shields, R. 1991: *Places on the Margin: Alternative Geographies of Modernity*. London: Routledge.

Siegert, M. 1970: 'Sade-Studien (Kommentar zu Sades Die Philosophie im Schlafzimmer)'. *Neues Forum*, 17(200–3), 848–54, 903–10, 964–70, 1041–6.

Silverstolpe, F. 1980: *En homosexuell arbetares memoarer: Järnbruksarbetaren Eric Thorsell berättar*. Stockholm: Barrikaden, 1981.

—— 1987: 'Benkert was not a Doctor: On the Non-medical Origin of the Homosexual Category in the Nineteenth Century'. In: *Homosexuality, Which Homosexuality? Conference Papers, History Volume*. Amsterdam: Free University, 206–20.

Simmel, G. 1903: 'The Metropolis and Mental Life'. In: Wolff, K. (ed.), *The Sociology of Georg Simmel*. New York: Free Press, 1950, 409–24.

Simon, W. and Gagnon, J. 1967: 'Homosexuality: The Formulation of a Sociological Perspective'. *Journal of Health and Social Behavior*, 8(3): 177–85.

Simpson, M. 1994: *Male Impersonators: Men Performing Masculinity*. London: Cassell.

Sinfield, A. 1991: 'Private Lives/Public Theatre: Noel Coward and the Politics of Homosexual Representation'. *Representations*, 36, 43–63.

—— 1994a: *Cultural Politics – Queer Reading*. London: Routledge.

—— 1994b: *The Wilde Century: Effeminacy, Oscar Wilde and the Queer Movement*. London: Cassell.

Smith, D. 1972: 'Sexual Practices in the Hippie Subculture'. *Medical Aspects of Human Sexuality*, 6(4), 142–51.
Smith, P. 1992: *Laws of Desire: Questions of Homosexuality in Spanish Writing and Film 1960–1990*. Oxford: Clarendon.
Smith, T. 1990: 'The Polls – A Report: The Sexual Revolution?' *Public Opinion Quarterly*, 54, 415–35.
Smith-Rosenberg, C. 1975: 'The Female World of Love and Ritual: Relations between Women in Nineteenth Century America'. *Signs*, 1(1), 1–29.
—— 1993: 'Exploring the Feminine Erotic: Some Reflections on the Social Purity Movement in Nineteenth-century America'. In: Liljeström, M. et al. (eds), *Kvinnohistoriens nya utmaningar*. Tampere: University of Tampere, 1994.
Smitt, J. 1951: 'Forsøg på en helhedsopfattelse af homoseksualiteten'. In: Smitt, J. (ed.), *Hvorfor er de sådan? En studie over homosexualitetens problemer*. Copenhagen: Reitzel, 11–153.
Socarides, C. 1968: *The Overt Homosexual*. New York: Gruen & Stratton.
—— 1978: *Homosexuality*. New York: Aronson.
—— 1990: 'The Homosexualities: A Psychoanalytical Classification'. In: Socarides, C. and Volkan, V. (eds), *The Homosexualities: Reality, Fantasy, and the Arts*. Madison, Conn.: International Universities Press, 9–46.
Sonenschein, D. 1968: 'The Ethnography of Male Homosexual Relationships'. *Journal of Sex Research*, 4(2), 69–83.
Sontag, S. 1964: 'Notes on "Camp" '. In: Sontag, *Against Interpretation*. New York: Farrar, Straus & Giroux, 1966, 275–92.
—— 1977: *On Photography*. New York: Farrar, Straus & Giroux.
—— 1978: *Illness as a Metaphor*. New York: Farrar, Straus & Giroux.
Spain, D. 1992: *Gendered Spaces*. Chapel Hill: University of North Carolina Press.
Spangler, L. 1992: 'Buddies and Pals: A History of Male Friendships on Prime-time Television'. In: Craig (ed.), 93–110.
Spartacus International Gay Guide, ed. J. Stamford. Annually since 1970.
Stangerup, H. 1966: 'Herman Bang'. In: Stangerup, H. and Billeskov Jansen, F., *Dansk litteraturhistorie*, vol. 3. Copenhagen: Politiken, 226–67.
Steakley, J. 1975: *The Homosexual Emancipation Movement in Germany (1863–1945)*. New York: Arno.
—— 1983: 'Iconography of a Scandal: Political Cartoons and the Eulenburg Affair'. *Visual Communication*, 9(2), 20–51.
Steinman, C. 1992: 'Gaze out of Bounds: Men Watching Men on Television'. In: Craig (ed.), 199–214.
Stewart, S. 1993: *Gay Hollywood Film & Video Guide: Over 75 Years of Male Homosexuality in the Movies*. Laguna Hills, CA.: Companion.
Stoddard, C. 1873: *South-Sea Idyls*. Boston: Osgood.
Stokes, A. 1956: 'Psycho-analytic Reflections on the Development of Ball

Games, particularly Cricket'. *International Journal of Psycho-analysis*, 37, 185–92.

Stone, L. 1977: *The Family, Sex and Marriage in England 1500–1800*. London: Weidenfeld & Nicolson.

Stubrin, J. 1994: *Sexualities and Homosexualities*. London: Carnac.

Stümke, H.-G. 1989: *Homosexuelle in Deutschland: Eine politische Geschichte*. Munich: Beck.

—— and Finkler, R. 1981: *Rosa Winkel, Rosa Listen: Homosexuelle und 'Gesundes Volksempfinden' von Auschwitz bis heute*. Reinbek: Rowohlt.

Sullivan, H. 1953: *The Interpersonal Theory of Psychiatry*. London: Tavistock, 1955.

Summers, C. 1990: *Gay Fictions: Wilde to Stonewall: Studies in a Male Literary Tradition*. New York: Continuum.

Sutherland, A. and Anderson, P. (eds) 1961: *Eros: An Anthology of Friendship*. New York: Arno, 1975.

Swain, S. 1989: 'Covert Intimacy: Closeness in Men's Friendships'. In: Risman, B. and Schwartz, P. (eds), *Gender in Intimate Relationships: A Microstructural Approach*. Belmont: Wadsworth, 71–86.

Szasz, T. 1970: *The Manufacture of Madness: A Comparative Study of the Inquisition and the Mental Health Movement*. London: RKP, 1971.

Taylor, A. 1981: *Male Novelists and their Female Voices: Literary Masquerades*. Troy, NY: Whitston.

Tewksbury, R. 1989: 'Measures of Sexual Behavior in an Ohio Prison'. *Social Science Research*, 74(1), 34–9.

Theis, W. 1984: 'Verdrängung und Travestie: Das vage Bild der Homosexualität im deutschen Film (1917–1957)'. In: Berlin Museum (ed.), 102–13.

—— and Sternweiler, A. 1984: 'Alltag im Kaiserreich und in der Weimarer Republik'. In: Berlin Museum (ed.), 48–73.

Third World Gay Revolution (Chicago) and Gay Liberation Front (Chicago) 1971: 'Gay Revolution and Sex Roles'. In: Jay and Young (eds), 1972, 252–9.

Thompson, M. (ed.) 1988: *Gay Spirit: Myth and Meaning*. New York: St Martin's Press.

Tóth, L. 1995: *The Politicization of Hungarian Gay Society in the '90s*. Paper for the Second European Sociology Conference, University of Budapest.

Trumbach, R. 1977: 'London's Sodomites: Homosexual Behavior and Western Culture in the Eighteenth Century'. *Journal of Social History*, 11, 1–33.

—— 1978: *The Rise of the Egalitarian Family: Aristocratic Kinship and Domestic Relations in Eighteenth-century England*. New York: Academic.

—— 1989a: 'The Birth of the Queen: Sodomy and the Emergence of Gender Equality in Modern Culture'. In: Duberman et al. (eds), 129–40.

—— 1989b: 'Gender and the Homosexual Role in Modern Western Culture: The 18th and 19th Centuries Compared'. In: Altman, D., Vance, C., Vicinus, M. and Weeks, J. (eds), *Homosexuality, Which Homosexuality*. London: GMP, 149–70.
Tucker, D. 1982: 'A Punk's Song: View from the Inside'. In: Scacco (ed.), 58–79.
Turner, V. 1969: *The Ritual Process: Structure and Anti-Structure*. London: Allen & Unwin.
Ufer, N. 1965: *§225 stk. 2. Meningsdannelser om et mindretal*. Copenhagen: Reitzel.
Ulrichs, K. 1864a: ' "Inclusa" '. In: Ulrichs 1994.
—— 1864b: ' "Vindex" '. In: Ulrichs 1994.
—— 1865a: ' "Vindicta" '. In: Ulrichs 1994.
—— 1865b: ' "Formatrix" '. In: Ulrichs 1994.
—— 1868: ' "Memnon" '. In: Ulrichs 1994.
—— 1870: ' "Prometheus" '. In: Ulrichs 1994.
—— 1879: ' "Critical Arrows" '. In: Ulrichs 1994.
—— 1994: *The Riddle of 'Man–Manly Love'*, tr. M. Lombardi-Nash. Buffalo: Prometheus.
Urry, J. 1990: *The Tourist Gaze: Leisure and Travel in Contemporary Societies*. London: Sage.
Vanggaard, T. 1962: 'Normal homoseksualitet og homoseksuel inversion'. *Ugeskrift for Læger*, 124(39), 1427–34.
Veldboer, L. 1994: 'Pleisterplaatsen van de roze leefwereld. Scenes, residenties en routes als vormen van ruimtelijke expressie'. In: Duyvendak, J. (ed.), *De verzuiling van de homobeweging*. Amsterdam: SUA, 94–107.
Vicinus, M. 1984: 'Distance and Desire: English Boarding School Friendships'. *Signs*, 9(4), 600–23.
—— 1985: *Independent Women: Work and Community for Single Women, 1850–1920*. Chicago: University of Chicago Press.
Vidal, G. 1948: *The City and the Pillar*. New York: Dutton.
Vinnai, G. 1970: *Fussballsport als Ideologie*. Frankfurt: Europäische.
—— 1977: *Das Elend der Männlichkeit: Heterosexualität, Homosexualität und ökonomische Struktur*. Reinbek: Rowohlt.
Vinterberg, S. 1987: 'Hergés Ufuldendte'. *Moderne tider/Information*, 16 January.
Walkowitz, J. 1992: *City of Dreadful Delight: Narratives of Sexual Danger in Late-Victorian London*. London: Virago.
Walter, A. (ed.) 1980: *Come Together: The Years of Gay Liberation (1970–1973)*. London: GMP.
Warner, M. 1993a: Introduction. In: Warner (ed.), vii–xxxi.
—— (ed.) 1993b: *Fear of a Queer Planet: Queer Politics and Social Theory*. Minneapolis: University of Minnesota Press.
Warren, C. 1974: *Identity and Community in the Gay World*. New York: Wiley.
—— and Johnson, J. 1972: 'A Critique of Labeling Theory from the

Phenomenological Perspective'. In: Douglas, J. and Scott, R. (eds) *Theoretical Perspectives on Deviance*. New York: Basic, 69–72.
—— and Ponse, B. 1977: 'The Existential Self in the Gay World'. In: Douglas and Johnson (eds), 173–290.
Watt, I. 1957: *The Rise of the Novel: Studies in Defoe, Richardson and Fielding*. London: Chatto & Windus.
Weeks, J. 1977: *Coming Out: Homosexual Politics in Britain, from the Nineteenth Century to the Present*. London: Quartet.
—— 1980: 'Capitalism and the Organisation of Sex'. In: Gay Left Collective (ed.), *Homosexuality: Power and Politics*. London: Allison & Busby, 11–20.
—— 1980–1: 'Inverts, Perverts and Mary-Annes: Male Prostitution and the Regulation of Homosexuality in the Nineteenth and Twentieth Centuries'. *Journal of Homosexuality*, 6(1/2).
—— 1981: 'Discourse, Desire and Sexual Deviance: Some Problems in a History of Homosexuality'. In: Plummer (ed.), 76–111.
—— 1991: 'Pretended Family Relationships'. In: Weeks, *Against Nature: Essays on History, Sexuality and Identity*. London: Rivers Oram, 134–56.
Weinberg, M. and Bell, A. (eds) 1972: *Homosexuality: An Annotated Bibliography*. New York: Harper & Row.
—— and Williams, C. 1975: 'Gay Baths and the Social Organization of Impersonal Sex'. In: Levine (ed.), 164–81.
Wellings, K., Field, J., Johnson, A. and Wadsworth, J. 1994: *Sexual Behaviour in Britain: The National Survey of Sexual Attitudes and Lifestyles*. London: Penguin.
Wellman, B. 1992: 'Men in Networks: Private Communities, Domestic Friendships'. In: Nardi (ed.), 74–114.
—— and Leighton, B. 1979: 'Networks, Neighborhoods, and Communities: Approaches to the Study of the Community Question'. *Urban Affairs Quarterly*, 14(3), 363–90.
—— et al. 1988: 'Networks as Personal Communities'. In: Wellman, B. and Berkowitz, S. (eds) *Social Structures: A Network Approach*. Cambridge: Cambridge UP, 19–61.
Welter, R. 1986: *Der Begriff der Lebenswelt: Theorien vortheoretischer Erfarungswelt*. Munich: Fink.
Weston, K. 1991: *Families we Choose: Lesbians, Gays, Kinship*. New York: Columbia UP.
Westphal, C. 1869: 'Die Conträre Sexualempfindung: Symptom eines neuropatischen (psychopatischen) Zustandes. *Archiv für Psychiatrie und Nervenkrankheiten*, 2, 72–108.
Westwood, G. 1960: *A Minority: A Report on the Life of the Male Homosexual in Great Britain*. London: Longman.
Whitam, F. and Mathy, R. 1986: *Male Homosexuality in Four Societies: A Cross-cultural Study of the US, Guatemala, Brazil, the Philippines*. New York: Praeger.

White, E. 1983: 'Paradise Found'. *Mother Jones*, 11, 10–16.
Whitehead, H. 1981: 'The Bow and the Burden Strap: A New Look at Institutionalized Homosexuality in Native North America'. In: Ortner, S. and Whitehead, H. (eds), *Sexual Meanings: The Cultural Construction of Gender and Sexuality*. Cambridge: Cambridge UP, 80–115.
Whitman, W. 1856: 'Song of The Open Road'. In: Whitman, *Leaves of Grass*. Photographs by Edward Weston. New York: Limited Editions, 1976.
Williams, W. 1985: 'Persistence and Change in the Berdache Tradition among Contemporary Lakota Indians'. *Journal of Homosexuality*, 11(3–4), 191–200.
—— 1986: *The Spirit and the Flesh: Sexual Diversity in American Indian Culture*. Boston: Beacon.
Wirth, L. 1938: 'Urbanism as a Way of Life'. In: Wirth, *On Cities and Social Life*. Chicago: University of Chicago Press, 1964, 60–83.
Wittman, C. 1970: 'A Gay Manifesto'. In: Jay and Young (eds), 330–42.
'Wolf' 1952: 'Da jeg fandt Gerard'. *Vennen*, 4(7), 136–8.
Wooden, S. and Parker, J. 1982: *Men Behind Bars: Sexual Exploitation in Prison*. New York: Plenum.
Wotherspoon, G. 1991: *City of the Plain: History of a Gay Subculture*. Sydney: Hale & Iremonger.
Wyneken, G. 1921: *Eros*. Lauenburg: Saal, 1921.
Yingling, T. 1990: *Hart Crane and the Homosexual Text: New Thresholds, New Anatomies*. Chicago: University of Chicago Press.
Zelený, J. 1962: *Die Wissenschaftslogik bei Marx und 'Das Kapital'*. Frankfurt: Europäische.

Index